WORKING CLASS RADICALISM
IN MID-VICTORIAN ENGLAND

Working Class Radicalism in Mid-Victorian England

TRYGVE R. THOLFSEN

HD
8390
.T5
1977

NEW YORK   COLUMBIA UNIVERSITY PRESS   1977

First published in 1977 in Great Britain by Croom Helm Ltd. and in the
United States of America by Columbia University Press
Printed in Great Britain

Library of Congress Cataloging in Publication Data

Tholfsen, Trygve R.
  Working-class radicalism in mid-Victorian England.

  Includes index.
  1. Labor and laboring classes – Great Britain –
Political Activity – History. 2. Radicalism – Great
Britain – History. 3. Great Britain – Social conditions –
19th century. I. Title.
HD8390.T5   1977   322'.2-0941   76-43323
ISBN 0-231-04234-S

CONTENTS

For Ellen, Barbara, and David

ACKNOWLEDGEMENTS

I am deeply indebted to my old friend David Roberts, who provided meticulous criticism of the first draft. As editor, John F.C. Harrison gave me the benefit of his unrivalled knowledge of Victorian social history. John Clive, Isabel Knight, and Douglas Sloan generously found the time to comment on parts of the first draft. I also wish to thank a number of other scholars who were helpful in various ways: Herman Ausubel, Mark Curtis, Robert Handy, Helene Roberts, Allen Staley, R.K. Webb, and Carl Woodring. Thanks are also owed to my wife Ann, who graced the enterprise with her presence.

A fellowship from the John Simon Guggenheim Foundation made possible a year of research in England in 1968–9 during a sabbatical from Teachers College. The research was also supported by a supplementary grant from the Columbia University Council for Research in the Social Sciences. Over the years Teachers College has provided a congenial environment for teaching and writing.

PREFACE

Historians of the Left have devoted a good deal of attention to the great formative period between 1789 and 1848 — from Paine and the Jacobins to Marx and the Chartists. They have also shown considerable interest in the development of organised labour and socialist movements beginning in the last quarter of the nineteenth century. On the whole, the post-1848 period has been treated as an interlude of quiescence, a brief pause in the movement towards a radical reconstruction of the established order. Viewed in a broader historical perspective, however, the mid-century decades, particularly in England, bring into focus aspects of the history of the Left that can be overlooked in an interpretation that presupposes a straight line advance towards clearly defined goals.

Working-class radicalism in mid-Victorian England experienced in concentrated form the predicament inherent in the historical development of the European Left — maintaining the impulse to radical change and preserving radical principles in the face of countervailing ideological, social, and economic circumstances. The mid-Victorian radicals encountered processes of stabilisation and deradicalisation that were to operate later in western Europe. In a difficult situation they preserved their commitment to democratic and egalitarian values and resisted the full consolidation of middle-class hegemony.

Looking back from the 1970s, we are aware of the vulnerability of the Left in the twentieth century — betrayed by Leninism, assaulted by fascism, and co-opted by liberalism. With the defeat of fascism, the fate of the Left has assumed one of two polar forms. In Russia and eastern Europe it has been transmogrified into the repressive ideology of a new ruling class. The events in Prague in 1968 symbolise the liquidation of the Left in the Soviet Union and its client states. In western Europe the Left has had the good fortune to survive, but under conditions that have made it difficult to sustain the impetus to radical change. Integrated into the structure of welfare capitalism and parliamentary democracy, it has undergone bureaucratisation and deradicalisation. In one sense the Left has been a victim of its success in compelling the removal of so many of the evils that afflicted European society in the nineteenth century. In this situation, however, the Left has been hard put to provide a genuine alternative to liberal reformism.

Because of its reformist, non-revolutionary orientation, working-class radicalism in England has had to face more directly the dilemma of the Left in the industrialised and democratic states of modern

Europe. On the one hand, democratic principles and institutions are an absolute prerequisite to the creation of a society characterised by genuine freedom and equality. The betrayal of the Left by Lenin and Sorel in the context of the pre-1914 attack on revisionist socialism was directly related to their obsession with the sins of liberalism. On the other hand, as the anti-revisionists correctly pointed out, parliamentary democracy in liberal capitalist society is inherently conservative and is unlikely to produce an electoral majority supporting radical social change. On the Continent this dilemma was obscured by revolutionary rhetoric.

Similarly, working-class radicalism in England has been more deeply involved in the ambivalent ideological relationship between liberalism and the Left. Partly under the influence of Marxism, the European Left tended to ignore the problem by treating liberalism merely as a middle-class ideology. In fact, however, middle-class liberalism and the Left had common origins and shared many values, aspirations, and assumptions. These historical affinities have made it difficult for the Left to maintain its ideological independence. In theory, the line between liberal reformism and the Left can be drawn easily enough, since the latter is committed to radical social and economic change. As a Victorian put it, the evil engendered by power 'cannot be eradicated until the power itself is withdrawn'. In practice, however, it has been hard to preserve a commitment to change in the structure of power.

Because of the reformist character of the English Left, it takes an effort of the historical imagination to recall the depth and intensity of the early-Victorian clash between working-class radicalism and a middle class that was aggressively seeking ideological and social dominion. In the new industrial cities there was a directness of social and ideological confrontation that was never to be duplicated on the Continent. Hence the swiftness and thoroughness of the ensuing processes of accommodation, which saw a modified liberalism established as a consensus creed, are all the more striking. Thus, basic elements in the history of modern Europe were telescoped and compressed in mid-nineteenth-century England, albeit in unique English form. And the historian is interested in mid-Victorian England, not as a foreshadowing of later developments elsewhere, but in its historical uniqueness and individuality.

1 PROBLEMS OF INTERPRETATION

This book deals with a well known episode in English social history: the swift transition from the militant working-class radicalism of the 1830s and 1840s to the relative quiescence of the age of equipoise. The older interpretation of these developments depicted a working-class surrender to middle-class ideology and the cult of respectability. In the light of recent scholarship, however, we have come to recognise a more complex phenomenon that poses a number of interesting problems of interpretation. The mid-Victorian working man no longer appears as the passive victim of ideological *embourgeoisement*; to a considerable degree he remained faithful to the values of the radical tradition. However muted, radicalism continued to be a bulwark against the triumph of middle-class ideology, despite numerous points of affinity between them. Yet working-class radicalism was very well integrated into a cohesive culture dominated by the middle-class. Hence, when we look at the mid-Victorian city, we see not only consensus and stability but unresolved ideological and social conflict: a stable culture in a state of inner tension.

The classic interpretation of the mid-Victorian period in the history of the working-class movement was laid down by the Webbs in their *History of Trade Unionism*. Surveying the trade union world in the late 1840s, they described the emergence of a 'new spirit', characterised by an acceptance of various aspects of middle-class ideology — individualism, respectability, self-help, and self-improvement. In the Webbs' account the 'New Model' trade unionist was a respectable working man, imbued with the middle-class economics and middle-class values. G.D.H. Cole, in his magisterial works of synthesis, described a similar shift in outlook in the working-class movement as a whole: 'The New Co-operation of 1844, the New Unionism of 1850, the new Friendly Society Movement . . . were all signs of this changed spirit — all attempts to work with and within the capitalist order instead of seeking its overthrow.' The nub of Cole's interpretation was the total domination of mid-Victorian society and culture by a newly ascendant capitalist class: 'Everything thus tended to impress on working-class organisation in the Victorian era the mood and character dominant in Victorianism itself — a mood of acquisitiveness, which measured man by money and reckoned virtues largely in monetary terms.'[1]

This interpretation, firmly based on a mass of supporting evidence, has not been overthrown or refuted. Yet the monochromatic picture painted by the Webbs has been modified by recent scholarship, which has depicted the mid-Victorian working man as a more complex and interesting figure. We have been reminded of his persisting radicalism, genuine independence, lack of servility, and imperviousness to crude political economy and middle-class propaganda. Without denying the prevalence of many of the traits singled out by the Webbs, historians have remarked on the presence of other characteristics which do not readily fit into the older stereotype. Geoffrey Best, for example, has commented on the ambiguity of trade unionist attitudes which often combined an extreme laissez faire individualism with 'elements of socialist idealism, class solidarity and pragmatic collectivism.'[2]

The situation of working-class radicalism in mid-Victorian urban culture provides more than enough material to satisfy the contemporary historian's appetite for ambiguity and paradox. Thus, although the mid-Victorian working man preserved his radicalism and independence, he was nevertheless well integrated into a remarkably cohesive culture — a tightly knit structure of values, institutions, roles and ritual — built on a social base dominated by the middle classes. A firm consensus on basic values had been established, especially on the overriding importance of the moral and intellectual improvement of the individual. Ordinary activity directed toward the common goals of the community was invested with the highest moral significance, and spokesmen for all classes took pleasure in celebrating each small instalment of progress. On the other hand, the mid-Victorian cities were the scene of continual class conflict, which manifested itself socially and ideologically. There was considerable working-class resistance to the middle-class and its pretensions. Yet criticism of middle-class propaganda was often accompanied by an affirmation of values which corresponded closely to official platform rhetoric, and working-class militancy assumed forms which were congruent with a culture that presupposed middle-class preeminence. These apparently contradictory characteristics are reflected in two successive sentences in a letter which Marx wrote to Engels after attending a working-class meeting in London in 1863. On the one hand, Marx noted that 'the workers themselves spoke *excellently*, with a complete absence of bourgeois rhetoric and without in the least concealing their opposition to capitalists.' Yet in the next breath he expressed the hope that the English workers would soon 'free themselves from their apparent bourgeois infection.'[3] Thus Marx noticed not only characteristics of mid-Victorian working men which the Webbs were later to emphasize, but also other traits which were to be momentarily forgotten.

When we turn to Chartism, the starting point for a discussion of the transition to mid-Victorian radicalism, we also have to take account of scholarship since the second World War. First and foremost, E.P. Thompson has demonstrated the richness and depth of the traditions of popular radicalism on which the Chartist movement rested. Studies of the unstamped press have shown the diffusion of new forms of working-class radicalism in the 1830s. At the same time other monographs have provided a much fuller picture of Owenism, so different from Chartism and yet very much a part of a broader working-class radical tradition. Local studies have contributed to a better understanding of Chartism in the provinces. We no longer see provincial Chartism in Hovell's terms as essentially a movement of hunger and desperation, dominated by handloom weavers, to be understood in contrast to the moderation and rationality of the movement that had originated with London artisans. Textbook accounts of a moderate London program transformed by the wild men of the North have been superseded. We now recognise the intellectual strength of the Chartist Left both in the provinces and in London. Within the framework of Chartism, working-class radicalism voiced a trenchant critique of the political and social order, explicitly rejecting the ideology that an aggressive bourgeoisie was trying to impose.[4]

This picture of early-Victorian radicalism lends new point to a question that a generation ago seemed to have been settled once and for all. How was it that so formidable a movement of reasoned protest, high aspiration, and proud class consciousness gave way so swiftly to mid-Victorian consensus? In that form, however, the question is misleading, since working-class radicalism did not merely dissolve into middle-class ideology, but persisted in a different form, continuing to resist propaganda from above and to foster a spirit of independence and pride among workingmen. Yet the traditions of radicalism were certainly softened by acculturation and accommodation. Thus, we are not dealing merely with the fading of protest but with a number of complex processes involving continuity and change, conflict and consensus, accommodation and resistance.

An inquiry into such matters will necessarily take as its point of departure Thompson's brilliant book; the notes give some indication of the extent to which this study is indebted to his work. As will be seen, however, this book deals not only with a later period but with a subject that is defined in different terms. First, it is limited to working-class radicalism, whereas Thompson examines a much broader topic, the 'working class' as a whole. Moreover, as a Marxist, Thompson treats working-class radicalism primarily in relation to the categories of class and class consciousness. Here the phenomenon is approached from a different vantage point.

The main body of the book (chapters 5–10) comprises a description of various aspects of working-class radicalism in the mid-Victorian period that followed its climactic early-Victorian phase (chapter 3). These chapters seek to describe the forms and conditions in which radical values and principles survived in an environment that was un-favourable in a number of different ways: the power and status structure required submission and deference; the culture put a premium on the ceremonial incantation of consensus ideals and sentiments that bore an affinity to many of the aims of radicalism; the moral and intellectual hegemony exercised by the middle classes tended to impose a middle-class form on consensus values. These phenomena are examined in the setting of mid-Victorian urban culture, with special reference to the ambivalent relationship between working-class radicalism and middle-class liberalism.

The processes that moulded these cultural and ideological patterns and mediated the transition from the early-Victorian to the mid-Victorian period are considered in chapters 2—5. It is suggested that the inner logic of the principles of working-class radicalism played a part in shaping its response to developments in middle-class liberalism and in the culture as a whole. From this angle chapter 2 outlines the intel-lectual and ideological origins of early-Victorian working-class radicalism. It is emphasized that Enlightenment liberalism provided the foundations of both working-class radicalism and the middle-class ideology against which it was directed. With the emergence of a more genial version of middle-class liberalism during the period of maximum social and ideological conflict (chapter 4), the road to rapprochement and con-sensus was open. Chapter 5 describes how the confluence of these ideological and intellectual currents contributed to the development of a cohesive culture, characterised by a pervasive consensus and a distinc-tive sensibility of aspiration. In the favourable setting provided by economic improvement and expansion, the same intellectual forces that had influenced the development of working-class radicalism and middle-class liberalism — the Enlightenment, evangelicalism, and romanticism — helped to shape the culture of which both were integral components. Working-class radicalism had to contend not only with middle-class predominance but with the attenuating and softening influence of a culture to whose creation diverse intellectual and social forces had contributed.

The argument of the book entails a number of conceptual and theoretical problems that call for some comment. At the most general level there is the difficulty, familiar to every historian, of conceptualising the elusive reality of phenomena characterised by constant change and endless diversity. Thus, 'working-class radicalism', for example, is not susceptible of summary definition. Not only was it changing over the years, but at any moment in time it displayed considerable variation. Yet it clearly embodied common characteristics. Hence in the following chapters such terms as 'salient' and 'distinctive' occasionally appear in tandem with metaphors of spectrum and continuum, permutation and combination. Another aspect of the problem of unity and diversity that is prominent in Victorian social history is geographical variation, especially from one city to another. In a definitive work this would be handled by comparative history on a large scale. This book, however, has the more limited objective of attempting to describe the 'central' features of working-class radicalism without, it is hoped, doing violence to regional variation.

Another recurring problem concerns the interplay between social and intellectual forces. In one sense there is no difficulty, since professional historians are committed to a methodological pluralism that treats as an open question the nature and effectiveness of the causal factors operating in a given situation. In practice, however, particularly when dealing with a subject like this one, there is a natural tendency to assign a sort of de facto primacy to social and economic forces. Such forces clearly played an important part in resolving the early Victorian crisis. The decline in Chartist agitation, together with the over-all 'relaxation of tension' and the achievement of 'stability', were in large measure the consequence of a relative improvement in the economic situation. Similarly, the apparent transformation of the militant Chartist into the 'respectable working man' can be understood in part in economic terms, including an expansion of the skilled segment of the labour force as a result of economic growth. In G.D.H. Cole's formulation, the mid-Victorian working-class adjusted to a mature capitalist economy. Since this line of explanation is so well grounded, one can hardly suggest that there is a prima facie case for the thesis that intellectual forces were of equivalent importance.

But there is a case to be made. To begin with, the character of the early-Victorian crisis itself cannot be explained simply by reference to economically determined conflict and unrest. Working-class radicalism embodied more than a protest against immediate grievances. It posed a profound challenge to the legitimacy of the social and political order. That challenge was based on solid intellectual and ideological foundations provided by the Enlightenment. Thus, although working-class radicalism was rooted in practical circumstances, such as economic dislocation and class conflict, these were not sufficient causes. The character and intensity of popular radicalism had been shaped by intellectual traditions inherited from the past. Moreover, since the challenge posed by working-class agitation in early-Victorian England was so deeply rooted, it could not be dispelled merely by a change in the economic situation. Similarly, when we turn to the 1850s and 1860s and consider the specific characteristics of mid-Victorian urban culture, especially its value system and its cohesiveness, we cannot explain it primarily in terms of its social and economic base.

Any attempt to describe the interplay between aspects of class and culture runs up against another difficulty. Although the two have to be separated for analytical purposes, they are in fact closely intertwined in their concrete historical manifestations. Thus, the character of a social class is determined not only by its socio-economic situation but also by cultural traditions; and a given culture bears the impress of class, past and present. For Marx, however, there was no problem; the essence of a social class is determined by socio-economic circumstances. His comment on the proletariat states his position with his usual clarity and precision: 'It is not a question of what this or that proletarian, or even the whole proletariat, at the moment *considers* as its aim. It is a question of *what* the proletariat is, and what in accordance with this *being*, it will historically be compelled to do. Its aim and historical action is irrevocably and clearly foreshadowed in its own life situation as well as in the whole organisation of bourgeois society today.'[5] In such statements as this and in his schematic formulation of the relationship between 'base' and 'superstructure', Marx forcefully asserted the primacy of social and economic forces in determining the character of a class. Hence his position can serve as a contrast to the methodological assumptions on which this book is based. It should be pointed out, however, that neo-Marxist thought in the twentieth century has abandoned the base-superstructure model for a more flexible formulation. Thus, Eugene Genovese has argued that the developing nature of a social class 'necessarily embraces the full range of its human experience in its manifold political, social, economic, and cultural manifestations.'[6]

The role of culture in shaping the character and outlook of social classes complicates the sort of discussion of 'middle-class values' that figures in the chapters that follow. On the one hand, it is clear that the mid-Victorian cities were permeated by values — such as the Protestant ethic and utilitarian individualism — that were nothing if not 'middle-class' in texture. They bore the stamp of a commercial bourgeoisie, separate and distinct from the landed class above and the working class below. Certain middle-class values, in turn, came under fire from working-class radicalism. While some such formulation is indispensable, however, it can be misleading if too much is made of it. Thus, we are not dealing with two discrete value systems, each socially determined, one of which was achieving domination over the other. Rather, there was a clash between divergent versions of common values, along with extensive overlapping as well as areas of unresolvable incompatibility. The aspiration to moral and intellectual improvement, for example, was not the creation of the middle-class as such, but was the end product of an historical process reaching back to the Greeks and Hebrews. Hence working men who accepted the ideal of individual improvement — or who esteemed rationality, education, and independence — cannot be said to have surrendered to middle-class values. On the contrary, just as the middle classes had fashioned a distinctive value system out of the ideas and beliefs of western culture, so working-class radicalism was a democratic and egalitarian version of inherited ideals.

A related aspect of this problem concerns the form in which the middle-class was attempting to impose its values on the working-class. It has often been noted, for example, that the middle-class wished to create the working-class in its own image. This image, however, was refracted through the prism of class. Hence the values which the middle-class preached to the working-class were by no means identical to the values to which they themselves subscribed. On the contrary, the 'middle-class values' which working men were invited to accept took on a form deemed appropriate to their station. This propaganda assumed that working men would accept their subordinate position, respect their superiors, work hard, and defer to authority, while at the same time moving gradually toward the moral and intellectual heights that had already been scaled by their superiors. Although the success myth came to figure prominently in such discourse, it was assumed that social advancement, for all practical purposes, would take place within the confines of the working-class.

While rejecting middle-class propaganda, working-class radicalism accepted the fundamental values of a culture that presupposed middle-class hegemony. Such ideological conflict within a framework of consensus was one of the more noteworthy aspects of the public life of the mid-Victorian cities. To describe that situation it is necessary to distinguish between the values of the culture as a whole, various versions of those values asserted by the dominant class, and the values of a working-class subculture based on resistance to a narrow class version of the official ethos. There is a great deal of overlapping here. While the same words recur, however, their meaning often varies with the social class of the speaker. In this context it is necessary to refer to 'middle-class values', but not as a set of fixed beliefs, determined primarily by the socio-economic characteristics of the class professing them. Although the value system of mid-Victorian urban culture had a distinctly middle-class coloration, most of its components were by no means intrinsically middle-class in character.

Of all the concepts essential to an understanding of class and culture in the mid-Victorian cities, respectability is at once the most indispensable and the most ambiguous. In a memorable phrase, G.M. Young observed that 'like Roman citizenship, it could be indefinitely extended, and every extension fortified the state'. An important biography of a mid-Victorian working-class leader has been aptly titled *Respectable Radical*. Geoffrey Best's account of the cult of respectability is a classic description of something quintessentially Victorian.[7] In using this concept, however, the historian has to make a distinction between the cult of respectability as it existed within the middle-class and the form that it assumed when extended to working men. He also has to distinguish between the 'respectable working men' of middle-class ideology and the radical workingmen who wished to be respected on terms of genuine independence. We are dealing with divergent versions of verbally similar values.

The notion of respectability had originated in pre-Victorian times as a device for validating in moral terms the social superiority of the middle-class to the mass of the population. The Victorian middle-class brought the idea to a climax and also gave it a new twist. Working men were now invited to enjoy the blessings of respectability. This was a rather odd invitation, since respectability had originally been a means of marking off the middle classes from the mass below. It required a certain ingenuity to invite even a segment of the working-class to enter these exclusive confines. But the Victorian middle classes developed a special brand of respectability suitable for their inferiors: the respectable working man was one who deferred to his betters, recognised their superior virtue and rationality, and set out to emulate them.

The middle-class definition of the 'respectable working man', embodied in the cult of respectability, was the polar opposite of the values of the working-class subculture, with its emphasis on self-respect and genuine independence. To be sure, it was easy to succumb to the middle-class version, and many mid-Victorian working men, eager to earn the respect and approval of their superiors, did so. At the same time, however, other working men, who displayed many of the specific traits commended to them by the middle-class, rejected the cult of respectability. That is, they insisted on genuine independence, and rejected the equivocal invitation being extended from above. The traditions of radicalism encouraged the rejection of the various forms of idolatry preached by the middle-class. Hence it was possible for working men to accept consensus values while repudiating the middle-class model of the 'respectable working man'.

One cannot be altogether comfortable with such terms as 'middle-class' and 'working-class', since each encompasses heterogeneous social groupings. Thus, the term 'working-class' must embrace a labour aristocracy at the top, an unskilled mass at the base, and various intermediate strata in between.[8] In what sense, then, can we use such terminology? The first thing to be said is that these terms have to be identified as methodological constructs, without any hint of reification. With that qualification, 'middle-class' is useful, and indeed necessary, to denote the common characteristics of the diverse social groups defined by their situation below the gentry and above the working-class. Occasionally the plural form serves to emphasise the diversity; in other contexts, segments of the larger group, such as the lower-middle-class, have to be identified. By the same token, all working men shared common characteristics determined by their relationship to employers and property owners. Certain traits of wage earners as such were fixed in law, which put 'servants' in one category and 'masters' in another. Moreover, although the middle-class was quite aware of social differences among working men, its ideological discourse tended to emphasize the common characteristics of the 'working-classes' as a whole. Finally, by the early 1830s, as Thompson has shown, working men of all strata had acquired a sense of their identity over against the middle-class. Even the labour aristocrats saw themselves as working men and as spokesmen for the working classes, despite the fact that they recognised — and often took pride in — the gulf that divided them from the unskilled.

What is the significance of the fact that the chief exponents of working-class radicalism were literate working men, many of them artisans who differed in skill, income and outlook from the less skilled majority? It would be a mistake to attempt to explain the main features of working-class radicalism primarily by reference to the socio-economic characteristics of this group. It would be even more misleading to interpret the transition to mid-Victorianism as a necessary manifestation of the response of an expanding labour aristocracy to changing economic circumstances. What is noteworthy about the leaders of working-class radicalism is that they maintained a democratic and egalitarian position and identified themselves with 'the working classes' against the middle-class, despite the fact that their socio-economic situation predisposed them to separate themselves from the mass of working men.

Any interpretation of working-class radicalism must take account of Marxism, a tradition of thought that from its inception has manifested a sustained interest in the social and ideological history of Victorian England. The development of Marxism itself, from Marx and Engels to Lenin and Gramsci, reflects a careful study of English capitalism. Marxist historians, beginning with Engels, have made valuable contributions to Victorian historiography. Moreover, certain categories, such as ideology and class conflict, which Marxists have singled out for emphasis, are indispensable in this area. In sum, in one way or another, historical scholarship has absorbed a great deal from the Marxist canon. The difficulty, of course, is that Marxist insights and concepts are not readily detached from the tightly interconnected theoretical structure in which they are embedded; since they permeate various interpretations of Victorian social history, a certain ambiguity has resulted. In addition the development of a more supple neo-Marxism leaves some doubt about just what remains of the original structure of classic Marxism. Under these circumstances, the non-Marxist historian has to comment on the difficulties posed by the classic Marxist view of working-class radicalism in Victorian England, with a view to clarifying some of the questions at issue.

The Marxist tendency to make class the master category, even when the base-superstructure model is abandoned, remains an obstacle to an acceptable interpretation of the history of working-class radicalism. The nub of the matter involves the relationship between liberalism and working-class radicalism. Classic Marxism treats liberalism in its various forms, from Locke to Mill, as a form of bourgeois ideology; that is, as essentially a reflection of the socio-economic 'being' of the bourgeoisie. So defined, it is counterposed to a revolutionary consciousness that is depicted as the inherent characteristic of the proletariat; deviation from the norm is treated as a form of 'false consciousness', induced by bourgeois ideology. Thus, both description and explanation presuppose two dichotomous and antithetical forms of socially determined consciousness. The fundamental weakness in this interpretation is that it neglects the historical fact that the attitudes and beliefs of working men and employers were shaped by the interplay between socio-economic structure and inherited cultural traditions, and cannot, therefore, be reduced to expressions of social class alone.

If the concept of hegemony, for example, is to be useful, it has to be pried loose from such remnants of classic Marxism. On the one hand, there is good reason to accept Marx's point — also made by Mill — that a dominant class tends to impose its values and self justification on society as a whole. Gramsci's formulation of hegemony to denote the intellectual and moral ascendancy exercised by a ruling class is even more useful, since it explicitly rejects any tendency to treat ideological superstructure as the mere reflection of the socio-economic base. On the other hand, the non-Marxist cannot accept the assumption that such hegemony is to be understood primarily as an instrument of bourgeois domination and as an obstacle to the development or revolutionary consciousness among the proletariat. It is preferable to take note of the hegemonic impulses of the middle-class, but without treating liberalism as essentially an instrument of class domination. Similarly, working-class radical resistance to middle-class hegemony can be understood without reference to the presumed existence of a latent revolutionary class consciousness in the proletariat.

Although the notion of class conflict is by no means uniquely Marxist, it has been assigned a role of pre-eminent importance in that view of history. If it is to be useful, however, it has to be dethroned from that eminence. In the case of Victorian England, to be sure, the omnipresence and importance of class conflict are plain enough without any recourse to theory. Precisely for that reason, however, it is necessary to incorporate the complementary insights of Emile Durkheim, who emphasised the tendency inherent in society as a whole to generate common values and endow them with a sacred character. When we look at the mid-Victorian cities, we see not only class interest and class conflict but other patterns that correspond to Durkheim's theory. Thus, the middle classes were certainly seeking to impose their values and ideas on the working classes and on the institutions of the society as a whole. The impulse to hegemony, in Gramsci's sense, is unmistakable. Yet the readiness to celebrate the high purposes of the community, both in ritual and in tacit assumption, represents something more than a middle-class confidence trick or a moral and intellectual victory for the middle classes. There was a powerful sense of community and common purpose which was not the creation of any one class.

The treatment of the middle-class in a book on working-class radicalism poses still another problem. There is a potentially misleading one-sidedness inherent in the need to concentrate on those aspects of middle-class attitudes and behaviour that are relevant to an understanding of working-class radicalism. In this context there is bound to be a great deal of emphasis on various manifestations of the middle-class inclination to preserve and justify its status, power, and privileges; quite apart from conscious ideological intent, the socio-economic situation coloured and limited its principles. Unfortunately, however, this means that the familiar virtues of the Victorian middle-class — seriousness, rectitude, and devotion to good works — tend to be taken for granted in the chapters that follow. Obviously, we are not dealing with a clash between a virtuous proletariat and a malevolent bourgeoisie. On the contrary, what is striking is the moral and intellectual quality displayed by both sides. To an impressive degree, the middle-class resisted the socially determined inclination to hostility and repression and sought instead to foster social harmony by promoting the cause of popular improvement. The virtues of men like Edward Baines and Sir James Kay-Shuttleworth are justly celebrated. For their part, the working-class radicals managed to avoid the rather different perils — *ressentiment*, envy, self pity — inherent in their situation. William Lovett and others maintained an exemplary integrity and grace in adversity. As this study is defined, however, we are not directly concerned with questions of relative virtue but with contending social philosophies. In that context the historian has to recognise the moral ambiguity of the position in which the middle-class found itself. Its moral ideals and aspirations were at odds with the imperatives of its socio-economic situation. Hence there was an inescapably ideological taint to the principles that it affirmed in good faith.

The historical situation of the Victorian middle-class not only imposed limits but also created possibilities that enabled it to achieve a distinctive fusion of moral and social energy. Its merits and achievements will stand comparison with any social group. Anyone inclined to dwell on its shortcomings need only cast his eyes across the Rhine and consider the German bourgeoisie as described, for example, by Friedrich Meinecke in *The German Catastrophe*.

Implicit in every interpretation of the history of working-class radicalism in England is some conception of its relationship to comparable movements in Europe. In that connection it has been customary to contrast the moderation and reformism of the English working-class movement with its more militant and even revolutionary European counterpart. There is, of course, substantial evidence to support the contrast, which constitutes a major theme in the comparative history of modern Europe. The familiar comparison to Germany is very much to the point. Although England was the first country to experience industrialisation, it went through a long period of Lib-Labism, and did not get a mass-based Labour Party until the twentieth century, and the party, in turn, did not subscribe to a socialist program until 1918. Germany, however, had a social democratic party in 1875, which in 1891, at Erfurt, adopted a Marxist program. By 1912 this party, officially committed to the class struggle and the proletarian revolution, was the largest in the Reichstag. If too much is made of this contrast, however, it may lead to a simplified view of working-class radicalism in England as an aberration from the mainstream of the European Left.

Detailed studies of the Social Democratic Party in Germany before the First World War have shown the extent to which revolutionary rhetoric concealed a hard core of reformism and labourism. Lenin recognised these tendencies and denounced them in his well known observations on 'trade union consciousness' in 1902. Events since then have confirmed his contention that the working-class, if permitted to develop 'spontaneously', will not become revolutionary, but reformist, labourist, and liberal. Reformism is the norm. As Lenin noted, revolutionary zeal is aberrant and has to be imposed from the outside. In Germany the extent to which the working-class took for granted democratic procedures became clear in the quasi-revolutionary situation in December 1918, when an election conducted by the workers and soldiers councils rejected revolution.[9] Viewed in this light, the English working-class movement no longer looks like a moderationist deviation from the main line of European radicalism. It has to be understood as an English manifestation of tendencies that were also present on the Continent, albeit with the usual national and chronological variations.

Chartism will be misunderstood if it is treated as just another instance of English reformism, in which England lagged behind the Continent despite its advanced industrialisation. To be sure, Chartism was neither revolutionary nor socialist, whereas a substantial number of French working men in the 1840s can be described in those terms;

the Six Points did not go beyond parliamentary reform. Hence it has been possible to depict Chartism as a primitive stage in working-class consciousness, which was to reach maturity in socialist form later. Such comparisons to a presumably more advanced European movement obscure the actual historical characteristics of Chartism, a working-class movement of a scope and magnitude that has not been approximated before or since. It was remarkable in the strength of its attack on class domination of the social and political system, in the extent to which it embodied what Marx called a demystification of middle-class ideology, and in the clarity of its demand for a democratic and egalitarian alternative to the existing order. It is against this background of militant radicalism that the emergence of mid-Victorian consensus has to be viewed.

Chartism has to be understood not only as a militant working-class movement but also as an expression of the nascent traditions of the Left which took shape within the framework of European culture and society in the age of the Enlightenment and the French Revolution. Chartist workingmen were not the passive creatures of forces that determined their 'being'. They chose values and principles from the legacy of the past and adapted them to their needs and aspirations.

Notes

1.   Sidney and Beatrice Webb, *The History of Trade Unionism,* London 1920, chapter 4; G.D.H. Cole, *A Short History of the British Working-Class Movement*, London 1948, pp. 144, 167. See also Raymond Postgate, *The Builders' History*, London 1923, pp. 190–2. Variants of the traditional emphasis on working-class acceptance of middle-class values will be found in my article, 'The Transition to Democracy in Victorian England', *International Review of Social History*, VI, 1961, 226–48, and in Harold Perkin, *The Origins of Modern English Society*, London 1969, chapters 8 and 9. For a Leninist interpretation of a labour aristocracy bought off by the bourgeoisie, see John Foster, *Class Struggle and the Industrial Revolution: Early Industrial Capitalism in Three English Towns*, London 1974.
2.   Geoffrey Best, *Mid-Victorian Britain*, London 1971, p. 268. For a good survey of the literature and a discussion of the problem of defining the characteristics of the mid-Victorian period in working-class history, see Royden Harrison, *Before the Socialists*, London 1965, chapter 1. Emphasising working-class independence are Brian Harrison, *Drink and the Victorians,* London 1971, Stan Shipley, *Club Life and Socialism in mid-Victorian London*, Oxford 1972, and J.F.C. Harrison, *Underground Education in the Nineteenth Century,* Leeds 1971, pp. 8–9. For revised interpretations of mid-Victorian trade unionism, see R.V. Clements, 'British Trade Unions and Popular Political Economy, 1850–1875', *Economic History Review*, XIV, 1961; Allan Flanders and H.A. Clegg, eds., *The System of Industrial Relations in Great Britain: Its History, Law and and Institutions*, Oxford 1967; A.E. Musson, *British Trade Unions, 1800–1875,* London 1972; H.A. Clegg et al., *A History of British Trade Unionism since 1889,*

vol. I, Oxford 1964, pp. 7–10. G.D.H. Cole began the process of revision with his article, 'Some Notes on British Trade Unionism in the Third Quarter of the Nineteenth Century', *International Review of Social History*, 1937. W. Hamish Fraser, *Trade Unions and Society: The Struggle for Acceptance 1850–1880*, London 1974, provides a balanced synthesis. See also E.J. Hobsbawm's comments on the Webbs' interpretation in *Labouring Men*, Anchor edition, New York 1967, p. 402.

3.   *Karl Marx and Frederick Engels on Britain*, London 1954, pp. 492–3.

4.   E.P. Thompson, *The Making of the English Working Class*, New York 1966; Patricia Hollis, *The Pauper Press: A Study in Working-Class Radicalism of the 1830s*, Oxford 1970; Joel H. Wiener, *The War of the Unstamped*, Ithaca 1969; Asa Briggs, ed., *Chartist Studies*, London 1969; Dorothy Thompson, ed., *The Early Chartists*, London 1971; Brian Harrison and Patricia Hollis, 'Chartism, Liberalism, and the Life of Robert Lowery', *English Historical Review*, LXXXII, 1967. See also the review article by Patricia Hollis, *Victorian Studies*, XVI, 1972, p. 238. Recent studies of Owenism include J.F.C. Harrison, *Robert Owen and the Owenites in Britain and America: The Quest for a New Moral World*, London 1969 and Sidney Pollard and John Salt, eds., *Robert Owen Prophet of the Poor*, London 1971.

5.   Istvan Meszaros, 'Contingent and Necessary Class Consciousness', in Meszaros, ed., *Aspects of History and Class Consciousness*, London 1971, p. 85, quoting Marx, *The Holy Family*. For a cogent formulation of the historical approach to class consciousness, see Tom Bottomore, 'Class Structure and Social Consciousness', in Meszaros, pp. 49–64.

6.   Eugene Genovese, *In Red and Black*, New York 1971, p. 323. See also E.P. Thompson, 'The Peculiarities of the English', in Ralph Miliband and John Saville, eds., *Socialist Register 1965*, New York 1965, pp. 337–59; E.J. Hobsbawm, 'Karl Marx's Contribution to Historiography', in Robin Blackburn, ed., *Ideology in Social Science*, London 1972. For a full theoretical statement of an Hegelianized neo-Marxism, see Karl Korsch, *Marxism and Philosophy*, New York 1971.

7.   F. M. Leventhal, *Respectable Radical: George Howell and Victorian Working-Class Politics*, Cambridge, Mass. 1971; G.M. Young, *Victorian England Portrait of an Age*, London 1953, p. 25; Best, pp. 256–63. See also Geoffrey Crossick, 'The Labour Aristocracy and Its Values', *Victorian Studies*, XX, 1976, and Richard N. Price, 'The Other Face of Respectability: Violence in the Manchester Brickmaking Trade 1859–1870', *Past and Present*, No. 66, 1975.

8.   For discussions of the problem of working-class stratification see Hobsbawm, chapter 15; E.P. Thompson, pp. 9–13, 193–4; J.F.C. Harrison, *The Early Victorians, 1832–51*, London 1971, chapter 2; Best, chapter 2; Royden Harrison, pp. 39–42.

9.   See Carl Schorske, *German Social Democracy, 1905–1917*, Cambridge, Mass. 1955; A.J. Ryder, *The German Revolution of 1918: A Study of German Socialism in War and Revolt*, Cambridge 1967, pp. 177–83; Hajo Holborn, *A History of Modern Germany 1840–1945*, New York 1969, pp. 298–532.

2 THE GENESIS OF WORKING-CLASS RADICALISM

Working-class radicalism in early-Victorian England embodied not only a protest against hunger and want, but also a demand for the creation of a new and better society. Chartism and Owenism expressed the new ideals and aspirations of the European Left in the formative period between 1789 and 1848. Looking beyond the removal of immediate grievances, working-class radicals envisaged an England transformed into a nation of truly free men, equal in rights; a nation in which every man could achieve full moral and intellectual development; a nation free from class domination. Although the Chartists were neither revolutionary nor socialist, their radicalism manifested a distinctive strength, shaped by historical circumstances in England. Unlike their European counterparts, English working men had experienced, directly and indirectly, the full impact of the first wave of industrialisation, which generated social conflicts that helped to create a new consciousness of working-class identity, defined in opposition to the employing classes. Drawing on well-established traditions of popular radicalism, English working men appropriated the inchoate principles of the Left and shaped them to their needs in a context of intense social and ideological conflict. Under these circumstances working-class radicalism developed a note-worthy concreteness, in direct confrontation with the new industrial middle-class and its ideology. Under the immediate pressure of economic deprivation and dislocation, the Chartists built a mass movement of unprecedented scope, duration, and intensity. A fusion of powerful social and intellectual forces sustained the formidable challenge that working-class radicalism posed to the established order in early-Victorian England.

In England as in Europe in the first half of the nineteenth century, the Left rested on an ideological base provided by Enlightenment liberalism. From that source came a trenchant rationalism, a vision of human emancipation, the expectation of progress based on reason, and an inclination to take the action necessary to bring society into conformity with rationally demonstrable principles. Without this intellectual legacy working-class protest probably would not have advanced beyond a demand for the remedy of immediate grievances and a primitive sense of class interest. Armed with the intellectual weapons of the Left, however, working-class radicalism developed into a powerful ideological force. The radicals judged their society in the light of the highest ideals of western culture and found it wanting. In England the first phase in the development of working-class radicalism came in the

1790s, with the spread of the doctrines of Paine and the English Jacobins. In the depression years after Waterloo the programme of political radicalism was taken up by working men in the new industrial towns who hoped that parliamentary reform would lead to economic improvement. Even at this early stage, working-class radicalism embraced not only a set of political demands, but a complex of egalitarian and rationalist principles that were to provide a matrix for the emergence of a new social and economic criticism in the 1820s. Anti-capitalist writings — rooted in the rationalist egalitarianism of the Enlightenment — added a new dimension to working-class radicalism. From this vantage point Chartists and Owenites were able to mount a powerful critique of the established order.

Working-class radicalism did not develop in a straight line, as a result of the unfolding of inherent social and ideological tendencies. It developed dialectically, in conflict with a middle-class liberal ideology that assumed a particularly aggressive and intransigent form in England during the generation after Waterloo. Working-class radicals confronted a middle-class that was not merely exercising power and defending its interests but was engaged in ideological warfare against the new threat from the Left. In their attack on popular radicalism middle-class spokesmen deployed a scientistic political economy derived from the Enlightenment and a self-righteous moralism derived from evangelical Christianity. Working-class radicalism developed in response to the ideological rigidity and bluster of the utilitarian liberalism of the early nineteenth century.

We turn first to Enlightenment liberalism, because it provided the intellectual foundations of both working-class radicalism and the middle-class ideology against which it was directed. In early-Victorian England this dynamic body of ideas contributed to an intensification of the social and ideological conflict between the middle and working classes. In mid-Victorian England, however, the legacy of the Enlightenment was to play an important role in the emergence of consensus.

(1) Enlightenment Liberalism and the Origins of the Left

By the 1780s a new corpus of ideals and principles was firmly established in the political consciousness of Europe and America. Based on ideological and institutional forms that had emerged in seventeenth-century England, the principles of liberalism took shape in the matrix of Enlightenment thought and found expression in the events of 1776 and 1789 and in the declarations that accompanied them. An exceedingly diverse phenomenon even before its subsequent proliferation, liberalism encompassed a whole new spectrum of aspirations, which were to inspire progressive and radical movements in the nineteenth century.

The genesis of Enlightenment liberalism reflected the interests and aspirations of the middle-class in a society dominated by the landed aristocracy. Its chief spokesmen came from that class, which, in turn, was the chief beneficiary of the principles of 1789. Yet liberalism was by no means merely a class doctrine, for it embodied the highest ideals of European culture at this stage of its development, and the liberals of the eighteenth century were agents of an historical process that extended into the remote past. Georges Lefebvre, who was not at all inclined to minimise the role of class, put the matter in proper perspective in his comment on the Declaration of the Rights of Man:

> In reality, America and France, like England before them, were alike tributaries to a great stream of ideas, which, while expressing the ascendancy of the bourgeoisie, constituted a common ideal that summarised the evolution of western civilisation. Through the course of centuries our Western world, formed by Christianity yet inheriting ancient thought, has directed its effort through a thousand vicissitudes towards the liberation of the human person.[1]

The long-standing concern for the individual, embodied in the Christian and humanist traditions, took on new life in the social and intellectual circumstances of the eighteenth century. The Enlightenment, with its confidence in reason as an inborn trait of humanity, proclaimed a faith in individual improvement and social progress in the present.

At the core of eighteenth-century liberalism were the twin principles of liberty and equality: the good society was composed of free men equal in rights. The goal of liberalism was the emancipation of *all* men; its principles were intended to apply equally to all. With good reason, equality has been described as 'one of the oldest and deepest elements in liberal thought'.[2] The principle of equal rights pointed towards a more egalitarian view of social and political life. A Virginian, the 'least egalitarian of Revolutionary leaders', put the point succinctly in 1766: '*Rights* imply *equality* without respect to the dignity of the persons concerned.'[3] In politics the concept of equal rights led readily to ideas of democracy and popular sovereignty. In Europe, as in America, the democratisation and radicalisation of Lockian liberalism did not take place as a result of the logic of ideas, however, but in the context of practical circumstances. As R.R. Palmer has shown, the idea of popular sovereignty — that governments should express the will of a sovereign people — was hammered out in the course of the struggle by the middle classes against the 'constituted bodies' dominated by the aristocracy of the old regime. Under the stimulus of the clash with the aristocracy, the middle classes spoke in the name of 'the people' and defined their position in terms of the universal principles of the Enlightenment. Although the movement was not socially egalitarian, it did signify, as Palmer pointed out, 'a new feeling for a kind of equality, or at least a discomfort with older forms of social stratification'.[4] The idea of popular sovereignty was articulated by the *philosophes*, most notably in Rousseau's conception of the general will. The Declaration of the Rights of Man was a crystallisation of the various elements that went into the making of Enlightenment liberalism — the principles of liberty, equality, and popular sovereignty, embedded in a rationalist structure.

From Enlightenment liberalism came the major ingredients that were to enter into the development of the traditions of the Left between 1789 and 1848: the notion that a good society ought to be characterised by genuine freedom and equality; the principle of popular sovereignty; and the conviction that the validity of these principles was rationally demonstrable. Merely to take seriously the principles of liberty and equality was radical enough, since no society could measure up to such standards. But the rationalist approach to politics vastly magnified the radical potential inherent in liberal and democratic principles; invested with the sanction of reason they possessed ever greater force. Franco Venturi has described the 'typical Enlightenment determination to create a paradise on this earth, to create a completely human society which was egalitarian and free'. Latent in Enlightenment liberalism was the new idea that the ills men suffered were the responsibility of society, and were not to be attributed to providential necessity; guided by reason, men could take control of their destiny. Ernst Cassirer summarised the new attitude as embodied in the writings of Rousseau: 'In its present form society has inflicted the deepest wounds on humanity; but society alone can and should heal those wounds. The burden of responsibility rests upon it from now on.'[5] This new utopian impulse was to inspire the democratic and socialist movements of the nineteenth century. Enlightenment liberalism was the fountainhead of the Left.[6]

Eighteenth-century liberalism, of course, also provided the intellectual weapons that propertied classes were to use against the threat from the democratic and socialist Left in the course of the nineteenth century. The events of the French Revolution between 1789 and 1794 set middle-class liberalism on a new course, quite different from the direction that appeared to have been fixed in 1789. With the beginnings of industrialisation and the emergence of socialist doctrines in the 1830s and 1840s, middle-class liberalism in Europe became even more defensive. Liberty came to mean economic freedom and laissez-faire individualism; in politics it came to mean representative government with a severely limited franchise. In the decades before 1848 in

Europe the socialist Left was to a large extent directed against middle-class liberalism. Hence the historian has to make a special effort to recall the shared assumptions underlying those clashing ideologies.

In England, as usual, these patterns took a somewhat different form. There, the commercial and professional classes were comfortable in social and constitutional circumstances that differed significantly from the situation in France. While the English middle classes accepted the substance of the principles of 1789, they had no reason to embrace them with the fervour displayed by the French. The tradition of the commonwealth men, so influential in its impact on republicanism in Europe and America, remained something of an aberration in eighteenth-century England. The radical temper of Enlightenment liberalism found expression in the limited circle of 'rational Dissenters', especially in Joseph Priestley and Richard Price. With such developments as these in mind, Venturi remarked that the rhythm of the Enlightenment was different in England: 'One has to wait until the eighties and nineties to find men such as Bentham, Price, Godwin and Paine.' The four men so singled out are, on the surface, quite heterogeneous, being both bourgeois and plebeian, and combining doctrines of utility and natural rights. But their social and intellectual heterogeneity makes all the more noteworthy the common ground of Enlightenment liberalism uniting them. For purposes of this study, Richard Price provides a convenient summary of the intellectual foundations common to both working-class radicals and middle-class liberals in England. With good reason Edmund Burke opened his attack on the philosophy underlying the French Revolution with a critique of Price; yet there is very little in Price that is not also to be found, in somewhat different form, in mid-Victorian liberalism.[7]

The basis of Price's meliorist liberalism was his conception of man as a rational and progressive creature, whose destiny it was to continue and accelerate the progress that had already been made. Like Joseph Priestley, he saw history as a pageant of progress, and was confident that the line of advance would continue since it was rooted in the very nature of man. But men could not rely passively on the unfolding of a providential plan, although they could count on continuing to be part of it. They had an obligation to contribute actively to the cause of improvement. The theme is summed up in the title of a discourse delivered by Price in 1787: *The Evidence for a Future Period of Improvement in the State of Mankind, with the Means and Duty of Promoting It.* In the sermon Price set out to show the grounds for his belief that there is a 'progressive improvement in human affairs which will terminate in greater degrees of light and virtue and happiness than have yet been known'. Despite ups and downs, the course of progress has been inexorable: recently 'an age of darkness and barbarism has been succeeded by ages of improvement more rapid than any that preceded them'. As a result of the discoveries of Newton and his pre-decessors, a 'barbarous philosophy' has been replaced by a 'more rational philosophy', which has now become 'the philosophy of the world'. In the present, there was overwhelming evidence that the process was con-tinuing. Price cited a number of developments which 'shew us man a milder animal than he was and the world outgrowing its evils, super-stition giving way, antichrist falling, and the *Millennium* hastening'. Finally, since 'it is the nature of improvement to increase itself', they could look forward to accelerating advances, for there are no 'limits beyond which knowledge and improvement could be carried'.

From these premises flowed activist conclusions. Price did not expect men to sit around waiting for the millennium. On the contrary, he emphasised that 'inactivity and sleep are fatal to improvement', and progress occurs only because of the 'investigations and active exertions of enlightened and honest men. These are aimed directly at the melioration of the world, and without them it would soon be degenerate'. In place of traditional acquiescence in the existing state of things, Price expected continuing action to effect nothing less than 'the melioration of the world'. If only men would take action, 'the world would make swift advances to a better state'. The first object of their exertions, wrote Price, must be 'an improvement in the state of civil government'. Two years later Price welcomed the French Revolution as the salutary consequence of the ideas of Milton and Locke, Montesquieu and Turgot. 'They sowed a seed which has since taken root, and is now growing up to a glorious harvest. To the information they conveyed by their writings we owe those revolutions in which every friend of mankind is now exulting . . . What an encouragement is this to us all in our endeavours to enlighten the world!'[8] This was a new and restless spirit, and no government was safe from it, as Burke was to complain in 1790.

Price's activism, of course, was not directed to the transformation of society, but concentrated on the political sphere. What really mattered was the battle against despotism. In the liberal mode, he welcomed revolutions which overthrew despotic governments and established freedom. For Price, free government was at once a manifestation of past progress and a precondition of further progress to come. A polity of free men, participating actively in the processes of governance, pro-vided the only proper environment for the development of the individual. Despotic government was incompatible with the traits of mind and character that a good society ought to foster. 'There is nothing so debasing as despotic government. They convert the governed into *beasts*, and the men who govern into *demons*.' Free governments, however, 'exalt the human character' and 'give a feeling of *dignity* and consequence to the governed'. Only in a free society can the processes of progress and improvement operate: 'It is only by diligent enquiry, by free discussion and the collision of different sentiments, that knowledge can be increased, truth struck out, and the dignity of our species promoted.' Liberal and rational values were inextricably connected. Knowledge and rationality were essential not only to progress but also to liberty. And liberty was a precondition of progress. All the elements fitted neatly together. 'Our first concern, as lovers of our country, must be to *enlighten* it . . . Why are the nations of the world so patient under despotism? . . . Why do they crouch to tyrants, and submit to be treated as if they were a herd of cattle? Is it not because they are kept in darkness, and want knowledge? Enlighten them and and you will elevate them. Shew them they are *men*, and they will act like *men*.' Like the authors of the Declaration of the Rights of Man, Price was sure that if only men were instructed in their rights they would not put up with the despotism: 'Ignorance is the parent of bigotry, intolerance, persecution and slavery. Inform and instruct mankind; and these evils will be excluded.'

English liberalism, steeped in nonconformity, stressed not only the intellectual but also the moral improvement of the individual, and the two are closely intertwined in Price's thought. On the one hand, of course, the individual, guided by reason, was the primary agent of progress, and his intellectual development was therefore of the highest importance. Of the three 'chief blessings of human nature', truth came first, followed by virtue and liberty. As a man of the Enlightenment, Price expected virtue to 'follow knowledge, and to be directed by it', and he noted that 'virtue without knowledge makes enthusiasts'. At the same time, however, Price also emphasised that 'knowledge without virtue makes devils'. It was the union of virtue and knowledge that 'elevates to the top of human dignity and perfection'. He explained what he meant in the accents of Puritanism: 'We must discourage vice in all its forms; and our endeavours to enlighten must have ultimately in view a reformation of manners and virtuous practice.' The moral improvement of the individual was one of the primary aims of public life. 'Every one of us ought to co-operate with his neighbour in this great work, and to contribute all he can to instruct and reform his fellow creatures.'

There was a distinctly middle-class coloration to Price's thought, which was to become more pronounced among the next generation of liberals. The actual reforms that he had in mind did not go beyond the establishment of representative government with an extended franchise. In the social sphere, the ascendancy of the middle-class was presupposed. In the economic sphere, Price took for granted Adam Smith's assumption that the exercise of freedom by profit-seeking businessmen would automatically redound to the well-being of the community as a whole.

Yet his premises also lent themselves to a more radical formulation, as for example, in William Godwin, who illustrates the close link between Enlightenment liberalism and the Left.

Godwin's *Inquiry Concerning Political Justice* is the incarnation of the spirit of the rationalist Left, as it emerged from the Enlightenment and the French Revolution. While the abstract and theoretical character of his thought ensured that his ideas would have little practical effect, it enabled him to proceed without constricting social presuppositions. Unburdened by a desire to build a political movement, he could pursue the logic inherent in the premises of eighteenth-century liberalism. Characteristically, he sums up the faith of the Enlightenment in five succinct propositions: 'Sound reasoning and truth, when adequately communicated, must always be victorious over error: Sound reasoning and truth are capable of being so communicated: Truth is omnipotent: The vices and moral weakness of man are not invincible: Man is perfectible, or in other words susceptible of perpetual improvement.' These presuppositions, in turn, supported the conclusion that the evils under which men suffer 'are not the inseparable condition of our existence, but admit of removal and remedy'. Godwin proceeded to the conclusion required by these principles, and argued that equal justice requires a 'system of equality'. Not even property remained exempt from his corrosive rationalism. Political remedies, he concluded, were insufficient to achieve justice and equality: 'Republicanism is not a remedy that strikes at the root of evil. Injustice, oppression, and misery can find an abode in those seeming happy seats. But what shall stop the progress of wisdom and improvement where the monopoly of property is unknown?'[9]

Although we are not concerned here with the impact of Godwin's thought on subsequent developments, two instances of his influence may be noted because they illustrate disparate aspects of the legacy of Enlightenment liberalism in Victorian England. As one would expect, both directly and indirectly Godwin's rationalism exercised an important influence on Robert Owen. On the other hand, Francis Place derived rather different conclusions from the *Inquiry*, which he described as his favourite book. Place found in it a 'rationalist gradualism' that ignored political activism in favour of an overriding preoccupation with the intellectual improvement of the individual.[10]

It was not Godwin but Tom Paine who in the 1790s brought English working men into contact with a democratic and egalitarian version of Enlightenment liberalism that was to provide the ideological base for the subsequent development of working-class radicalism.[11] Paine's radicalism also reflected a rather different social world from that of Price and Godwin — embracing artisans, craftsmen, and small businessmen, ranging from skilled working men to the lower middle and middling classes of the eighteenth century. In France these groups provided the social base of *sans-culotte* radicalism. In England they supported the republicanism of Paine and the English Jacobins. In this social milieu liberal principles took on a plebeian coloration.

Paine's republicanism illustrates the mixed legacy that radical working men inherited from the eighteenth century. On the one hand, his ideas were to make possible a sustained assault on the ideological and political structure of the established order: a confident rationalism that insisted on putting received ideas and practices to the test of reason, a total lack of reverence for traditional authority, a deep commitment to popular sovereignty, a truculent egalitarianism, and an eagerness for swift renovation based on universal principles. The logic inherent in Paine's radicalism pointed clearly in the direction of Owen and Bray as well as the Chartist Left. On the other hand, of course, the specific programmatic content of *The Rights of Man* remained very much within the confines of classical liberalism and the principles of 1789, albeit with a number of 'Welfare State' proposals in Part Two. Its orientation was primarily political and anti-aristocratic and assumed an identity of interests among the non-aristocratic classes. Concerned about 'the greedy hand of government', Paine shared the traditional liberal view of the state as an obstacle to progress. The traditionalist aspects of such radicalism and its stabilising function in the mid-nineteenth century are well known. Hence it is necessary at this point to emphasise Paine's affinity with the mainstream of the Left.

Paine took the doctrines of Enlightenment liberalism and applied them to the established order of his day in an irreverent and egalitarian spirit. Sharing the *philosophes'* supreme confidence in reason, he had in mind 'a system of principles as universal as truth and the existence of man'. Foremost among these principles was 'the unity or equality of man'. By the unity of man he meant that 'man is all of *one degree*, and consequently that all men are born equal, and with equal natural rights'. Unlike the exponents of moderate liberalism, with whom he had so much in common, Paine was unwavering in his commitment to the principle of equality and its implications. Hence his demand for a republic was by no means narrowly political in character. In a republic the talents of the citizenry — which are not hereditary — would be fully employed: 'The human faculties act with boldness, and acquire, under this form of government, a gigantic manliness.' The people would be truly sovereign. Fully aware of the extent of social and economic deprivation, he took it for granted that a properly organised republic would deal with it. He deplored the 'poverty and wretchedness prevailing in England and Europe' and the fact that 'we see age going to the work-house, and youth to the gallows' in countries that are called civilised. In his *Agrarian Justice* (1796) he firmly rejected the notion that the distribution of wealth between rich and poor had any rational basis and depicted property as a social product that ought not to be monopolised by a small group of individuals. Such broader aspirations as these were latent in Paine's egalitarian republicanism. However circumscribed the particular reforms that he had in mind, he breathed the confidence of the Left: 'From what we now see, nothing of reform in political world ought to be held improbable. It is an age of revolutions, in which everything may be looked for.' Above all, he was certain of the triumph of 'the principles of universal reformation'.[12]

After the Napoleonic wars the ideas of Paine and the English Jacobins provided the ideological basis of a powerful radical movement in the English towns. During the same period, however, partly in response to the new threat on the Left, middle-class liberalism turned in a different direction, deeply hostile to the egalitarian and democratic spirit of popular radicalism and concerned with defending the interests of the new industrial and commerical élites. The narrowness, rigidity, and class consciousness of the liberal creed in the generation after Waterloo contributed to the radicalisation of the working-class movement in the 1820s and 1830s.

(2) 'The Political-Economic Form of Liberalism', 1798–1834

In trying to see early nineteenth-century liberalism 'as it really was', the historian has to be wary of the usual pitfalls. If he approaches it by way of the high Victorians, he may perceive it as an anticipation of the ideas of Cobden, Gladstone, and Asquith; in that case he may rub off the rough edges as adventitious and ephemeral phenomena. If his approach is Marxist, he may reduce early nineteenth-century liberalism to nothing more than an instance of bourgeois ideology. Even the historicist tradition, with its insistence on the empathetic understanding of historically unique phenomena, does not provide unequivocal guidance, for the anti-Voltairean orientation of historicism can encourage the notion that the sign of a proper empathy is the absence of an interpretation that might be construed as an adverse moral judgement; there has been a tendency to label as 'unhistorical' descriptions of the propertied classes that appear to be critical, reproachful, or left-wing. Yet an attitude of homogenising blandness is not likely to be of much help in getting at the salient characteristics of this harsh and intransigent interlude in the history of English liberalism. It was the class-conscious rigidity of middle-class liberalism in the post-Waterloo generation that directly affected the development of working-class radicalism.

Central to the outlook of the new commercial and industrial middle-class of the 1830s were the doctrines that John Stuart Mill called a 'Benthamic and political-economic form of Liberalism'.[13] It has also been called 'utilitarianism with a small "u" ', a useful label, provided that we keep in mind that the utilitarian liberalism of the provincial middle-class was overlaid with nonconformist piety; Benthamite secularism had little appeal for the men who dominated the new industrial towns. Their world view fused utilitarian and Christian principles. But the cherished principles of early nineteenth-century liberalism were universal only in theory. In practice they were used as weapons to turn back every working-class demand for justice or redress. The 'science' of political economy was invoked to refute proposals for legislative regulation of the working day and to counter dissatisfaction with low wages. Traditionally repressive attitudes towards the poor were now wrapped in the mantle of scientific law and Christian precept, intended to demonstrate that the primary cause of poverty was the ignorance and depravity of the poor. Education became an instrument of propaganda and social control as the middle classes set on foot a large-scale campaign to convince working men of the eternal validity of the social prejudices of their superiors. Ideologues like Andrew Ure debased the liberal and Christian values of western culture by bending them to the service of class interest.

Certain aspects of utilitarian ideology had their origin in circumstances that antedated the ascendancy of the new industrial middle-class. The character of early nineteenth-century liberalism was shaped by the interplay between a body of inherited ideas and traditions and the socio-economic characteristics of that class. The 1790s was the critical decade in shaping the character of the inheritance transmitted by the eighteenth century. As was noted above, the commercial and professional classes of eighteenth-century England, by virtue of the relatively favourable social and constitutional situation that they enjoyed, never embraced the principles of 1789 with the enthusiasm of their French counterparts. After the Revolution, in reaction against Jacobinism, the English middle classes turned aside from the militant liberalism of the Enlightenment and joined the aristocracy and gentry in a policy of repression and reaction. They continued to accept the fundamental principles of liberalism, but in limited and negative form. Also during the 1790s, as part of this literally 'reactionary' trend, all segments of the propertied classes embraced a new and harsher version of traditional attitudes towards the poor. In 1798 both of these ideological patterns received sharp theoretical formulation in T.R. Malthus' *Essay on the Principle of Population*, which left its imprint on the utilitarian liberalism of the next generation.

Malthus' *Essay* combined two aspects of the social and ideological currents of the 1790s and gave them a distinctive form. First, he linked the problems of poor relief and population. He gave a demographic slant to the new concern about poor relief that developed among the propertied classes after the bad harvest of 1795. At the same time Malthus joined his economic and demographic analysis to a frontal attack on the meliorist aspirations of Enlightenment liberalism. In developing his two themes Malthus invoked the authority of science and the Enlightenment in a critique of the Left, both reformist and radical. More influential than Malthus' specific conclusions was the fact that for a generation social issues tended to be perceived in terms of his categories and temper of mind.

The full title of Malthus' essay underlines the link between his interest in the problem of population and his rejection of meliorist liberalism: *An Essay on the Principle of Population, as it Affects the Future Improvement of Society, With Remarks on the Speculations of Mr Godwin, M. Condorcet and Other Writers.* In fact, Malthus was concerned not only with Godwin's more utopian speculations but with the basic principles of Enlightenment liberalism, common to Price, Condorcet, and the 1789 Declaration. Thus he explicitly rejected the assumption that 'the greatest part of the vices and weaknesses of men proceed from the injustice of their political and social institutions, and that if these were removed and the understandings of men more enlightened, there would be little or no temptation in the world to evil'. He took pride in demonstrating that this was 'entirely a false conception'. He made it plain that he was refuting not merely Godwin's aberrant notions about property and equality but their underlying premises. Malthus devoted a whole chapter to a trenchant critique of Godwin's five propositions, which were quoted above, and insisted on the futility of any schemes of improvement based on such premises. At once foreshadowing and influencing the middle-class liberalism of the next generation, Malthus turned to the Enlightenment for arguments to use against the Left. Even a society founded on the most exemplary principles, he argued, would necessarily degenerate as a result of the operation of 'the inevitable laws of nature'.[14] This Malthusian scientism was to be prominent in the political-economic form of liberalism.

Malthus incorporated into the *Essay*, in seemingly scientific and objective form, the increasingly severe attitudes towards the poor that had developed among the propertied classes since the Restoration. Those classes had operated on the traditional assumption that 'the poor' or 'the lower orders' were inherently lazy and inclined to any number of disagreeable habits. Under the impact of Restoration Puritanism they were easily persuaded that the primary cause of poverty was the personal deficiencies of the poor. These socially determined attitudes, in turn, inspired sporadic attempts by the propertied classes to do something about what they perceived to be the problem of the poor. Of the various vices to which the poor were believed to be prone, idleness came to loom larger and larger in the consciousness of the

propertied classes in the eighteenth century. The charity school movement was intended to inculcate habits of diligence and obedience. It
was generally assumed that the most intense discipline and indoctrination were necessary to overcome the natural disposition of the poor to
be idle. By the closing decades of the eighteenth century, under the
impact of evangelicalism, the prevailing view of the poor became exceedingly moralistic. Doubts were expressed about the desirability of
continuing to grant poor relief, since it tended only to further weaken
the moral character of the poor.[15]

Malthus added new cause for concern about the vices of the poor,
and gave the propertied classes more reason to believe that the
labouring poor constituted a major threat to the well-being of society.
Viewed from the standpoint of 'the principle of population', their
rapid reproduction threatened to put an intolerable pressure on the food
supply. In this context, Malthus objected to the meliorist theories of
Godwin and Condorcet on the grounds that their well-intentioned
efforts to improve the condition of 'the lower classes of people' were
bound to be counter-productive. The chief example of misguided
benevolence that Malthus had in mind was the English poor laws, which
he denounced for reasons that were soon to be known as 'Malthusian':
such poor relief defeated its own purpose by encouraging the poor to
excessive and premature procreation, thus putting pressure on a food
supply that was increasing only arithmetically. In disarmingly quiet
tones, noting that it was after all only a 'palliative', Malthus proposed
'the total abolition of all the present parish-laws'. He explained his
position in a well-known passage: 'Hard as it may appear in individual
instances, dependent poverty ought to be held disgraceful. Such a
stimulus appears to be absolutely necessary to promote the happiness of
the great mass of mankind and every general attempt to weaken this
stimulus, however benevolent its apparent intention, will always defeat
its own purpose.'[16] Although Malthus' proposal for abolition of the
poor laws did not win general acceptance, a number of Malthusian
attitudes entered into utilitarianism and the doctrines of political
economy.[17] It was generally agreed that demographic and economic
considerations militated against the existing system of poor relief,
which provided potentially disastrous inducements both to sloth and
to premature procreation.

The next stage in the development of the Malthusian side of middle-
class liberalism can be seen in an influential book published in 1821 by
Thomas Chalmers, a Scottish Presbyterian minister who developed a
programme that foreshadowed middle-class liberal policies that were to
be adopted in many industrial towns in the 1830s, partly in response to
his writings.[18] In Chalmers the moralistic element, which had been only
latent in Malthus, was very much in the foreground and his main theme

was the need to raise the moral level of the working classes. To this end, he recommended that the methods of the country parish be brought to the town and that ministers of religion make a joint effort with political economists. The primary objective of the enterprise was unmistakably Malthusian: 'The tendency to excessive population can only find its thorough and decisive counteraction among the amended characters and the moralised characters of the people themselves.' More specifically, the working classes had to be taught to curb their sensuality. 'So long as there is generally a low and grovelling taste among the people', they will rush into premature marriages. Hence the urgent need 'to go forth among the people' and 'deliver lessons'. The point was to make the working man 'a more reflective and a less sensual being than before; and, altogether, impress a higher cast of respectability on all his habits and on all his ways'. Chalmers' message was to be delivered by the provident societies a decade later: 'The high road to the secure and permanent prosperity of labourers, is through the medium of their own sobriety, and intelligence, and virtue.' They must put their confidence in the 'virtues and frugalities of private life'.

Writing in 1821, Chalmers also had very much in mind the need to combat the errors and vices of popular radicalism. He pointed out 'the affinity which subsists between the cause of popular education and that of popular tranquillity'. He was eloquent on the subject of the ideological value of 'the truths and doctrines of political economy'. He could not conceive of a 'likelier instrument than a judicious course of economical doctrine, for tranquillising the popular mind, and removing from it all those delusions which are the main causes of popular disaffection and discontent'. Once the people absorb sound economic knowledge it will prove to be 'a sedative to all sorts of turbulence and disorder'. Convinced that political economists and Christian philanthropists had hitherto 'maintained an unfortunate distance from each other', he wanted them to join forces, in order to convey interlocking moral and economic truths to the working classes.[19] In fact, that alliance was to be very much in evidence in the provident societies, which looked to Chalmers, among others, for inspiration.

In a number of the larger towns in the early 1830s 'anxious solicitude' about the poor led to the formation of new institutions intended to deal with the problem. The provident societies took as their premise the long-standing belief of the middle and upper classes that many of the 'evils' which affect the poor might be 'alleviated or removed by a judicious management of the resources within their own power'. Hence the new societies proposed to instruct the poor in habits of 'forethought and economy'. An elaborate system of visitors was set up to bring this instruction directly to the homes of the poor. These visitors were also equipped to collect small deposits, so as to stimulate regular saving, and a premium higher than the regular rate of interest was to be paid. In addition, the visitors were assigned another function which reflected deep-seated middle-class attitudes towards the poor. They were to seek out the 'deserving' poor, so that the 'occasional relief of sickness and unavoidable misfortune' would not be misplaced. In the blunt language of the societies, the visitors were charged with 'the suppression of mendicity and imposture'. Along with 'the desire to elevate the character and condition of the working population' was a determination not to be cheated by the depraved creatures whose vices had led them into poverty. From this social and moral perspective, the societies set out 'to encourage the lower orders by pecuniary rewards and the personal inculcation of religious and moral obligations so to economise their money and improve their habits as to elevate themselves above the condition of pauperism, and to regard it eventually as an odious means of subsistence'.[20]

The provident societies brought to a climax the moralistic view of the poor that had been developing among the propertied classes since the Restoration. By 1830 it had been reinforced by evangelical censoriousness. Animated by a sincere desire to 'diffuse the blessing of religious truth through populous districts of the town', the middle classes organised an assault on indigent working men. Their basic attitude was that of the master suspicious of his servants, and the apparatus of visitors — the innovation of which they were so proud — was intended simply to ensure that the working classes did not deceive their betters. But this crude class attitude had been overlaid with a self-righteous revulsion from the 'vices' of the poor. 'Not satisfied with the mere detection of mendicant imposture, the District Provident Society proposes measures to check the vicious disposition that engenders it.' They were in hot pursuit of nothing less than 'a *permanent* cure of the great moral disorder of mendicity'. Hence visitors would have to get detailed knowledge of potential recipients of relief, 'for the artifices of hypocrisy and cunning can only be baffled by information obtained through long acquaintance and habits of confidential intercourse'. Thus, along with Christianity, personal relations were to be enlisted in the service of the suspicions and prejudices of the propertied classes. This was the social reality behind the announcement of the Liverpool society that it intended 'to rescue the lower orders from the miseries of poverty and vice, and to make them the authors of their own independence and virtue by encouraging them to form prudent and moral habits'.[21]

As the propertied classes became convinced that handouts under the poor law were immoral and dangerous, the poor rates continued to rise. Under these circumstances, the Whig government felt impelled to take action, and in 1833 appointed a Royal Commission to make recommendations. The result was the Poor Law Amendment Act of 1834, a statute which enacted the prejudices of the propertied classes in the rigid and doctrinaire form dictated by Benthamite utilitarianism.[22] Its approach was summed up in the principles of less eligibility and the workhouse test, although these were not provisions of the Act. The law – and the 'Bastilles' that were to be constructed in its name – was seared into the consciousness of the working classes. They recognised its true character as a savage piece of class legislation. The working classes were united in detesting the 'principles of 1834'.

The individual most responsible for the new poor law was Edwin Chadwick, the Benthamite who dominated the deliberations of the Royal Commission. He was not a Malthusian in the strict sense, for he rejected out of hand any suggestion that poor relief be abolished. Chadwick's idea was that the poor relief system might be used as a deterrent and a stimulus so as to create a truly free labour market, which would benefit everyone, including the poor. In brief, the natural indolence of the poor was to be overcome by compelling them to seek work first and to ask for relief only as a last resort. To that end, outdoor relief was to be abolished, and relief would be given only in the workhouse, where, as Chadwick remarked in the Commission's Report, the pauper's 'situation on the whole shall not be made really or apparently so eligible as the situation of the independent labourer of the lowest class'. This was certainly a plausible recommendation in the light of the social attitudes of the propertied classes. With bureaucratic and technocratic zeal, however, Chadwick spelled out the character of a 'system' which was expected to work wonders in handling 'the idle and the dissolute', a phrase which underlines the moralism beneath the veneer of officialese. 'By the workhouse system', wrote Chadwick, 'is meant having all relief in the workhouse, and making this workhouse an uninviting place of wholesome restraint . . . '[23]

Parliament did not accept the commission's recommendation for the abolition of outdoor relief, nor did it enact the principle of less eligibility or the workhouse test. But it established a Poor Law Commission and empowered it to issue regulations for the administration of poor relief, and set in motion an administrative revolution to make sure that the desired changes would be brought about. The commission, spurred on by its secretary, Edwin Chadwick, made plain its commitment to the workhouse test and the principle of less eligibility. One of their policies was the separation of husband and wife in the workhouse. In replying to working-class protests against this practice, the commissioners expressed the attitudes that made the new poor law a symbol of class rule at its worst. They denied that the purpose of the regulation was population control. Since they did not in fact share Malthus' concern about population growth, their reply had a certain plausibility. Yet the regulation clearly reflected the Malthusian feeling that the working classes were mired in 'sensuality' that had to be curbed on moral and demographic grounds. The commissioners also explained that the separation of husband and wife was part of the discipline intended to persuade the inmates to leave as soon as possible. That reply at least had the virtue of candour. Other replies to protests were simply smug. The commissioners provided testimonials from elderly couples about how glad they were to be separated, pointed out that soldiers and sailors were separated from their wives, and noted that families were, after all, separated only at night.[24]

When the assistant commissioners went into the industrial areas to introduce the new law in 1837, they were greeted with the resistance that they deserved. To be sure, neither the law nor the commissioners' regulations were ever carried out with full rigour. The workhouse test was enforced only sporadically. In fact, as Michael Rose has shown, in the industrial areas allowances continued to be paid out in support of inadequate wages.[25] There was considerable variation from one board of guardians to another. Generosity and compassion were by no means absent. It would be misleading, to say the least, to suggest that the early-Victorian bourgeoisie made the law the occasion for an all-out assault on the working classes. On the other hand, in order to understand the social and ideological conflict of the 1830s and 1840s, it is important not to whitewash the law and its underlying principles.

The new poor law received substantial support from many prominent middle-class liberals in the industrial towns. In the *Leeds Mercury* Edward Baines, Jr. acclaimed the importance of the new legislation. After the law had been in operation for two years he announced that it would remain 'a monument to the honour of Political Economy'. In Nottingham the law was greeted with enthusiasm by Absalom Barnett, an overseer whose stern view of the poor was compounded of utilitarianism and evangelicalism. He was supported by men of a similar outlook, such as William Felkin, a lace manufacturer of humble origins who was later to be mayor. The chairman of the board of guardians of Ashton Union in industrial Lancashire was Samuel Robinson, a humane and benevolent man devoted to mechanics' institutes and other philanthropic causes. In 1837 he wrote a pamphlet in defence of the new law against criticism by Charles Hindley, who had said that 'poverty ought not to be treated as a crime'. Robinson argued that such a statement was irrelevant, because 'the New Poor Law nowhere, that I am aware, proposes to punish poverty as a crime'. Having scored that debating point, however, he made plain his acceptance of the principles of 1834 and showed why supporters of the statute laid themselves open to Hindley's accusation: 'Poverty, in itself, is indeed no crime; but the improvidence and profligacy which are the common causes of poverty are crimes, and crimes of considerable magnitude.' Robinson's confidence in the law reflected the usual dogmatism of its proponents: 'But I firmly and conscientiously believe, that in the principles of the law is involved the social regeneration of an immense portion of the country, the agricultural, which has been degraded into the most debasing pauperism under the influence of the old system; and that it is only by a rigid adherence to the same principles that the manufacturing portion can be preserved from a like degradation.'[26] For good reason working men in 'the manufacturing portion' of the country regarded those principles as anathema. Robinson's good works could not remove the stigma.

The middle classes were, of course, by no means united in support of the new poor law.[27] Charles Hindley was a manufacturer, a patron of mechanics' institutes, and a friend of Brougham himself. His liberalism led him to denounce the law. In the anti-poor law movement as a whole in the 1830s there was an active middle-class element. Very often local men who served as guardians mitigated the harshness of the law. On the other hand, there were also guardians whose niggardliness and meanness had to be curbed by the commissioners, well-intentioned and humane men who cannot be written off as callous 'utilitarians'. While this diversity must be kept in mind, however, it should not be permitted to obscure the prime importance of the new poor law in the development of working-class radicalism in the 1830s. The law expressed with administrative lucidity the prevailing attitudes of the propertied classes towards the poor. On the one hand the poor were perceived as a vicious and ignorant lot whose intellectual and moral deficiencies made them personally responsible for their poverty. On the other hand, with little regard for consistency, the poor were also treated as things — objects in the labour market — whose behaviour had to be manipulated in accordance with the laws of political economy. These were the same principles that underlay the provident societies of the 1830s. Even middle-class critics of the new poor law, who invoked the standard of common sense and compassion in calling for a more moderate implementation, were by no means free of its underlying assumptions. Thus, the 1834 poor law presented in stark form the bourgeois liberal vision of society — the negation of the basic values and aspirations of working-class radicalism.

Working-class radicals also encountered middle-class liberalism in the form of incessant propaganda, handed down from above.[28] Implicit in the Malthusian view of the poor was the notion that if they were to be rescued from their low state they had to be instructed in various important matters of which they were woefully ignorant, above all the principles of political economy. While the political economists themselves were more flexible and various in their views than was once supposed, there is no mistaking the patently ideological character of the political economy being disseminated to the working classes in the 1820s and 1830s by the likes of Mrs Marcet, Harriet Martineau, Charles Knight, and countless lecturers at mechanics' institutes. They were intent on helping benighted working men to understand a corpus of economic principles whose absolute validity was beyond question. Behind the facade of economic science was a total commitment to the social predominance and moral pre-eminence of the middle classes in relation to a subordinate working-class. Also fundamental to political economy in its early-Victorian form was some version of the principles of 1834, perceiving 'the poor' as inherently inclined to sloth and vice. In this and in other areas the principles of economic science were inseparable from unexamined social and moral assumptions. On this base rested such doctrines as laissez faire and the wages fund theory. Most important, however, was the whole complex of ideas and assumptions subsumed under the rubric of political economy. It posed a clear alternative to the egalitarian aspirations of working-class radicalism. Radical working men accurately perceived political economy as an elaborate rationalisation of inequality and middle-class domination.

Perhaps the most significant aspect of the writings of Mrs Marcet and Harriet Martineau is the tone of condescending self-assurance. In Mrs Marcet's *Conversations on Political Economy* the misconceptions to be refuted by a 'Mrs B' are presented by a child, whose questions are 'such as would be likely to arise in the mind of an intelligent young person, fluctuating between the impulse of her heart and the progress of her reason, and naturally imbued with all the prejudices and popular feelings of uninformed benevolence'. Mrs B patiently explains to Caroline that 'diversity of rank and condition' is highly beneficial, since it tends to 'stimulate the industry and bring into action the various faculties of mankind'. She depicts a well-ordered society in which the industrious become rich, the less industrious remain poor, and 'the idle are reduced to positive indigence'.[29] Like Harriet Martineau, Mrs Marcet was obsessed with a Malthusian anxiety about pauperism, ignorance, and vice. The villains are 'the idle and the profligate'. For her part, Harriet Martineau was more verbose, turning out nine volumes of *Illustrations of Political Economy*, and more relentlessly didactic. In her ninth volume, *The Moral of Many Fables*, she regales the reader with summaries of principles. Among these the 'wages fund' or 'subsistence fund' figures prominently. In no-nonsense fashion she explains the simple and self-evident truth that there is a fixed fund available for wages. Hence it follows inexorably that the *only* way to raise wages is to decrease the labour supply. She presents her teachings in a highly personal tone. 'There is a very cheering moral involved in every melancholy story that we hear of the contentions of masters and men, and of the sufferings which thence arise. The fact is that, so far from the masters having any natural power — even if they had the wish, — to oppress the working classes, the working classes hold a power which may make them the equals in independence of any class in society.' The working classes have the power to determine 'whether the sub-sistence fund shall be divided among a moderate number or among a scrambling multitude'.[30] They can delay procreation — or they can emigrate.

Andrew Ure, a staunch supporter of mechanics' institutes and provident societies, in 1835 wrote a classic apologia for the new indus-trialism of Lancashire and Yorkshire. His *The Philosophy of Manufactures* is of interest as an example of the ideological inclinations of the middle classes in their most blatant form, for it expresses the middle-class outlook almost to the point of parody. Ure takes for granted the virtue of manufacturers and the absolute validity of laissez-faire philosophy. He approaches the working classes as an enemy, and applies Christian and utilitarian principles in a mean and narrow spirit. The poor must be rescued from pauperism and subversion and trained to be docile and diligent workers. That is the primary purpose of popular education. While affirming the 'paramount importance to the state of providing good education for the children of the poor', he emphasised that it must be of the proper sort. In well-ordered schools the children 'learn to be obedient and orderly, and to restrain their passions'; when they move on into the factory they invariably are 'most obedient and docile'. Ure carried into the early nineteenth century many eighteenth-century attitudes towards the poor. The workers must be educated to be submissive and contented with their lot; they must be taught to look to the future life for rewards that it would be immoral to expect in this world. Above all, they must not be educated above their station. He quoted with approval strictures against those who have been 'continually instilling into the minds of the people, that education is the way to advancement, that "knowledge is power", that a man cannot "better himself" without some learning!' And the factory owners certainly must not be compelled to provide schooling for the children in their mills. In one of his best passages, Ure expatiated on the dire consequences of the education clauses of the Factory Act of 1833. Because of this impracticable provision the mill owners, according to Ure, had been obliged to dismiss children under twelve, with disastrous results: 'The children so discharged from their light and profitable labour, instead of receiving the education promised by parliament, get none at all; they are thrown out of the warm spinning-rooms upon the cold world, to exist by beggary or plunder, in idleness and vice — a life woefully contrasted with their former improving state at the factory, and its Sunday-school.'[31]

Ure depicted Christianity as an invaluable instrument for the production of a docile work force. First of all, as a sort of opium of the people, it might console working men for present misery by holding forth the prospect of bliss in the after life. The first and great lesson of the Gospel, Ure argues, 'is that man must expect his chief happiness, not in the present, but in a future state of existence. He alone who acts on this principle will possess his mind in peace under every sublunary vicissitude, and will not care to scramble with feverish envy or angry contention for the idol phantoms which the dupes of pleasure and ambition pursue'. But Christianity was also assigned a more positive function in making the working classes safe for capitalism. 'How speedily would the tumults which now agitate almost every class of society, in the several states of Christendom, subside, were that sublime doctrine cordially embraced as it ought to be!' Only Christianity could furnish 'restraints powerful enough to stem the torrents of passion and appetite which roll over nations'. This transformation of the sinner into a man of virtue could not be accomplished by 'sentimental theism', however. 'Where then shall mankind find this transforming power? — in the cross of Christ. It is the sacrifice which removes the guilt of sin: it is the motive which removes the love of sin.'[32] Thus Ure enlisted Christianity in the service of capitalism in the war against envious, indolent, and predatory working men.

In a marvellous passage Ure urged the manufacturers to apply the principles of Christianity in their factories: 'It is, therefore, excessively the interest of every mill-owner, to organise his moral machinery on equally sound principles with his mechanical, for otherwise he will never command the steady hands, watchful eyes, and prompt co-operation, essential to excellence of product. Improvident workpeople are apt to be reckless, and dissolute ones to be diseased: thus both are ill-qualified to discharge the delicate labours of automatic industry . . . There is in fact no case to which the Gospel truth, "Godliness is great gain", is more applicable than to the administration of an extensive factory.'[33] This was the talk of an ideologue, who carried middle-class fantasies to an extreme. Any extended attempt to use Christianity as he recommended would have been counter-productive. But Ure's spirit is plainly visible in a good deal of the propaganda put out by the early-Victorian middle classes.

Chambers' Edinburgh Journal is a good example of the middle-class liberal view of the working classes and the sort of propaganda based on it. Tract No. 170, 'Hints to Workmen', issued by the Chambers brothers in 1846, was hardly calculated to win converts, but it certainly made plain the hard-nosed liberal perception of the working classes. 'The working classes generally are remarkable for their credulity. They too often believe, and allow themselves to be carried away, by opinions propounded by individuals of their own body, although these opinions are at variance with the experience, or with principles professed by the wisest men in the country.' This line was set forth in the name of 'independence of thought and action'. Presumably intended to persuade working men of the virtues of laissez-faire capitalism, the *Journal* was in fact a perfect embodiment of just those middle-class attitudes which radical working men were trying to combat. The smug tone of the *Chambers' Journal* is noteworthy, because it reveals class attitudes so directly and vividly. An 1845 comment on the original purpose of the publication is innocent of any sense that working men had legitimate grievances. 'We felt that by this means a vast amount of unequivocal good might be effected amongst the humbler classes in particular . . . Gaining the heart of the poor man, always inclined to jealousy, it might force reproofs and maxims upon him which he would take from no other hand. By such a work the young might be, even in the receipt of amusement, actuated to industrious and honourable courses.'[34] The same point of view pervades an 1844 tract, 'The Employer and Employed', cast in the form of a dialogue between an employer and a workman. In the first sentence, the mill owner speaks: 'I am glad to see you Mr Jackson; step into my house, and let us have a little conversation on the present unhappy differences on the subject of wages. Perhaps I may show you that the ideas entertained respecting employers are not, by any means just.'[35] The *Northern Star* devoted a long review article to a denunciation of the tract. The tract — and the *Chambers' Journal* — exemplified the middle-class smugness and arrogance that reinforced Chartist militancy.

Just as the Christian and liberal ideal of elevating the character and condition of the people was bent into a narrowly middle-class shape, so the ideal of popular education was overborne by the socially determined impulse to indoctrination and propaganda. James Kay, who in the 1840s was to preside over a great expansion of government activity in support of popular education, at the outset approached the matter in a Malthusian and utilitarian spirit of social control. Education was essential to raise the level of the poor who were 'too often consumed by vice and improvidence' as well as 'selfish profligacy'. The poor had to be persuaded to be provident and delay marriage. Only a general system of education could rescue the poor from dissipation, idleness, and ignorance. Kay also saw popular education as a means of combating the spread of subversive ideas among the working classes. In 1832 he was concerned that 'political desperadoes' would tempt the 'turbulent population' of the poorer sections of Manchester to 'the hazards of the swindling game of revolution'. In 1839 he saw the Chartists in the same terms: ignorant and unprincipled men, taking advantage of the ignorance and discontent of the working classes. He saw education as the best means of inculcating sound principles and showing the poor that 'their interests are inseparable from those of other orders of society'.[36]

The elementary schools established by the religious societies shared many of Kay's social and educational objectives. That is, they perceived popular education in terms of some form of indoctrination and social control. Their reading books are a case in point. Daily Lesson Book Number 3 of the British and Foreign School Society was an anthology to teach reading. The poetry was selected with a view to the 'cultivation of a humble, contented, and domestic spirit'. The prose included extracts relating to 'elements of political economy, slavery, war, temperance, economy, cleanliness, trust-worthiness, obedience to laws, sanctification of the Sabbath, piety, etc.'. The lesson outline for 'improvement of the mind', the first in the book, read in part as follows: 'Great end of knowledge, not worldly advantage, — merely to get on, — not mere gratification, — not display, — but to make us happier and better, — to do good to others, — to lead to God.' The selection on wages from Archbishop Whately's *Money Matters*, explained that 'the rate of wages does not depend on the hardness of the labour, but on the value of the work done'. It was preceded by a text from Proverbs: 'Slothfulness casteth into a deep sleep: and an idle soul shall suffer hunger.' Benjamin Franklin was included under the heading 'The Way to Wealth'. 'If we are industrious, we shall never starve, as poor Richard says, for, "At the working man's house hunger looks in, but dares not enter".' The lesson outline for 'Happiness' read in part as follows: 'How to be found. — In performance of duty — esteem of wise and good — approval of conscience — favour of God.' It concluded with a brief summary: 'Happiness is in the mind — not in outward circumstances, il.: contented poor man — miserable rich — if indolent and useless; . . . '[37]

In the area of adult education also liberal idealism was tainted by the omnipresence of socially determined impulses. Thus, the mechanics' institutes were intended not only to diffuse useful knowledge but also to wean working men away from subversive ideas and to inculcate the social philosophy of the middle classes. The first proponents of the institutes, partly in order to refute the arguments of Tories who viewed with alarm any sort of popular education, depicted them as instruments of social order, intended to teach the working classes their place in society. The institutes would make working men 'more intelligent and useful in their several stations of life, better acquainted with their duties and responsibility'. It was argued that the 'greater degree of knowledge an individual possesses, the more easily he can calculate upon what the duties of society and of his station, impose upon him'. Although religion and politics were formally excluded from the curriculum to begin with, the founders assumed that students attending the institutes would absorb the principles of political economy. Brougham edited a course of lectures on political economy that were read at Manchester and Liverpool; the lectures were also available to member branches from the Yorkshire Union of Mechanics' Institutes. Benjamin Heywood, a leader of the movement in Manchester, drew up a list of the topics that ought to be delivered at a series of 'plain and popular lectures'; they included the security of property, the necessity for differences in fortune and condition, the circumstances which regulate wages, the advantages of provident societies, and the operation of the poor laws.[38]

Sir Robert Peel's *Address on the Establishment of a Library and a Reading-Room at Tamworth* in January 1841 illustrates the condescending tone of the ideology being disseminated by the patrons of mechanics' institutes and reading rooms. 'It will not be our fault if the ample page of knowledge, rich with the spoils of time, is not unrolled to you. You will not be able to say that "chill penury" has "frozen the genial current" of your aspirations for knowledge and distinction. We tell you that here is access for you to that information which may at the same time facilitate your advance in your worldly occupations, and lay the foundation for mental improvement.' Thus Peel gave an ideological cast to the ideal of the pursuit of knowledge by attributing poverty to the failure of working men to take advantage of educational opportunities that would enable them to get on in the world. He reduced adult education to a crass materialism: if working men would give up 'vulgar amusements' and find time for 'rational recreation' they would be richly rewarded. Among the rewards would be the opportunity to escape from 'heartless associates' to which they were condemned by their class position. Behind the rhetoric of the mechanics' institutes lay the standard social attitudes of the early-Victorian middle classes.

The liberal ideology of the 1830s reflected a new and intense class consciousness on the part of the middle classes.[39] In confrontation with the aristocracy above and the working-class below they had developed a strong sense of identity and a deep pride in their achievements. They affirmed the justice of their case against the aristocracy in two agitations, first for the franchise and then for the repeal of the Corn Laws. Against the claims of the working-class the middle-class liberals took up an intransigent position on every issue; drawing a line at the £10 householder, exalting laissez faire in the Halifax resolutions and like documents, and smashing the trade unionism of 1833–4. They proclaimed their own rectitude in contrast to the privileged luxury of the aristocracy and the depravity of the poor.

It was in reaction against a self-righteous bourgeois liberalism that working-class radicalism developed, taking as its point of departure the egalitarianism of Paine and the English Jacobins.

(3) The Growth of Working-Class Radicalism, 1816–36

During the turbulent decades that followed the Napoleonic wars, working-class radicalism developed into a formidable ideological force.[40] The first phase, which came to a climax in 1819, reflected the outlook of Paine. As articulated by men like Wooler, Carlile, Cobbett and Hunt, post-war radicalism was plebeian and populist in tone, and vehemently hostile to established forms of authority. In this form English working men appropriated the traditions of the Left, rooted in the Enlightenment and the French Revolution. This post-war radicalism was for the most part confined within the social and political categories of the eighteenth-century liberal attack on an aristocratic constitution. Beginning in the 1830s, however, a number of interconnected developments contributed to the gradual transformation of the radicalism of 1819; it absorbed the new social and economic critique developed by Owen and the anti-capitalist economists; it became more class conscious, oriented to a conflict between working-class and middle-class. Moreover, like other movements on the Left in Europe and America in the pre-1848 period. working-class radicalism in England absorbed a romantic impulse to social regeneration that raised to an even higher power the aspirations fostered by the Enlightenment. The distinctive feature of the development of the Left in England was the active participation of working men, who had a direct experience of exploitation and deprivation in the new industrial society. From their ranks came men who brought to the radical cause strong intelligence and deep commitment.

Over twenty years before the first Chartist petition working-class radicalism was firmly established in the cities and towns of the midlands and the north. Between 1816 and 1819 the radicals covered the manufacturing districts with a network of clubs devoted to political discussion and agitation. The great demonstrations of those years constituted the visible expression of a solidly based grass-roots movement, composed of men who had come to political consciousness under the spur of trade depression. In the traditions of popular radicalism they found a vehicle of protest and hope. The Hampden clubs were first, founded with striking rapidity in the late summer of 1816. The initial impetus had come from Major John Cartwright, who since 1812 had made a number of tours of the provinces preaching manhood suffrage. The movement struck a responsive chord, and six months after the founding of the first of the provincial Hampden clubs there were forty in the Lancashire area alone. They were also strong in a number of urban centres, with connections in the surrounding districts — among them Leicester, Birmingham, Nottingham, and Sheffield. Although the Hampden clubs disappeared quickly in response to the repression mounted by the government and the propertied classes, new political clubs soon re-emerged in 1818 in different form. Some took as their model the Political Protestants of

Hull; others, variously called Union Societies or Political Unions, bore an affinity to the Stockport Union for the Promotion of Human Happiness. Whereas the Hampden clubs had been concerned primarily with organising political activity and demonstrations, their successors concentrated on discussion, debate, and propaganda. They were closely linked to the new radical press, of which the *Black Dwarf* was the most influential representative at this time. From the Methodists they took their main institutional mechanism, the weekly class meeting. Despite their primary orientation to discussion rather than action, they were swept up into the agitation that reached its climax at Peterloo. Although the radicals were inactive in the 1820s, they had created an enduring tradition. During the Reform Bill crisis independent working-class political groups were very much in evidence in the provincial cities, some of them affiliated with the London-based National Union of the Working Classes. They provided continuity of ideology and personnel between 1819 and 1839.[41]

By 1819, then, English working men had seized the traditions of the Left, made them their own, and established the foundations of working-class radicalism. Elements of the legacy of 1819 were to remain firmly lodged in the consciousness of Victorian working men. What were its characteristics? The first point to be noted is that at the outset it was not specifically 'working-class' in character, but populist, plebeian, and *sans-culotte*. The primary social category of the ideology of 1819 was 'the People', rather than 'the working-class' or 'working men', and it approached 'the rights of all men' in political rather than class terms. Its leadership reflected the typical *sans-culotte* alliance of artisans, craftsmen, small masters and shopkeepers. E.P. Thompson has described the varied social composition of the post-war radical movement: ' "the industrious classes" — stockingers, hand-loom weavers, cotton-spinners, artisans', and also 'a widespread scattering of small masters, tradesmen, publicans, booksellers and professional men, from among which groups the officers of local political societies were sometimes drawn'.[42] Despite the presence of these lower-middle-class elements, however, the spirit of the movement was aggressively plebeian rather than petty bourgeois. These disparate social groups were united by a common hostility to the domination exercised by the aristocracy, the gentry, and the urban patriciate. They expressed their protest in terms of the political egalitarianism of Painite radicalism. Here was the ideological point of departure for the subsequent development of working-class radicalism.

Two aspects of the legacy of 1819 were to exercise an important formative influence in the shaping of early-Victorian working-class radicalism. First of all, it embodied a militant activism, derived from Enlightenment liberalism fused with plebeian energy and egalitarianism. The rationalist impatience and irreverence of the eighteenth-century

Left had been harnessed to the endemic discontents of working men subject to old forms of exploitation in a new urban and industrial setting. By 1819 an incipient working-class Left was in being, ready to absorb the new social and economic radicalism of the 1820s and 1830s. In confrontation with the bourgeois liberalism that was to culminate in the principles of 1834, the radicalism of 1819 responded with a swift move to the Left. At the same time, however, other aspects of the legacy of 1819 deflected the attention of radical working men to ancillary and obsolete issues and objectives, exemplified by the continuing attack on 'Old Corruption' and the world of sinecurists and placemen. In fact, this aspect of traditional radicalism is so conspicuous that it can easily obscure the latent subversiveness of the spirit of 1819 and its affinities with the new ideological currents of the 1830s. We shall turn first to the archaic elements of the radicalism of 1819.

The main impetus behind the 1819 agitation was economic distress: the 'chilling hand of penury' had been felt in the manufacturing towns, and the radicals knew all too well that 'the children were in rags and the fathers were destitute'. But the men of 1819 perceived the economic problem and its solution in terms derived from the eighteenth-century liberal attack on aristocratic government. A Leeds meeting reported that 'in reviewing the causes which have led to this state of unexampled misery, we find that an immense taxation, co-operating with the corn-laws and other infamous legislative enactments of the same nature, have materially operated to produce it'. Such high taxes were necessary only to pay for wars contracted by the 'borough tyrants', to keep a standing army, and to maintain 'sinecurists and pensioned minions who live in every species of luxury at the expense of a starving people'. Denunciations of 'Placemen and Pensioners' were routine, on the assumption that excessive taxation was the cause of mass poverty. Compounding the ideological confusion was an overlapping of arguments based on natural rights and historic rights. A Newcastle meeting defended 'our own natural and imprescriptible rights, which we conceive to be our birthright as Britons, and to be guaranteed to us by the wise laws and constitution of our ancestors'.[43]

Along with such elements however, the radicalism of 1819 also embodied a firm assertion of the egalitarian and democratic values that were to be so fundamental to the new proto-socialist ideas of the 1820s and 1830s. Implicit in the spirit of Peterloo was a rejection of the various forms of subordination and deference. There was more than political rhetoric in the first of the resolutions carried at a Leeds meeting in 1819: 'That there is no such thing as servitude in nature, therefore all statutes, or enactments that have a tendency to injure one part of society for the benefit of another, are a gross violation of the immutable law of God.' That denunciation of servitude as unnatural, with its overtones of Rousseau or Godwin, reflects just the sort of rationalist radicalism that Burke found so explosive. Its radical potential was magnified by the presence of a plebeian pride expressed by a speaker at the meeting who announced that the 'lower classes of society' would have to rely on their own efforts alone: 'If you are not rich men, you are not on that account less useful members of society: you compose what has contemptuously been styled the mob; and I address you as a member of that mob.' Despite their preoccupation with placemen and sinecurists, the radical reformers at Nottingham issued a clear statement of economically egalitarian objectives in this resolution: 'That the friends of the present system wish the produce of the People's Labour to be consumed by a few rich men; that moderate reformers wish that produce to be consumed by a greater number of the rich; but radical Reformers wish it to be consumed by the People themselves.'[44] The men of 1819 were very much in the mainstream of the Left — eager for a change of system in the direction of rationality and equality.

In that spirit the editor of the *Black Dwarf* did not confine himself to an attack on Old Corruption, although this was his prime target. Without using the language of class, he nevertheless developed a cogent critique of existing patterns of social domination and subordination. Characteristically, he took as his text a standard Enlightenment statement of abstract equality: 'That "all men are equal" is a philosophic truth no man will deny. That they are all equal in the eye of heaven, and before the *just laws* of man, is the basis of all morality and religion.' But this truth, he went on, is only confessed with the lips; the master cotton spinners, for example, refuse to recognise that their servants 'have a right to as much as they can eat for their labour'. Class domination was incompatible with the principle of equality: 'A compact seems to pervade certain gradations of society, that all may be mutually degraded, for the liberty of degrading others.' The lord bows and scrapes to the king; gentlemen, manufacturers, and merchants kowtow to the lord, and in turn 'exact obedience and submission, from the artisan, the tradesman, and the mechanic'. Wooler did not stop there, but took note of the base of the social pyramid: 'Thus at last all the weight of tyranny falls upon the great mass of the people, who cannot shift it from their shoulders.' Taking his stand with the trade unions against the masters, Wooler pointed out that 'the poor man who happens to imagine that he has a right to live by his labour is transformed into a criminal, if he dares associate himself with any other man to ascertain what his labour is worth'.[45] In Wooler and in the popular radical movement as a whole such social criticism developed within the framework of eighteenth-century political categories.

William Benbow, the Manchester radical whose activity extended from Peterloo through Chartism, illustrates the way in which the old-style radicalism of Paine and Cobbett was moving in a more class-conscious and socially egalitarian direction in the 1820s while preserving the language of 1819. His 1832 pamphlet, *Grand National Holiday and Congress of the Productive Classes,* continued the orthodox ultra-radical dichotomy of aristocracy versus the people. At the same time, however, the pamphlet shows the beginnings of a redefinition of 'the people' so as to denote working or labouring people. Moreover, Benbow also is an example of the way in which the old distinction between the idle and the industrious, originally used to distinguish between a ruling aristocracy and the rest of the population, could lead to a conception of the labour theory of value. In the pamphlet Benbow wrote, 'The only class of persons in society, as it is now constituted, who enjoy any considerable portion of ease, pleasure, and happiness, are those who do the least towards producing anything good or necessary for the community at large . . . It is ignorance that makes us incessantly toil, not for ourselves, but for others . . . They have fattened upon the sweat of our body.' Iorwerth Prothero, in a perceptive article, has emphasised that Benbow's statement that labourers 'will be no longer robbed of the fruits of their toil' sprang from a well-established tradition and need not be explained by reference to the influence of Owen, whose ideas Benbow rejected.[46]

While Owenism did not convert English working men to the labour theory of value, it played an important part in the process that deepened and extended the social content of working-class radicalism in the 1820s and 1830s. Operating outside the framework of radicalism, Robert Owen himself helped to set the process in motion. Bypassing politics entirely, he inveighed against the iniquity of the social and economic system and called for a total transformation. The theme was taken up and sharpened by the anti-capitalist economists. As a result, a new content was infused into working-class radicalism. The old political demands remained, but they were set in a socially radical context. The end product — the consciousness of the working-class Left in early-Victorian England — was the consequence of the interplay between the traditions of 1819 and the social and ideological developments of the 1820s and 1830s.

Robert Owen was first and foremost a man of the Enlightenment. He took the ideas and principles of eighteenth-century rationalism and turned them against a society that narrowly restricted the values that it professed to esteem. The great force of Owen's social thought sprang from his ingenuous insistence on judging social and economic arrangements by what he regarded as universally valid scientific principles. Beneath the surface of Owen's positivism and secularism, however, lay a moral passion that had been nurtured by generations of Puritanism. He was appalled by the misery that he saw around him not only because it was irrational but also because it was immoral. He was outraged at social and economic arrangements that blighted man's capacity for moral and intellectual development. In Owen, as in so many exponents of working-class radicalism, the religious and intellectual traditions of western culture were central to his response to industrialism. From this vantage point he articulated three interconnected themes that were to echo through the disparate forms of working-class protest in the 1830s and 1840s — denunciation of a society based on the principle of competitive individualism, a rejection of political economy and other forms of middle-class ideology, and an insistence of the labour theory of value.

In his *Report to New Lanark* Owen indicted existing social and economic arrangements because they fell so far short of the rational standard that all reasonable men were bound to accept. He singled out the principle of individual interest as the chief source of the deficiencies of English society. That principle 'acts like an immense weight to repress the most valuable faculties and dispositions, and to give a wrong direction to all human powers'. Owen laid bare the disastrous consequences of a commercial system devoted to producing at the lowest cost and selling at the highest: 'It has made man ignorantly, individually selfish; placed him in opposition to his fellows; engendered fraud and deceit; blindly urged him forward to create, but deprived him of the wisdom to enjoy. In striving to take advantage of others he has over-reached himself.' A few years before Owen had denounced a society in which a man had been 'individualised' to the point where 'he cannot but be an enemy to all men, and all men must be in enmity and opposed to him'.[47]

Owen carried the attack into the enemy camp and denounced the political economists for preaching an acquisitive individualism that corrupted the common life and destroyed the possibility of genuine community. He treated their doctrines with contempt, as ideological fantasies whose grandiose claims bore no relation to the real world. Thus, Owen himself contributed at the very outset to the deep scepticism of the working-class movement towards the propaganda of the middle classes. Owen summarised the views of the political economists with the air of a man shaking his head at the thought that intelligent men could believe such things: 'It has been, and still is, a received opinion among theorists in political economy, that man can provide better for himself, and more advantageously for the public, when left to his own individual exertions, opposed to and in competition with his fellows, than when aided by any social arrangement which shall unite his interests individually and generally with society. This principle of individual interest, opposed as it is perpetually to the public good, is considered, by the most celebrated political economists, to be the corner-stone to the social system, and without which society could not subsist.' For all their learning, however, they were simply wrong and Owen blandly dismissed their basic principle with an appositional phrase, 'opposed as it is perpetually to the public good'. For Owen it was all too obvious that 'the present arrangement of society is the most anti-social, impolitic, and irrational that can be devised'. That was the voice of Enlightenment radicalism — the spirit of Paine, emancipated from preoccupation with placemen, and turned loose on social and economic arrangements. In the name of reason Owen indignantly depicted the actual characteristics of a society devoted exclusively to individual gain: 'Under its influence all the superior and valuable qualities of human nature are repressed from infancy, and . . . the most unnatural means are used to bring out the most injurious propensities; in short . . . the utmost pains are taken to make that which by nature is the most delightful compound for producing excellence and happiness, absurd, imbecile, and wretched.' *Pace* the political economists, competitive individualism was irrational and unnatural. Hence the need for a totally new social system, based on 'the principle of union and mutual co-operation'.[48]

One of the doctrines that Owen laid down in the *Report to New Lanark* — the labour theory of value — was to become a sort of ideological truncheon for the working-class movement as a whole. With one heavy blow it could demolish the moral and economic pretensions of the propertied classes. Owen stated the first of his premises with the starkness of an axiom in geometry: 'Manual labour, properly directed, is the source of all wealth, and of national prosperity.' Yet the labourer received only a fraction of the value of what he produced. Owen proposed to put into 'immediate practice' the principle that had been established by thirty years of experience and study: 'THAT THE NATURAL STANDARD OF VALUE IS, IN PRINCIPLE, HUMAN LABOUR, OR THE COMBINED MANUAL AND MENTAL POWERS OF MEN CALLED INTO ACTION.' When that principle was put into effect there would be a total transformation of the abominable system of wages that had prevailed for so long: 'The demand for human labour would no longer be subject to caprice, nor would the support of human life be made, as at present, a perpetually varying article of commerce, and the working classes made the slaves of an artificial system of wages, more cruel in its effects than any slavery ever practised by society, either barbarous or civilised.'[49] Owen's denunciation was to recur in the working-class movement for a generation and more, even among men who were by no means Owenites.

During the 1820s Owen attracted a devoted band of working-class supporters who made his ideas the basis of a flourishing co-operative movement. As more and more working men took up Owenism, it tended to shed the paternalistic orientation that was so characteristic of

Owen himself, and a more democratic and egalitarian version took shape. At the same time, the original corpus of Owenite doctrine was considerably enriched by an efflorescence of anti-capitalist writings, which owed a great deal to Owen's inspiration. This new body of theory was to influence the ideological development of both Owenism and the working-class movement as a whole.

The anti-capitalist economists provided the working-class movement with new intellectual and ideological weapons. In brief, they took the economic and political science developed by Enlightenment liberalism, removed the middle-class bias, and produced an egalitarian economics with a working-class slant. Whereas Owen had concentrated on the false principles underlying existing social arrangements, they provided an economic and social analysis of a system that exploited labourers for the benefit of capitalists. The title of Thomas Hodgskin's book, *Labour Defended against the Claims of Capital* (1825), tells the story. The scientific claims of the employing classes were to be subjected to rigorous and sceptical analysis. As a one-time Benthamite who had grown disenchanted with the rigidity of his master's doctrines, Hodgskin turned the science of political economy against its previous beneficiaries. He set out to show that capital has 'no just claim to any share of the labourer's produce, and that what it actually receives is the cause of the poverty of the labourer'. The capitalist was merely an 'oppressive middleman, who eats up the produce of labour and prevents the labourer from knowing on what *natural* laws his existence and happiness depend'. In view of the 'serious contest between capital and labour', there was no point in continuing to talk as if the aristocracy was the enemy. 'It is, therefore, now time that the reproaches so long cast on the feudal aristocracy should be heaped on capital and capitalists; or on that still more oppressive aristocracy which is founded on wealth, and which is nourished by profit.'[50] The anti-Establishment spirit of 1819 had been turned in a new direction, and the moralistic outlook of Owen had been given a sharp social and economic focus. William Thompson's *An Inquiry into the Principles of the Distribution of Wealth most Conducive to Human Happiness* (1824) started from the premise that 'labour is the parent of wealth', and moved on from there to set forth a fusion of Owenism and egalitarian utilitarianism. Writing with the authority of positivist rationalism, Thompson set forth propositions that claimed the force of natural law: 'Wealth should be so distributed as to produce the greatest *equality*, consistent with the greatest production.' He was especially concerned with correcting the unequal distribution of education, which had so frequently 'served to corrupt, to extinguish, or to shut out knowledge from the productive and useful members of a community'.[51] Like Thompson and Hodgskin, John Gray affirmed the labour theory of value in his *Lecture on Human*

Happiness (1825).

As the Owenite co-operative movement grew during the 1820s, it spread the ideas of the anti-capitalist economists along with Owen's vision of a new community. In London George Mudie organised a group of working-class Owenites and in 1821 founded the *Economist,* the first of a profusion of journals spawned by the movement. In 1824 another propagandist group, the London Co-Operative Society, entered the field, and put out the *Co-operative Magazine* two years later. The most influential publicist and theoretician of the movement was Dr William King of Brighton, who established the *Co-operator* in 1828. He suggested retail storekeeping, on a co-operative basis, as a means of raising the capital necessary to build Owenite communities. King's writings on co-operatives preserved the moral and rationalistic orientation of the master, but added a more realistic social and economic analysis that showed the influence of the anti-capitalist economists: 'The capitalists produce nothing themselves; they are fed, clothed and lodged by the working classes.' While renewing Owen's denunciation of the principle of competition, King also emphasised capitalist exploitation of workmen. Along with this criticism of capitalists, however, King spelled out the broader aspiration that was to be at the heart of the working-class movement for the next two generations. The point of the movement was not narrowly economic, even in the sense of effecting a juster distribution of goods. The point was to create a society in which all men might achieve their full humanity and develop all their powers: 'We claim for the workman the rights of a rational and moral agent . . . the being whose exertions produce all the wealth of the world — we claim for him the rights of a man, and deprecate the philosophy which would make him an article of mere merchandise to be bought and sold, multiplied and diminished, by no other rules than those which serve to decide the manufacture of a hat.'[52] In 1829 the British Association for the Promotion of Co-operative Knowledge joined King in propagating Owenite ideas. Its founders had read and admired the works of Owen, Thompson, Gray, and others and set out to disseminate their doctrines.

The propaganda sent out from London and Brighton found a receptive audience in the manufacturing areas, where an indigenous co-operative movement developed, possessing its own network of publications. It has been estimated that by the end of 1831 over 500 societies were in existence. The movement boasted a number of journals, held regional conferences and innumerable local meetings. One important centre was at Birmingham, where the Birmingham Co-operative Society announced in its rules in 1828 that 'community of Property in Lands and Goods' was its great goal, and a year later was publishing a lively journal. In Lancashire too the movement was booming in the early 1830s, as

A.E. Musson has shown.[53] The co-operators in Lancashire and Cheshire had read the various publications emanating from London, particularly the Society for the Promotion of Co-operative Knowledge, and from Brighton and Birmingham. Musson has provided a number of examples that illustrate the dominance of such ideas as the labour theory of value and the superiority of co-operation to capitalist competition. The *Lancashire Co-operator* stated the standard argument that working men remained impoverished despite the fact that 'the workman is the source of all wealth' and 'there can be no wealth without labour'. Drawing on the Owenite idiom, the Lancashire co-operators traced the origins of this situation to 'the erroneous arrangement of our domestic, social, and commercial affairs, by means of which machinery is made to compete with and against human labour, and of course to the detriment of the human labour, instead of co-operating with him and for him, to his advantage and comfort'. While asserting the superiority of social arrangements based on the principle of co-operation, the Lancashire co-operators also perceived the problem in terms of economic categories, which may reflect the newer anti-capitalist writings complementing Owenism: 'We can fairly trace that all the miseries which society suffers are mostly owing to the unfair distribution of wealth', wrote the *Lancashire and Yorkshire Co-operator*. In any case, the co-operators subscribed to the Owenite remedy, the creation of a 'New System of Society' based on co-operation. The rejection of competitive capitalism could not have been more total.

The British Association for Promoting Co-operative Knowledge, whose publications were read so avidly by working men in Lancashire and Cheshire, included in its leadership a group of exceptionally able men who were to play an important role in the prehistory of Chartism: William Lovett, James Watson, Henry Hetherington, and John Cleave. While profoundly influenced by Owenism, these men maintained their allegiance to traditional political radicalism, which found expression in the National Union of the Working Classes, the unstamped agitation, and the London Workingmen's Association, which drafted the Charter. Although these men never became sectarian Owenites, their radicalism reflected the new social and economic criticism of the 1820s. Lovett and his colleagues perceived the N.U.W.C. as an attempt at 'blending their own peculiar views of society, more especially of production and distribution of wealth, with those of the Radical Reformers'. They illustrate some of the ideological cross-currents that entered into the development of a new working-class radicalism in the 1830s.[54]

As a leader of the N.U.W.C. (and its predecessor the Radical Reform Association) Lovett was firmly committed to the political radicalism that had persisted in unbroken continuity since 1816. In the early 1830s he was also taking a strong line against the competitive system and its ideology. At an Owenite congress in 1832 he introduced the first resolution, attributing the ills of society to the dominance of the competitive principle. In the course of his speech he singled out for special criticism the views of the Society for the Diffusion of Useful Knowledge. He left no doubt that he and his colleagues had in mind a totally different sort of society: 'The system which they sought to establish was the reverse of the competitive − it was all for each, and each for all: and if carried into execution would sweep away all this world's cares and troubles, and make it bloom a terrestrial paradise.' Unlike most Owenites, however, Lovett delivered his critique in the more aggressive accents of popular radicalism: 'If, therefore, in spite of our reasoning and petitioning, the possessors of property turn from us with indifference or treat us with contempt, even the multitude will be fully justified in undermining and destroying a system productive of such mischief, *as is the system of private property*.' At one of the early meetings of the N.U.W.C. Lovett introduced a resolution that summed up his social and political radicalism: 'This meeting is of the opinion that most of the present evils of Society are to be attributed to corrupt legislation, coupled with uncontrolled machinery, and individual competition; and that the only permanent remedy was to be found in a new system in which there shall be equal laws and equal justice, − when machinery shall be turned to the advantage of the whole people, and where individual competition in the pursuit of riches, shall be unknown.' In the course of his speech he criticised an S.D.U.K. pamphlet in which Charles Knight praised the virtues of machinery.[55]

Beginning in 1830 Lovett, Hetherington and their fellow-radicals were also active in the unstamped press, the movement 'to resist the efforts of a corrupt government to suppress the voice of the people'. Lovett helped to organise the sale and distribution of the *Poor Man's Guardian,* edited by Henry Hetherington, which fused political radicalism with the new anti-capitalist ideas that had emerged in the 1820s. In addition to the *Guardian* a host of other unstamped periodicals flooded the working classes with a stream of radical ideas and doctrines. Old and new ideas jostled in constantly shifting patterns. No single body of doctrine emerged triumphant. As Patricia Hollis has shown, the *Guardian* was unsuccessful in its attempt 'to deflect the working-class analysis away from an attack on taxation and Old Corruption and on to Property and Power, the oppression of capital and the exploitation of labour'. Despite the continuing presence of the obsolete remnants of eighteenth-century radicalism, however, there can be no doubt that the unstamped press had raised the social and political consciousness of the working classes to a higher level of sophistication. Thus, hostility to political economy was almost universal among the unstamped news-papers.[56]

By the mid-1830s then, a distinct working-class radical subculture had come into being, comprising diverse ideas and attitudes that were not always consistent. In striking contrast to the ideological situation twenty years earlier, however, a trenchant critique of the social and economic system was now possible. The extent of that change can be seen in a brilliant expression of the new subculture, John Francis Bray's *Labour's Wrongs and Labour's Remedy; or the Age of Might and the Age of Right*, published in Leeds in 1839. A compositor, Bray was active in working-class radicalism in Leeds in the 1830s. In 1837 he became the treasurer of the newly-formed Leeds Working Men's Association, which was soon to be the chief organ of Chartism in the town. Despite this involvement with politics, however, Bray did not become a Chartist, for he had come to the conclusion − after an extensive inquiry into 'first principles' − that mere political changes were insufficient to accomplish the social transformation that was called for. In November 1837 he set forth his ideas in three lectures that outlined the argument that he was to expand into a book in the following year. Bray did not win much support for his views, which were published at a time when radical working men were about to pin their hopes on the Charter. Hence his book is important not because of its influence, but because it illustrates what J.F.C. Harrison has called 'the quality of the best contemporary working-class thought'.[57]

Bray's analysis is noteworthy, first of all, in its rejection of partial reforms and its insistence on nothing less than 'a change of system'. He called on working men to reject any 'partial alleviation' of their ills and to do something about 'that social whole which keeps them poor'. Secondly, Bray forcefully refuted the arguments advanced by middle-class ideologists, with their 'cold-blooded calculating liberality'. He denounced the political economists not merely on technical grounds but because of their 'doctrines of inequality'. He identified the class system as the critical area for radical change. Bray was scornful of those who were so eager 'to preach up things as they are' in an effort to convince the people that 'the present gradations of society, which cause so much discontentment among the poor and the oppressed' are part of the natural order of things. These professed reformers were intent on preserving social and economic inequality: 'We have seen that these men contemplate nothing more than what they conceive to be the improvement of the present system − that they would keep the whole human race divided into two classes, into rich and poor, or capitalists and producers − the one class wallowing in wealth, and the other placed just beyond "the verge of starvation".' For his part, Bray denounced that society, composed as it was of 'a high class and a low class − the former enjoying the greater part of the wealth produced by the incessant activity and toil of the latter'. He took his stand on the

Enlightenment premises of the Left: 'All existing wrongs are wrongs on principle — wrongs on reason, and justice, and equal rights and must therefore be subverted on principle.'[58]

(4) The Enlightenment, Evangelicalism, and Individual Improvement

By the 1830s a coherent working-class radical tradition had taken shape, comprising not only specific demands but also a broader complex of ideas, beliefs, and values. Two aspects of that complex were especially important both for radicalism itself and for the working-class sub-culture to which it contributed: first, the belief in individual improvement, moulded by the interplay between the Enlightenment and evangelicalism; second, the outlook and temper of Enlightenment rationalism, complemented by later accretions from romanticism. Although these intellectual forces have to be separated for purposes of analysis, they were, of course, closely intertwined in historical actuality. Thus the Enlightenment itself had not developed in isolation in the crucible of science and rationalism; in England it bore the special impress of the intellectual and moral traditions of Puritanism. Eighteenth-century Christianity, in turn, had been profoundly affected, both positively and negatively, by rationalist currents of thought. Romanticism germinated in soil that had been prepared by religion. It was the Enlightenment, however, which was of pre-eminent importance in the traditions of the Left, both as a causal factor and as a constituent element.

At the core of working-class radicalism was a profound commitment to the intellectual and moral development of the individual. Both the radical critique of existing society and its vision of the future presupposed the intrinsic value of individual improvement. The established order was under attack not only for its political and economic inequalities but also for its failure to bring within reach of the mass of the people values that were proclaimed with a formal universality by preachers and publicists who claimed to speak for society as a whole. In this area, as in others, working-class radicals asserted the professed ideals of the culture in egalitarian and class-conscious form, without the qualifications inherent in unstated assumptions that presupposed vast class differences. On the rhetorical level the ideal of individual improvement certainly enjoyed an unchallenged pre-eminence by the end of the eighteenth century. It had received the sanction of both the Enlightenment and evangelicalism, two movements that were otherwise polar opposites.

The same intellectual forces also influenced the development of the improvement ethic within working-class radicalism. Most important, of course, was the Enlightenment, for it provided the intellectual foundations of the Left as a whole; the radical and egalitarian version of the improvement ideal was expressed in rationalist terms. But Christianity also played an important part at various stages in the process. For one thing, as has been noted, the English Enlightenment bore the stamp of its Puritan and Nonconformist background. Moreover, in the early nineteenth century many working men came to radicalism from the world of the chapel and evangelical religion. Later, many working-class radicals also proved responsive to more romantic formulations of the intellectual and moral improvement of the individual.

The primary source of the working-class radical commitment to the improvement of the individual was the idea so familiar to *philosophes* and Jacobins that intellectual development was to be cherished both for its own sake and as a means of advancing the cause of liberty and progress. The two goals were inseparable. The more a man pursued knowledge and cultivated his mental powers the more active would he be as a critic of obscurantism and injustice; thus he would contribute to the creation of a society in which such intellectual possibilities were open to all men. Furthermore, since the rationalists equated reason and virtue, it followed that moral improvement would be an inevitable consequence. This cluster of assumptions underlay the *Black Dwarf's* criticism of Malthusianism in 1823: 'It is not by diminishing their numbers but by sharpening their intellects that the condition of the human race is to be bettered.' This comment reflects a long-standing radical concern with the intellectual deprivation suffered by working men as well as the conviction that the spread of knowledge and virtue would strengthen the forces of progress.[59]

The tradition of self-education was very much a part of English Jacobinism in the 1790s. As a matter of course the Failsworth Jacobins, for example, included the study of Euclid and Shakespeare in their programme of activities. The radical preoccupation with popular education also reflected broader traditions of self-culture that had taken root among the working-class by the early nineteenth century. During the early decades of the century a minority of working men, chiefly artisans, went to extraordinary lengths to educate themselves. The time, energy, and willpower required to do this while working full time were remarkable. These were the men who exercised leadership in the working-class communities; many of them have told their stories in autobiographies and memoirs. The study of natural history proved to be especially appealing and the workman-naturalist became a familiar figure. In the age of Wordsworth and Shelley the workman-poet also found a place. An offshoot of this robust autodidact culture was an efflorescence of mutual improvement societies, in which working men met for informal discussion of selected books and topics. Radical clubs and reading societies also devoted themselves to mutual improvement. Carlile and Wooler were read not only for their politics but for a broader intellectual stimulation. Thus, 'the tradition of mutual study, disputation, and improvement' was firmly established as an aspect of working-class life in the manufacturing areas.[60]

A preoccupation with morality and moral improvement was a prominent feature of the radical-rationalist tradition, which embodied a sobriety and seriousness that antedated the impact of the evangelical revival. This was in part the consequence of a secularised Puritanism, which was woven into English rationalism and radicalism. E.P. Thompson has noted how much 'the Jacobins and Deists owed to the traditions of old Dissent'. Another source of the rationalist stress on morality was the even older Socratic faith that knowledge of the good would necessarily lead to the practice of virtue. Furthermore, the moral earnestness so characteristic of the radical movement was also in part the result of a desire, particularly among the infidels of the Paine-Carlile camp, to refute the charge that attacks on Christianity fostered immorality and vice. A case in point, as Thompson has shown, is the extensive reprinting of the works of Volney by the radicals of the early nineteenth century.[61] These reprints included not only the *Ruins of Empire*, a deist critique of Christianity, but also *The Law of Nature*, which presented an orthodox and traditional moral code in the language of the Enlightenment. The 'individual virtues' described by Volney would not have been out of place in a Latitudinarian sermon: '1. Science, which comprises prudence and wisdom; 2. Temperance, comprising sobriety and chastity; 3. Courage, or strength of body and mind; 4. Activity, that is to say, love of labour and employment of time; 5. And finally, cleanliness, or purity of body, as well in dress as in habitation.' A good deal less orthodox, however, was Volney's account the 'social virtues', where the accent of rationalist radicalism is unmistakable. All the social virtues may be reduced to one fundamental principle — justice. He made it plain, moreover, that 'equality and justice are but one and the same word, and same law of nature, of which the social virtues are only applications and derivatives'.[62] Volney's 'law of nature' comprised not only the traditional virtues but also the basic premises of the Left.

Very much in that tradition, as developed in the thought of the 1820s and 1830s, John Francis Bray was to stress the importance of the intellectual and moral development of all men. He took it for granted that one of the primary characteristics of a properly socialist society was an equal provision for the 'physical, moral, and intellectual cultivation of all its members'. Implicit in that positively stated objective is a strong sense of the extent of vice to be overcome: 'There is in man no intellectual deprivation which may not be elevated and refined — no brutal propensity which may not be tamed and humanised.' In the spirit of Owenite environmentalism, Bray expressed his confidence that 'a high elevation and a general uniformity of character can exist amongst the people of a nation'. Education in the fullest sense would include 'the formation of character upon the best principles and from the best models known — the practice as well as the knowledge of morality and charity — the love of truth, and virtue, and social harmony — the establishment of institutions for relaxation and amusement'.[63]

A belief in education was a major article of faith in the radical creed. An educated populace knowing its rights would resist oppression; the spread of knowledge would lead inexorably to progress. The radicals envisaged a society in which educational opportunities would no longer be restricted to the propertied classes. They had in mind a real education, not charity-school training in deference; nor were they willing to accept middle-class indoctrination in political economy. Inevitably, the radicals came into conflict with middle-class efforts to use adult education as a vehicle of propaganda. Such conflicts reinforced the radical preoccupation with education. In Manchester in 1829, for example, Rowland Detrosier, a self-educated cotton spinner, led a movement to establish a breakaway mechanics' institute under working-class control. Like other working-class radicals, he saw lack of popular education as part of a broader pattern of exploitation and deprivation. 'Our labouring population are indeed no longer the serfs of the land — but they are the slaves of commerce, and the victims of bad government.' For the mass of the people, the whole of their education 'presents to them scarcely any thing more edifying than the examples of ignorance and brutality'. The master class is interested in cultivating only one of their virtues — their industry. To develop that virtue 'no pains are spared, no means left untried, that avarice can dictate, or poverty oblige its victims to submit to'. It is generally assumed that a working man should receive just enough education to do his job, and no more. 'To govern, is assumed to be the peculiar province of the few; to labour and submit, the becoming duty of the many.' Detrosier demanded education for independence, not submission: it is time to chase all 'debasing humility' from the working man's cottage and 'to teach its too humble inhabitants a proper and becoming pride'. That was a theme that was to re-echo in popular radicalism.[64]

From this radical perspective, Detrosier affirmed the progressive faith in education. 'Man is not born wise or good; his wisdom and goodness are the result of education . . . It is in the circumstances by which he is surrounded — it is in the erroneous education of which he is the victim, that originate his misery and self-degradation.' Hence a proper education can be the means of 'moral and political regeneration'. Detrosier was particularly interested in the moral aspects of education, and resisted the worship of science that was so characteristic of the mainstream of the Enlightenment. He warned against being so dazzled by the discoveries of science and the rapid creation of industrial wealth that 'we forget, in our delirium of joy, to ask the important question, whether morality, in the most extended signification of the word, has progressed in the ratio of scientific acquirement?' England's mechanical skill is not enough; she must cultivate moral excellence as well: 'SCIENCE CREATES WEALTH; BUT IT IS MORALITY THAT PERFECTS MAN.' Inevitably, he came to focus on the deficiences of the working classes, whose 'moral degradation' he viewed with alarm. To be sure, he was careful not to blame them for their condition. Nevertheless, one of the prime purposes of sound education was to rescue those thousands who were 'uncivilised, degraded, and inhuman'.[65]

Like so many working-class radicals, Detrosier's Enlightenment ideas had developed in a Nonconformist matrix. To this source may be traced the preoccupation with morality that characterised his approach to education. He argued for an extension of 'moral and political knowledge among the working classes', and invoked the authority of history in support of the proposition that 'POLITICAL MELIORATION IS THE RESULTING CONSEQUENCE OF MORAL PROGRESSION'. He saw the Sunday schools as a 'medium of moral and political regeneration'. While recognising their defects, he was confident that they could be put to good use. 'When our youth shall be taught in the Sunday-school, the philosophy of nature, of morality, and of politics, – then indeed will it become the full-grown Hercules of Truth, that will strangle the reptiles of corruption and vice, if it be supported by a proper education at home.' He was carried away by the prospect: 'Let our Sunday-schools become the UNIVERSITIES OF THE POOR, in which the infant mind shall be taught to look through nature up to nature's source, by teaching it the simple elements and rudimental facts of natural philosophy; . . . Teach it the dignifying truth, that the only acceptable service to that source is – to love and serve their fellowmen.'[66]

In England in the second half of the eighteenth century the belief in individual improvement was nurtured not only by Enlightenment rationalism but also by the parallel influence of the evangelical revival, which began with a series of conversions in the 1730s, brought Methodism into being, and permeated the Church of England and the old Dissent. An English manifestation of a broader religious movement, embracing Pietism in Germany and the Great Awakening in the American colonies, evangelicalism had a profound effect on the culture as a whole. While fundamentally Protestant and Puritan in character, evangelical theology renewed traditional doctrines by working them into the heart through a conversion experience and making them the basis of a revitalised spiritual life. Evangelicalism provided new theological and psychological foundations for Puritan activism. The evangelical Christian was to do good not only in direct obedience to a transcendent God, but also in response to the presence of the divine, as the Holy Spirit, 'rectifying our wills and affections, renewing our natures, uniting our person to Christ . . . leading us into actions, purifying and sanctifying our souls and bodies'. The sanctifying influence of the Holy Spirit was to make itself felt now, in this world.[67]

The evangelical doctrine of progressive sanctification constituted a major point of affinity with the progressive and improving outlook of the Enlightenment. Evangelicalism strengthened the nascent ethic of improvement and focused it on traits of moral character. After his conversion, the individual was expected to be 'constantly growing in grace' and striving for a 'progress in holiness'. Writing at the beginning of the nineteenth century, Hannah More summed up a well-established creed: 'Let us be solicitous that no day pass without some augmentation of our holiness, some added height to our aspirations, some wider expansion in the compass of our virtues. Let us strive every day for some superiority to the preceding day, something that shall distinctly mark the passing scene with progress.' Thus evangelicalism, which had originated in part in reaction against rationalist Christianity nevertheless reinforced the secular faith in progress and individual improvement.[68]

Through the chapel, evangelicalism exercised a more direct influence on the outlook of many working men who were active in radical movements. There is abundant evidence, from the Political Protestants on to the Chartists, of the readiness of working men to borrow organisational forms and rituals from Methodism in particular.[69] They were actively involved not only in the various branches of Methodism but also in some Baptist congregations and the more obscure sects of popular religion. Such working men found in the chapel a severe moral discipline, which sustained their self-respect and independence. Both formally and informally the full force of the institution was directed to the maintenance of standards of behaviour. Those who strayed from the path were reproved and expelled if they were refractory. At the Surrey Street Methodist Chapel in Sheffield an applicant for membership would first be given a 'ticket on Trial', to be admitted to full membership after a probationary period of two or three months. Then a deputation would visit him and his family 'requesting their union with the society'. Subsequent failure to observe the code, however, brought swift action. Deputations would visit members whose attendance or behaviour left something to be desired. It would be duly recorded that a member had 'dismembered herself from this Society' as a result of non-attendance. The minute book would note instances of improper conduct by some of the singers during the service. A member charged with intoxication was tried in formal proceedings, pronounced 'guilty of the charges preferred against him', and sentenced: 'That he be put on trial for three months and that Dr Handley be requested affectionately to admonish him on the subject.' Reports of such visits and admonitions recur throughout the minute book. Another offender, found guilty of 'disgraceful conduct and wicked language in the public street', was ordered not to 'have a seat any longer in our Singers' Pew', and it was directed that 'this resolution be read to him by John Scholfield, the leading singer'. A Baptist Church in Keighley, whose minister had been a rope maker, took a more positive view of the pursuit of improvement: 'April 3rd, 1844. Several of the members having signified a wish to have a class or experience meeting of the members and inquirers for mutual improvement, agreed that one be held on Tuesday evenings.'[70]

The conversion experience, that central event in the religious development of the evangelical, required the moral transformation of the individual. Variations on the standard pattern can be followed in the biographies printed in denominational periodicals. A weaver's apprentice in early nineteenth-century Rochdale recalled that he had led a carnal life until the age of eighteen, when 'I was then convinced by the Spirit of my sinful state and danger before Almighty God'. Eventually he became a Methodist class leader. A Leeds man who started work in 1812 at the age of seven, entered a Sunday school at the age of sixteen and learned to read. Three years later he 'became the subject of deep conviction of sin, and for nine months sought the Lord, but not in good earnest, as he was drawn aside from the great object of salvation by his companions'. But then he renounced these companions and 'with all his heart applied to the Mercy-seat'. It was reported that his life in the workshop 'diffused a salutary and Christian influence among his fellow-workmen', and that his manner was 'kind, gentle, and very forebearing'. A Primitive Methodist who became a 'new creature' in 1842 turned to self-improvement as part of the process of transformation: 'One of the first results of the conversion was, his setting himself earnestly to the work of self-culture, attending an evening school, giving attention to reading, writing etc.'[71]

Perhaps the most striking manifestation of the working-class commitment to the moral improvement of the individual was the extensive participation by working men in the teetotal movement of the 1830s. The movement is also of interest as an indication of the extent to which many working men who remained outside the sphere of organised radicalism were nevertheless imbued with a proud class consciousness, a sense of the worth and dignity of their class, and a hostility to social superiors who refused them the respect to which they were entitled. Teetotal working men, however, readily co-operated with middle-class leaders like Joseph Livesey.

The teetotal movement appeared suddenly early in the 1830s and swiftly gathered a following of dedicated working men.[72] By 1837 over a hundred societies had come into being and were actively engaged in the cause. The dominant figure in teetotalism was Joseph Livesey, a Preston cheese merchant who had been active since 1825 in the cause of the moral and intellectual improvement of the working classes. Supported by young working men from his Adult School, he took over the Preston Temperance Society and transformed it into a militant teetotal group in the autumn of 1832. In the next few years Livesey and his working-class followers conducted a remarkably successful campaign in Lancashire and surrounding areas. 'By far the greatest number of our active spirits were workingmen', he was to write later. 'Our workingmen — sawyers, mechanics, and men of all trades — were constant speakers at the meetings; they went everywhere, and no others were listened to with equal attention.' Livesey had no doubt that 'for penetrating the masses and benefiting the millions, there is no agency equal to the plain, pointed, short, unvarnished speech of the teetotal artisan'.[73]

Teetotalism was a response to the anti-spirits movement which had sprung up in 1829 in the provincial towns. That movement had been led by the local patriciate, and followed the traditional pattern of charitable activity, in which the upper and upper middle classes — both Anglican and Nonconformist — joined together to elevate the masses below. Descending from above was a steady stream of visitors, tracts, and exhortations. The doctrine of the movement was correspondingly moderate. Adherents were asked merely to refrain from the use of hard liquor; beer and wine were acceptable. By 1832 the temperance movement had found a comfortable niche in the public life of the provincial towns. Suddenly, however, this peaceful scene was disturbed by the irruption of teetotalism, which not only proclaimed total abstinence, but preached it with unbecoming fervour. The most unusual feature of the new movement was the fact that most of the teetotal lecturers were working men. The pattern of exhortation from on high had been broken. Working men themselves became actively engaged in a great missionary enterprise, aimed at reclaiming other working men who had fallen victim of drink, and converting them to the cause of continuing personal renewal and improvement. As the anti-spirits societies were won over to teetotalism, they also enrolled the activist working men. At this point the social élites that had founded the temperance societies on the conventional model withdrew. As Brian Harrison has put it, 'When an anti-spirits society adopted the teetotal pledge, gentility usually departed in a hurry.' But a good deal of respectability stayed behind. Those who remained formed a social configuration quite different from that of the provident societies or the religious societies devoted to education. In the teetotal societies, working men were actively involved, in association with the lower middle and middling classes.[74]

Livesey's teetotal 'advocates' met with considerable success in their encounter with the anti-spirits societies of the north of England. In Leeds the adoption of the teetotal position came in 1836 by vote at a public meeting after a vigorous debate. The parent society established a number of branches in the town, and working men flocked into them. In Rochdale also the teetotal cause triumphed, although debate continued. In 1839 the minute book took official notice of 'the disaffected state of the society'. One visible sign of the impact of the teetotal movement was the appearance in the minute book in 1837 of the crabbed handwriting of a new secretary who had not had the benefit of an extended education. In Newcastle-on-Tyne, a somewhat different pattern developed. In 1835 teetotallers broke away from the anti-spirits group and formed a separate organisation, the Newcastle Tee-Total Society. According to the official account, after preparatory work by outsiders, including a visit from Livesey and a varnish maker from Preston, 'a few working men in this town were induced to attach their names to an agreement, which one of them had drawn out upon the improved principle'. A year later it boasted almost 1,000 members. When Thomas Whittaker, the former cotton worker, addressed a Newcastle teetotal meeting in 1836, he was preceded by local working men, 'three of our zealous advocates'. In Newcastle, as elsewhere, the leadership was in the hands of the middling and lower middle classes.[75]

While the social range of the teetotal movement extended well into the middling classes, it was imbued with a somewhat plebeian spirit in the 1830s, and this accounts for much of the opposition that it ran into. In 1840 the Newcastle Society reported that at first it had been 'almost unanimously rejected as a compound of fanaticism and infidelity', and that the opposition to it had been 'long and desperate'. In Rochdale in 1839 the Methodists refused the Temperance Society the use of their chapel because of complaints about 'harsh language used by many of the Temperance Advocates'. Small businessmen who came from a working-class background often took pride in their plebeian accent and demeanour. The Andrews brothers, Leeds business-men who visited Newcastle on a successful temperance mission in 1835, were described as being 'altogether of unpolished manners and un-cultivated mind'. There was good reason for the sort of opposition which Livesey described in his memoirs: 'The conflict was fierce; and the resistance manifested in hostile opposition, served only to fire our zeal. We seemed as if we would turn the world upside down.'[76]

Although Livesey was not likely to turn the world upside down, his ideas were well calculated to appeal to class-conscious working men committed to the improvement ethic. His working-class background — he worked for a time as a weaver — certainly contributed to his rapport with working men. But he was solidly established in the middle-class when he launched his temperance career; and his outlook embodied the fusion of evangelicalism and utilitarianism so characteristic of the provincial middle classes. Starting from a social and intellectual background similar to that of the provident societies, however, Livesey developed a social· doctrine that was in many respects antithetical to theirs. Whereas working-class depravity was the premise of their charitable activity, Livesey took an almost populist view of the latent virtue of the common people. He insisted that working men had just as much native talent as their social superiors: 'With all your scanty means, and limited opportunities, if you begin in earnest today, and persevere, your improvement this day twelvemonth, should you be spared, will be to yourself an ample reward. In *artificial* acquirements you are at great distance behind the rich, but, in *natural* endowments, you are equal to any: let this consideration, also, stimulate you to exertion.' From this point of view, he called on working men to undertake the cause of moral improvement both in themselves and in their less fortunate fellows: 'You have minds naturally as capacious as those above you, and it is by improving these, intellectually and morally, that your value in society becomes more and more manifest. While you grovel like the brutes, and seek no higher pleasures than the inebriating draught, your degradation is sure, and a state of vassalage is the most appropriate to your habits of debauch.'[77]

Livesey embodied the broad impulse to renovation and improvement, so prevalent in the 1830s, in a form to which class-conscious but non-political working men could respond. When he wrote in 1830 that his new journal would keep one object constantly in view, 'the reformation and happiness of mankind', he was repeating one of those standard phrases that express the aspirations of a period. In commenting that his only reward was 'the pleasure and satisfaction of attempting to better the condition of man', he could point to his own efforts to 'improve the condition of the working people'. In the utilitarian mode, he set up a general reading room for the working classes in 1827; the next year he helped form the Institution for the Diffusion of Knowledge. Hoping to advance both 'an increase of knowledge and the promotion of godliness', he founded a 'Youth's Sunday School' for poor youths aged fourteen to twenty-one. In the *Moral Reformer*, which he founded in 1831, Livesey put his primary emphasis on the moral and religious impulse to improvement. While praising the widespread interest in improving the condition of society, Livesey argued that reformers had not accomplished much so far, because they were 'working at the wrong end'. In a machine it is the power of the main spring that is really essential, and reformers have been concentrating too much on external regulations. For Livesey the weakness in existing reform efforts was all too apparent: '*Religious principle and moral character are wanting*'; these are the true base of every improvement.' Theoretical perfection is not enough. What is called for is more attention to 'the lifegiving vigour of moral principle and moral feeling'. Since Livesey was a moralist, not an ideologue, he was by no means preoccupied with the vices of the poor. Turning from the poor to the sons of the rich, Livesey concluded that they 'eagerly pursue the same sins in a more polite shape' and merely try to avoid 'the vulgar forms under which vice is practised by the lower classes'. Like the working-class radicals, Livesey had no doubt that 'the characters of the different classes of the people in this country, are the same, whatever be their station in life'.[78] This was the version of the improvement ethic that working men like Thomas Whittaker took up with such enthusiasm.

Thomas Whittaker, the most famous of the working-class temperance lecturers, exemplified the religious basis of the teetotal movement. He perceived the temperance movement as a way for men 'to find the House of God, and to obtain the salvation which would make them fit for the kingdom of Heaven'. Whittaker entered the teetotal movement from a Methodist background and embraced it as a religious experience. Born in 1813, he started work in a cotton mill when he was six. He never went to day school, but in Sunday school he received enough instruction to be able to read the Bible. As 'the son of a mother in Methodism', he felt the full force of evangelical Christianity. Although he had not prayed in the three years prior to signing the pledge, he responded in religious terms to the temperance meeting that he attended with his brother, 'a strictly sober and God-fearing young man'. He found 'an earnest purpose and a religious power in that meeting which lives with me to this day'. In the meetings that he attended that week Whittaker experienced 'a manifestation of the power of God that I and many others had never seen or felt before; it was a pentecostal week, our hearts were touched, and the Holy Ghost fell upon us'. Signing the pledge was a 'great deliverance achieved by God'. When he returned home after signing the pledge, he informed his wife and they knelt in prayer together — 'the grandest prayer meeting I was ever at'.[79] In the most literal sense then, Whittaker had undergone a conversion experience. He conducted his teetotal work with missionary zeal. For many other working men also the temperance movement tapped a latent religiosity.

While teetotalism was quite distinct from working-class radicalism, it illustrates the presence of attitudes and ideas that many working men carried with them into the radical movement. It reflects an important aspect of the outlook of working men newly conscious of their own identity and worth, over against a middle-class that was not only bent on ruling them but on derogating their qualities as men. But it was neither anti-bourgeois nor politically radical. The class consciousness of the working-class in the early 1830s also took the form of a determination to enable individual working men — as an expression of their class pride — to bring about their own improvement in the short run, without waiting for social and political changes. Teetotalism would not have established itself so quickly if it had not touched deep chords in working-class consciousness. The spectrum of working-class values on the eve of Chartism ran from teetotalism to the unstamped. Although the teetotal movement was closer to the world of the chapel and the Sunday school than to the radical reading room, it shared some of the outlook of radicalism. The teetotallers shared the radical faith in knowledge and reason, but they linked it to the improvement of the individual, especially in morality, rather than to a criticism of the social and political order. Working-class participation in the teetotal movement in the 1830s was not conventional or respectable, and working men pursued the cause with a militancy and aggressiveness not unlike that of the radicals.

(5) *Rationalism and Romanticism*

Interwoven in the texture of working-class radicalism was the legacy of Enlightenment rationalism, which provided a distinctive temper of mind and a characteristic approach to politics and society. From the Enlightenment the radicals derived the conception of man that under-girded their critique of the established order. For *philosophes*, Jacobins, and their radical heirs man was essentially a rational creature, held in thrall by institutions and customs that violated the principles established by reason. It followed that if only men could be instructed in such principles, they would move swiftly to overthrow the old regime of ignorance and despotism. Once ignorance and superstition were over-come, men of good will could build a free society based on reason. Thus the radical movement became a vehicle for maintaining and transmitting Enlightenment values and the rationalist view of life. This included the tendency to equate reason and virtue; once a man under-stood moral principles he would follow in the path of truth and goodness.

The rationalist faith echoed through the radical movement from Paine and the English Jacobins to Carlile, Lovett, and Harney. When working men in the industrial towns formed Hampden clubs and political unions after the Napoleonic wars, they met not only to make demands for reform but also to engage in discussion, debate, and the diffusion of political knowledge. Reading societies, news rooms, reading rooms and discussion groups proliferated as an integral part of the radical move-ment; here the workers could read the radical publications. They shared a premise stated in a resolution passed by the Political Protestants of Leicester: 'Convinced that the diffusion of political information is the best means of obtaining these objects, we have formed ourselves into

Societies for this purpose.' A member of another group of Political Protestants put the same point in more lyrical terms: 'The sun of Reason, which once shed its benign influence over the metropolis only, is now giving its exhilarating beams of universal expansion; and the industrial peasant will soon know that he is oppressed, as well as his pampered oppressors, who are revelling in the fruits of his labour.' In the years after Peterloo such political societies discussed the writings of Richard Carlile, who helped keep alive the spirit of 1789 and 1819. Like so many other militant radicals, Carlile had no doubt that 'when the political principles laid down by Thomas Paine are well understood by the great body of the people, everything that is necessary to put them in practice will suggest itself'. A major figure in the struggle for freedom of the press, Carlile also voiced the hope of the unstamped movement: 'Let us endeavour to progress in knowledge, since knowledge is demonstrably proved to be power.'[80]

The bonds between rationalism and the working-class Left were drawn still closer by the unstamped press, which combined new and more corrosive forms of political and social criticism with a struggle against the crudest sort of intellectual repression. The agitation helped to rivet on working-class radicalism what has been called the 'rationalist illusion', the notion that the diffusion of knowledge would soon 'emancipate the whole human family from the reign of ignorance and slavery in which they are now benighted'. At his trial for the sale of unstamped periodicals, Joshua Hobson explained that he hoped to demonstrate to the working classes how 'they might extricate themselves from their degraded state of thraldom'. It had long been an article of radical faith that once working men understood their rights they would take the action necessary to get them. Tyranny of any kind could not withstand the spread of political knowledge. That theme was often sounded in the grandiloquent language so characteristic of the period: 'Ah! Sanguinary traitors, well ye know we want but knowledge to direct the blow! That taught by an unshackled press, the people quietly would *command* redress for all their wrongs.' William Lovett even hoped that 'if cheap knowledge were universally distributed, it would work its way in effecting a more useful distribution of that property which now lay in great heaps'. The courage and enterprise displayed by the men of the unstamped movement reflected the conviction that 'the brutal tyranny of a single man or of any set of men now-a-day could not possibly exist a single week, under the omnipotent cannonade of the untaxed press'.[81]

A fuller statement of the rationalist faith underlying the radicalism of the 1830s is to be found in a tract by William Carpenter, one of the initiators of the unstamped agitation. Articulating a familiar theme of Enlightenment thought, he depicts history as a struggle between 'knowledge and ignorance, good and evil'. He is optimistic, because he assumes that man is fundamentally a rational creature, constantly growing in knowledge and rationality, which, in turn, lead to unending progress. 'The children of humanity have . . . advanced in social and intellectual being. This has resulted from the impulse of rational nature, constantly endeavouring to expand itself into activity and exaltation.' Given this view of man, Carpenter logically concludes that 'revolutions are but the outward signs and necessary effects of the general progression of intellect'. So far, however, the triumphs of the human mind have been confined to the realm of science and invention, while the social condition of man, 'remains anomalous and unimproved'. At present, despite a great increase in the powers of machinery, poverty and destitution pervade one part of society, 'and redundant luxury the other'. Carpenter calls for the application of knowledge to the develop-ment of an 'improved system of social economy'. He is confident that this is inevitable, and that the new order which results will be based on the principles of co-operation and equality. Thus the action of reason on the facts of social life will 'perpetually extend the dominion and blessings of truth'. To be sure, just as the scientific truths of Galileo ran into resistance in the past, so the truths of social economy will encounter prejudice and opposition. But their triumph is inevitable. For Nature endowed men with 'constitutions capable of "progressive virtue", and endless expansion of intellect'. To know the character of the human mind is to be 'blessed with visions of the prospective exaltation and happiness of the future generations of man'.[82] While Carpenter's confidence in the power of the human mind is very much of the Enlightenment, the sense of exaltation reflects the presence of a rather different cast of mind.

While working-class radicalism was firmly anchored in the Enlighten-ment it also came under the influence of romantic currents that im-parted a somewhat different temper. As in the pre-1848 Left in Europe, there emerged a more emotional, utopian, and even sentimental out-look. A more extravagant rhetoric expressed a sense of heightened expectation. Nothing less than the social and moral regeneration of mankind now appeared to be a feasible objective, well within reach. While romantic utopianism faded swiftly on the Continent after 1848, it persisted for another generation in England, albeit in modified form, as an ingredient in mid-Victorianism. Hence this aspect of working-class radicalism has to be kept in mind, despite the pre-eminent importance of the traditions of the Enlightenment.

Of all the intellectual forces in modern Europe, romanticism is the most difficult to identify and pin down. In order to use the term at all the historian must first enter a few preliminary qualifications. The basic difficulty is the extreme diversity of the phenomenon, as indicated in

A.O. Lovejoy's suggestion that we refer to various 'romanticisms' rather than to a single body of ideas. The diverse manifestations of 'romanticism' stand out in contrast to the relative unity of the Enlightenment, which can be defined in terms of a common core of ideas and principles. The problem of national and chronological variations, substantial even in the case of the Enlightenment, is compounded by the multifariousness of romanticism itself. The social and ideological aspects of romanticism display a similar pattern of variation. Initially, it lent itself to an aristocratic attack on Enlightenment liberalism, as in the writings of Burke, deMaistre, and Adam Müller. In Germany, it remained the basis of an anti-liberal conservatism that became part of what has been called the 'Germanic ideology'. In France, after the initial impulse of romantic conservatism had passed, romanticism influenced not only liberalism but also Left attacks on liberal individualism. Finally, in addition to handling the problem of diversity, the historian also has to be wary of permitting his description of romanticism to imply an acceptance of the romantic stereotype of the Enlightenment. The *philosophes* did not in fact subscribe to the simplistic rationalism imputed to them by their romantic critics. Romanticism was not a sudden intellectual revolution, but a recombination, in a new context, of elements already present in eighteenth-century thought. Moreover, the Enlightenment was never displaced by romanticism, even in Germany, while in England there was a complex interplay between aspects of the two intellectual traditions.[83]

Romanticism remains the most convenient term to denote the new currents of thought that developed in reaction against the dominant ideas of the Enlightenment. Its most conspicuous feature was an emphasis on emotion, feeling, and sentiment in an attempt to overcome what were perceived to be the limitations of eighteenth-century rationalism. Romanticism tended to glorify the impulses of the heart rather than the 'fallible and feeble contrivances of reason'. This broad stream, with its eddies and counter-currents, entered into European culture in various ways.

The link between romanticism and the Left was most pronounced in France, where the extraordinary socialist ferment of the 1830s and 1840s had been profoundly affected by romantic ideas and attitudes. The historian of 1848 in France has commented on the widespread belief in 'the swift and splendid transformation of society', often accompanied by a 'maudlin and hysterical idealism'. In Germany romanticism fed the impulses that contributed to the revolutions of March 1848, and the term *vormärzlich* denotes the utopian pre-1848 mood. Similar attitudes found expression in America, not among revolutionaries but among moral and social reformers who now insisted on 'immediate liberation', instead of waiting for gradual improvement. John Higham has described the boundlessness of aspiration so typical of pre-Civil War America: 'The characteristic accent of the age sounded in the apocalyptic note the reformers struck over and over again. Fired by perfectionist and millenialist ideas, they tended to feel that the last days of the unrighteous had arrived.'[84]

In England too, as W.L. Burn put it, it was easy to believe that 'an attainable paradise was just around the corner'. In his suggestive essay, 'The Romantic Element — 1830 to 1850', G.K. Clark noted the connection between romanticism and social protest in England: 'If romanticism had taught men to contrast, to imagine or to feel, then the feelings which the world of the nineteenth century was most likely to excite were disgust, pity and anger.' He pointed out that Chartist exuberance and vehemence corresponded to other aspects of early Victorian culture — melodrama on the stage, the conventions of romantic oratory, and sentimentality in literature.[85]

In the unstamped press, where the faith of Paine and Carlile was undimmed, a new spirit was visible. The repeal of the taxes of knowledge was depicted as much more than the remedy for a specific grievance: 'Peace will follow with her olive, and plenty with her horn; profuse of comfort and prodigal good the arts and sciences will follow in their train.' Then 'the millenium . . . will be realised'. In the same vein a Walsall correspondent of William Carpenter's wrote that repeal would 'free the immortal mind'. His metaphors reflect a shift in diction and sensibility: 'I need not describe to you, who feel the intellectual flame, the burning and intense desire of attaining knowledge, which every man must feel and experience who has tasted its sweetness . . . We are here obliged to submit to receive it drop by drop, which, like the imaginary appearance of water in the burning sandy desert, only increases the thirst.' To be sure, grandiloquence was by no means unknown to the English Jacobins. But there is a different texture to the expectation that once the taxes on knowledge were repealed the millennium would be at hand.[86]

English romanticism found its most brilliant expression in poetry, and in this form it exercised a direct influence on the temper of working-class radicalism. In the 1830s and 1840s the Lake poets still enjoyed a great popularity among the reading public. Moreover an unusually large number of ordinary people had taken to writing verse themselves. As Martha Vicinus has shown, the Chartist movement produced a vast out-pouring of radical poetry. There was good reason for the affinity between romantic poetry and early-Victorian radicalism. At the very beginning of the nineteenth century, when French and German romanticism was deeply reactionary, the Lake poets were articulating a populist view of the common people that ran against the grain of established opinion, both aristocratic and middle-class. Although by 1802 Wordsworth had abandoned his initial enthusiasm for the French

Revolution, he retained much of the idealism of his youth. In the preface to *Lyrical Ballads* he announced that he had chosen 'low and rustic life' as his subject, because 'in that condition the essential passions of the heart find a better soil in which they can attain their maturity'.[87] The socially heretical character of this position is vividly evident in Francis Jeffrey's vehement repudiation of Wordsworth's suggestion: 'It is absurd to suppose, that an author should make use of the language of the vulgar, to express the sentiments of the refined.' Jeffrey returned to the attack twelve years later in a denunciation of Wordsworth's 'unlucky habit of debasing pathos with vulgarity' and his insistence on 'choosing his examples of intellectual dignity and tenderness exclusively from the lowest ranks of society'.[88] What appalled this spokesman of middle-class Whiggery had a corresponding appeal to the radicals. The populist theme is even more prominent in Shelley, where it is embedded in a full-blown radicalism that fused rationalism and romanticism.

In *Queen Mab* Shelley combined Godwin's rationalist radicalism with newer currents of romanticism. He envisaged a world where 'reason and passion cease to combat . . . Whilst each unfettered o'er the earth extend/Their all subduing energies, and wield/The sceptre of vast dominion there'. Shelley took the Enlightenment faith in human perfectibility and expressed it in terms of the more romantic notion that 'every heart contains perfection's germ'. In the tradition of Enlightenment radicalism, he judged the world by an absolute standard of freedom but in a warmer idiom: 'The man/Of virtuous soul commands not, nor obeys. /Power, like a desolating pestilence, Pollutes whate'er it touches; and obedience, /Bane of all genius, virtue, freedom, truth, /Makes slaves of men, and of the human frame, /A mechanised automaton.' Shelley was very popular with the Chartists and their tributes to him reflect the sensibility that he had done so much to fashion: 'The nobleness and independence of his soul was even surpassed by his expansive, disinterested, overflowing benevolence.' Of the few who had been called ' "Poets of the People", assuredly the first and noblest name is that of Shelley'.[89]

Romanticism, of course, had little to do with the genesis of the Chartist movement. Chartism took shape in a setting of direct social and ideological conflict intensified by economic distress. Working-class radicals confronted employers who withheld the vote in 1832, who set out to crush trade unionism in 1833—4, and who fought every demand for factory legislation. Such grievances took on a sharper edge with the onset of mass unemployment. The impact of distress, in turn, was vastly magnified by the decision to introduce the new poor law into the manufacturing areas. Historians have been unanimous in emphasising the importance of the protest against the new poor law as a decisive factor in the immediate origins of Chartism. The law was not only a direct economic threat but also a symbol of middle-class ideology at its harshest. The anti-poor law movement was at the centre of the social and ideological currents that flowed into Chartism.

But Chartism was not merely an instinctive class response to external pressures; nor was it simply the reflection of socially determined class conflict. It embodied formidable traditions of working-class radicalism that had developed in the years since Waterloo. The Chartists were responding to their situation not only as class-conscious working men but as free-born Englishmen and radicals whose outlook had been shaped by the interplay between immediate experience and the intellectual legacy of western culture. Various forces, religious and secular, rationalist and romantic, had gone into the making of the working-class radical consciousness in all its complexity and variousness.

Notes

1.   Georges Lefebvre, *The Coming of the French Revolution*, Princeton 1947, pp. 214–15. See also Franco Venturi's comment on the relationship between the middle-class and the Enlightenment as a whole: 'I believe that, wherever one looks, the relations between the bourgeois forces, however active or static, and the movement of the Enlightenment, must remain a problem; they cannot be taken for granted or used as an historical presupposition.' *Utopia and Reform in the Enlightenment*, Cambridge 1971, p. 11.
2.   Isaiah Berlin, 'Equality', *Proceedings of the Aristotelian Society*, LVI, 1956, pp. 301–26.
3.   Bernard Bailyn, *The Ideological Origins of the American Revolution*, Cambridge 1967, p. 307.
4.   R.R. Palmer, *The Age of the Democratic Revolution: A Political History of Europe and America*, 1760–1800, vol. I, Princeton 1959. See also Palmer's analysis of popular sovereignty as an *idée force* in his article, 'Reflections on the French Revolution', *Political Science Quarterly*, LXVII, 1952. For a discussion of republican ideas and the Enlightenment, with particular reference to their English origins, see Venturi, pp. 70–94.
5.   Venturi, p. 97; Ernst Cassirer, *The Question of Jean-Jacques Rousseau*, Bloomington, Indiana 1963, pp. 69–77, and *The Philosophy of the Enlightenment*, Princeton 1951, pp. 234–74.
6.   From Burke's *Reflections* to Michael Oakeshott, *Rationalism in Politics*, New York 1962, the connection between Enlightenment rationalism and the Left has been a staple of conservative thought. But the connection has also been examined by historians on the Left, as, for example, in Lucio Colletti, *From Rousseau to Lenin*, London 1972, and George Lichtheim, *The Origins of Socialism*, London 1969, pp. 3–25, and *Marxism*, New York 1961, pp. 13–30. Liberal historians have tended to emphasise the reformist aspect of Enlightenment thought, particularly in reaction against the perverse interpretation advanced in J.L. Talmon, *The Origins of Totalitarian Democracy*, London 1952. The concept 'totalitarian democracy' is a contradiction in terms that distorts the history of the twentieth century; the distortion is compounded when it is projected back into the eighteenth century. Talmon's interpretation obscures the fundamental point that totalitarianism represented an explicit repudiation of Enlightenment rationalism,

liberalism, and democracy. Talmon's thesis has been well refuted by Peter Gay, *The Party of Humanity*, New York 1964, pp. 279—82 and Alfred Cobban, *In Search of Humanity*, New York 1960, pp. 182—4. Nevertheless, if Talmon's conceptual superstructure is ignored, his book provides an excellent analysis of the radical implications of Enlightenment thought. In dealing with this problem Sheldon Wolin draws a sharp distinction between liberalism, as exemplified in Locke, and the rationalist radicalism of Mably, Paine and Godwin: *Politics and Vision*, New York 1960, pp. 286—314. While such a distinction is useful in Wolin's perceptive history of political theory, the historian of social and ideological movements has to put more emphasis on combinations and over-lappings of disparate ideas and traditions, as indicated in Lefebvre's comment, p. 181, that the Declaration of 1789 could become a 'charter of political and even social democracy'. See also the suggestive study by Steven Lukes, *Individualism*, New York 1973.

7.   Venturi, p. 132. See also Venturi, *Italy and the Enlightenment: Studies in a Cosmopolitan Century*, New York 1972, pp. 1—32. On the rational dissenters, see Anthony Lincoln, *Some Political and Social Ideas of English Dissent, 1763—1800*, Cambridge 1938; Elie Halévy, *The Growth of Philosophic Radicalism*, London 1928, pp. 120—58.

8.   Richard Price, *Discourse on Love of Our Country*, London 1789.

9.   William Godwin, *Enquiry Concerning Political Justice*, 3rd edition, London 1797, book I, chapter 5; book VIII, chapter 6; Halévy, pp. 181—224.

10.   Brian Harrison and Patricia Hollis, 'Chartism, Liberalism, and the Life of Robert Lowery', *English Historical Review*, LXXXII, 1967.

11.   See E.P. Thompson, *The Making of the English Working Class*, pp. 86—113, 498—9; E.J. Hobsbawm, *Labouring Men*, pp. 1—5; Eric Foner, 'Founding Father Tom', *New York Review*, 15 May 1975; Halévy, pp. 120—50, 181—91.

12.   Thomas Paine, *Rights of Man*, New York 1942, pp. 35, 128, 147; Halévy, pp. 205—8.

13.   Halévy, pp. 153—372; Mill is quoted in John Clive, *Macaulay*, New York 1973, p. 62. In his *Autobiography*, New York 1924, p. 54, Mill refers to the 'Benthamic and politico-economic form' of liberalism.

14.   Malthus, *Essay on Population*, Penguin edition, 1970, chapter X. See also Halévy, *History of the English People in the Nineteenth Century* I, New York 1949, pp. 572—4.

15.   See A.R. Poynter, *Society and Pauperism*, Toronto 1969.

16.   Malthus, chapter V.

17.   Halévy, *Philosophic Radicalism*, pp. 204—48.

18.   Thomas Chalmers, *The Christian and Civic Economy of Large Towns*, London 1856. See also L.J. Saunders, *Scottish Democracy, 1815—1840*, London 1950, pp. 208—21.

19.   Chalmers, pp. 573—86.

20.   *The Fourth Annual Report of the Manchester and Salford District Provident Society*, Manchester 1837.

21.   *First Annual Report of the Liverpool District Provident Society*, Liverpool 1831.

22.   S.E. Finer, *The Life and Times of Sir Edwin Chadwick*, London 1952, pp. 39—49, 69—114. K. Smith, *The Malthusian Controversy*, London 1951, p. 301, describes the new Poor Law as 'the victory of Malthus'.

23.   Michael E. Rose, *The English Poor Law 1780—1930*, Newton Abbot 1971, p. 85; Sidney and Beatrice Webb, *English Local Government*, vol. VIII, London 1927—9, p. 67.

24.   Ursula Henriques, 'How Cruel Was the Victorian Poor Law?', *Historical Journal*, XI, 1968, 365—71; see also David Roberts, 'How Cruel Was the

Victorian Poor Law?', ibid., VI, 1963.

25. Michael E. Rose, 'The Allowance System under the New Poor Law', *Economic History Review,* 2nd ser. XIX, 1966. See also Norman McCord, 'The Implementation of the 1834 Poor Law Amendment Act on Tyneside', *International Review of Social History,* 1969.

26. Donald Read, *Press and People,* 1790–1815, London 1961; Roy A. Church, *Economic and Social Change in a Midland Town: Victorian Nottingham 1815– 1900,* London 1966, pp. 12–13, 105–21; Samuel Robinson, *A Letter to Charles Hindley, M.P. on the Subject of the New Poor Law,* Ashton-under-Lyne 1837.

27. See Michael E. Rose, 'The Anti-Poor Law Movement in the North of England', *Northern History,* I, 1966. But the success of local guardians in preserving the practices of the old Poor Law was hardly a victory for humanitarianism. As Rose has observed, 'inhumanity was by no means the new found prerogative of Chadwick and the "three Bashaws of Somerset House" '. 'The New Poor Law in an Industrial Area', in R. Hartwell, ed., *The Industrial Revolution,* New York 1970, p. 135.

28. See J.F.C. Harrison, *Learning and Living 1790–1960,* Toronto 1961, pp. 38–89, 203–310.

29. Mrs Marcet, *Conversations on Political Economy,* 7th edition, London 1839, pp. 68–73, 152.

30. Harriet Martineau, *Illustrations of Political Economy,* vol. IX, London 1834, p. 44; see also R.K. Webb, *Harriet Martineau: A Radical Victorian,* London 1960, pp. 91–133.

31. Andrew Ure, *The Philosophy of Manufactures,* London 1835, pp. 407, 423, 427, 406.

32. Ibid., pp. 423–5.

33. Ibid., p. 417.

34. *Chambers' Edinburgh Journal,* Tract No. 170, *Hints to Workmen,* 1846.

35. *The Employer and Employed,* 1844.

36. Trygve R. Tholfsen, ed., *Sir James Kay-Shuttleworth on Popular Education,* New York 1974. See also Richard Johnson, 'Educational Policy and Social Control in Early Victorian England', *Past and Present,* no. 49, 1970.

37. British and Foreign School Society, *Daily Lesson Book Number Three,* London 1842. See J.M. Goldstrom, *The Social Content of Education,* 1808–1870, Shannon 1972.

38. Mabel Tylecote, *The Mechanics' Institutes of Lancashire and Yorkshire before 1851,* Manchester 1951, pp. 44–9.

39. See Asa Briggs and John Saville, eds., *Essays in Labour History,* London 1960, pp. 43–73.

40. Thompson, pp. 603–700.

41. Ibid., pp. 631–49, 669–94; Donald Read, *Peterloo,* London 1954, pp. 41–7, 210–16; A. Temple Patterson, *Radical Leicester,* Leicester 1954, pp. 107–27. On working-class radicalism in the Reform Bill period, see Asa Briggs, 'The Background of Parliamentary Reform in Three English Cities', *Cambridge Historical Journal,* 1952; Asa Briggs, ed., *Chartist Studies,* London 1959, pp. 17– 20, 66–7; Joel Wiener, *The War of the Unstamped,* Ithaca 1969, pp. 248–9; *Poor Man's Guardian,* 5 November 1831, 24 March 1832, 19 May 1832.

42. Thompson, p. 610.

43. *Black Dwarf,* 28 July, 3 and 11 August 1819.

44. Ibid., 28 July 1819.

45. Ibid., 16 September and 19 August 1818.

46. Iorwerth Prothero, 'William Benbow and the Concept of the General Strike', *Past and Present,* No. 63, 1974, pp. 132–71. See also Prothero's comments on the problem of understanding Benbow's ideas in their contemporary context rather

than in terms of later developments.

47. Robert Owen, *A New View of Society and other Writings*, London 1927, pp. 262, 292. See J.F.C. Harrison, *Robert Owen and the Owenites in Britain and America*, London 1969, pp. 1–87; G.D.H. Cole, *A History of Socialist Thought*, I, London 1962, pp. 86–101.
48. Owen, p. 269.
49. Ibid., pp. 246–51.
50. Thomas Hodgskin, *Labour Defended against the Claims of Capital*, London 1825, p. 67. See also Cole, pp. 110–12.
51. William Thompson, *An Inquiry into the Principles of the Distribution of Wealth Most Conducive to Human Happiness*, London 1824, p. 279. See Cole, pp. 114–19.
52. Patricia Hollis, *The Pauper Press*, Oxford 1970, p. 216.
53. A.E. Musson, 'Ideology of Early Co-operation in Lancashire and Cheshire', *Transactions of the Lancashire and Cheshire Antiquarian Society*, LXVIII, 1958.
54. British Museum, Add. MSS., 27822, f. 20. See also Briggs, *Chartist Studies*, pp. 17–19.
55. *Poor Man's Guardian*, 5 May 1832 and 24 December 1831; the quotation with the reference to 'reasoning and petitioning' is from Joel Wiener, *The War of the Unstamped*, Ithaca 1969, p. 225. See also David Large, 'William Lovett', in Patricia Hollis, ed., *Pressure from Without in Early Victorian England*, London 1974.
56. Hollis, *Pauper Press*, pp. 220, 286; see also Wiener, *passim*, and Thompson, pp. 726–9.
57. J.F.C. Harrison, 'Chartism in Leeds', in Asa Briggs, ed., *Chartist Studies*, London 1959, p. 70.
58. John Francis Bray, *Labour's Wrongs and Labour's Remedy*, Leeds 1839, pp. 137–8, 215.
59. Thompson, p. 776.
60. Ibid., p. 743; Harrison, *Learning and Living*, pp. 43–57.
61. Thompson, pp. 741–3.
62. Comte de Volney, *Law of Nature*, pp. 197, 213, in *Ruins of Empire*, New York 1853.
63. Bray, *Labour's Wrongs*, pp. 111, 124.
64. R. Detrosier, *An Address Delivered to the Members of the New Mechanics' Institution, . . . Manchester, . . . March 25, 1831, on the Necessity of an Extension of Moral and Political Instruction among the Working Classes*, London 1831, pp. 1–4. See also Gwyn Williams, *Rowland Detrosier*, York 1965; Eileen Yeo, 'Robert Owen and Radical Culture', in Sidney Pollard and John Salt, eds., *Robert Owen Prophet of the Poor*, London 1971, p. 90.
65. Detrosier, pp. 3–5.
66. Ibid., pp. 7–10.
67. Albert C. Outler, ed., *John Wesley*, New York 1964, p. 495.
68. Hannah More, *Practical Piety*, London 1830, pp. 2–3.
69. Robert F. Wearmouth, *Methodism and the Working-Class Movements of England, 1800–1850*, London 1937.
70. Surrey Street Chapel, Sheffield, Leaders' Meeting Minutes, 1850, MS N.R. 32, Sheffield Reference Library; Joseph Rhodes, *A Century of Keighley Baptist History 1810–1910*, Keighley 1910, p. 52.
71. *United Free Church Magazine*, May, June, July 1858; *Primitive Methodist Magazine*, January 1859.
72. Brian Harrison, *Drink and the Victorians: The Temperance Question in England 1815–1872*, London 1971, pp. 107–26.
73. Joseph Livesey, *Reminiscences of Early Teetotalism* (n.p,n.d.), pp. 29, 37–8.

74. Brian Harrison, p. 137.
75. *Leeds Temperance Herald,* 22 July 1837; Leeds Temperance Society, Minute Book, 1830–45, Archives Department, Leeds Reference Library; Rochdale Temperance Society, Minute Books, vol. I, 1832–42, vol. II, 1842–53, Rochdale Reference Library; *First Annual Address of the Newcastle Tee-Total Society . . . 30 December 1836.*
76. *Fifth Annual Report of the Newcastle Temperance Society . . . 29 December 1840*; Livesey, *Reminiscences,* pp. 37–8; Rochdale Temperance Society, Minute Book, 6 September 1839.
77. *Moral Reformer,* III, 1833, 8.
78. Ibid., 357–8.
79. Thomas Whittaker, *Life's Battles,* London 1888, pp. 50–7.
80. *Black Dwarf,* 11 November 1818, 20 October 1819; Thompson, pp. 764–5.
81. Wiener, pp. 119–23.
82. William Carpenter, 'The Progress and Influence of Knowledge', *Political Tracts,* No. 6, 1831. See Wiener, pp. 139–42, 244–6, and Hollis, pp. 232–7.
83. On the problem of constructing a useful concept of romanticism, see Rene Wellek, 'The Concept of "Romanticism" in Literary History', *Comparative Literature,* vol. I, 1949; A.O. Lovejoy, *Essays in the History of Ideas,* Baltimore 1948, pp. 228–53.
84. George Lichtheim, *The Origins of Socialism,* London 1969, pp. 26–82; H.J. Hunt, *Le Socialisme et le Romantisme en France,* Oxford 1935; J.L. Talmon, *Political Messianism,* New York 1960, pp. 17–131; Georges Duveau, *1848: The Making of a Revolution,* New York 1968, p. 203; John Higham, *From Boundlessness to Consolidation: The Transformation of American Culture 1848– 1860,* Ann Arbor 1969, pp. 12–13.
85. W.L. Burn, *The Age of Equipoise,* New York 1964, p. 66; G.K. Clark, 'The Romantic Element, 1830 to 1850', in J.H. Plumb, ed., *Studies in Social History,* London 1955, pp. 217–37.
86. Wiener, p. 123; Hollis, pp. 296–7.
87. Carl R. Woodring, ed., *Prose of the Romantic Period,* Boston 1961, pp. 49– 68; Clark, pp. 224–6; Martha Vicinus, *The Industrial Muse: A Study of Nineteenth Century British Working-Class Literature,* New York 1974, pp. 94– 112.
88. Woodring, pp. 581–94; John Clive, *Scotch Reviewers,* Cambridge, Mass. 1957, pp. 151–65.
89. Sir Henry Newbolt, ed., *Poems of Shelley,* London, (n.d.), pp. 63, 26 ; Graham Hough, *The Romantic Poets,* London 1958, pp. 122–55; Y.V. Kovalev, *An Anthology of Chartist Literature,* Moscow 1956, pp. 295–7; Carl Woodring, *Politics in English Romantic Poetry,* Cambridge, Mass. 1970, pp. 230–325.

3 THE CHALLENGE OF WORKING-CLASS RADICALISM

Working-class radicalism came to a climax in Chartism, which gathered up the ideas and aspirations of the early-Victorian Left into a single mass movement that demanded the enactment of the Charter. Along with the Six Points, the Chartists were committed to the whole complex of principles and values that had been woven into the traditions of popular radicalism during the previous generation. In its various forms Chartism embodied a formidable critique of the established order, denying the legitimacy of existing political and social arrangements, and rejecting both the traditional deference ideology and the new ideological forms of middle-class liberalism. Chartism conducted an ideological counter-offensive against a middle-class that was aggressively seeking intellectual, moral, and social hegemony. Implicit in the agitation was the hope that radical political change would somehow lead to the creation of a society free from the incubus of class.

On a much smaller scale, but in concentrated form, the local Owenite societies of the late 1830s and early 1840s brought into sharp focus a single aspect of the ideology of working-class radicalism. Confined to a devoted group of followers, quite unpolitical in outlook, Owenism mounted a sustained attack on the principles and values of a competitive and acquisitive industrial society. In the manner of a sect, Owenism proclaimed a new faith, socialist and rationalist. In their quest for new forms of community, in which men might live together in fellowship and co-operation, the Owenites set out to spread new social principles to replace the capitalist creed of competition and profit.

Chartists and Owenites alike resisted the efforts of their superiors to impose a narrowly bourgeois version of liberalism as the value system of the industrial towns. They rejected out of hand the utilitarian-evangelical doctrine that the poor had to be delivered from depravity and educated to industrious and 'rational' subordination. In opposing the ideological dominion sought by the middle-class, radicalism affirmed an egalitarian and class-conscious version of the improvement ethic and insisted on the inherent capacity of all men to achieve a personal development hitherto restricted to the few. Emphasising the virtues and achievements of working men was an integral part of the radical defence of the worth and dignity of the working-class. As egalitarians the radicals insisted on the right of every man to develop his powers to the fullest. Thus, the radical belief in individual improvement was indissolubly connected with the critique of a society that denied working men opportunities monopolised by their superiors.

During the years of radical agitation, debate, and propaganda these values became firmly lodged at the core of a working-class subculture that was developing in opposition to the cultural and social claims of the middle-class. This subculture embraced not only those who put their hopes in political or social change but also other working men who, while remaining aloof from the radical movement, accepted the aspiration to improvement in a spirit of class consciousness and in rejection of middle-class efforts to keep them in their place. In the years after 1848 radical values — democratic and egalitarian — persisted in a subculture that had been shaped by Chartism, Owenism, and the older traditions of radicalism.

In the 1830s, as in the 1840s, working-class radicalism stood in an ambivalent relationship to middle-class liberalism. In the early-Victorian years the radical movement was directed against the excesses of the utilitarian liberalism that was in the ascendant in the 1830s. Under those circumstances shared ideas and principles necessarily remained in the background. By the 1850s, however, elements of consensus had become more prominent, and overt conflict between radicalism and liberalism became muted. In the course of those mid-Victorian processes of accommodation, the values of the working-class subculture turned in an unintended and unexpected direction — assimilation to the cultural patterns of a society dominated by the middle-class. That process is central to an understanding of the transition from early Victorian conflict to the more complex situation of consensus and conflict in the mid-Victorian decades. In considering Chartism and Owenism, however, it is desirable to keep our knowledge of subsequent developments in the background and try to see them as they were in their own time.

Although the Chartist programme was primarily political, the movement displayed the same preoccupation with social issues and phenomena that contributed to the emergence of the socialist Left in Europe in the decade before 1848. Socialism rested on a new awareness of social and economic obstacles to freedom and equality along with a strong sense of the limitations of political liberalism and laissez-faire economics. In Paris the social republicans fused socialism and the French revolutionary tradition and produced a working-class radical movement that illustrates the familiar contrast to the less 'advanced' or more moderate character of the English Left. It would be misleading to leave the matter there, however. Both in France and Germany the working classes participated in revolutionary activity only under middle-class auspices. Political circumstances, combined with the 1848 mood of romantic optimism, produced a momentary unity among the middle and working classes that disintegrated a few months later. In contrast, the Chartists remained aloof from the anti-Corn Law movement and kept up a heavy fire against middle-class liberal ideology. Hence the contrast between England and Europe should not be depicted in a way that obscures the fact that working-class radicals in England before 1848 expressed the fundamental position of the Left more profoundly and directly than their counterparts across the Channel.

(1) *Chartist Ideology*

The profoundly radical and subversive character of Chartism sprang from a number of interconnected aspects of the movement.[1] First of all, the Six Points themselves encompassed more than a set of narrowly political reforms. Implicit in the Charter was both a demand for the transformation of the structure of politics and the broader principle that working men ought to exercise control over every aspect of their lives. Moreover, the Chartist agitation was conducted in an ideological context that was even more radical in its implications; the Six Points and the surrounding ideology have to be understood together as manifestations of the radicalism that had developed since the Napoleonic wars. Thus, Chartism was an intensely class-conscious movement directed against all forms of deference and subordination. In particular, it refused to accept the newer ideological and institutional forms of middle-class domination in an industrial society. Finally, Chartism embodied an aspiration to fundamental change – the hope that the enactment of the Six Points would lead to a radically different England. There was good reason for the middle-class to be anxious and appalled at the movement that erupted in 1839.

If our view of the Charter is filtered through the prism of the mid-Victorian decades, we might see nothing more than six demands for parliamentary reform, five of which were subsequently adopted without any disruption. of the body politic; we might be inclined to minimise the unruly aspects of the movement as momentary side-effects of economic and social dislocation. In fact, however, the demand for manhood suffrage had a totally different significance for Chartism than for the Reform League in 1866. For one thing, the Charter represented an uncompromising assertion of the principle of popular sovereignty in a context that envisaged the destruction of the political domination exercised by the propertied classes. The Charter was directly concerned with class and power, whereas the mid-Victorian radicals perceived the problem in terms of the more abstract categories of reform and progress. Demanding the vote as part of a frontal attack on the power structure, the Chartists saw political democracy as a means to a shift in power relations. Similarly, the democratic and egalitarian principles underlying the Charter were not confined to the electoral system. They reflected the concern with genuine equality that had characterised the Left since Paine and the Jacobins. In this class-conscious setting ideas of 'democracy' and 'equality' retained their full force; they had not yet undergone mid-Victorian domestication. Moreover, democratic and egalitarian values were part of a broader radical creed.

If we see Chartism as an anticipation of, or deviation from, more 'mature' or 'advanced' positions subsequently developed on the Left, we shall miss the ideological force of the movement in its own day. In fact, on a number of issues it achieved a concreteness and sharpness of formulation that was weakened in the more elaborate programmatic statements of the socialist movements that came later. As a class-conscious movement in a society dominated by the propertied classes, Chartism confronted directly the reality of power, status, and class. Affirming working-class pride in a society that exalted status and money, Chartism had clearly in mind the quality of human relationships that must be brought into existence, whereas socialists were later likely to assume that changing the economic structure would automatically take care of everything. Moreover, the Chartist understanding of the mechanisms of class domination and exploitation had a solid intellectual basis in the body of radical thought that reached full development in the unstamped press. From the same sources the Chartists had absorbed a sophisticated grasp of the ideological devices used to rationalise injustice and inequality. The Chartists were adept at unmasking attempts at ideological mystification. They had no patience with 'the humbug set up by the middle classes, to cajole and deceive us'. With a first-hand knowledge of the poor law and the behaviour of employers, the Chartists rejected the fantasies purveyed by middle-class propagandists. Although not socialist, the Chartists had absorbed the proto-socialist critique of capitalist economics, which they applied trenchantly to liberal ideology and the social order that it rationalised. Despite the lack of specific programmatic proposals, the impulse to some sort of change of system was strong.

What set Chartism ideologically apart from middle-class liberalism, despite numerous affinities, was the conviction — often only tacit — that class was the crux of the problem of progress and justice. Hence the Chartist assertion of familiar liberal principles — liberty, equality, and individual improvement — differed significantly in context and connotation from middle-class individualism and utilitarianism. Unlike the liberals, the Chartists were convinced, however vaguely and imprecisely, that some action ought to be taken to deal with class domination. They expected and hoped for some sort of social and economic change that would end working-class powerlessness and exploitation.

These generalisations about the character of Chartism ran up against an obvious difficulty — the diversity and multifariousness of the movement. Local studies have demonstrated the range of geographical variations. The movement as a whole assumed diverse forms, as indicated by such labels as knowledge Chartism, improvement Chartism, self-help Chartism, teetotal Chartism, protest Chartism, etc. There was also the cleavage, variously labelled, between militants and moderates, physical force and moral force, followers of O'Connor and Lovett. Moreover, this heterogeneity cannot be handled analytically merely by locating individuals on a scale running from left to right, from militancy to moderation. The historian has to contend with shifting combinations and permutations of ideas and attitudes.

With these qualifications in mind, however, the brief account of Chartism that follows will concentrate none the less on the underlying social and ideological unity of the movement. It enlisted the support of all strata of a 'working class' that was stratified and variegated. Without minimising the significance of the differences in tactics, temperament and ideology that divided the 'militants' from the 'moderates', we shall single out the shared radicalism that brought them together in a great national movement. Harney and Lovett, who symbolise the two poles of Chartism, were united in deploring the injustices and imperfections of the established order. Chartists of every persuasion saw the Charter as a means of bringing about substantial change. Left and centre alike were committed to individual improvement in a radical and egalitarian spirit. Henry Hetherington, editor of the *Poor Man's Guardian* in the 1830s, remained firmly on the Left as a 'moderate' Chartist a few years later. Chartists agreed in denouncing present ills and in demanding fundamental remedies. Even after the split developed in 1839, both sides accepted the substance of the resolutions passed by the Convention that spring.

The delegates to the Convention in 1839 were united in the conviction that the economic and social ills afflicting the country required drastic remedies. They agreed that the point of the Charter was to get a Parliament that would take whatever action was necessary. Among the delegates who were soon to be in the moderate camp in opposition to O'Connor and doctrines of 'physical force', there was little sign of moderation in their denunciation of the social and political system. In response to a moving account of distress in Lancashire, John Cleave drew a broadly radical conclusion: 'And was not the existence of such distress quite enough to convince every man that there was something diseased and rotten at the core of society — something which, if not removed, would cut deeper and deeper until the whole world would become equally diseased and rotten.' Cleave was speaking in support of Richard Marsden, a cotton worker representing Preston. The London artisan was in total agreement with the Lancashire weaver's analysis of 'the evils which press upon the industrious classes'. Two weeks later a resolution against the factory system was passed unanimously: 'This convention is of the opinion that neither peace, comfort, nor happiness

can exist in this country, so long as this system is allowed to continue.'
In a seconding speech Henry Hetherington denounced 'so accursed and
pernicious a system as that now existing in the manufacturing districts'.
William Carpenter, who had urged working-class co-operation with
middle-class reformers in 1831, now referred to the 'frightful character
of that system which the manufacturers were desirous of extending,
through the repeal of the Corn Laws'.[2]

Chartists of various shades of opinion shared a distaste for the seamy
side of industrial capitalism. Moderates and militants alike could support
the bellicose language of the manifesto issued by the convention in May.
'Men and women of Britain, will you tamely submit to insult? Will you
submit to incessant toil from birth to death, to give in tax and plunder,
out of every *twelve* hours' labour, the proceeds of hours to support your
idle and insolent oppressors? . . . Will you allow your wives and
daughters to be degraded, your children to be nursed in misery,
stultified by toil, and to become the victims of the vice our corrupt
institutions have engendered?' The delegates were concerned with
interlocking 'political burthens and social grievances'. High on the list
of such grievances was the new poor law. The manifesto stated a theme
that was to re-echo in the agitation to come: 'Will you permit the
stroke of affliction, the misfortunes of poverty and the infirmities of
age to be branded and punished as crimes, and give our selfish oppressors
an excuse for rending asunder man and wife, parent and child, and
continue passive observers till you and yours become the victims?'[3]

Many of the moderates who opted for Lovett rather than O'Connor
in the split that developed in the spring and summer of 1839 remained
faithful to the political and social radicalism underlying the movement
as a whole. Rejection of physical force by no means meant an abandonment of a class-conscious critique of the established order. Lovett himself is a case in point. Even in 1841, after a wretched period of
imprisonment that would have crushed the will of a lesser man, he
stood firmly on the Left. Despite his obsession with the sins of
O'Connor, his article on the 'State and Condition of the Millions'
articulated a number of the ideas that were being expressed more
heatedly by the militants before great crowds in the manufacturing
districts.[4] The central elements of Chartist radicalism are conspicuously
present in Lovett's article: a scathing denunciation of the social and
economic ills suffered by the working classes, an awareness that these
were not merely knife and fork issues but matters of power and class
relations, and an unremitting attack on all efforts at ideological
obfuscation. Lovett denounced poverty not only because it meant lack
of money, but because it 'engenders a spirit of tame servility', which
in turn, helps to perpetuate the 'slavery and wretchedness' of the poor.
Keenly aware of the links between socio-economic power and what

Marx was to call false consciousness, Lovett regretted that working men foolishly believed that 'the rich man's gold is the grand pivot on which the circle of production revolves' and even came to consider him their 'benefactor'. If only they had inquired a little further they would have found that his gold 'is the result of the poor man's industry'. But it was difficult for working men to realise this, because wealth and power are 'united to mislead and misdirect them'. Only the greatest vigilance could enable working men to detect 'the deceptions and sophistries of those who are so intent on deceiving them'.

Lovett painted a bleak picture of the life of working men in the industrial areas, which he described as a 'continuous round of toil, anxiety, poverty and woe' from the cradle to the grave. Like the Chartists of the north, Lovett was appalled by child labour and the spectacle of children 'being impressed into the service of some labour-grinding personage, as *fitting instruments* or *tools of production*, or moulded into little domestic slaves to clean, scour, and drudge away the prime of existence, midst the taunts of the idle and the threats of the wealthy'. Like O'Connor and the fustian jackets of the north, Lovett inveighed against the new poor law and all that it stood for. Working men, after having spent 'an apprenticeship to slavery — too often of body and mind', find that 'even the wretched asylum of the poor-house is likely to be denied them, or rendered so odious that death would be a happier boon'. He derided the Malthusian pap handed down from above in response to working-class complaints. If working men 'look for help to those who have profited by *their* toils, and who by *their* labour have been raised to affluence', they find that their employers 'point to the number of their children as proofs of their folly and imprudence, and to the uncultivated wastes of distant climes as havens of refuge for the destitute'. Working men who 'turn to the *laws* of the country for redress', find that they 'proclaim the sons of poverty as "vagrants, idlers, and impostors", allied against the *prosperity* they are made to protect'. If they turn to the press, they find that 'it too delights to blacken with infamy the struggles of honest labour, and lauds their oppressors as bountiful dispensers of benefits to whom they should gratefully bow in silent subjection'. For Lovett, as for Harney, the Charter meant an end to subjection and oppression.[5]

When we turn to the Chartist speeches and manifestos in the manufacturing districts in 1839, we find a similar critique of the established order. But protest had a sharper edge to it among men who had first-hand experience of the new poor law and the factory system. Richard Marsden's lament about distress was concrete and specific, whereas Lovett's approach by comparison seems more remote and theoretical. In the speeches by O'Connor and others, addressed to the 'fustian jackets' of the north, the middle-class and its ideology appear more vividly, and come more directly under attack. On the other hand, the persistence of the old radical rhetoric, with its emphasis on the 'corruption' of a system dominated by lords and parsons, often tended to blur the attack on the new industrialism. Chartism was never an ideologically homogenous movement, but a mosaic of disparate elements. Yet that ideological amalgam was nevertheless an effective vehicle of social and political criticism. Together, the various radical rhetorics conveyed a firm sense of what was wrong with England in 1839. The traditions of 1819 had been supplemented and extended by the ideological developments of the 1820s and 1830s.

A mixture of old and new appears, for example, in a broadside inviting the working men of Ashton to contribute to the National Rent in December 1838. On the one hand, the direct link between political change and economic improvement is reminiscent of 1819, as is the language of 'liberty' and 'bondage'. At the same time, however, an implicit attention to class relations invests the idea of liberty with a new social content: 'The time has come to prevent the working classes from starving — an object that can never be accomplished until every man has a voice in making the laws that govern him; . . . We are now arrived at that *crisis* — that we must either enjoy glorious liberty, or live in the most abject bondage for ever; Therefore, if you love your home — if you wish to save your children from being slaves — if you desire to live by your labours, rally round the standard of independence, and prove to your merciless Taskmasters that the people are the source of legitimate power.' A similar melange of social and ideological categories appears in a statement of grievances prepared by the Knaresborough Working Men's Association in reply to a questionnaire sent out by William Lovett on behalf of the convention. What is noteworthy, however, is not the inconsistency, but the firm grasp of the overall situation that underlies the document as a whole: 'Competition and Machinery appear to have been the most fruitful causes of want and misery — the National Debt with vast numbers of other bad Laws have caused competition among the productive millions — However in a few words it appears to us quite evident that the primary cause of all the evils under which we labour is Class Legislation. Universal suffrage alone can remedy the evils under which we labour.' While the ideas of Owen and Cobbett jostle uneasily, the aspiration to fundamental change is clear enough. Similarly, the Nottingham Chartists combined 1819-style denunciations of 'aristocrat factions' and 'despotism' with references to the results of 'middle-class legislation' since 1832 and called for the cessation of attempts to 'plunder or debase the great mass of the people under the wily pretence of Liberal Reform'. At a Chartist meeting in Leeds the arrest of Joseph Rayner Stephens was denounced as an attempt to 'perpetuate the slavery, starvation and misery of the millions for the benefit of the idle aristocracy and of the money-loving capitalist'. Although the aristocratic villains of the radical scenario of 1819 had not disappeared, the centre of the stage had been pre-empted by bourgeois figures.[6]

Chartist attacks on the middle-class, which were especially strong in areas of the anti-poor law or factory agitations, reflected the new social criticism of the 1820s and 1830s. Here also there was the usual variation ranging from anti-capitalist principle to disappointment over failure of middle-class reformers to deliver on the promises implicit in the 1831–2 movement. Nevertheless, some sort of disaffection with the middle-class and its ideology was a leading motif in the Chartist movement as a whole. In rejecting proposals for co-operation with the middle-class in a demand for repeal of the Corn Laws, the secretary of the Sheffield Working Men's Association expressed views that were prevalent in the early years of the movement: 'We feel assured that such is the sympathy of your class – the Corn-law-repeal-agitators for us, the working-men, that you would, in case you got a repeal of those laws before we got the suffrage, render every assistance to the faction to screw the iron-collar about our necks, and tether us down to the rock. Starvation for ever! We cannot forget raising that class to the franchise in 1832.' In Leeds it was 'Neddy' Baines who drew fire as the most convenient local symbol of the 'millocracy' and 'money-hunting millowners'. At Chartist meetings in the West Riding in 1839 Richard Oastler received frequent praise for his work against the new poor law and on behalf of factory legislation, albeit with expressions of regret for his Toryism. In Lancashire the mill towns were placarded with broadsides denouncing mill owners and their economic doctrines. In Bolton the committee of the Working Men's Association denounced as 'Whig lickspittles' a few working men who had joined up with the corn law repealers. Although the Committee opposed the corn laws, it insisted that the repeal movement should not divert working men from 'their hitherto undeviating crusade against oppression'.[7]

James Mitchell, a militant Chartist from Stockport, echoed a number of recurring themes in blunt language castigating both segments of the propertied classes. While contrasting 'we poor working people' with the rich, the 'oppressors of the poor', Mitchell evinced a special animus against 'those who were with us during the passing of the Reform Bill' but who were no longer allies: 'Bolton has been duped by the Whig faction, like Stockport; but they have excluded all the middle-class men, and now know each other and are getting on.' The long struggles of the 1830s were reflected in his denunciation of the mill owners: 'The people have resolved not to be as mere machinery at the disposal of the cotton lords, or other lords, but were determined to associate them-selves in one common bond for the purpose of ameliorating their condition.' Nor was Queen Victoria exempt from Mitchell's scorn. He pointed out that the President of the United States managed on £5,000 a year, 'whilst your young and lovely Queen (laughter) — your youthful and virgin Queen (laughter) — has £300,000 a year'.[8]

At a great meeting in Nottingham in May 1839, John Deegan, delegate to the convention from Hyde, delivered a speech that illustrates a number of elements in the Chartist outlook at the time. He began with conventional radical rhetoric about the loss of their birthright as Englishmen. Then, in non-abstract language he expressed the essence of the new social and economic criticism of the 1820s and 1830s: 'We are going to determine that those who produce the steaks, shall eat and enjoy them, and those men who never produce steaks, shall have no steaks. How can we do that? By obtaining Universal Suffrage by every man shewing to his employers, and the Government, that he has a little of the blood that animated his forefathers circulating in his veins, and a little of the milk of his mother warming his bosom.' They would use legal means first, but if those failed, they would arm themselves. He depicted the basic issue not only in economic terms but in class terms as well. Without universal suffrage, he argued, you will be 'liable to be turned out of work, and your masters taking advantage of your poverty, and their wrath will send orders all round the country that you may not get employment'.[9] To create the sort of society that Deegan had in mind required a radical social and economic transformation. Although Deegan and other Chartist militants had not formulated a programme to carry all this out, their critique was no less trenchant for that. They left no doubt that the point of universal suffrage was to get a society characterised by radically different economic and social relations.

Some form of the labour theory of value, which Deegan summed up so neatly in his Nottingham speech, was a staple of Chartist discourse. The year before a Nottingham Chartist had said that Chartism would 'give us the means of keeping the produce of our labour to those who toil and produce it'. A few years later a leader of Nottingham Chartism described the proposition that 'labour is the source of all wealth' as so self-evident that even a Conservative artisan would have to accept it. Taking that principle as his premise, he asked the sort of question that other Chartists were asking: 'Then . . . how is it that the men who labour, and have raised all the wealth of the country, should be starving and ready to perish in a land said to be the most Christian and enlightened?' His conclusion followed logically: 'Let us not nibble at the effect, but go to the root of the evil.'[10]

For the Chartists as a whole the new poor law was the most hated expression of the social and ideological system against which they were in revolt. Feargus O'Connor had made his reputation as a leader of the anti-poor law agitation of the mid-1830s. His popularity among the 'unshorn chins' of the manufacturing areas was enhanced by his continuing attacks on the new poor law and the middle-class liberal ideology behind it. O'Connor could draw on a reservoir of anger and bitterness about the principles of 1834. The Chartist delegate from Loughborough, for example, derided the 'elegant buildings' that had been built to house men who had spent their lives working fourteen to sixteen hours a day for six or seven shillings a week. 'And for fear any indiscretion might take place between the men and their wives they had made comfortable apartments for them to live separate. (Laughter).' A letter to the convention from a Mansfield Chartist reported that the unemployed knitters had 'no other place of refuge but the Hellish Bastille'. The Mansfield Working Men's Association issued public thanks to Oastler for his 'decided opposition to the devil's own law, the Poor Law Amendment Act', and hoped that he would continue his efforts ' . . . until the Somerset-House monsters are dethroned, the devil's law sent to its native home, and the poor placed in a situation to live by their labour'.[11]

After the mass jailings of Chartist leaders in 1839, the movement suffered a momentary setback. By the middle of 1840, however, a resurgence was well under way. This phase of Chartism spawned a number of rival groups, but it was the National Charter Association that attracted mass support and organised a campaign that culminated in the presentation of another national petition in 1842. The association was formally established in Manchester in July 1840 and was most active in the manufacturing districts of Lancashire and Yorkshire. Although it looked to O'Connor for inspiration, the association was not simply his creature, but was the expression of a broadly-based working-class movement that refused to be deflected from the cause to which it had been committed for so long.

The aggressive posture of the N.C.A. leadership appears in an address issued by the executive in March 1841 congratulating the working classes on their 'noble stand' in the eight months since the association had been established. It dismissed the existing House of Commons in a sentence: 'We have, in the collective wisdom of the nation, assembled in St Stephens, the conflicting parties of the manufacturing and agricultural interest, contending only who shall have most of the productions of your labour.' The middle classes and their ideology received short shrift: 'We have given a broadside to every humbug set up by the middle classes, to cajole and deceive us.' They needed money, because their opponents were spending so freely: 'How do Whig, Tory, Sham-Radical, and other factions act towards us? Why, by the money they suck and screw out of our labour, they bribe the base hirelings of a prostituted press to misrepresent us, and our principles.' The address praised not only O'Connor, but also 'the schoolmaster of Chartism, . . . the father of the new ideas, J.B. O'Brien'.[12]

Although the N.C.A. was based chiefly in the north, it also had a loyal following in the rather different social and economic setting of Birmingham. An address to the working classes issued in January 1841 by the Birmingham National Charter Association would not have been at all out of place among the 'workies' of South Lancashire or the West Riding: 'FELLOW VICTIMS, BROTHER SLAVES . . . We now ask you what benefit you have received from the other classes who move above you as task-masters — and oppressors, but their legalised demand for plunder, the labour of your hands? Who, now, will deliver you from the degraded position you occupy? Will a middle-class crew who frown on all equality? Whose misdeeds make them to be as vicious and corrupt as the Government they uphold?' A year later the 'male and female Chartists of Birmingham' spelled out the same message in an address to O'Connor celebrating his 'glorious triumph over middle-class expediency', at a time when 'the meretricious glare of respectability, and the specious pretences of middle-class hypocrisy, are thrown out as lures to entrap our fellow white slaves'. Farther north, at a meeting in Gateshead, a local N.C.A. leader expressed the hope that 'the working men then present would trust no man above his own sphere of life, without testing him well first. We know them only as enemies. Let us have a good proof of their real friendship before we put any reliance in them'.[13]

As in Gateshead, it was the possibility of collaboration with middle-class radicals that evoked strong counterattacks by Chartist militants. In January 1841 a group of thirty delegates met in Leeds to organise an effort to persuade the Chartists to join forces with the middle classes in a campaign for parliamentary reform and a repeal of the Corn Laws. The Chartist militants in Leeds denounced the proposal out of hand. William Hick's comment reflected the proudly working-class character of the Chartist Left: the 'middle-class men' had refused to join Chartism on equal terms and were inviting working men to give up their own movement and trust in their superiors. But to do that would be to abandon the whole point of an agitation aimed at working-class emancipation. 'By such a compromise, we must give up the leadership out of our own hands, into those of our former betrayers, who would glory to repeat the dose, no matter by what amount of cajolery . . . the power is obtained . . . Can we make such overtures, without giving the direction of our affairs to "our superiors"? I answer, no! never, never!' Hick would have nothing to do with those who 'come to treat us with their wheedling twaddle — half censure — half rub-down flattery'. He indignantly rejected the suggestion that working men moderate their language so as to make a better impression on the middle and upper classes; 'And why, then, stay now to "soften our speech and smooth our tongues"? Is it less necessary to speak the truth — to call things by their right names, than formerly?' There was to be no 'mincing the description of crying evils'. Hick's advice was to 'stick to the real "workies" ' and distrust the middle classes: 'Having wormed themselves, at the expense of working men, into an aristocratic niche in society, they think to carry their obnoxious nonsense of "superiority" along with them, remain apart, or bring us over to the notion that we ought still to do their bidding, and remain slaves.'[14]

In February 1841 a proposal for a union between middle-class and working-class reformers, presented by Arthur O'Neill and John Collins on behalf of the Christian Chartists in Birmingham, drew a powerful counterblast from William Rider. A leader of working-class radicalism in Leeds throughout the 1830s — secretary of the Radical Political Union in 1831 and founding member of the Leeds Working Men's Association in 1838 — Rider rejected co-operation with middle-class radicals or with working men who were too moderate or collaborationist. He saw no virtue in 'a union between the profit-hunters and the pro- ductive classes, at the expense of the least scintilla of Chartist principle'. He was on the side of 'the fustian-jacketed Chartists' against the 'profitocracy'. Rider directed his most scornful barbs at Samuel Smiles, editor of the *Leeds Times*, who had invited the Chartists to co-operate with middle-class radicals. Rider was confident that such an alliance would be rejected, 'as the people, the "workies", are wide awake'. Warning the Chartists against 'the sophisms of those pseudo-Liberals', Rider dismissed Smiles and his group as 'political adventurers, trading politicans, the Jim Crow fraternity, and a few soft-handed political spouters'. He described the 'lessons' to be learned from a recent meeting: 'That King Humbug is dethroned, and cannot be reinstated — a sure and certain sign that the Messrs Marshall, Stansfeld, and Co. must speedily commence some other line of business than that of twaddle-spinning — such stuff being too fragile to hold the tottering system together.' He was furious with Smiles' suggestion that the Leaguers were but Chartists under another name. The purpose of repeal was 'to enable the millocrats, merchants, or slaughter-house gents to compete with the foreign manufacturer'. The purpose of their scheme was 'to reduce the price of bread, so that the "workey" may get his morsel at a cheaper rate, and the grinder be thus enabled to turn the wage-screw a little lower'.[15]

The men of South Lancashire had every reason to be bitter about 'the system' in the dismal autumn of 1842. There is no need to look beyond the immediate economic situation to find the cause of their anger and frustration. What is of more interest, however, is the categories and principles in terms of which they expressed their rage. In an address to their constituents and to 'the Chartists generally' the

South Lancashire Chartist delegates turned their fire directly on the capitalist middle classes: 'During the past few weeks in particular, the monstrous power of the capital in the hands of the middle classes has been most wickedly arrayed against the parents of that capital – the toiling millions of Great Britain. After enjoying all the comforts of life – rioting in luxury as the swine wallows in mire – the middle-class, alike Whig and Tory, have unitedly endeavoured to reduce the honest artisan to a worse than Egyptian state of bondage.' In this context the point of the Charter was not merely to raise wages and end economic depression, but to bring political power to bear in an effort to correct the gross imbalance in class relations between capital and labour. 'Nothing short of political power to *protect* our *labour* will satisfy us, the working classes of this country.' They had to 'support the rights of labour against the heartless aggressions of capitalists', protect working men against 'middle-class juries', and 'bring this unrighteous system of class legislation to an end'. While their conception of specific remedies was imprecise, their diagnosis of the social and economic ills of the working classes was clear enough. The basic problem was 'the aggression of class-constituted tyranny'.[16] The force of their critique reflected the sophisticated social and political consciousness that had developed during the previous generation.

The national petition of 1842 was written in much quieter language than the address of the South Lancashire Chartists. Yet it expressed no less clearly the social content of the Charter. The petition recognised that the ultimate cause of the manifold ills that afflicted working men was a power structure that produced a particular social and economic system, buttressed by coercive legislation that invoked the authority of the sovereign state. If the language was rhetorical and conventional, its specific meaning was quite clear in the context of the document as a whole: 'Your honourable House has enacted laws contrary to the expressed wishes of the people, and by unconstitutional means enforced obedience to them, thereby creating an unbearable despotism on the one hand, and degrading slavery on the other.' In addition to the familiar references to the national debt and excessive taxation, the petition focused sharply on specific working-class grievances – wages, hours, unemployment, and the system of poor relief. Because of lack of popular representation, the House of Commons had insisted on continuing the 1834 Poor Law, 'notwithstanding the many proofs which have been afforded by sad experience of the unconstitutional principle of that bill, of its unchristian character, and of the cruel and murderous effects produced upon the wages of working men, and the lives of the subjects of this realm'. Thousands were dying from 'actual want'. Even those who were working received wages that were woefully low, while 'those whose comparative usefulness ought to be questioned' received high salaries. 'Riches and luxury prevail amongst the rulers, and poverty and starvation amongst the ruled.'[17] Once the ruled got the vote, these social and economic conditions would be transformed.

A number of the other Chartist groups that emerged in 1840 remained apart from the N.C.A. Among them were Lovett's National Association for Promoting the Political and Social Improvement of the People, Teetotal Chartism and Christian Chartism. On the whole, they were less militant than the N.C.A., more inclined to seek alliances with the middle classes, and more hopeful of long-run changes in 'public opinion'. They turned away from direct petitioning and pressure and put their faith in efforts to raise the moral and intellectual level of the working classes in the short run while continuing to make a case for the extension of the suffrage. They were all strenuously opposed to physical force, an important symbolic issue separating them from O'Connor and his followers, although the N.C.A. was not in fact committed to physical force. The outlook of these improvement Chartists is summed up in the title of the book written by Lovett and John Collins while they were in prison: *Chartism: A New organisation of the People, Embracing a Plan for the Education and Improvement of the People, Politically and Socially; Addressed to the Working-Classes of the United Kingdom, and more especially to the Advocates of the Rights and Liberties of the Whole People as set forth in the 'People's Charter'.* Defining a twofold objective for Chartism — gaining equality of political rights and placing people in 'such a *social condition* as shall best develop and preserve all their faculties, physical, moral and intellectual' — Lovett and Collins chose to concentrate on the second. Through education they proposed to prepare their brethren 'to enjoy all the *social* advantages of the political power they are now seeking to obtain'. They also hoped to win increasing co-operation from the middle classes in working towards both their political and educational goals.

Although the Chartists of the centre had diluted somewhat the spirit of protest and militancy that had been so pronounced in 1839, they nevertheless remained faithful to the central values and principles underlying the movement. Their conspicuously moderate tone should not be permitted to obscure the fact that they had by no means abandoned the radical goals of Chartism. Thus, Lovett and Collins continued to assert working-class rights and egalitarian aspirations and to criticise the excessive concentration of social and economic power that prevented their realisation. While hoping to convince the middle classes of the validity of the Chartist position, they refused to bid for support on middle-class terms. Lovett and Collins made it plain that the basic problem was 'wealth and class domination', whether one was considering black slavery in America or 'its damning brother, *the infant slavery of England*'. At a Chartist meeting in 1841, Collins said that 'the anomaly of immense wealth and great poverty' must not be allowed to continue; 'they would put a stop to it, let the consequence be what it might'.[18] Pointing with pride to working-class efforts in support of the unstamped agitation and in the establishment of mechanics' institutions, reading rooms and libraries, Collins and Lovett noted that 'the middle classes, too intent on buying, selling, and speculating, have remained apathetic or sneering spectators of the efforts of the many; till success showed the prospect of advantage, and patronage appeared profitable'. While they welcomed 'the co-operation of good men among all classes', they could not count on much of it. Hence 'the necessity of self-reliance'.[19]

Even in 1842, when Collins and Lovett gave enthusiastic support to Joseph Sturge's attempt to unite the middle and working classes behind a manhood suffrage programme in the Complete Suffrage Union, they refused to hedge their principles in order to curry favour with the middle classes. In April, at the first conference of the C.S.U., Collins criticised those who ignored the miseries of the working classes and did nothing 'to obtain justice for the masses, so long as they could ease themselves by shifting the burdens upon the shoulders of their workmen, by reducing wages and various other means'. He told the story of a gentleman who asked him how, as a reasonable man, he could propose to 'give a vote to all the riff-raff . . . the thimble riggers and those kind of men who attend races and fairs'. Collins' reply rejected the double standard of 'respectability' that the propertied classes were wont to apply in such matters, and pointed to the number of 'riff-raff', not to mention swindlers and liars, who were already installed in £10 houses. His defence of the working classes was not delivered in a docile or deferential spirit, but with scorn for the cant that usually characterised middle-class comments on the subject. In reply to a smug statement by John Bright, Collins defended the ballot in class terms, and in the process affirmed the Chartist vision of a society free from the pressures and coercions of concentrated power: 'Neither the landlord under whom I live, nor the master for whom I work, nor the banker with whom I do business, ought in the slightest degree to exercise any coercion towards me, or dictate in what way I shall give my vote.' He made it plain that in this instance, as in others, the point at issue was not narrowly political, but embraced the moral quality of relations between men: 'And if there be one thing more humiliating than another — more soul-degrading, it is to be compelled to do a thing at which your mind revolts, and yet to do that act as if it was of your own free will.'[20] Collins had put his finger on an issue that was to be a good deal more urgent in the coming decades, when the middle classes took up more urbane forms of domination and sought voluntary support for their views on every issue.

At the C.S.U. conference in April both Lovett and Collins demanded a 'full measure of justice' as the basis for co-operation with the middle classes. Their defence of the Six Points as well as the name of the 'Charter' symbolised a determination to preserve the integrity of Chartism as a working-class movement. 'I think we should be doing outrage to the cherished feelings of the many,' said Lovett, 'were we to discard — to contemptuously spurn that name, because of the prejudices of the few.' In a spirit of conciliation, however, he withdrew a reference to the people's charter in his resolution. Even this did not satisfy John Bright, who brusquely introduced a weakening amendment whose curtness reflected, if not 'contempt', then something close to it. Although Bright's amendment was lost, the spirit underlying it contributed to the irreparable schism between the middle- and working-class delegates that developed at the December conference of the C.S.U. Even Thomas Cooper, writing later in a mood of mid-Victorian moderation and tranquillity, described in stark class terms the issue at that meeting. If there had been 'words of real kindness and hearty conciliation' from the middle-class side, they would have had no trouble winning over the working men. 'But there was no attempt to bring about a union — no effort for conciliation — no generous offer of the right hand of friendship. We soon found that it was determined to keep poor Chartists "at arm's length". We were not to come between the wind and *their* nobility.' In insisting on the Charter and nothing less and in rejecting the terms that had been condescendingly offered by the other side, Lovett remained true to his radical creed. Like other Chartists who believed in rationality, improvement, and class harmony, he did so in an egalitarian and working-class context.[21]

William James Linton, who was closely associated with Lovett in the 1840s, combined a belief in individual improvement with a vision of a social order radically transformed. Although he exercised little influence in the movement, Linton exemplifies the profoundly radical outlook of many Chartists who were moderate in tactics and temperament but not in principle. He took the doctrine of popular sovereignty and carried it to its logical conclusion in social democracy. What led him to the Left was his penchant for thinking in theoretical terms and taking literally the principles of equality and democracy. Among the Six Points, he concentrated on universal suffrage, which he justified in the language of Paine and Godwin: 'First, and far above all else — treating this question as not only political but moral, we base the right — the rightness of Universal Suffrage upon the *natural equality of humankind*.' He treated the question in social terms as well. Since humanity is the 'sole sovereign', such sovereignty could not be surrendered to a monarch or to a class. 'It is not within the scope of human rights to divide men into slaves and tyrants, under any pretence of employment.' It followed that 'republicanism is not republican unless it is social as well as democratic'. Universal suffrage would correct the evils of 'class government', in which 'the *respectables* hate and fear the productive class' and use their position to defraud the community. Like so many other Chartists, Linton looked forward to a truly democratic and egalitarian society.[22]

Although Linton was active in the Chartist cause as an editor, poet, and engraver, he never became a major figure in the movement. He is of considerable historical interest none the less, because as a writer and autodidact he articulated attitudes and ideas that usually remained beneath the surface, finding expression only sporadically or implicitly. In particular, Linton exemplifies the romantic strand that ran through Chartism. Unlike the solidly rationalist Lovett, Linton combined rationalism and romanticism. He took the egalitarian radicalism of the Paine-Carlile-Hetherington tradition and infused it with romantic attitudes and sentiments. F.B. Smith, in an excellent biography, has characterised Linton's outlook as 'mystical republicanism'.[23]

The elements that went into the making of this doctrine can be seen in the first issue of the *National*, a weekly edited by Linton. The frontispiece was 'Tintern Abbey', drawn and engraved by the editor. Smith points out that 'the presiding genius of the magazine was Shelley in his offensive, anti-clerical, anti-authoritarian, homiletic strain'. Like the Shelley of 'Queen Mab', Linton also drew on the rationalist radicalism of the eighteenth century. In support of his belief in the inherent perfectibility of man, he quoted Godwin, Condorcet, and Rousseau; in an issue devoted to religion Voltaire and Paine figured prominently. But Linton's tone also reflected the romanticism of the 1840s. He extended his most intense enthusiasm to Lamennais and Channing, and he translated Lamennais' *Modern Slavery*. His radical vision of the future rested on a distinctly romantic conception of man and his limitless potentialities. 'Between the God-like Shakespeare and the poorest and most imbruted slave, there are more points of likeness than of difference. *Each is a man*.' Every human being is born with 'a life which it is his business to build up towards the most perfect beauty of which his nature is capable, which it is his business to endow with the completest nobility his natural powers can acquire'. In the perfect society of the future individuals would be bound together 'in a holy and ardent love'. Linton's Chartism was pervaded by romantic utopianism.[24]

Although grass-roots Chartism did not adopt such Lintonian rhetoric, the movement as a whole reflected the early-Victorian mood of heightened expectation and aspiration. The Chartist demand for the enactment of the Six Points was overlaid with a romantic hope that fundamental change was imminent. 'You are now called upon by your Fellow Operatives to set your hand to the great and glorious work of National Regeneration', announced a circular issued by order of the Shrewsbury Working Men's Association. For the evils of society 'there is a certain and happy cure in the PEOPLE'S CHARTER'. A working men's committee in Bolton indulged in the rhetoric of romantic radicalism: 'The past is but a record of the woes that ye have endured. The present exhibits society as a dark despairing chaos, where the poor are dashed to and fro like useless atoms. The future is dawning upon you with deliverance: to make that deliverance complete depends on yourselves.' Hoping for regeneration and deliverance, the Working Men's Association at Hull thanked their delegate to the convention: 'May your endeavours to obtain redress prove successful; and may "Peace and happiness, truth and justice, be established amongst us to all generations".' The banners at the great demonstration displayed romantic and sentimental slogans. Grandiloquent and impassioned oratory reflected the conventions of the stage and the pulpit.[25]

Chartists like Lowery, Cooper, and Linton had been profoundly influenced by the romantic poets. Lowery was writing poetry in his teens. Many of the Chartist poems, by Linton among others, reflect a distinctly Shelleyan diction. Ernest Jones' 'Onward and Upward' illustrates the exalted tone of high aspiration:

> Right onward the great thoughts are going,
> Upkindling the hearts of the brave.
> Right upward the Eagle is winging, −
> (Leaves serpents to crawl on the sod)
> Right upward the spirit is springing
> From priestcraft − to nature and God.[26]

Actual conditions of life among the working classes offered ample stimulus for expression of sympathy in the romantic idiom. The reviewer of a volume of poems by Gerald Massey commented on the poet's work in a factory as a child: 'Imagine this poor child at the age of eight or nine years forced by imperious poverty from his bed at five o'clock on a winter's morning to toil through darkness, storm, and snow, to the child-slaying den where Moloch and Mammon sat enthroned on bleeding hearts and ruined souls.' He pointed out that the poet had first-hand knowledge of 'those wrongs which spring from the unbridled tyranny of heartless employers, and their brutal underlings'. The reviewer looked forward to a day 'when all the abominations of the Factory System shall be swept away, and women and children shall be finally freed from the bondage which made the childhood of Gerald Massey a term of suffering and sorrow'. Massey himself wrote in the same key in the dedication of the volume under review: 'Who can see the masses ruthlessly robbed of all the fruits of their industry, of all the sweet pleasures of life, and of that nobleness which should crown human nature as with a crown of glory, and not strive to arouse them to a sense of their degradation, and urge them to end the bitter bondage and the murderous martyrdom of toil?'[27]

The most consistently romantic rhetoric came from George Julian Harney on the far Left of the movement. This tendency was doubtless reinforced by his close ties with the French socialists and radicals. Typical was his denunciation of mere reform and his demand for 'absolute social revolution': ' If the REPUBLIC – DEMOCRATIC – SOCIAL, AND UNIVERSAL be indeed an "Utopia", then it is utopian to hope for the regeneration of the vast mass of mankind, at present plunged in slavery, misery, and degradation. Time is not more certain, or Death more sure, than that there is no salvation for the down-trodden millions, but by and through THE REPUBLIC – DEMOCRATIC – SOCIAL – AND UNIVERSAL.' His expression of sympathy for the downtrodden was expressed in a standard idiom: 'How wretched the lot of the immense body of the people in all lands, compelled to toil like beasts of burden . . . Denied the possession and exercise of those rights which should distinguish them from the brute creation, and set to labour, not for their own support, but for the profit of those who live upon their toil, they are used up without pity, and flung away—like vilest weeds trampled upon – without remorse.' In ringing tones he identified the issue: 'Death or life, slavery or freedom, misery or happiness.' He concluded with a fervent appeal to the working classes: 'By the wrongs of your class and the miseries of your order throughout the world – By the blood of the martyrs, sacrificed on scaffold, barricade, and battle-field – . . . By the principles you love, the hopes you cherish, the hatred you bear to tyrants and their tyranny . . . ' He adjured them to 'hasten the glorious time when . . . the *Reign of Justice* shall be inaugurated to the jubilant cry of "*Vive la République Universelle, Democratique, et Sociale*".'[28]

(2) *Chartism and Improvement*

The Chartist movement was not only an agitation to demand the enactment of the Six Points but also an expression of the values and aspirations of working-class radicalism. Above all, the Chartists believed in the intellectual and moral improvement of the individual; and this belief was inextricably linked to their class-conscious radicalism. They decried the existing order not merely because it left men hungry and reduced them to servility, but also because it deprived them of the opportunity to develop fully as human beings endowed with moral and intellectual powers of the highest order. The Chartist stress on the educability of the common people was intended, in part, to combat the tendency among the propertied classes to treat working men as a class of inferior beings, capable only of manual labour. The Chartist version of the improvement ethic was embedded in a populist and egalitarian context that was often anti-bourgeois. And one of the primary purposes of intellectual improvement was to enable working men to see through the specious arguments of the political economists. Hence the Chartists devoted a good deal of time to educational activity, including the establishment of their own schools. Through its varied activities Chartism contributed to the creation of a working-class subculture, committed to a radical version of values professed by the culture as a whole.[29]

Inevitably, there was a good deal of overlapping between the Chartist faith in improvement and the preachments of middle-class improvers. This overlapping was to contribute to a growing consensus. It does not follow, however, that the self-improvement side of Chartism was a proto-bourgeois element, portending *embourgeoisement* to come. In the following account we shall emphasise the radical and class-conscious aspect of Chartist values. We shall turn first to some of the more militant Chartists who early in 1841 were actively engaged on behalf of the National Charter Association. Intent on preserving the working-class character of the movement, the men of the N.C.A. were quite hostile to the middle classes, and were determined to prevent defections to the other side. From this perspective they affirmed a familiar cluster of radical values.

The Chartist affirmation of the improvement ethic usually came in the context of a defence of working men against middle-class strictures. William Hick, for example, in urging the Chartists to stick to the real 'workies' and steer clear of the 'wheedling twaddle' of the middle-class, emphasised the intelligence and skill with which working men conducted their meetings: 'Hitherto, have we not done our own work — done it well; and are we not progressing gloriously? What, then, may hinder us from proceeding? We increase numerically, and more abundantly in real knowledge and mental capability. Look at our union, sobriety, the anointed but unsophisticated eloquence of our speakers! What body of politicians, or of anything else, can get up and conduct meetings, write and pass resolutions, in such business-like order and ability as the Chartists?' Hick called on working men to turn away from the middle-class and put their faith in 'the divine power of strong truth, boldly spoken, as manifested in the proud and exalted attitude we now hold, as a respectable, powerful and intellectual political body of working men; in their onward career, able and willing to work out, in defiance of every obstacle, their own political redemption'. In repudiating 'obnoxious nonsense of "superiority"', Hick drew on the romantic idiom so characteristic of early-Victorian radicalism: 'Our position is a truly godlike and primitive one; obtained, too, by dint of much painful labour and cost: intellect and virtue alone can rule among us; and we are better able, nay, almighty to conquer without the middle-class men.'[30]

Similarly, the Birmingham branch of the National Charter Association, whose anti-bourgeois attitudes were noted above, vehemently asserted the 'moral worth' and 'intellectual greatness' of working men. Addressing their 'brother slaves' as 'the most virtuous classes in society', they catalogued the virtues esteemed by working-class radicalism: 'We pledge ourselves to give way for more honesty of purpose, to more intellect, to more democracy, to more knowledge; yea, and to more power to do good. We will school those of our brethren who are ignorant that they may advocate their political equality.' Pre-eminent among the virtues to which they laid claim was rationality. Firm in their rationalist confidence in the inherently progressive character of knowledge, they put their faith in reason, even to the point of hoping to convert the middle classes, of whom they held so low an opinion: 'Make converts to Universal Suffrage, obtain justice by demanding your rights, question those who plunder you and live by your labour. Do so, on all occasions; just ask them to shew their superior intellectual endowments, their right to trample on you or your order. Dispute with them their right to a vote, whilst you are not represented at all. Shew them how their property is protected, whilst your labour is swallowed up by their hungry wolves, their idlers.' If their cogent arguments did not have effect, they would at least have the satisfaction of demonstrating their intellectual and moral capacity to their detractors: 'Fellow countrymen, your moral worth, your intellectual greatness must shine forth in every company you enter.'[31]

Since the Chartist militants ran into a great deal of apathy among working men, they readily assumed a posture of exhortation in relation to the working classes as a whole. If only they could overcome the ignorance of the mass, then the movement would get the support it needed; if working men could be persuaded to give up the pot house or other 'sensual' diversions, they might be won over to the Chartist cause. Thus many Chartist leaders came to see themselves as 'improvers' in relation to the working classes as a whole; inevitably, they often echoed middle-class preaching in that area. In Newcastle-upon-Tyne a Chartist leader delivered a stirring appeal to apathetic working men: 'Can you reflect on the condition of your class, (if you have a single virtue to excite reflection,) without contemplating the fatal consequences of your sullen, soulless, yes, your criminal apathy? We demand your immediate exertions; in the name of every principle sacred to man, we call upon you to delay not another moment, in proving that you have integrity, virtue, patriotism, and honour, to contribute your share of influence in this magnificent struggle, for the salvation of our common country.' He pointed out that every district of the country was appointing 'able and virtuous men to enlighten and instruct the working classes', but that the Newcastle area still did not have a missionary. In Leeds William Hick warned against 'the least approach to vulgarity, much less brutality, in the advocacy of our cause'. Standards of decorum had to be maintained. Not without a degree of inconsistency, present in other Chartists also, Hick often seemed eager for working men to win the good opinion of their social superiors. It was easy to cross the line from defending the worth of the working-class to exhorting working men to prove that they possessed all the virtues demanded by middle-class ideologues. Reports of Chartist meetings often drew attention to their orderliness and respectability, noting that 'the business was done in a manner which reflected great credit upon the working men'.[32]

The presence within Chartist radicalism of attitudes that were later to be part of mid-Victorian consensus can also be seen in Bradford, which was still a centre of militant Chartism in the spring of 1848. The Bradford Chartists were certainly as forceful as ever in demonstrating their support for the movement. Despite the presence of special constables, who had been making a show of force, the Chartists held a series of meetings and processions in support of the national convention. They protested when the police seized eight guns from one of their supporters. There was drilling on the moors. One speaker professed to be undisturbed at the fact that they had been accused of treason: 'It was treason on the part of the Americans to wage the war of independence. It was treason to arm themselves against their rulers.' As for the special constables, he was ready to do battle with them: 'They cared not for the crouching tigers at the Court House. They were waiting for an opportunity to ride rough shod over them.'[33] After ten long years the Bradford Chartists were still holding their ground.

The Bradford militants argued their case in terms of the political rationalism that had long been part of the radical tradition. It provided a convenient way of refuting the charges that justified the enrolling of the special constables. 'The working people of this country were desirous of governing the nation intellectually, not by physical force; and when a people were bent upon demanding their legitimate rights peaceably, from a government that was sustained by physical force, that government could not put down an intellectual people.' To be sure, this was a debating ploy, used against the other side. But it voiced a faith that was built into the structure of working-class radicalism. Regardless of how the constables behaved, the Chartists 'were determined to exercise themselves intellectually, by meeting in the manner they were doing. He believed that intelligence would yet put down tyranny ("It always has done.").' The speaker was not taking a consciously moderationist line by any means; he complained that manufacturers were taking advantage of their position to persuade their working people to be sworn in as special constables 'to fight against the interests of their fellow men'. He was simply expressing a faith in rationality which was central to radicalism and the working-class subculture.

The *Northern Star* combined militant politics with a firm commitment to the improvement ethic. An editorial praised the Sunderland tailors for forming a trade union which was also intended to perform friendly society functions, thus fostering 'sentiments of manly independence, (free from the insolence of ignorance)' and promoting 'physical, moral, and intellectual improvement'. When George Julian Harney became sub-editor and took over the literary page, he devoted a great deal of sympathetic attention to distinctly non-proletarian improving literature. He frequently printed the poetry of Eliza Cook and gave high praise to the *Illustrated Family Journal*. The editor of the *Family Herald* was classified with Carlyle as one of the 'most original thinkers of our time', and the journal itself received a favourable puff: 'Of all the cheap miscellanies combining information and amusement for the "million", we know of none worthier of approval than the *Family Herald*.' The first issue of *Douglas Jerrold's Shilling Magazine* was greeted with great enthusiasm. The reviewer quoted with approval a sentence from the prospectus, ' "It is also our faith that the present social contest, if carried out on all sides with conscience and tender heart, must end in a more equitable allotment of the good provided for all men." ' This sentiment, so very much in tune with the romantic-rationalist sensibility, found a very favourable response indeed: 'We add, Amen! and may the success of Mr Jerrold's undertaking be commensurate with his hopeful aspirations, and the mighty good he sets himself to help accomplish.' Having found the new journal so appealing, the reviewer was surprised when it received generally favourable notices; he had expected it to 'excite the hostility of all those pimps of power who . . . prostitute their glorious privilege of the . . . perpetuation of wrong and oppression'.[34]

Harney had nothing but scorn for the propaganda churned out by Charles Knight for the Society for the Diffusion of Useful Knowledge: 'A political economist and Malthusian, he has hardly issued a solitary publication in which he has not done his best to promulgate the damnable doctrines of the heartless political school to which he belongs.' Yet Harney believed in the diffusion of genuinely useful knowledge, for he shared the rationalist radicalism of Paine and Carlile: 'Knowledge *is* power; and the result of its present widespread diffusion must be the political, and ultimately the social, emancipation of the masses.' That was the theme of a review published on Harney's literary page, of *Daily Lesson Book Number 4*, issued by the British and Foreign School Society. The book received the highest praise: 'A better book, we think, the society could not have selected.' The reviewer went on: 'Very possibly the getters up of this publication have but little sympathy with that great party of the movement with whom we are connected; but be that as it may, we tell them, that they are serving us in the most effectual way they could do, by preparing the mind of "Young England" for the full accomplishment of those changes which a portion of their fathers are at present seeking.' While the book itself was innocuous enough — consisting of snippets of miscellaneous information on every conceivable topic — the aims of the society that published it were totally antithetical to those of Harney. *Daily Lesson Book Number 3*, for example, was patently propagandist and included a large dose of popular political economy. The Chartist belief in knowledge as such was so great that the society's textbooks were not considered to be tainted by their source. The point was that once the people were educated they could not possibly remain 'political serfs and bondsmen in the proud land of their birth'.[35]

The Chartist faith in education did not extend to the kind being purveyed to the poor by the propertied classes. Hence the Chartists founded a network of educational institutions of their own. A familiar feature of the movement was the acquisition of a hall or meeting place, which became the centre for a multitude of activities. Working men scraped up enough pence to build or rent a hall, which often housed libraries, reading rooms, and news rooms. Here the Chartists conducted Sunday schools, day schools, evening schools, and mutual improvement societies, which constituted an alternative to the popular education provided from above. They were an integral part of a radical movement concerned not only with agitation but also with the affirmation of fundamental values and principles. Brian Simon has described the nature and extent of the Chartist educational enterprise, in large towns and small, in rural and urban areas. The Chartist hall at Oldham provided 'lectures and discussions on Science, Literature, and Fine Arts, Theology, Morals, Social and Political Economy, etc.' and 'schools for children of all parties and denominations'. In addition to a large meeting room it included a school room, a newsroom, a library, and a 'depot' for books and newspapers. Leeds had a new Chartists' hall, with a Charter debating society, as well as the usual reading room and library. The Stalybridge Chartists founded a people's institute, which included a Sunday school and a day school. By the early 1840s the founding of Chartist halls was in full spate.[36]

The Bolton Chartists illustrate the pattern of educational activity. In 1840 a few of the younger operatives in Bolton established a working men's Sunday and evening school. The evening school met four nights a week from 7.30 to 9.30. Each night three members attended as teachers, and one as a superintendent. There was a charge of a penny a week for instruction in reading only, and two pence for reading, writing, and arithmetic. Beneath the school room were two other rooms, one of them a reading room, which stocked Chartist literature. According to the writer of a letter to the *English Chartist Circular*, that journal was 'an especial favourite'. After reading an article there on 'Democratic Improvement Societies', the members decided to establish a discussion class along the lines recommended in the article. The first question discussed was whether excessively long hours gave working men any opportunity for education. The members concluded that although working conditions were certainly wretched, 'education might become more general than it is, providing *employers* would assist, and the *employed* were reasonably determined to obtain it'.[37]

This group of earnest Chartists in Bolton, associated with the temperance wing of the movement, displayed various affinities with middle-class liberalism. The Bolton Chartists blamed the working classes for their plight and treated education as something of a panacea. In a discussion session they decided that the lack of determination to obtain an education among the working classes was 'the great obstacle in the way of our much desired object — social and political emancipation; and which now renders them the slaves of whatever other class may choose to oppress them. Were not this the fact, we should have more night schools in existence than we have — Mechanics' Institutions, and Mutual Instruction Societies would be better, and such resorts as "Star Inn" and "Finley Fraziers" less attended'. Thanks were extended to the 'liberal gentlemen of Bolton' for their contribution of 119 volumes to the library. There was a Nonconformist liberal flavour to the *English Chartist Circular*'s praise of the Bolton working men for doing something concrete to achieve independence for themselves instead of relying on the schools provided by the Anglican establishment: 'Let us have *self*-supporting, not *charity*-supported schools; let us impregnate the minds of our children with the spirit of independence, and not degrade them by compelling or allowing them to wear the *badge* of an "obey the powers that be", falsely called "National" schools; — let us teach them now to clothe themselves in the comfortable garments of honest Freemen, instead of donning the filthy rags of dishonoured slaves.' The editorial came close to the suggestion that since ignorance is the primary cause of injustice, education is the best remedy. The young Chartists of Bolton were praised for showing the 'ready possibility of working men gaining *by* and *in* themselves that "knowledge" which is truly "power" '. As soon as every district had one such school as this 'popular intelligence will surely become the welcome and the sure harbinger of popular freedom'. All the phrases expressing the rationalist faith of the Left were there, but they had been bent in a middle-class liberal direction.[38]

The *English Chartist Circular* was the organ of teetotal Chartism, a movement that stands at the moderate end of the working-class radical spectrum. Its outlook is clearly defined in an address written by Henry Vincent in 1841. Signed by the leading Chartists of the day, including a number of militants, it urged the establishment of Chartist teetotal societies. While reflecting the class-conscious radicalism of the movement as a whole, the address is oriented in the direction of liberalism and mid-Victorian consensus. Although it denounced the 'flood of national wrongs' and the 'rapacious cupidity' of England's rulers, the main emphasis was on the shortcomings of working men. The first sentence of the address, if taken literally, denied the whole point of the Chartist agitation: 'The ignorance and vices of the people are the chief impediments in the way of all political and social improvement.' In this context the address deplored the tendency of drunkenness to 'debase and still further pauperise a politically oppressed and pauperised people'. Individual improvement was exalted at the expense of political action: 'And though we admit that *class legislation* has inflicted upon us ills innumerable, and blighted the intellect and broken the hearts of whole generations of the sons of toil, we cannot shut our eyes to the truth THAT NO STATE OF FREEDOM CAN IMPROVE THE MAN WHO IS THE SLAVE OF HIS OWN VICES.' Moreover, the address echoed the middle-class liberal line that the aristocracy was the chief obstacle to progress. 'Aristocratic institutions' must be superseded by 'enlightened democracy'; the love of intoxicating drinks was stigmatised as 'the mainstay of aristocracy'. In an idiom indistinguishable from that of the middle-class improvers, working men were warned against 'the *time* wasted over the pint and pipe — time which ought to be devoted to SELF-CULTURE or the EDUCATION OF CHILDREN'.[39]

(3) Owenism, 1835–45

Owenism was not only a major factor in the ideological origins of Chartism but also important in its own right as an expression of working-class radicalism. Shortly after the collapse of the Grand National Consolidated Trades Union, the Owenites organised themselves into a network of branches in the cities and towns of the manufacturing areas.[40] During the peak years of 1839–41 there were sixty branches with 50,000 members in regular attendance. Members participated in a diverse round of activities — educational, cultural, religious, and ceremonial. As a sect rather than a mass movement Owenism brought into sharp focus aspects of radicalism that were expressed only implicitly or sporadically in Chartism. The Owenites explicitly rejected the ideological and institutional forms that an ascendant middle-class was seeking to impose; they proclaimed alternative principles and sought to demonstrate their truth both in theory and in practice. Unlike the Chartists, they did not convene mass meetings of protest in an attempt to persuade − or intimidate − the governing classes to enact measures of reform. Instead of trying to convince the unconverted of the merit of specific measures, they put their faith in persuasion and preaching over the very long run. In the short run, they carried out a limited withdrawal into the shelter of the group, where principles could be maintained in their purity. Determined to live by the principles they preached, they pursued the activities of the branch as a first step towards the creation of a new way of life. Thus, Owenism was in the best sense a sectarian movement, concerned with the proclamation and propagation of social and moral truths.

It was precisely because of their utopian concern with values and principles, to the exclusion of practical issues of class and politics, that the Owenites moved so readily beyond the Chartists in insisting on a total reconstruction of the social order. They preached a gospel that envisaged a new social and moral world, from which the vices of capitalist competitiveness had been banished once and for all. Their preoccupation with principles, however, fostered a soft and rhetorical cast of mind. While the Owenites were well aware of class differences and economic exploitation, they tended to assume that such matters would be disposed of automatically as soon as their ideas won general acceptance. They were 'utopian' in the pejorative sense. Their warm idealism lacked the realism of the Chartists. Conscious of the obligation to be fair to those who had not yet seen the light, the Owenites preferred not to speak harshly of individuals or classes. They were admirably gentle idealists, looking hopefully to the future. Yet they were uncompromising in their total rejection of a social order that fell so far short of their ideals.

Local Owenite societies developed an active life of their own within a new institutional framework established by Owen himself after the debacle of 1834. He founded a journal, the *New Moral World*, and a national executive that presided over the local branches. Owen maintained continuity of leadership from London throughout several changes in the name of the organisation, which in 1835 was known as the Association of All Classes of All Nations, in 1839 as the Universal Community of Rational Religionists, and in 1842 simply as the Rational Society. In 1839 the national executive created a system of social missionaries, each of whom was assigned a district, to work with the local branches. Two and a half million tracts were provided for local distribution between 1839 and 1841. Several of the branches built their own meeting places, first known as social institutions and then as halls of science. In the cities the Owenites created a network of institutions and activities: Sunday schools, adult classes, mutual improvement classes, lectures, and even social festivals. The weekly lectures were delivered by social missionaries, stationed lecturers, or Owenite activists from the surrounding areas. Some of the branches hired their own lecturers for full-time educational and propaganda work. In these various ways the faithful practised their rational religion.

At the core of the 'rational religion' were the principles of Owenite socialism. Insisting on nothing less than a 'total reconstruction of Society', the Owenites dismissed 'the panaceas advocated by the political reformers' on the grounds that these would leave untouched 'the roots of evil of which they so much complained'. For their part, they confidently applied a few basic principles in almost syllogistic form: 'Labour was the source of all wealth; and the equal distribution of its results the only way of producing universal contentment.'[41] The Owenites were equally firm in rejecting out of hand the whole of orthodox Christianity. In an age still under the influence of the evangelical revival this was indeed an expression of an intense radicalism of mind and spirit. Having rejected both the economic and intellectual structures of their society, it was natural for the Owenites to constuct their own institutions and ceremonies – halls of science, mutual improvement societies, hymns, sermons, festivals – embodying their principles in pure form, uncorrupted by the world of competition.

The Owenites saw themselves engaged in 'peaceful warfare against the errors of the old society'.[42] Explicitly and implicitly, in thought and in action, the Owenites were repudiating the culture and values of capitalist society. With good reason, their programme has been characterised as an attempt to create an alternative culture, free from the domination of the master class. Hence they had to have their own schools, to instruct the young in sound values, untainted by the acquisitive selfishness of the world based on the principle of competition. The branches themselves were organised on a radically democratic basis, which undercut the paternalistic inclinations of Owen himself. As Eileen Yeo has pointed out in an important article, 'Branch activity was directed towards creating a participatory and democratic radical culture.'[43] Like Chartism, Owenism reflected the outlook of class-conscious working men, committed to democratic and egalitarian values. For the Owenites, however, those principles entailed a rejection of the social and economic system.

At the regular meetings of their branches, the Owenites renewed their commitment to 'the cause of socialism'. Lecturers inveighed against the vices of competition and extolled the virtues of harmony and co-operation. Sometimes the speaker was a social lecturer, despatched by higher headquarters, like Joseph Southall, who was sent to Oldham by the Manchester board in June 1840. He delivered a talk in which he contrasted the 'social degradation' of England and Ireland with the 'economic arrangements proposed by Mr Owen'. At Rochdale a similar lecture, delivered by a man from a neighbouring town, was reported to have been 'a powerful analysis of the evils resulting from the institution of private property, which was ably contrasted with the opposing system of Community'. The labour theory of value was a potent weapon for attacking a social and economic system that reduced its most useful and productive members to a state of misery. After a few weeks of residence in the Wigan area, the social missionary found abundant evidence to confirm the Owenite critique: working men, 'who produce all wealth . . . are generally speaking, *miserably poor*; they are in fact, *comfortless*, *joyless*, and *neglected*; and as a natural consequence degraded and debased'. Attempts by political economists to defend the competitive system were dismissed out of hand, as in a lecture delivered by a social missionary in Liverpool. Deploring 'the lamentable effects of their heartless, wretched principles', he rejected emigration, the only remedy suggested by the political economists. For Owenism, only a truly fundamental change would do any good: 'The evil is too deep for emigration to cure. The basis and framework of society are bad. Individualisation of property must be destroyed; and antagonism of competition must be annihilated.'[44]

A fuller statement of the Owenite critique of political economy is to be found in a book written in 1842 by John Watts, the social missionary for the Manchester area. The basic principles of Owenite economics were summed up in the title of his first chapter: 'LABOUR THE ONLY SOURCE OF WEALTH. – APPROPRIATION UNJUST. – RENT IS ROBBERY.' Watts also provided a capsule summary of what political economy was all about: 'If political economy as it now stands in the fashionable world be called justice, it must be acknowledged that it is a great misnomer, . . . ; the many are now condemned by and from their birth, while the few are exalted to riches and honour, regardless of their worth.' Like other Owenites – and many Chartists too, for that matter – Watts stressed the absurdity of the doctrines that working men were asked to accept as scientific truth: 'All this is *Political Economy*. Economy forsooth! it is as if some demon had made the world, taught us from youth to call the truth a lie, and the grossest falsehood, truth! In our economy, there is a most extravagant waste of life and labour, and waste of everything valuable, and a saving only of what is worthless!' Drawing a familiar comparison between the Negro slaves in America and the factory workers in England, Watts noted the absence of comparable philanthropic efforts on behalf of factory workers: 'Is this condition so much better than that of negroes, that it deserves no exhibition of philanthropy, that it demands no sympathy?

Yet the tendency of our Political Economy in the doctrine of wages, is to perpetuate this state of things.' While attributing the evils of English society directly to the workings of the capitalist economy, Watts' approach was characteristically moral: 'The nature of trade is evil, and to it more than to aught else, we owe what we have of natural depravity; and it is evil, so evil that a good man entering into it is necessarily spoiled.' As for profit, it was simply a form of theft. In the Owenite mode, he had no qualms about selecting an illustrative example from Scripture: Jesus himself drove the money changers from the temple because they had made it into a 'den of thieves'. Watts spelled out the social consequences of an economic system based on private profit: 'Thus is it clear, that the tendency of our system of competitive society, and division of interests, under any form, is to make one class rich and the other poor; and ultimately, to reduce the poor to the condition of serfs.' Watts concluded his pamphlet with a sweeping indictment of the total economic system: 'We dislike the principle of trade altogether; we dislike the vast inequality now existing between the different members of the human family.' He looked forward to a totally different society, 'when none shall be worshipped as Gods, and none treated as dogs; but when all shall be honoured as men; when their vices and failings shall be prevented, or cured not revenged; in short, when MORAL shall take the place of POLITICAL ECONOMY'.[45]

Watts' counterpart as social missionary in Sheffield in 1841 was George Jacob Holyoake, who had begun what he was later to describe as 'sixty years of an agitator's life'.[46] One of the most militant Owenites of the early 1840s, Holyoake later became a prominent figure in mid-Victorian radical movements, particularly secularism and co-operation. His ideological development is central to an understanding of working-class radicalism both in its early- and mid-Victorian phases. At this point, he is of interest as an exemplar of Owenism at its most radical. Born in Birmingham in 1818, Holyoake learned the trade of a whitesmith as a boy and worked in a foundry for thirteen years. By the late 1830s he was actively involved in the adult education movement. For three years he taught literature and mathematics in the Birmingham mechanics' institute. He then became conductor of the scientific and literary classes at the Owenite branch there. He was also attending Owenite lectures and making a record of them in his notebook. In April 1838 he noted the theme of an 'argumentative and well delivered' lecture delivered by Frederick Hollick, social missionary: 'It is the system that must be changed and not the Rulers alone.'[47] Holyoake accepted that principle for some years to come. In 1840 he was appointed lecturer at the hall of science in Worcester at a salary of sixteen shillings a week. Until he moved his family to Worcester, he often walked the twenty-six miles to Birmingham to visit them. In addition to his lecturing Holyoake also participated in the various activities of the branch, including 'little festivals of the families of members'.[48] In 1841 the national executive appointed him social missionary for the Sheffield area.

Holyoake's Owenism was deeply radical, both in its critique of existing society and in its aspiration towards a total social and economic transformation. In a letter of March 1842 asking his father's opinion about his 'exertions in reform', Holyoake described his social and political views, and summarised a lecture that he had delivered the night before: 'I took up the position that the now much-talked-of reconciliation between the middle and working classes was worse than a chimaera, a dangerous chimaera — First I said we must do away with class distinctions — *middle men* and *working men* may unite, and cordially, but the *two classes* never can.' Among the 'monster evils' of his day he singled out 'not mere aristocracy but *all social inequalities*'; and in politics, the problem was not simply the exclusiveness of the governing classes but 'the absence of perfect self-government'. He took his stand with the 'most advanced democratical party' and warned against the danger of again being left in the lurch by the sort of reformers who had got the vote for the middle classes. As the Owenite movement faded away, Holyoake turned to radical journalism as a vehicle for carrying on the work of spreading the ideas of Owenism and other forms of radicalism. In 1844 he became co-editor of *The Movement* and announced the objects of his 'little revolutionary journal': 'The Destruction of religion and Class rule and Private Property. The Substitution of Morality and Republicanism and Communism.' He praised Harney and defended O'Connor against criticism from the Complete Suffrage group. Holyoake knew the predicament of the working man, who was sure to be a loser regardless of what he decided to do: 'The way of a working man is hard — if he sinks under his fetters he is called a slave and a coward — if he breaks them off, the law grasps at him with bloody fangs.' In the first issue of a new journal that came out in June 1846, Holyoake maintained his position on the far Left of working-class radicalism: 'The *Reasoner* will be Communistic in Social Economy — Utilitarian in Morals — Republican in Politics — and Anti-theological in Religion.'[49]

Even in 1851 Holyoake refused to be taken in by the general euphoria surrounding the Creat Exhibition of 1851. Instead, he made it the occasion for an impassioned — and often sentimental — account of the misery that lay behind the facade of opulence and prosperity. 'Does the fair lady who admires that exquisite piece of cutlery, whose polish rivals her mirror, remember that he who gave it its lustre spit blood? . . . Would that lord in white waistcoat suppose that the article he is so much delighted with, was fashioned by a man pale with consumption and grim with want?' Not even among the brass workers of Birmingham did Holyoake find class harmony: 'He who made that brass bedstead, cursed his employer all the day long.' And in Lancashire, 'the capitalist spins humanity up in his mills, weaves into his calico the hopes, affections, and aspirations of the poor, and then moves heaven and earth for new markets to sell them in'. Mocking those who saw the exhibition as 'an object of wholesome glory' Holyoake suggested that they ought to exhibit the producers as well as the products: 'Let the young factory man be there as he is to be found at home, without knowledge or emulation, the young factory woman without self-respect; manhood and womanhood without content or hope; old age trembling at its decay of power, and at the workhouse destiny before it.' He had heard enough about economic growth. 'Talk of the development of industry: it is the development of curvature of the spine, concave chests, and deformities of mind more hideous even than deformity of body.' Holyoake spoke the language of class struggle and social change: 'Yet there are people who get rich not merely *in spite* of this misery – that were a thing to be glad at; but people get rich *out of* this misery and because of it – and this is a thing to be looked into and to be altered.' Holyoake was not thinking in narrowly economic terms. 'It is not the misery of this, so much as the demoralisation of it, which has to be deplored. The working-class are a stricken race. Their native energy seems bled out of them. They live as men should never live and they die as men should never die . . . They have not even the dignity of despair. Despair is at least a manly desolation', implying that 'the struggler yields to a fate he has fought against bravely'. But 'the modern workman has not even this gloomy example to bequeath to his children'. Working men 'slink into the garret or the cellar, or to that public stable, the poor-law union, and lay themselves down on the pauper's bier, and from his ignoble grave bequeath to their brethren the legacy of a dishonourable example of ignorance, supineness, submission, and cowardice'.[50]

Like their Chartist brethren, then, the Owenites saw through the ideological mystification practised by the propertied classes; even more than the Chartists they accompanied their indictment of the established order with an aspiration to the radical transformation of the social and economic system. Like the Chartists, but more consciously and systematically, the Owenites were also concerned with affirming the values and principles that ought to be actualised in a properly organised society. Recognising that there was little likelihood of fundamental change in the near future, the Owenites concentrated on disseminating their principles and putting them into practice on a small scale in their own lives. In this way they hoped to 'promote the success of the social cause' and carry forward 'the great work of human redemption'. What really mattered was strengthening their own faith and spreading 'social' principles to others. As a devoted Owenite perceived the situation in 1844, 'Considering the small chance there is for the greater number of our members ever becoming residents at Harmony, we should devise some plan for bettering our condition under the present arrangements of society, and at the same time demonstrate to the world the truth of our principles.'[51]

Among the principles that the Owenites inherited from the 'Social Father' was the idea of unlimited improvement for the individual in a society based on the principle of co-operation. Owen's determination to transform the character of the individual reflected a fusion of Enlightenment environmentalism with the evangelical concern with the moral re-birth of the individual. In the spirit of a rationalist revivalism, he argued that 'the whole man must be re-formed on fundamental principles the very reverse of those in which he had been trained; in short, that the minds of all men must be born again, and their knowledge and practice commence on a new foundation'. Throughout his life Owen considered it essential to 'remoralise and improve the working classes'. Owen's approach to improvement was highly paternalistic; the working-class character was to be re-formed from above. He saw the problem in terms of 'rationally forming the character of that immense mass of the population which is now allowed to be so formed as to fill the world with crimes'. In accents that had affinities to the attitudes of the propertied classes as a whole in the early nineteenth century, he was concerned about 'the poor and the uneducated profligate among the working classes'.[52]

The Owenite branches excised Owen's paternalism and developed an egalitarian version of the improvement ethic. A Huddersfield Owenite expressed the ideal in the glowing language so characteristic of the movement. While noting with regret that little had been accomplished recently by the Huddersfield branch in the area of 'intellectual and moral improvement', he concluded with a hopeful exhortation that sums up the values and aspirations of Owenism:

> Be true to yourselves and the system ye advocate; carry on your school with spirit and energy — organise yourselves into classes for mutual improvement — store your minds for useful knowledge — become lovers of science — develop each other's moral, social, and sympathetic feelings — commune with each other a little oftener than you have hitherto done, and instead of being, as ye now are, a desponding body of men, you will become morally and intellectually strong — your Society will be renovated — your Hall will become of some utility.

The speaker suggested 'the reducing to practice, by each member, of the principles of the Society, in his daily conduct, and the cultivation of his mental faculties — his moral and sympathetic feelings'.[53]

Formally committed to the cause of 'rational reform', the Owenites energetically propagated the cluster of values derived from Enlightenment rationalism. They did so, first of all, in the traditionally radical manner, by depicting intellectual advance as the indispensable prerequisite to political and social progress. The Owenites subscribed to one of the fundamental articles of the radical creed: 'Recollect, if the world is to be regenerated, ignorance must be removed. Let us endeavour, then, to give each other as much information as possible.'[54] Ignorance was the great obstacle to working-class freedom and political progress. G.J. Holyoake put the point neatly in his *Practical Grammar*, published in 1844: 'Intellectual bondage is worse than physical, because the physical chain is riveted by others, the mental by ourselves. The ignorant man is at the mercy of educated opinion. To be free, we should be in a position to dare the judgement of the wise.'[55] This was an area where working men could take action for themselves here and now, with cumulatively beneficial results in the future. There was every reason to believe that instructional activity would contribute to the regeneration of the world.

Owenites shared the radical faith in education, even to the point of hoping that a 'good education' would contribute to a solution of the problem of 'the unequal distribution of the means of physical comfort'.[56] The sort of education that they had in mind — 'full, free, and equal, without distinction of class or caste' — could come only after the creation of a socialist society. In the short run, they had to settle for much less, as at Birmingham in 1841, where they established a social institution, 'for the educational and moral improvement of the producers of wealth, without regard to class, sect, or party'. Thus while they continued to affirm their grandiose expectations for education, the Owenites worked on a modest scale. In Stalybridge, a small group hired a room 'for the purpose of improving themselves in the leading branches of education, and of holding occasional meetings for the advancement of Social principles'.[57] Elsewhere, Owenites set up schools to instruct members in 'the general elements of useful knowledge'. Believing in 'rational amusement', they arranged 'scientific entertainments'. The Owenites built schools and halls of science to advance intellectual improvement in the present.

The Owenites were no less concerned with bringing about the maximum moral improvement of the working classes in the short run. Unlike the middle-class improvers, however, they blamed the social system for creating the conditions that led to intemperance and vice. If depravity abounded, it was evidence of the corruption inherent in the system of competition. Thus, a Huddersfield socialist, after attending a Christmas festival organised by the local Owenite branch contrasted 'the sobriety and civil manners of those who had participated in our "Feast of Reason" with the brutal language and bullying conduct of the unfortunates .who were reeling from the public houses'. The Owenites also contrasted their own neatness and cleanliness with the disorder and dirt to be found in the world that they were bent on transforming. One branch proudly noted the fact that in its Saturday amusement class 'a spirit of neat cleanliness and order is evidently on the increase', since members were no longer attending the meetings 'in their greasy jackets and working gowns'. This improvement was described in socialist terms, in a way that had no visible connection with the respectability preached by the middle classes. The 'greasy jackets' were treated as part of the Old World — the world of competition and acquisitiveness that was to be replaced by the new moral world of co-operation. According to this account, when members arrived at meetings they also had been accustomed 'to run from their seats and jostle each other to obtain what the Old World's teaching made them believe was a preferable place, viz. the head or top of the dance, which could only make them objects of *envy* to others who had been trained equally erroneously with themselves'. This also needed to be corrected. Along with the new cleanliness, it was felt, came a heightened social awareness that 'in order that *all* may enjoy happiness it is necessary each would endeavour to give up as much of their Old World feelings as possible on such occasions'. Cleanliness — like the spirit of unselfishness and co-operation — was depicted as one of the essential characteristics of the new socialist order.[58]

In its theory and practice, then, Owenism was a cogent expression of the traditions of working-class radicalism. It is from this perspective that we have been discussing it as well as Chartism. If we shift our point of view, however, and look at Owenism in relation to mid-Victorian ideological and social patterns, other aspects of it come more prominently into view. Above all, one is struck by the numerous points of affinity with the early-Victorian culture, of which the Owenites remained very much a part.

Despite their determination to free themselves from the old world of competition, the Owenites were keen on doing many of the same sort of things that were soon to be sponsored, on a growing scale, by middle-class improvers and by non-radical working-class groups. Not only what they did but the manner in which they did it reflected patterns characteristic of the culture as a whole. The Owenite halls of science, for example, while thoroughly socialist and working-class in orientation, were announced as a means of enabling working men and their families 'to acquire and communicate useful knowledge, and . . .

have innocent recreation and rational amusement at so trifling an expense as to be within the means of the poorest when employed'.[59] A contemporary working man's institution operated by Owenite socialists arranged a programme which corresponded closely in form to non-socialist programmes at the same time: lectures on Sunday, a tea party on Monday, and a concert on Tuesday. To be sure, the Owenites were insistent on maintaining their independence from middle-class control, and socialist lectures were radical in the extreme; but the rest of this apparatus of improvement fitted in comfortably with the culture of which it was in fact a part. It was even possible for one Owenite to argue that the movement ought to be given credit for having originated tea meetings and other worthwhile improvement activities: 'The clergy and the Dissenters have copied the infant schools and tea meetings from the Socialists; and the Chartists are, by their excellent leaders, Lovett and Collins, being taught to copy their general organis-ation, and to imitate their peaceful efforts to improve the condition of all.' Such peaceful efforts, of course, fell far short of achieving the utopia that they had in mind. But the author of these remarks, like many of his brethren, consoled himself with a quasi-religious hope: 'Knowledge and peaceful efforts will make them "wise unto salvation", which, being translated, is deliverance from evil.'[60]

The aggressively secularist outlook of Owenism retained a distinctly nonconformist flavour. The Owenites were only too eager to adapt traditional religious forms to their purpose: they developed their own service, complete with hymns. A description of a meeting at the hall of science in Manchester in 1844 conveys the atmosphere of revivalist fervour: 'In a few minutes the steam was up; the feeling of the meeting was truly enthusiastic, and their countenances were lit up with a glowing feeling of joyous emotion.' The evening had been set aside for 'a *demonstration* and a *revival* of that active and life-stirring agitation which once lived amongst us in the youthful days of our movement'. The report of the meeting noted that the 152nd hymn had been sung with spirit.[61]

Thus the Owenites set about constructing an alternative way of life with forms derived from a culture of which they were very much a part. While their intention was to detach inherently sound values from a setting that constricted and perverted them, and reconstitute them in a more congenial milieu, they could not avoid reinforcing — if not actually sanctifying — values that were becoming part of an emerging consensus. Many of the virtues that the Owenites were urging in a radical and class-conscious context lent themselves to assimilation to a culture that cast them in a different mould. Thus, when the Owenites stressed the need for civility, courtesy, fellowship and brotherly love among men, they did so in terms of their rejection of a social and economic system that nurtured antithetical qualities: selfishness, egotism, competitiveness, and lack of consideration for others. The Owenites had celebrated social harmony in criticism of a society marred by constant conflict; they called for courtesy as part of a new pattern of social relations between equals. By the 1850s, however, middle-class spokesmen were preaching many of the same virtues, but in the context of an inegalitarian and acquisitive society.

The utopian side of Owenism was to be especially vulnerable to assimilation to mid-Victorianism. The Owenites were so absolute in their aspirations — urging the transformation of not merely the economic system but also the character of the mass of the people who had been degraded by that system — that they had to settle for extravagant rhetoric and limited short-run improvements. Their concern with improving the character of the individual constituted an important point of contact with the main thrust of the culture as a whole. Their sentimental utopianism, rooted in radical protest, came to overlap with the sentimental optimism of a culture based on progressive liberalism. Hence the Owenism of the 1840s, a manifestation of the heroic period of working-class militancy and class consciousness, also provides the best preview of the coming period of accommodation and acquiescence — when it was to be difficult indeed to maintain the values and principles of radicalism.

Chartism, even more than Owenism, contributed to the creation of a working-class subculture, embodying a radical and egalitarian formulation of the values of the culture as a whole. A totally unanticipated consequence of this development was a gradual broadening of the area of consensus shared with the middle-class. As the middle classes developed a more benign version of liberal ideology and reduced the overt signs of self-serving class interest (see chapter 4 below), there came to be more and more overlapping with the values of working-class radicalism. Ironically, then, it was during the most militant and class-conscious period in their history that the English working classes became firmly committed to the values which were to provide the basis of mid-Victorian consensus and equilibrium. In the very act of attacking the middle classes and asserting the worth and dignity of their own class working men were affirming many of the values which, in slightly modified form, were to undergird a culture that presupposed middle-class pre-eminence. Their questioning of the legitimacy of the social and political order was based on values which, in a different form and context, were to legitimise the mid-Victorian polity. The early Victorian working man chose his own values and shaped his own social character as part of a quest for dignity and freedom, only to find his efforts enmeshed in a larger process which assimilated his hard-won virtues to a culture characterised by middle-class hegemony. It was no longer a matter of asserting radical values: they had to be preserved from the embrace of a competing middle-class version.

In other ways also some of the more militant aspects of early-Victorian working-class radicalism were to prove to be readily assimilable to mid-Victorian cultural patterns that shifted their function and significance. The utopian hopefulness of Chartists and Owenites, quite out of proportion to the objective possibilities of the situation, lent itself to the ritual expression of noble sentiments and aspirations so characteristic of mid-Victorianism. The sometimes sentimental optimism of working-class radicalism turned out to possess affinities with the official earnestness and idealism of the new culture that was taking shape beneath the surface of agitation and protest. The radical temper of the faith in individual improvement was later to facilitate acquiescence in a subtly different consensus version. These unexpected potentialities, latent in working-class radicalism, were to be exploited by the simultaneous development of new forms of middle-class liberalism.

Notes

1.   In addition to the works cited in note 4, chapter 1, see also Mark Hovell, *The Chartist Movement*, Manchester 1918; A.R. Schoyen, *The Chartist Challenge: A Portrait of George Julian Harney*, London 1959; F.B. Smith, *Radical Artisan: William James Linton 1812–97*, Manchester 1973; G.D.H. Cole, *Chartist Portraits*, introduction by Asa Briggs, London 1965; John Saville, *Ernest Jones: Chartist,*, London 1952; Donald Read and Eric Glasgow, *Feargus O'Connor, Irishman and Chartist*, London 1961; J.T. Ward, *Chartism*, London 1973; J.F.C. Harrison, *The Early Victorians 1832–1851*, London 1971, pp. 153–67.
2.   *Charter*, 3 and 17 March 1839. For Marsden's speech see Thompson, *Early Chartists*, pp. 181–4.
3.   William Lovett, *My Life and Struggles,* London 1967, p. 174.
4.   *English Chartist Circular*, I, no. 11. For an interpretation that stresses Lovett's acceptance of industrialism, see the excellent article by David Large in Patricia Hollis, ed., *Pressure from Without*, London 1974, pp. 105–30.
5.   *English Chartist Circular*, I, no. 11.
6.   H.O. 40/44; British Museum, Add. MS 34245B, f. 288; H.O. 40/47; *Northern Star*, 5 January 1839.
7.   *Charter*, 19 May 1839; *Northern Star*, 11, 18, and 25 May 1839; HO 40/43; see also Briggs, *Chartist Studies*, pp. 29–60, 65–84, 294–7.
8.   *Northern Star*, 18 May 1839.
9.   H.O. 40/47.
10.   *Nottingham Review*, 26 August 1842.
11.   H.O. 40/47; Add. MS 34245A; *Northern Star*, 5 January 1839.
12.   *Northern Star*, 20 March 1841.
13.   Ibid., 30 January 1941, 21 May and 16 April 1842.
14.   Ibid., 30 January 1841.
15.   *Northern Star*, 6 and 27 February 1841; see also Briggs, *Chartist Studies*, pp. 66–84.
16.   *English Chartist Circular*, II, no. 85.

17. Patricia Hollis, ed., *Class and Conflict in Nineteenth Century England*, London 1973, pp. 217–23.

18. *Birmingham Journal*, 29 March 1841.

19. Collins and Lovett, *Chartism*, pp. 8, 14.

20. *Report of the Proceedings at the Conference of Delegates, of the Middle and Working Classes, held at Birmingham, April 5, 1842, and Three Following Days*, London 1842, pp. 9, 25, 36.

21. Ibid., pp. 55, 67; Thomas Cooper, *Life Written by Himself*, Leicester 1971, p. 222.

22. F.B. Smith, *Radical Artisan: William James Linton 1812–97*, Manchester 1973, Appendix, pp. 219–39, consists of excerpts from the *English Republic*, vols. I–III (1851–5). Linton indicates that most of the argument on universal suffrage, pp. 227–31, published in 1854–5, was written fifteen years before.

23. Ibid., p. 30.

24. Ibid., pp. 1–45, 227–8.

25. Add. MS 34245B; H.O. 40/44; *Northern Star*, 20 February 1839, 19 March 1842; see also Clark, 'Romantic Element', loc. cit., p. 220, and Burn, *Age of Equipoise*, p. 62.

26. Ernest Jones, *Chartist Songs and Fugitive Pieces* (n.d.).

27. *Friend of the People*, 26 April 1851.

28. Ibid., 26 July 1851.

29. F.B. Smith, p. 21, notes the presence of many references to Channing and self-culture in Chartist documents.

30. *Northern Star*, 30 January 1841.

31. Ibid.

32. Ibid.

33. *Bradford Observer*, 13 April 1848.

34. *Northern Star*, 27 February 1841, 8 February 1845.

35. Ibid., 8 February 1845.

36. Brian Simon, *Studies in the History of Education 1780–1870*, London 1960, pp. 243–76.

37. *English Chartist Circular*, vol. II, no. 110.

38. Ibid.

39. Ibid., vol. I, no. 9; see also Brian Harrison, 'Teetotal Chartism', *History*, LVIII, 1973.

40. See J.F.C. Harrison, *Robert Owen and the Owenites in Europe and America*, London 1969.

41. *New Moral World*, 3 July 1841.

42. Ibid.

43. Eileen Yeo, 'Robert Owen and Radical Culture', in Sidney Pollard and John Salt, eds., *Robert Owen: Prophet of the Poor*, London 1971, p. 89.

44. *New Moral World*, 11 July and 8 August 1840; John Green, *The Emigrants*, Manchester 1838.

45. John Watts, *Facts and Fictions of Political Economists,* Manchester 1842, pp. iv, 30–1, 60.

46. George Jacob Holyoake, *Sixty Years of an Agitator's Life*, London 1906, pp. 15–19.

47. Holyoake Notebook, 1838–9, MS, Bishopsgate Institute.

48. *Sixty Years*, pp. 133–4.

49. Holyoake to his father, 11 March 1842, MS, Holyoake House, Manchester; *The Movement*, 1 January and 17 February 1844; *Reasoner*, June 1846.

50. *Leader*, 21 June 1851.

51. The Holyoake collection, Bishopsgate Institute, has a number of interesting letters from Owenite activists in the early 1840s. The last passage quoted is from

New Moral World, 27 July 1844.
52. Robert Owen, *A New View of Society and Other Writings*, London 1927, pp. 94, 212, 21, 14.
53. *New Moral World*, 20 July 1844.
54. Ibid., 27 July 1844.
55. Edward Royle, 'Mechanics' Institutes and the Working Classes, 1840–1860', *Historical Journal*, XIV, 1971, 316.
56. Ibid.
57. *New Moral World*, 13 July 1844.
58. This paragraph is based on Yeo, pp. 95–6.
59. Ibid., p. 92.
60. *New Moral World*, 9 January 1841.
61. Ibid., 29 June 1844.

4 THE MELLOWING OF MIDDLE-CLASS LIBERALISM, 1834–51

During the period of confrontation with working-class radicalism, the middle classes were gradually developing a more benign social philosophy, which presupposed a continuation of their predominance while taking a more positive view of the classes below. In the course of time the repressive spirit of 1834 was replaced by the genial optimism of 1851. No longer obsessed with the coercion and indoctrination of refractory working men, the middle classes instead invited them to join in the common enterprise of social and economic advancement and intellectual and moral improvement. Instead of merely deploring the vices of the working classes, middle-class spokesmen began to talk of the avenues to virtue and knowledge that were open to all men in a society devoted primarily to the improvement of the individual. The class character of their ideology receded into the background in the wake of a new emphasis on values which, in form, applied equally to all.

At first glance, this shift in middle-class attitudes hardly seems worthy of notice. Since we know that every dominant class tends to develop an ideology that justifies and rationalises its privileges, it would seem that the early-Victorian middle classes were simply responding to the logic of their situation by improving the ideological effectiveness of the liberal creed. In fact, however, the response dictated by the socio-economic situation was to dig in, make no concessions, and simply redouble attacks on the 'demagogues' who had misled the working classes and prevented them from recognising their true interests. The 'natural' line for the middle classes — implicit in both social and ideological circumstances — was the one laid down by Andrew Ure: use Christianity and utilitarianism as instruments of indoctrination to compel the working classes to recognise the validity of laissez faire and acknowledge the legitimacy of middle-class domination. Yet Ure's policy of manipulating available intellectual materials for crudely ideological purposes was bound to be counter-productive. As John Stuart Mill observed a few years later, the idea of a society 'only held together by the relations and feelings arising out of pecuniary interests' was 'essentially repulsive'.[1] In any case, popular political economy had been unmasked by working-class radicalism. In effect, it had been recognised as a new variant of an old opium-of-the-people doctrine. To the extent that Ure's ideas were being actively preached, they were not tranquillising the working classes but alienating them.

Yet the English middle classes rejected Ure's plausible advice and smoothed off the jagged edges of utilitarian liberalism. The same intellectual forces that had contributed to the moralistic and dogmatic spirit of 1834 now helped the middle classes to find their way out of the predicament in which they had been caught up. During the 1830s and 1840s there took place a gradual shift in the direction of an idealism that had lain dormant during the era of anti-Jacobinism and Malthusianism. Once the middle classes got over their initial shock at the new working-class presence in the industrial towns, they were able to assume the more congenial role of spokesmen for the universal aspirations of liberalism and practical Christianity. Another ingredient in the process was that traditional stimulus to middle-class idealism — hostility to the gentry and aristocracy. With characteristic ambivalence, the merchants and manufacturers also displayed an inclination to emulate the paternalist ideal of the landed classes. As a result, without sacrificing one jot of the substance of power the middle classes defined their role and social values in terms of the highest ideals of the culture. Having bent Christian and liberal ideas into narrowly ideological shape in the generation of 1834, they permitted the hopefulness and optimism of those traditions to unfold in the generation of 1851.

In this chapter the term 'liberalism' is used in a rather broad sense to denote the social outlook and values of the new middle class of merchants and manufacturers who dominated the industrial towns of early-Victorian England. Two strands have been singled out for discussion. The first is utilitarianism, a secular middle-class creed based on the Enlightenment with a large admixture of political economy; with respect to the working classes, it stressed the diffusion of useful knowledge and the development of popular education. The second strand, closely intertwined with utilitarianism in the consciousness of predominantly Nonconformist businessmen, included a complex of attitudes derived from evangelical Christianity. The founders of the provident societies in the 1830s were men of piety who perceived the social and economic world in the categories of political economy. Utilitarian and Christian elements were fused in early-Victorian liberalism.

But the character of a culture, as well as the processes of change within it, is disclosed not only in its dominant forms but also in its more eccentric manifestations. The last two sections of this chapter deal with a numerically small group of advanced reformers, conscious of their location well ahead of the main body of middle-class liberalism. These men asserted liberal ideals and aspirations in genuinely universal form; their position was very close indeed to that of working-class radicalism in the next generation. The reformers reflect a pattern that has recurred in English society and politics since the middle of the nineteenth century — the steady incorporation of ideological and programmatic elements from the left-of-centre segment of the consensus prevailing in a given period. In this instance, mid-Victorian liberal consensus was to reflect the idiom and sensibility of the advanced reformers of the 1840s, who mediated the transition to a new culture in which their ideas were assimilated and domesticated.

(1) *'The Inestimable Blessing of Knowledge'*

Utilitarianism had never been a mere ideology, justifying middle-class predominance. It also carried the ideals of Enlightenment liberalism — opposition to privilege, commitment to progress for all, confidence in the beneficence of reason, and an insistence on applying principles uniformly, without regard to creed or class.[2] Despite the Malthusian cast of early-nineteenth-century utilitarianism, it retained the broadly liberal aspirations inherited from the eighteenth century. In the generation after 1834 this heritage was an important factor in the formation of the mid-Victorian ethos. Latent idealism that had been inhibited by the Malthusian and anti-Jacobin tide took on new life and contributed to the emergence of a new version of meliorist liberalism, wedded as firmly as ever to private property and middle-class supremacy, but emphasising the benefits that everyone, working men included, would derive from the diffusion of knowledge and rationality.

Thus, the chief intellectual force behind the spirit of 1834 also played a major role in its transformation. The principle of self-help and independence, removed from the harsh context of the new poor law, moved closer to what many radical working men themselves had in mind, namely emancipation from traditional dependence and servility. The utilitarian faith in reason, especially when expressed in criticism of the more obscurantist forms of toryism, led the liberals to put their confidence in the independent and intelligent working man, capable of making up his own mind, an ideal that received classic expression in 1848 in John Stuart Mill's *Political Economy*. The chief institutional vehicle in the shift in liberal ideology was the mechanics' institutes. Even in the 1820s, when they were dominated by the 'political-economic form of liberalism' and a will to indoctrinate, the institutes embodied the great hopes of utilitarian rationalism. In the coming decades this side came to the fore, and also took on the warmth of evangelical and romantic currents of feeling.

James Mill, the most influential expositor of utilitarianism in its formative phase, was imbued with the meliorist and egalitarian outlook of Enlightenment liberalism. Although he was second to none in his assertion of the virtues of the middle classes, he sought to apply his principles equally to all men. When he referred to 'man' or 'the individual' he employed these terms as genuinely universal categories, not as fictions masking middle-class interests. In the Enlightenment tradition, Mill's article on education for the *Encyclopaedia Britannica* in 1818 rested on the assumption that all men are endowed with reason and are capable of profiting from education, the basis of progress for all. Commenting favourably on Helvetius' environmentalism, Mill reached a conclusion that was to be central to Owenism and the Left: 'All the difference which exists, or can ever be made to exist, between one *class* of men, and another, is wholly owing to education.' While conceding the existence of significant inborn variations in ability from one person to another, Mill insisted nevertheless that it is differential education which is responsible for the fact that 'large numbers or bodies of men are raised to a high degree of mental excellence; and might, without doubt, be raised still higher'. At one point, carried away by his premises, he drew a radical conclusion with utopian gusto: 'Whatever is made of any *class* of men, we may then be sure is possible to be made for the whole human race. What a field for exertion! What a prize to be won!' Mill insisted that such traits as intelligence, temperance, and benevolence ought to be developed to an 'equal degree' in all men, 'in the poor as in the rich'. If it were possible to develop them 'in the highest possible degree in all men, so much the more would human nature be exalted'.[3]

Mill illustrates another aspect of utilitarianism that was to be prominent in the liberalism of the next generation. His rationalism and his radicalism flourished in opposition to the obscurantism of traditional toryism: 'Till recently, it was denied, that intelligence was a desirable quality in the great body of the people; and as intelligence is power, such as an unavoidable opinion in the breasts of those who think that the human race ought to consist of two classes – one that of oppressors, another that of the oppressed.' Unlike the tories, who would compel deference and obedience, the utilitarians would submit their policies to the test of reason and debate. Whereas the tories would use education to train the people 'to habits of servility and toleration of arbitrary power', the liberals would educate the people in rationality, independence, and freedom. Mid-nineteenth-century liberalism shared Mill's rationalist assurance: 'Grant a reading people and a free press, and the prejudices on which misrule supports itself will gradually and silently disappear.'[4] While Mill concentrated on a middle-class attack on the ruling oligarchy, utilitarian radicalism could also recognise that working men were an 'oppressed' class.

Samuel Smiles was full of utilitarian idealism when he came to Leeds as a young doctor in 1838. He immediately established close ties with radical working men and clashed sharply with those liberals who seemed interested only in indoctrinating the working classes with middle-class ideology. In an editorial in the *Leeds Times* he denounced 'teachers of useful knowledge' who taught political economy and self help as doctrine that would reconcile the working classes to their miserable lot and keep them from subversive temptations. Sympathetic with working-class critics of the new poor law, he was repelled by the crudely middle-class orientation of Edward Baines, whose attitude towards the working classes he found to be coloured by a 'prurient and diseased imagination'.[5] In February 1842, when the middle classes were looking anxiously at growing working-class unrest, Smiles supported the Complete Suffrage Union's programme of manhood suffrage. Although never a Chartist himself, he hailed Chartism as 'one of the most notable steps in the march of modern civilisation. I cannot look on it with the fear and trembling some people do, but consider it to be one of the most hopeful of all the signs of the times'. Rejecting the notion that Chartism was the product of unreason, he described it as 'the result of knowledge — political knowledge if you will — flowing in upon the minds of. men who find themselves living in the midst of wealth and civilisation a degraded and an oppressed class'. Lancastrian schools, Cobbett, and the Reform Bill had all made their contribution to 'the diffusion of intelligence' underlying the Chartist movement. 'It is the result of that desire which the Creator has implanted in every bosom — the desire after increase of human happiness; and constitutes the very spring and fountain of all human progression and improvement. It is a thing, therefore, not to be put down, or despised; but to be guided and directed towards great and noble purposes.'[6]

From this radical perspective Smiles proposed measures that would enable working men to 'extricate themselves from their degraded state'. His utilitarianism tinged with romanticism, he painted a glowing picture of the infinite capacities latent in working men. He reminded them that 'they have been created for other and for higher purposes than mere animal existence — that they, too, have been made "infinite in faculties", — not merely a mass of brute agency by which to do the bidding of the few, but "the reasonable creatures of God", who have a reason, and feeling, and sensibility, by which to derive enjoyment and happiness from all those finer inlets which are the access of nature and genius to the human soul'. He praised 'the Spirit of Enquiry which pervades the industrious classes of society and expressed his satisfaction that 'the intelligent portion of the working classes, at the present day, hate patronage of any kind'. When Smiles advocated education and self-help in 1845 as a means of improving the condition of the working classes, he was speaking as a middle-class radical who had proved his devotion to the working-class cause. He envisaged education as a means to genuine freedom and independence, and scornfully dismissed the notion that popular education would give working men 'aspirations to rise above their present position and might endanger institutions now established among us, and held to be "glorious" '. In the spirit of utilitarian optimism he reversed the reactionary arguments: 'Welcome the education which shall make men respect themselves, and aim at higher privileges and greater liberties than they now enjoy.'[7]

The most cogent formulation of this utilitarian vision of the good society is to be found in John Stuart Mill's *Principles of Political Economy*, first published in 1848. Taking a less sanguine view of the middle-class than did his father, who extolled it as an ornament to civilisation, he made a strenuous effort to apply utilitarian principles uniformly without class bias. In his chapter 'On the Probable Futurity of the Labouring Classes', John Stuart Mill defined the characteristics of the social ideal that liberalism proposed to put in place of the old regime. Genuine independence for the working classes was to be the goal of social policy: 'The poor have come out of leading-strings, and cannot any longer be governed or treated like children. To their own qualities must now be commended the care of their destiny.' He rejoiced in the disappearance of the 'ancient deference and sub-mission of the poor' and welcomed the principle of equality in class relations: 'Whatever advice, exhortation, or guidance is held out to the labouring classes, must henceforth be tendered to them as equals, and accepted by them with their eyes open.' The goal was to make them above all 'rational beings'. He was confident that the mass of the people would advance 'in mental cultivation, and in the virtues which are dependent on it'. As a result of such progress, involving not only education but also participation in working-class organisations, working men would become 'even less willing than at present to be led and governed, and directed into the way they should go, by the mere authority and prestige of superiors'. No longer would they have any 'deferential awe, or religious principle of obedience, holding them in mental subjection to a class above them'.[8] For good reason Mill's position found a great deal of support among working-class radicals of the next generation.

To be sure, the middle classes did not subscribe to the social ideal of John Stuart Mill. He was noteworthy in his readiness to accept the implications of liberal principles. Even Mill, for that matter, could not shake off his social presuppositions. He expected working men to 'feel respect for superiority of intellect and knowledge, and defer much to the opinions, on any subject of those whom they think well acquainted with it. Such deference is deeply grounded in human nature; but they will judge for themselves of the persons who are, and are not, entitled to it'.[9] Mill hoped that the middle-class would earn such respect and deference. Even more than Mill, Smiles was committed to middle-class predominance. While praising the Chartist agitation, he was afraid that it would get out of hand. He quoted with approval Channing's comment: 'It is from the free and enlightened spirit of the middle classes that help is to come to the Chartists. Nothing will soothe and tranquillise the Chartists like sympathy, like some proof that they are not abandoned by the more prosperous, and to tranquillise them is a great end.'[10] The emergence of a more benign liberalism in the early-Victorian decades was never free from middle-class presuppositions and ideological motives. But the overt intention to tranquillise working-class radicals tended to recede into the background as the middle-class drifted towards a social philosophy more congenial to the spirit of the age. This trend can be seen in the mechanics' institutes, which were more than mere instruments of utilitarian propaganda.

Henry Brougham, founder of the Society for the Diffusion of Useful Knowledge and leader of the mechanics' institute movement, was in the vanguard of the utilitarian effort to enlighten the working classes. A staunch supporter of the new poor law and the principles of political economy, he set out to show working men both the necessity and the beneficence of capitalism. Even in Brougham's narrowly middle-class version of utilitarianism, however, the positive side of the utilitarian-rationalist tradition is plainly visible. Thus, in his widely read pamphlet of 1825, addressed to the working classes in behalf of adult education, he took the high ground of idealism: 'To the working classes I would say, that this is the time when by a great effort they may secure the inestimable blessing of knowledge.' Taking for granted the 'moral and intellectual improvement of the people' as a goal on which all men of good will agreed, he acclaimed it in the grandiloquent terms that were to be so familiar a generation later: 'What higher achievement did the most sublime philosophy ever aspire after than to elevate the views and refine the character of the great mass of mankind?'[11]

Brougham combined an appeal to working-class independence and middle-class idealism. Working men ought to have the 'principal share' in the management of mechanics' institutes. 'The people themselves must be the great agents in accomplishing the work of their own instruction.' This would encourage working-class independence and strength of character. Although greater efficiency in instruction might be achieved in the short run by middle-class domination of the institutes, it was not worth the price of increased dependence of working men on their superiors. In phrases that were to be common-place in the 1850s Brougham flattered working men on their success in managing other institutions: 'If benefit societies are on the whole, well managed, we may rely upon institutions being still better conducted, where the improvement of the mind being the object, those only will ever take an active part, who are desirous of their own advancement in knowledge, and of the general instruction of the class to which they belong.' When he called on the middle classes to help working men in this great enterprise, Brougham brought his rhetoric to a higher pitch: 'A well-informed man of good sense, filled with the resolution to obtain for the great body of his fellow creatures, that high improvement which both their understandings and their morals are by nature fitted to receive . . . may in all quiet and innocence enjoy the noblest gratification of which the most aspiring nature is susceptible; he may influence by his single exertions the character and fortunes of a whole generation, and thus wield a power to be envied even by vulgar ambition for the extent of its dominion — to be cherished by virtue for the unalloyed blessings it bestows.'[12]

In the quarter century following the publication of Brougham's pamphlet, the middle classes gave considerable support to the movement for the establishment of mechanics' institutes. Quite apart from the question of the impact of the institutes on working men, there can be no doubt of their importance in stimulating the middle-class to develop a more positive version of utilitarianism along with a more benevolent social role for itself. At a time when the propertied classes as a whole were preoccupied with the inherent depravity of the poor, the institutes emphasised the intellectual potentialities of working men. Instead of censuring working men for their deficiencies, the founders of the institutes invited them to acquire useful knowledge, as in Newcastle-on-Tyne in 1824: 'One great object of this Institution is the formation of a Library to promote the intellectual and moral improvement of the various classes of the community, especially apprentices and mechanics, whose means prevent their admission into more expensive establishments.' Those who enrolled would be enriched by a number of benefits: 'Their skill will thereby be increased, their taste improved, their character exalted, and their happiness augmented.' By 1839, when a similar institution was founded in Oldham, such phrases had already achieved the status of cultural cliches. The founders wished to provide to 'various classes facilities for friendly intercourse, wholesome recreation, and the cultivation of intelligence and refinement'.[13]

The manufacturers and merchants who lent their support to the early-Victorian mechanics' institutes were hard-headed men accustomed to getting value for money. And they left no doubt that the return they expected was a working population that could understand sympathetically the middle-class point of view. But these men also perceived themselves as benevolent and idealistic progressives. The language of the annual report of the Manchester District Association of Literary and Scientific Institutions was an expression of deeply held values and aspirations: 'The truth is, the mass of intellect uncultivated is so enormous, the value and dignity of the human mind is so great, and the beauty and utility of knowledge so conspicuous and unquestioned, that no philanthropist . . . will ever dream of inconvenience or trouble if by any means he can accomplish, even in the slightest degree, the honourable object of his ambition — the mental culture and elevation of any portion of his fellow-citizens.'[14] While the men who subscribed to these high ideals were totally committed to a social structure which reduced to a minimum the possibility of realising them, that fact does not lessen the significance of their presence.

As some of these quotations make clear, utilitarianism by the 1830s had already felt the influence of romanticism and had taken on a brighter hue. Education in the mechanics' institutes was not intended merely to convey information but 'to form the character, to enlighten the mind, to soften the manners, to refine the taste, to enlarge the views, and to improve and civilise the whole man'. There are more and more references to 'the way the mind is filled with images of everything that is noble, beautiful, and good'.[15] The legacy of evangelicalism joined with romanticism in contributing to the development of a more exalted and even sentimental version of the utilitarian ideal of intellectual improvement, as, for example, in a speech, 'On Mental Elevation and Progress', delivered by the Rev. J. Aspinall to the Huddersfield Mechanics' Institute in 1848. Aspinall saw 'signs in the moral sky . . . which proclaim the social, intellectual and spiritual tendencies of the age, to be all bearing towards the time when mind shall be the acknowledged legislator of the world'. Education was co-operating with commerce for 'the same glorious end, pouring forth its enlightening, elevating, civilising waters in ten thousand rills, from ten thousand points, to converge and meet in one mighty ocean, the universal mind of man. And, above all and before all the Gospel of life, with its stronger and holier influences, is sanctioning, cementing, and riveting the same blessed work, and stamping as Christian what otherwise would only be a human hope and undertaking'. Aspinall preached the gospel of salvation through intellectual effort: 'Seek, by painstaking and hard-working efforts, to elevate yourselves, on the wings of industry, into the highest regions of literature and science.'[16] To be sure, he also assured his audience that they could expect certain practical rewards for their virtue. But the primary emphasis was in the realm of the spirit.

(2) *'To Expand the Intellect and Ennoble the Character'*

Perhaps the cruellest aspect of the social philosophy of the middle-class in the early nineteenth century was the notion that the primary cause of poverty was the moral defects of the poor themselves. Utilitarian theorists had codified evangelical moralism and the scientism of political economy into the principles of 1834. Even here, however, the idea that the way to cure poverty was to rescue the poor from their vices was to give rise to the more positive policy of 'elevating the masses', which postulated the fulfilment of the highest moral and intellectual potentialities. No longer content merely with teaching habits of thrift in order to save working men from improvidence, middle-class improvers were to envisage more grandiose objectives concerned with man's 'higher nature'. Evangelicalism and utilitarianism together helped to shape this new ideal.

The provident societies of the 1830s mediated the transition between the harshness of the Malthusian era and the softer social values of the 1850s. While repelled by the depravity of the poor, they also embarked on a policy of reformation that presupposed a more favourable view of the potentialities of the impoverished. The intellectual ingredients that were to enter into the more positive view of the obligation to elevate the masses can be seen in the writings of Thomas Chalmers, to whom the provident societies looked for inspiration. Writing in 1821 in the wake of the post-war working-class radicalism and in an ideological atmosphere impregnated by Malthusianism, Chalmers assumed the negative and defensive posture characteristic of early-nineteenth-century liberalism. At the same time, however, he blended evangelicalism and utilitarianism into a hopeful creed that foreshadowed the outlook of the mid-Victorian consensus. Writing in the spirit of high aspiration that was to be so prevalent a generation later, his aim was nothing less than to make man 'a more reflective and a less sensual being than before'. Educating the poor would 'call forth the aspirations of that higher nature which has so long been over-borne by the urgency of their animal wants, and the unchastened violence of their mere animal propensities'. He proposed to use every instrument that might be 'pressed into the service of forming to ourselves a loftier population'.[17]

Chalmers illustrates an early stage in the process that was to invest the social vision of the middle classes with the glow of moral and religious principle. Accepting the social structure without question, he sought merely to bend it to the service of moral ends: 'The social fabric would still have its orders and its gradations and its blazing pinnacles. But it would present a more elevated basis. At least the ground floor would be higher, while, in the augmented worth and respectability of the people, it would have a far deeper and surer foundation.' Chalmers' functionally conservative position was significantly different from the traditional conservatism of the squire-archy, for it was built with liberal and progressive materials. Ever aware of the importance of 'tranquillising the popular mind', he saw that this could be done, not by exacting automatic deference and docility, but in the liberal mode. Thus, he argued that 'reason will make anything palatable to the lower orders; and, if only permitted to lift her voice in some cool place, as in the class-room of a school of arts, she will attain as firm authority over the popular mind, as she wields now within the walls of parliament'. Chalmers' ideology presupposed a very favourable view of working-class rationality. 'To make the multitude rational,' he wrote, 'we have only to treat them as if they were fit subjects for being discoursed with rationally.'[18] Eventually the middle classes were to take up this velvet-glove policy.

While the provident societies did not abandon the spirit of 1834 (see chapter 2(2)), they also came to put more emphasis on the desirability of raising the poor to a higher level. Their 'great principle', announced the officers of the Manchester and Salford Provident Society, was 'the desire to elevate the character and condition of the working population by which we are surrounded'. While this principle was usually invoked in a spirit of class superiority and condescension, it represented a shift away from primary reliance on repression, coercion, and indoctrination. Similarly, the practice of visiting the poor, so prominent in the programme of the societies, while renewing old patterns of deference and subordination, also opened the door to a more benevolent middle-class role than the one inherent in the principle of the workhouse test. The Liverpool society, which provided a model that was imitated in other towns in the 1830s, urged the rich to enter into 'more frequent communication with the poor; not simply thro' the mercenary relations of giving or receiving alms, which leave dormant or keep down the best points of the human character, but by an interchange of those kind feelings which must spring from a system of judicious benevolence on one side, and justifiable confidence on the other'. The ideal of judicious benevolence and the desire for something more than merely mercenary relations between the classes were to be recurring themes in the gradual transition from 1834 to 1851.[19]

The early-Victorian bourgeoisie was never completely comfortable with the cash nexus. Class contact arising from 'the mere relations of business' fell short of the truly harmonious relations between the classes that they hoped for. The elaborate programme of visitations established by the provident societies was intended to produce 'mutual good-will' and 'reciprocal improvement': 'It is in the obscure walks of such visitations that sympathies are formed, which beget the union and prejudices are counteracted which tend to the *dis*-union of the different classes: the rich become acquainted with the real wants, and real good qualities of the poor; the poor learn to appreciate the good feelings of those, whom they are too frequently taught to regard as their oppressors instead of their benefactors, their enemies instead of their friends.'[20] While the middle classes never permitted such sentiments to interfere with the exercise of their social and economic power, the desire for mutual goodwill between the classes was genuine, and it contributed to the development of a more genial liberal creed, aspiring to cordiality.

In Nottingham one of the founders of the local provident society was William Felkin, a merchant and manufacturer who later became mayor.[21] He supported the new poor law and served on the first board of guardians until 1839. Even in the 1830s, however, he was developing a more positive social philosophy that moved beyond the limits imposed by the principles of 1834. Without reducing the prerogatives of the middle classes, Felkin found room for the aspirations of the working classes. He enables us to trace the process that converted unpromising ideological material into the stuff of mid-Victorian consensus.

Starting from a position very similar to Andrew Ure's, Felkin soon moved in a different direction. Both men viewed the world from a distinctly middle-class perspective; both were enthusiastic supporters of the provident societies; both accepted the truths of evangelical Christianity and political economy. Whereas Ure developed a narrow class version of the liberal and Christian creed, however, Felkin took a broader view of the principles that he had inherited. Instead of perceiving the working classes as an enemy force, threatening civilised society, Felkin saw them as individuals open to unlimited moral and intellectual improvement. Putting all his emphasis on potentialities to be developed, he invited working men to join in the ongoing enterprise of individual advancement. In a pamphlet on the Great Exhibition, Felkin expressed his social philosophy in the buoyant mood of 1851. Abandoning the remnants of Malthusian pessimism, he sounded a note of mid-Victorian affirmation: 'Barren and cheerless speculations will be replaced by energetic and healthy action.'[22] Although his faith in political economy was undimmed, he propounded a more benevolent version, which he contrasted with the 'calculating and heartless political economy' of the earlier part of the century. He saw 'a brighter page . . . now opening before us', and it was in this confident frame of mind that he approached the working classes. Unlike Ure, he saw no need to set out to create a docile work force; he was sure that working men would not only come to understand sympathetically the needs of their employers and the economy, but also embrace the ideal of unending improvement. Felkin in 1851 had left the spirit of 1834 far behind.

By what road did Felkin arrive at the ideology which was so characteristic of the mid-Victorian middle classes? What forces shaped his development? A discussion of those questions may cast some light on the broader problem: how did the Victorian bourgeoisie move from the principles of 1834 to the consensus that was already close to realisation by 1851? How did they create a sense of community and common purpose while committed to a creed that exalted individual acquisition and profit?

William Felkin was born in 1795 in an industrial village west of Nottingham.[23] His father and his grandfather were framework knitters. At the age of twelve he was apprenticed to a baker. A year later he moved to his grandfather's and began an apprenticeship as a framework knitter. In 1809 he was apprenticed to a Nottingham merchant. Upon completing his apprenticeship he spent six years in London in the commercial end of the hosiery business. In 1822 he began to work for John Heathcoat, a Nottingham manufacturer who had invented a bobbin-net lace machine. In 1826 he became Heathcoat's agent in Nottingham. While continuing in that capacity, Felkin in 1832 formed a business of his own in partnership with a Nottingham lace manufacturer. He was a commission agent, selling unfinished brown net to small manufacturers for processing. Soon his firm began the manufacture of lace, with Felkin concentrating on the sales end of the business. In 1848 the partnership was dissolved and Felkin formed a lace manufacturing business of his own. In 1864 he went out of business as a result of financial difficulties; his friends raised enough money to save him from bankruptcy. Throughout his life Felkin was active in local affairs. He was an organiser of the relief committees which sought to mitigate the effects of cyclical unemployment in the 1830s. He took a leading part in the work of the Nottingham Provident Society, which had been formed on the Liverpool model. He was the superintendent of a Baptist Sunday school, served for a short time on the committee of the Lancastrian school, and helped found a mechanics' institute. Thus, he devoted abundant time and energy to the cause of elevating the condition of the working classes.

Felkin came from a deeply evangelical background. His father, one of the first converts to the evangelical Baptists in Ilkerton, became a lay preacher while working as a framework knitter. In 1797 his congregation sent him to London to study at the Baptist Academy operated by the founder of the sect. Two years later he was ordained and returned to the congregation. William Felkin, born five years after his father's conversion, was reared in an atmosphere of evangelical piety. In his autobiographical recollections of his mother, Felkin recalled 'her looks of love and caressing endearments, when preparing for bed, I knelt before her to repeat my evening hymn and prayer'. After he left home to follow his apprenticeship Felkin received 'lively and instructive' letters from his father, calling on him to 'make the salvation of the soul the chief concern, with the whole heart sincerely, earnestly and with perseverance. This *must* be crowned with success. See your own sins. See God and Christ co-operating for your salvation'. This was standard evangelical doctrine: it was the state of the individual soul that mattered, and it must be cultivated. The culmination of the process of personal sanctification would be Felkin's becoming 'a new creature'.

From his father and from the evangelical employer to whom he was apprenticed, young Felkin absorbed that deep regard for learning so characteristic of the early nineteenth century. His father's letters made it plain that study was to be pursued as an activity of the highest value in itself, although its practical value was also noted: 'Instead of reading with others in a desultory way, study Latin with Mr McLeod. That would lay the foundation for future progress in learning and usefulness and respectability. Do not aim at too much at once; that issues in superficiality in all and distracts our present thoughts.' When Felkin received this letter he was in his fourth year as an apprentice in a business managed by Nathan Hurst, whose precept and example reinforced parental exhortation. In his autobiography Felkin recalled that in Hurst was 'one of the closest thinkers and best read men in the place'. As Hurst checked the work of the apprentices, he would pause and 'ask what works we were reading, what we thought of them, and to throw out ideas often of value in drawing attention to important or difficult points'. Felkin wrote several short papers that were read and discussed at weekly meetings with some of his fellow apprentices 'in a school room supplied with dim tallow candles, barely sufficient to make the manuscript legible'. In his autobiography he described the process of self-education in the warehouse: 'But to sit down and put thoughts and reasonings on paper and then examine their accuracy, diction and effect was, after the long hours and fatiguing business of the day, a very great effort, especially being in opposition to a very naturally intense desire for outdoor recreation. However it became by practice somewhat less difficult.'

Along with these religious and intellectual values, the young Felkin also imbibed the principles of political economy. Throughout his life he maintained a profound faith in the beneficence of untrammelled economic activity. 'Commercial intercourse has, in every age and clime, given the first impulse to improvement of the physical, and mental, and the moral condition of our race. – It is the handmaid of Christianity.'[24] There could be no doubting the basic validity of the 'philosophy of production' expounded by Adam Smith and his successors.

Felkin's advice to the working classes in the 1830s reflected the bleak principles of political economy and the moralistic outlook of the provident societies. To working men he offered the conventional exhortation: be diligent and thrifty and you will find your reward. In 1837, in a pamphlet reporting the results of an elaborate inquiry into the economic situation of the working classes, he concluded that the statistics showed that unless working men were induced to practise prudent economy and foresight 'their fire-sides will be altogether deserted, and their domestic habits and comforts destroyed'.[25] The remedy for poverty and unemployment was not to be found in legislative action but in the character of the individual workman. Felkin insisted that the working man, like the merchant, must practise thrift as the first step towards independence.

Even in the 1837 pamphlet, however, Felkin took a positive view of the potentialities of the working classes. While exhorting working men to buckle down and be thrifty or else suffer the consequences, he also presented a glowing vision of higher goals than the mere avoidance of poverty. He pointed out that 'many from amongst the labouring classes have exhibited vast mental and imaginative power, and have attained to high moral elevation'. He invited working men to develop habits of prudence and forethought not merely for the sake of economic benefits, but because the resulting lack of worldly cares 'would facilitate the exertions of the mind'. He wrote lyrically of 'mental occupations' that would 'expand the intellect and ennoble the character of those engaged in them'. While moving away from the early-nineteenth-century view of the labouring poor, however, Felkin did not preach the gospel of success. On the basis of his own knowledge and experience, he candidly pointed out that few working men were in fact going to change their status. Hence he did not hold forth the hope of social mobility but invited them to become 'an ornament to their station'.[26]

By 1851 Felkin's belief in the elevation of the working classes had been set in the context of an all-embracing and optimistic mid-Victorian liberalism. Like Cobden and Tennyson, he saw the world moving onward and upward in an endless ascent. In international relations, peace and universal progress would flow from expanding commerce between the nations: 'To trade together is the first step. It is to civilise the barbarous, and to soften the rude; to restrain the lawless, and to bless the industrious.' In domestic affairs, working-class improvement was part of this liberalising and progressive process. Felkin saw the Great Exhibition itself as 'a fine opportunity for "levering up" the average level of the mind and taste of our mechanics and of the people at large'. Since large numbers of working men had already achieved a high moral and intellectual level, Felkin envisaged a missionary role for them in relation to their less fortunate fellows. He suggested that 'the working people should select their own choice men' to attend the exhibition and report back. 'Give these picked representatives of their class plenty of time and space for their examination; press them to make it minute, as well as general; above all, to repeat it after intervals in which they may see and inoculate their fellow workmen, with the views of the marvels they may have investigated.'[27] The mid-Victorian liberals were to envisage a similar role for the working-class élite.

Felkin readily conceded that the working classes had cause for complaint and that existing society fell short of the standards that he had in mind. He was not at all comfortable with the reality of class conflict. In his 1837 pamphlet he was sensitive to the charge of 'supposed partiality in favour of the opulent and employing classes, and prejudice against the labourers in manufacture'. He went out of his way to refute the charge by noting his own working-class origins and by demonstrating his readiness to recognise the shortcomings of the middle classes. He went so far as to suggest that if the habits of the propertied classes were investigated in the manner of his own investigation of the working classes, it would probably be found that they had been setting a bad example for the labourer, who had merely copied the vices of the classes above him. In 1851 he chided employers for their snobbish attitudes: 'Let not the men of wealth, energy, and foresight appear to condemn their strong-handed, honest-hearted brethren, who apply their power and skill to the productions before us.' He accepted the working men's complaint of 'the excessively broad line of demarcation drawn between them and their employers', and even put much of the blame for this state of affairs on the employers: 'The adviser, protector, and friend, have too frequently been displaced by the severe, and harsh, and haughty master.' Inevitably, therefore, the 'commanding attitude of the employer had been met by untractable indifference and reckless-ness on the part of the man'. Felkin denounced 'the voice of harsh authority, addressing itself as if to slaves rather than free men'.[28]

Here also Felkin was articulating salient themes of mid-Victorian liberalism. Even-handedness required a recognition of shortcomings on both sides. As the old obsession with working-class depravity faded away, however, new ideological forms emerged. Having recognised the objective existence of class conflict without attempting to blame the working classes for it, Felkin suggested that if only masters and men would behave properly discord would vanish. Thus he reaffirmed the classic liberal belief in harmony of interests in moralistic and high-minded form. If employers would help their men to be thrifty, the latter would respond gratefully: 'Happily, employers, as well as others, are awakening to a sense of the important duty owing to their work-people; and it may be hoped that by a union of justice in regard to the amount of wages, kindness by assisting to effect the best appropriation of them, and faithfulness in pointing out the folly and wickedness of idleness and extravagance, the former will regain the confidence and regard of those of the workpeople who may have been estranged from them, and the latter made grateful for so important an obligation.' Both classes must make an effort to overcome the unfortunate attitudes into which they had lapsed. The harsh words of employers and employees should be 'hushed in expressions of confidence and mutual respect'. No class should act 'selfishly or immorally'; each should remember that 'privilege and duty are correlative'.[29]

Felkin's irenic liberalism presupposed the existing class structure.

He expected working men to know their place and act accordingly. The prudent working man 'learns to understand clearly and appreciate carefully his own position in society; he knows and feels that independent labour is honourable as it is useful'. He was critical of working men who showed an unbecoming zeal for 'the cause of political and social regeneration'.[30] But he was confident that they would soon see the virtue of individual improvement. Hence he celebrated the opportunities for improvement and advancement, not as a means of tranquillising the working classes, but to awaken them to the possibility of progress without end. Many working men also envisaged a society of that sort. While the class structure was in fact incompatible with such an achievement, nevertheless the shared vision was to create a sense of community among classes divided by conflicting interests.

(3) *Social Reformers and the Religion of Improvement*

Felkin approached early-Victorian society from the point of view of an active businessman who was at ease with the system of which he was a part, and who sought to remedy some of its shortcomings. As such he was representative of a substantial and important segment of the middle classes. To his left — to use that term somewhat loosely in this connection — was a group of reformers who were numerically not nearly so representative of the middle-class as a whole, but who nevertheless played quite an important part in the development of the ideological forms of mid-Victorian urban culture. These social reformers — publicists, editors, writers, lecturers, and leaders of good causes — operated on the fringes of the middle-class. Not involved in running, or profiting from, the commercial and industrial system, they were not inclined to take for granted its inherent virtue. On the contrary, their somewhat undefined social situation predisposed them to think and act in terms of principle, at a time when principled behaviour was highly esteemed. Hence these reformers — and the word reform carried a credal lustre for them — devoted themselves earnestly to a discussion of the shortcomings of Victorian society and the ways in which it might be improved. They conducted a continual criticism of its weaknesses and demonstrated genuine sympathy with the plight of the working classes. From this perspective they preached the new secular religion of improvement. They reshaped traditional Christian and utilitarian beliefs into a creed that reflected the warmer currents of romanticism.

These social reformers supported all the good causes of their day. Some of them, like Mary and William Howitt, embraced a whole gamut of forward movements with equal fervour. Their address to friends and readers in 1847 is a vivid precipitate of the variegated social and political ideals of the middle-class improvers and progressives:

To all the onward and sound movements of the time — a great
and glorious time! — to the cause of Peace, of Temperance, of
Sanitary reform, of Schools for every class — to all the efforts
of Free Trade, free opinion; to abolition of obstructive Monopolies,
and the recognition of those great rights which belong to every
individual of the great British people — our most cordial support
shall be lent.

Everything which can shorten the hours of mere physical
labour, and extend those of relaxation, mental cultivation, and
social, domestic enjoyment . . . must have our best and most unremitting exertions for its establishment.

We shall say to the people, inform your minds on your rights;
combine to maintain them; be industrious and get money; be
temperate and save it; be prudent and invest it to the best
advantage; but learn at the same time to respect the rights of your
fellow-men.[31]

Some of the reformers concentrated their attention on one or more
good causes, such as temperance or mechanics' institutes. But all of
them shared a belief in the mystique of reform, a concern for the well-
being of the working classes, and a faith in moral and intellectual
improvement through education. In periodicals such as the *People's
Journal, Howitt's Journal, Eliza Cook's Journal,* and the *Truth Seeker*
they approached the social and political world of their day with the zeal
of devoted votaries of reform and improvement.[32]

The social reformers articulated a progressive creed which, in muted
and often insipid form, was to become the mid-Victorian consensus.
Mediating the transition to mid-Victorianism, these progressives and
radicals expressed their ideals in the more emotional and even
sentimental mode imparted by romanticism. The commonplaces of
utilitarianism were clothed in language remote from the bureaucratic
and calculating spirit of Benthamism. The virtues of reason were now
preached in a mystical spirit, stressing the grand and glorious unfolding
of the individual soul. The appetite for nobility of sentiment was
insatiable, and easily degenerated into sentimentality. The reformers —
like so many of the Chartists — gave free rein to the romantic inclination
to exalt the heart and the feelings. An indication of the strength of these
new currents was the enthusiastic response of English reformers to
Transcendentalism, which had developed in America from the ideas of
German romantic idealism. William Ellery Channing and his conception
of self-culture as the highest activity of the human soul played a part
in deepening the ethic of improvement in England. Channing conceived the human soul as an embodiment of the divine, whose highest
purpose was moral and intellectual development. The idea of self-help,

which originated in the constricting atmosphere of neo-Malthusianism, took on a more exalted look when propounded by Emerson in *Man the Reformer*. Self-help lost its narrow bourgeois cast and acquired a more universal lustre, connoting the achievement of genuine independence and freedom. Such Transcendentalist ideas were taken up with such alacrity because they corresponded to intellectual and spiritual currents already at work in England.[33]

W.J. Fox, who was active among the social reformers of the 1840s, illustrates the impact of romantic and Transcendentalist ideas on someone committed to the rationalism of Priestley and Bentham. As editor of the *Monthly Repository* Fox had emerged by 1830 as one of the leaders of Unitarianism, a sect firmly rooted in Enlightenment rationalism. Fox found that heritage inadequate, however, and consciously sought to go beyond it by incorporating ideas and beliefs from the rather different tradition of Unitarianism represented by William Ellery Channing. What appealed to Fox in Channing was his sense of 'the grand and the beautiful'. He emphasised the need for an extension of the 'dominion of pure religion from the head to the heart'. Fox hoped that the poets would heed Channing's injunction to explore 'the mystery within ourselves, the mystery of our spiritual, accountable, immortal nature'.[34] This romantic sensibility is all the more noteworthy since Fox continued to take Benthamite principles as his guide to social and economic life. But Fox had been put off not only by the narrowness of Priestleyan rationalism from a religious point of view, but also by the lack of reforming zeal in the traditional Unitarianism based on it. He welcomed the more emotional creed of Channing, because it offered the prospect of application to the secular world, where its aim would be the elevation of the human character and the improvement of the social order. The development of the individual soul was linked to the reform of society as a whole.

Samuel Smiles' conception of self-help in the 1840s also owed a great deal to the Transcendentalists, Channing and Emerson. Smiles' intellectual base was a democratic version of Benthamite radicalism. That body of ideas included the notion of working-class self-help of the sort propagated by the Society for the Diffusion of Useful Knowledge and expounded in G.L. Craik's *Pursuit of Knowledge under Difficulties*, which Smiles had read before coming to Leeds. The book consisted of a series of biographies of men who had educated themselves and then achieved success — a literary formula that Smiles himself was to use with great effectiveness in later years. In the early 1840s, however, Smiles was much too radical to accept Craik's aridly propagandist version of working-class self-help and independence. It was the Emerson-Channing version of self-help that appealed to him. Like Smiles, they were reformers and critics of early-nineteenth-century industrial society; hence their ideas were free from the note of apologetics so prominent in Craik and the SDUK. Equally important, Emerson presented the idea of self-help in the framework of his vision of the development of the human soul. It was in this spirit that Emerson in *Man the Reformer* asked the question, 'Can we not learn the lessons of self-help?' In his review of the book Smiles agreed that there was indeed a lesson to be learned, and praised Emerson for teaching 'the nobility of manhood, the dignity of labour, the honourableness of industry, economy, and the domestic virtues'. Thus Smiles clothed the idea of self-help with higher aspirations, so that it was something more than merely an exhortation to work hard and avoid poverty. Smiles envisaged it as part of a much grander process: 'The progress of man towards sobriety, temperance, self-control and self-emancipation.'[35]

George Searle Phillips was secretary of the Huddersfield Mechanics' Institution from 1846 to 1854; as editor of the *Truth Seeker* in the late 1840s, he was in close touch with other advanced reformers, including Owenites. He embraced the ideas of Transcendentalism more fully and profoundly than Smiles. When Emerson lectured at the Huddersfield Mechanics' Institution in 1847, he stayed at Phillips' house. In Phillips we find the romantic-progressive-utopian mentality of the 1840s at its most extravagent and engaging. It is exemplified in his description of his pupils:

> I love each honest face, tho' scarred with fire,
> And trenched with indigo and sooty stains;
> For through their darkened lineaments I see
> The Maker's Image, gleaming like the light
> Of sunshine 'mid the ruins of the storm,
> And know that heaven doth compass them.

Phillips wanted education to 'reach down into the depths of the moral nature of man'. In the purest Transcendentalist spirit he saw the divine life within men, and urged that this be cultivated: 'They have a Kingdom of heaven within them.' He envisaged 'improvement' of a profound and mystical sort. It was in this sense that he described self-improvement as 'the main business of life'. Even Leeds he saw as 'an effusion of the Eternal mind'. Walking its streets he heard 'the songs of happy children and the shouts of a regenerated world'. Phillips was unique, even among the social reformers. Yet he remains of interest to the historian, precisely because he embodied in such extreme form the intellectual and spiritual currents characteristic of his age.[36]

The *People's Journal* illustrates the posture of many of the social reformers of the 1840s: a combination of sentimental idealism with sharp critical comment on the social and political order. Having established its disinterested concern for the welfare of the working classes and its readiness to reprove the powerful, the journal confidently preached the virtues and principles that lay at the core of the culture as a whole. An article by J. Goodwin on 'Mutual Dependence and Responsibility' is a case in point. On the one hand, the author's critique of early-Victorian society was thoroughgoing enough to satisfy an Owenite socialist, if not Marx himself. His denunciation of the principle of 'independence' — by which he meant laissez-faire individualism — and his plea for a society characterised by 'mutual dependence' was unequivocal: 'The principle called independence has been misapplied and turned into the direst curse. It has been used as a covering for those twin demons *pride and selfishness*, which have prevented the improvement and blasted the happiness of mankind in all ages; it has given rise to class-politics, class-commerce, and class-religion, it has split up the community into fragments, dividing the true interests and sympathies of man from man by gulfs all but impassable.' He condemned the worship of money in the intensely acquisitive society of his day: 'Who does not know that money is become synonymous with power, dignity, independence, and even worth? . . . A man without "brass" is no man at all.' In a characteristic anti-climax, however, Goodwin's philippic led up to a call for 'a mutual effort on the part of the various classes to promote the general interest and happiness of the community as a whole'. He announced that employers 'are bound by the eternal law of moral justice to make due provision, or such as their means will allow, for the general welfare and advancement of those in their service'. He appealed to the idealism of employers as the solution to the evils that he had denounced: 'You have a right to exercise authority over those you employ; but you have not a right to regard them as beasts of burden, created only to serve your interest and pleasure. You may regard them as your inferiors — for they are so conventionally and circumstantially, not intrinsically; but you must regard them as *men*.' He asked employers not merely to observe the law in their relation with their employees but to follow the dictates of 'conscience, reason and religion'. Such high-mindedness would be amply rewarded: 'Then will you make your dependents thankful, prosperous, and happy They will look up to you with humble deference.'[37]

The *People's Journal* illustrates the process that transmuted early-Victorian utopianism into mid-Victorianism. In a mode soon to be dominant, it is unrelenting in the sentimental exaltation of culturally esteemed virtues. A story, 'Rose Linwood, or the Spirit of Charity', strikes a familiar note, when, at the conclusion, the husband, 'his face glowing with delight at the noble conduct of his bride', says: 'I am prouder of her virtues than I am of her beauty. And the blessing of those whom she has forgiven and protected will, I trust, cling to us through after life, to add to the sunshine of our happiness and lighten the burthen of our cares.' The moral pointed by another piece of fiction reflects the Victorian preference for what a later age was to call positive thinking: 'Beware, how you indulge hard thoughts and unkind feelings.' Soft thoughts and kind feelings were to be actively cultivated. An essay by the temperance reformer, Passmore Edwards, discusses 'The Advantages of Knowledge' in this spirit. The acquisition of knowledge is depicted as a religious obligation, part of the ennobling process of self-cult·ire and self-development. The man of knowledge 'fulfills the behests of nature, and passes forward on the eventful stream of life, with a determination to perform his duty, in obedience to a high conception and appreciation of his destiny'. In the course of his article on knowledge, Edwards presents a model of the ideal man for emulation. The catalogue of virtues is overwhelming: 'While firm in his holdfast of the truth, and unflinching in its defence . . . he would extend his benevolence to all men.' He would be 'disinterested in his generousness, because selfishness was contrary to the ennobling purposes of the universe'. Like other social reformers, Edwards was inviting his readers to scale the moral heights.[38]

An article by Clara Walby on 'Works of Fiction' reaches great heights of earnestness and utopianism. Sternly dismissing books written merely for entertainment and not designed specifically to contribute to 'the great work of moral regeneration', the author refuses to recognise any middle ground: 'Whatever does not propel us forward on the hallowed track of improvement must — imperceptibly perhaps, but not less certainly, — compel us to retrograde.' She then proceeds to her main theme: the need to apply high ideals to 'the obvious, tangible duties of life, the realities that surround us on every side'. Time should be spent 'in gathering spiritual treasures to be stored in Eternity, whose track is the track of true IMPROVEMENT, and whose voices instruct in the unmistakable language of immortal TRUTH!'[39]

Clara Walby's article is of interest, not because of the number of persons who may be assumed to have taken it literally, but because it could have been produced only in this culture. Without by any means being typical in a statistical sense or even in a typological sense, it gives us an insight into the *Zeitgeist*. In other words, even those who would have found this effusion a bit much were nevertheless under the influence of a culture in which such an effusion was possible. For the author of the article works with common assumptions, and if she highlights them to the point of caricature, the historian can easily strip away the excess and get at what lies beneath. And what lies beneath was widely shared in that broad spectrum of improving-progressive opinion among both the middle and working classes.

While *Eliza Cook's Journal* was not devoted specifically to reform causes, it preached the gospel of improvement from the standpoint of an ostentatious devotion to the working classes and a readiness to judge the rich even more severely than the poor. Eliza Cook saw the working classes in the warmest terms, not as threats to social order, but as potential converts to the true, the good, and the beautiful. In 'A Word to My Readers' in the first issue she stated her purpose: 'I am only anxious to give my feeble aid to the gigantic struggle for intellectual elevation now going on, and fling my energies and will into a cause where my heart will zealously animate my duty.' The emotional and sentimental tone marked her off from her predecessors in the battle against ignorance. She preached utilitarian values in the idiom of a romantic sensibility: 'It is too true that there are dense clouds of Ignorance yet to be dissipated — huge mountains of Error yet to be removed; but, there is a stirring development of progressive mind in "the mass" which only requires steady and free communion with Truth to expand itself into the enlightened and practical wisdom on which ever rests the perfection of social and political civilisation.'[40]

Eliza Cook and others of the same outlook made a strenuous effort to apply their principles equally, without class bias. She was acutely aware of the corruption and hypocrisy associated with 'this inhuman and and unchristian spirit of class and caste'. She denounced the 'false respectable' — that is, the prevailing socially determined notions of respectability — and hoped for the day 'when industry and usefulness shall be pronounced as truly honourable, and intelligence and moral worth be stamped as the only true respectability'. She had no illusions about the prevailing scale of values at any social level: 'To be rich, or to have the appearance of it, is esteemed as a merit of a higher order, whereas, to be poor, or to seem so ranks as something like an unpardonable offence.' She traced the false notion of respectability to 'the overweening estimate which we form in this country, of two things well enough in their place — rank and wealth'. This is remote in spirit from Andrew Ure, eager to persuade the working classes to ape their betters. It is also remote from the success myths put out by some propagandists of the mechanics' institutes. Eliza Cook treated the inclination to rise in the world as a vice, the source of 'the false and demoralising habit' of respectability: 'We all of us feel as if we belonged to some rank or caste, out of which we are always struggling to rise into some other above it. You find this spirit of caste as keenly at work among the humblest as among the highest ranks.' She denounced the whole 'desperate scramble'.[41]

The ultimate remedy for society's ills envisaged in her *Journal* was similar to that of many, if not most, Victorian reformers: if only both sides to every dispute would be rational, if only employers and employees would do their duty and observe sound principles, then progress and harmony would ensue. There was no hint of an aspiration to radical social and political change of the sort that had seized the Chartist imagination. 'Shall we say, then, with the anarchist and the leveller, that the well-being of the poor is incompatible with the existence of the rich? Not so; but it is incompatible with their neglect of duty.' To be sure, the propertied classes get their knuckles rapped regularly: 'How sinful it is for the employer to grudge the labourer his due reward.' There has been 'injustice and avarice on the part of individuals among the higher classes'. Unfortunately, 'ambition has taken the place of benevolence, and mutual rivalry has put an end to mutual co-operation'. But this criticism of the propertied classes, despite its affinities in tone and in idiom with some Owenite thought, leads only to an extremely favourable view of the existing society and its potentiality for improvement. Radical language has been turned around and used to buttress the social order: 'Our argument is simply this — the antagonism of classes is a delusion. Rich and poor are mutually dependent, and mutually entitled to respect. Their true equality consists not in similarity of position, but in equality of social rights as fellow-men and brethren.' Populist sentiment and noble aspirations are invoked to justify extreme inequality in fact: 'We would not abase the rich to the poverty of the poor, but we would exalt the poor to the *honourable* position of the rich.'[42] There was to be a great deal more of this in the ideology of the mid-Victorian middle-class.

Temperance was one of the causes that attracted middle-class social reformers of the 1840s. For Thomas Beggs it was for a time the focal point of his commitment to social reform. Born in Edinburgh in 1808, he later moved to Leeds, where he was apprenticed to a bookbinder. There he took the total abstinence pledge in 1838. Active on the left wing of middle-class radicalism, Beggs advocated manhood suffrage at a time when the vast majority of the propertied classes viewed Chartism with consternation and alarm. In 1842 he became secretary of the Nottingham branch of the Complete Suffrage Union and lectured for the C.S.U. in a number of towns. His lectures on 'The Moral Elevation of the People' were published in the *National Temperance Magazine* in 1845 and 1846. In 1846 he became secretary of the National Temperance League. A year and a half later he took a position in the Health of Towns Association.[43]

Like many of the social reformers of the 1840s, Beggs decried the evils of competitive capitalism and was appalled by the consequences of the unrestrained quest for profits: 'Facility and cheapness of production are the considerations taking precedence of every other. The highest interests of humanity must yield before this fierce and unregulated competition for gain, leaving its traces behind it, in the vice, misery, and destitution of the large bulk of the people.'[44] Beggs also denounced the moral and intellectual consequences of the competitive economy: 'The moralist is confined to his study, whilst the political economist is enthroned; he talks for ever about capital and labour, new markets and advanced improvements – his constant theme is profit – as if man had no higher purpose to serve than to become a mere money-making machine, and pay never-ceasing homage to the idol that rusts his very heart.' Among the 'influences for evil peculiar to our own times', he singled out 'the defects inseparable from our competitive system'. Noting that working men 'are offered up as victims to the monster god of avarice and selfishness', Beggs denounced 'the immolation of our youth to the factory system'. He was equally firm in his rejection of traditional ideology, especially 'the belief that Providence has placed us in our different spheres, and that the mass of the people are suffering in obedience to His arrangement'. He had no sympathy for the idea that 'the bulk of society [are] intended to be slaves to toil, from which there is no hope of escape – made to create wealth, pay taxes, and eat the smallest possible share of that which they produce – go to church and adopt the opinions of their taskmasters'. Beggs took a more egalitarian position, and invoked both science and Christianity in support of it.

Having delivered a devastating critique of the social and economic system, Beggs proceeded to suggest remedies – education in general and temperance in particular – which offered no immediate prospect of removing the fundamental defects that he had described. He indulged in the long-range aspiration that the social reformers found so appealing: 'By shewing the real nature and true causes of the evils which press upon society, it [temperance] points to a remedy. It teaches the value of self-reform, as an indispensable preliminary to those great social changes which we hope to see, but which we must not expect, but as the result of the increased morality and intelligence of the people.' Education is the answer, and 'the temperance cause is an educational movement'. Education will elevate the working classes and influence public opinion as a whole, so that eventually better policies will be adopted. He even included the factory problem in this formula, and argued that a ten-hours bill was not the answer to the 'immolation of our youth'. His own proposal in this area was feeble in the extreme: 'A remedy would be easy if society felt its importance – for the people would refrain from patronising those shops where late hours are kept.' He went so far as to suggest that it would be a mistake to shorten hours until the proper 'rational amusement' had been arranged. Thus, beginning with a critique of capitalist materialism and acquisitiveness, Beggs ended up dealing with the social problem – in what was to become typical Victorian fashion – by trying to spiritualise, elevate, and refine the working classes.

(4) *Joseph Cowen, Jr. and 'Onward Movements for Intelligence and Virtue'*

Joseph Cowen, Jr. by the late 1850s was a commanding figure in the public life of the Newcastle-on-Tyne area. The son of a self-made manufacturer and newspaper proprietor, he staked out a position on the far left of middle-class radicalism and won a great deal of working-class support for his Northern Political Union. In his youth he was an avid reader of the *People's Journal* and an admirer of William Howitt and W.J. Linton. In 1854 he founded the *Northern Tribune* and included on his contributors' list such men as F.R. Lees, Thomas Cooper, and G.S. Phillips. He was in contact with such working-class radicals as G.J. Harney and G.J. Holyoake. When the *Tribune* ceased publication it was taken over by Holyoake's *The Reasoner*. Thus, a number of strands come together in Cowen, who was in the vanguard of what he called 'the onward movements for intelligence and virtue'.[45] His radicalism rested on an egalitarian affirmation of the consensus ideals of the early-Victorian cities. If we wish to understand the transition from 1834 to 1851, we have to pay some attention to Cowen.

It must be said plainly at the outset that Cowen was in no sense a typical representative of the provincial middle classes. In fact, he was if anything somewhat aberrant. Certainly only a tiny minority of his class subscribed to his views. What, then, is Cowen's significance for the social historian, who is interested in widespread patterns rather than idiosyncratic behaviour? For one thing, Cowen's fundamental values and beliefs came from the common stock of assumptions available to the early-Victorian middle classes. He simply seized on certain of their ideals more vehemently and intensely, and tried to apply them without the inhibitions of class. Cowen shows us one extreme of the arc of cultural possibility open to the Victorian middle classes. In Cowen we see the brightest and most vivid hues of the value system. If we limit ourselves to individuals who embody the values of culture in the average form, we may fail to realise the strength of the religious and intellectual forces at work. The ideas and values which we see so starkly in Cowen were also in operation, albeit not in such concentrated form, among the middle classes as a whole. They contributed to the genesis of a new culture, endowed with a sense of community and common purpose remote from the spirit of 1834.

We have quite a full picture of Cowen's intellectual orientation at the age of sixteen from a journal that he kept while a student at the University of Edinburgh. Although he was later to adopt a secularist position he was very much an evangelical Christian in his youth. 'The writer of the following pages *professes* to be a *Christian* . . . Christ is his hope – his Redeemer from sin – his triumph in joy – his glory in affliction.' Along with Christianity, however, Cowen had also embraced the democratic religion of humanity, the creed of Howitt and Beggs, Michelet and Mazzini. In between a number of excerpts from Hebrews, he included some ringing words from Michelet: 'Freedom! Glorious word! comprising indeed all human dignity. There is no virtue without Liberty.' His 'Ultra Radicalism', as he called his political position, was infused with the spirit and even the idiom of his Christianity, and he noted that his principles were 'founded on Scripture and common sense'. If one followed the dictates of 'common sense and humanity', one was obliged to be a radical. At the outset his radicalism was inseparable – and indeed indistinguishable – from his Christianity. Among the 'causes' enjoined by God and scripture were voluntarism (opposition to the established church), radicalism (including universal suffrage), Garrisonian abolitionism, teetotalism, and pacifism. He stressed their interconnectedness: 'To advance the cause of sobriety or in other words to advance the cause of religion, humanity, freedom, and happiness together – this I do in being teetotaller . . . '[46] His account of 'my Christianity' included all the familiar principles of the social reformers of the 1840s.

On leaving the university Cowen turned his youthful idealism to the cause of popular education and in 1849 helped found the Winlaton Literary and Mechanics' Institution. The first annual report of the new organisation was splendidly grandiloquent even by the standards of the day: 'Our object if we know it is a noble one – our mission if we are not mistaken is a holy one. Humanity demands such an enterprise. Life requires such an oblation. Conscience anathametises the craven. Truth and right claim our championship and ensure our success. With ignorance and immorality of whatever cast or grade and wherever found we wage a war of extermination.' The same themes echo, albeit in muted form, in other Victorian documents. Here, in the excitement of a youth of eighteen, there are no limits: 'What we have effected heralds mightier conquests. Mind will be emancipated. The true soul loathes all shackles. Mental might and moral majesty are marching to sovereignty. The day dawns with nobler triumphs for *man* than ever greeted the Imperial Caesar in the Roman Capitol returning from his million murders.' By any objective and realistic standard, the language was out of proportion to the limited activities of the organisation. But the historian cannot limit himself to a judgement of significance based primarily on such a standard. The point is that the language reflects, in exaggerated form, an important aspect of a distinctive historical reality. Every sentence reflects the characteristic fusion of rationalist and Christian values in

the new secular religion of the cities: 'Our responsibilities are great but
we eschew retrogression. The 19th Century is not the time for going
back . . . The gorgeous predictions of the Ancient seers will soon be
realised – intelligence and virtue will be law. Myrtles will supplant
thorns and thistles and this sin-planted earth again become a Paradise.
To assist in this great good work is our task. To the consummation of
this glorious end is our labour directed.'[47]

Although Cowen's outlook reflected his social situation, he was in no
sense an apologist for the middle classes. On the contrary, as a man who
was not above a certain self-righteousness, he took pleasure in reproving
them for their shortcomings. He clearly did not hold up the successful
members of the middle classes as models for emulation. On the contrary,
he made it plain that he saw 'little nobility and but small chivalry
amongst them'. 'They trample on the rights – they despise and insult
the principles and feelings of those who in worldly circumstances are
below them; and then they *ape* the aristocrat. Their God is gentility and
their worship Mammon.' Cowen had no illusions about middle-class
notions of respectability: 'The company of the vain, the unthinking,
the dissolute and even the immoral if they be but "respectable" they
can keep, but the companionship of the poor but honest man who
dares to think and speak for himself on matters of politics and religion
they shrink from as from the Prince of all evil.' 'The influentials', as
Cowen called them, had shown very little interest in the cause of
improvement. Because of their 'accursed snobbery', they 'never can do
either themselves or the working classes, morally or mentally any
good'. If anything the younger ones were worse than their elders, for
they 'spend more on decorating and bedaubing their external man [?]
with all the tomfooleries of misnamed respectability than would more
than half keep our institution in operation. They feed their dogs on
better food than many [a] working man can obtain for himself and
family'.[48]

It is in the context of such principled radicalism, innocent of any
inclination to rationalise the interests of the middle classes, that
Cowen's advice to the working classes – so similar in substance to
orthodox middle-class propaganda – has to be understood. Thus, his
exhortation to the working classes to help themselves comes immediately
after his denunciation of the vices and apathy of the middle classes.
His message is that working men better help themselves, because they
would be foolish to count on much help from their social superiors.
'I beseech you, then my friends of the working classes, rely on your own
efforts – depend for success on your own exertions and not on the
spasmodic aid you may by chance derive from either one class or
another.'[49] Thus, Cowen's version of self-help expressed the ideal of
genuine independence rather than the achievement of a respectability.

As such it was very close to the values of the working-class subculture.

For all his genuinely radical and populist spirit, the substance of Cowen's social teaching corresponded closely to that of the middle classes that he criticised so severely. His assumptions were profoundly conservative from the point of view of their attitude towards the structure of power. Yet these attitudes subsisted side by side with genuinely radical demands. Cowen, for example, believed in the Charter and manhood suffrage – an extremely radical position in the 1840s. But his commitment to the ethic of mental and moral improvement was so strong that he chose to belittle the hopes of those who expected the Six Points to bring about sudden improvement. Thus, he did not depreciate the Charter from the point of view of an opponent, and there was realism in his recognition that a franchise change was bound to be of limited impact. But the whole burden of his case for moral and intellectual improvement, and for working-class self-help, functioned in fact, although not in intention, to weaken Chartist militancy and to reinforce stabilising elements in the society. 'Give us the Charter tomorrow & what will it accomplish by itself? Will it make one drunken man sober – will it by itself make one ignorant man wise – one vicious man virtuous – one bad and avaricious man good and benevolent?'[50]

Some of Cowen's observations to working men, from the point of view of a radical who was unsparing in his criticism of the middle classes and their false values, provide a reminder of the limits imposed on social thought, not by the immediate pressure of class interest, but by the range of opinion in the society as a whole at this time. 'The working men of Winlaton, poor though they are, if they would use the means within their reach, can do more for themselves in a mental and moral point of view, than all the Acts of Parliament can or will do for them this side of 1900.' Not content with this way of emphasising self-improvement, however, Cowen went much further: 'My friends depend upon it, the root of the evils under which you labour you have brought upon yourselves. The roots of your diseases like your sins are your own faults. Granted what you say is true – that our social system is bad. The best way to cure it is to reform yourselves.'[51]

Cowen exemplifies, almost to the point of caricature, the theme that the improving creed constituted a religious faith, in the sense that it received an unqualified commitment, was beyond criticism and of self-evident validity, and gave meaning and significance to the life of the individual committed to it. Merely its affirmation – as well as its defence against unbelieving Tories – was an act of high importance: that is, not a mere political act, but a statement of transcendent values. Cowen delighted in invoking a religious mood in his addresses to mechanics' institutes: 'In a celebration like the present, I recognise a something not limited to the spectacle of the moment, however beautiful and radiant it may be . . . but extending from this place to swarms of toiling men elsewhere, cheering and stimulating them in the onward and upward path that lies before us all.' Wherever the hammer beats or the factory chimneys smoke, and wherever there are human beings into whom 'their wise Creator did not see fit to constitute all body but into each and every one of them He breathed a mind – there I would fain believe some touch of sympathy and encouragement is felt from our collective pulse'.[52]

The religion of improvement presupposed the existing social structure and the social roles that it prescribed. Cowen's idealism often did no more than put a gloss on existing patterns of class relations: 'And thus by the happy union of both rich and poor, great and small, a triple cord of duty, interest and affection will be woven over the broad gulf that now so unhappily divides society; and both parties be led to see that as children of a common parent and members of a common family the welfare of the one is the welfare of the other.' Mechanics' institutes would bring together rich and poor and overcome the conflict between them. By working together on behalf of the great goals of knowledge and improvement, they would achieve social harmony and order and overcome the discord of the 1830s and 1840s. 'And each and every one shall be disposed to reach out the hand of catholicity and good feeling to his neighbour and say what we can do to promote each other's mutual moral well-being.'[53] Here was an admirable ideal, which Cowen pursued with fervour. But it was clear that Cowen's conception of proper social roles in the pursuit of high ideals did not differ from that of the middle-class as a whole.

By 1850 many middle-class and working-class radicals shared a romantic-progressive sensibility. W.E. Adams, the compositor of W.J. Linton's *English Republic*, has described the outlook of such a group: 'We were dreamers, enthusiasts, fanatics, what you will – we Republicans of the middle of the century.' From the outset their politics had been inseparably connected with the high ideals of the religion of improvement: 'With the desire for culture there had come a passion for politics.' Chartism had failed to satisfy Adams and other improving working men in Cheltenham. 'Higher aspirations entered our heads, suffused our thoughts, coloured our dreams.' When they turned to Harney's *Democratic Review*, they 'found a programme, but we wanted a religion'. That religion came to them from Italy, by way of W.J. Linton, who published a series of articles on republicanism in Harney's *Friend of the People*. Linton's articles had been based on a proclamation issued by Mazzini's Central Democratic Committee in July 1850 in London. Mazzini's romantic liberalism struck a responsive chord in Linton and Adams. Adams quoted 'a few of its inspiring passages': 'We believe in the progressive development of human faculties and forces in the direction of the moral law which has been imposed upon us.' 'We believe that the interpretation of the moral law and rule of progress . . . ought to be confided to the people enlightened by national education, directed by those among them whom virtue and genius point out to them at their best.'[54] That ringing affirmation expressed values and attitudes that lay at the core of a new ethos.

Notes

1. John Stuart Mill, *Principles of Political Economy*, London 1892, p. 456.
2. Elie Halévy, *The Growth of Philosophic Radicalism*, London 1928, pp. 3—34.
3. F.A. Cavenagh, ed., *James and John Stuart Mill on Education*, Cambridge 1931, pp. 12, 29, 59.
4. Ibid., p. 59.
5. Alexander Tyrrell, 'Class Consciousness in Early Victorian Britain: Samuel Smiles, Leeds Politics, and the Self-Help Creed', *Journal of British Studies*, X, 1970, 105—14. See also Donald Read, *Press and Public*, London 1961, pp. 177—9, and Asa Briggs, *Victorian People,* London 1954, pp. 124—49.
6. Samuel Smiles, *The Diffusion of Political Knowledge Among the Working Classes* 1842.
7. Ibid., pp. 4, 17; Tyrrell, pp. 116—17, quoting Smiles, *The Education of the Working Classes*, 1845.
8. Mill, *Principles of Political Economy*, p. 458.
9. Ibid., p. 459.
10. Smiles, *Diffusion of Political Knowledge*, p. 19.
11. Henry Brougham, *Practical Observations upon the Education of the People, Addressed to the Working Classes and Their Employers,* London 1825.
12. Ibid.
13. Newcastle Mechanics' Institute, Minute Book, 1862—9, Newcastle Reference Library, quotes the 1824 manifesto; A. Tait, *History of the Oldham Lyceum 1839—1897*, Oldham 1897, p. 11. See also Mabel Tylecote, *The Mechanics' Institutes of Lancashire and Yorkshire before 1851*, Manchester 1957.
14. *Report of the Manchester District Association of Literary and Scientific Institutions*, Manchester 1840, p. 40.
15. *Speech Delivered at the Annual Meeting of the Friends of the Manchester Lyceum*, London 1840, p. 5.
16. *Bradford Observer*, 16 March 1848.
17. Thomas Chalmers, *The Christian and Civic Economy of Large Towns,* London 1856, pp. 569—71.
18. Chalmers, p. 585.
19. *The Fourth Annual Report of the Manchester and Salford District Provident Society*, Manchester 1837; *First Annual Report of the Liverpool District Provident Society*, Liverpool 1831.
20. *Second Annual Report of the Liverpool District Provident Society*, Liverpool 1832.
21. See the biographical introduction by Stanley D. Chapman to William Felkin, *History of the Machine-Wrought Hosiery and Lace Manufactures*, New York 1967; see also Roy A. Church, *Economic and Social Change in a Midland Town: Victorian Nottingham, 1815—1900*, London 1966, pp. 105—24, 326—31.

22. William Felkin, *The Exhibition in 1851 of the Products and Industry of All Nations*, London 1851.
23. The biographical information in the following paragraphs is based on the fine University of Nottingham M.A. thesis, 1960, by Stanley D. Chapman.
24. Felkin, *The Exhibition in 1851*.
25. *Remarks upon the Importance of an Inquiry into the Amount and Appropriation of Wages by the Working Classes*, London 1837.
26. Ibid.
27. *The Exhibition in 1851*.
28. Ibid.; *Remarks upon the Importance . . .*
29. *The Exhibition in 1851*.
30. Ibid.
31. Carl Woodring, *Victorian Samplers: William and Mary Howitt*, Lawrence, Kansas 1952, pp. 115–33.
32. J.F.C. Harrison, *Learning and Living*, Toronto 1961, pp. 144–51.
33. Ibid., pp. 137–45.
34. Francis E. Mineka, *The Dissidence of Dissent*, Chapel Hill 1944, pp. 216, 309–11.
35. Alexander Tyrrell, 'The Origins of a Victorian Best-Seller – An Unacknowledged Debt', *Notes and Queries*, new series, XVII, 1970, 347–9.
36. Harrison, *Learning and Living*, p. 118; Tylecote, pp. 213–15.
37. *People's Journal*, vol. VII, 1849, 44.
38. Ibid., pp. 127–32.
39. Ibid., p. 199.
40. *Eliza Cook's Journal*, 5 May 1849.
41. Ibid., 1 December 1849.
42. Ibid., 16 June 1849.
43. Thomas Beggs, 'The Moral Elevation of the People', *National Temperance Magazine*, January 1845 – May 1846.
44. *National Temperance Magazine*, January and May 1845.
45. Joseph Cowen, Jr., 'The Substance of two addresses delivered at the Winlaton L. and M. Institution soirée 18 June and the Blaydon and Stella Reading Room soirée 26 August 1850', MS, Cowen Collection, Newcastle Reference Library, item D42. This superb collection is equipped with a first-rate index. See also D.G.E. Harris, 'Joseph Cowen', in Joyce Bellamy and John Saville, eds., *Dictionary of Labour Biography*; E.R. Jones, *Life and Speeches of Joseph Cowen*, London 1885; W. Duncan, *Life of Joseph Cowen*, London 1904.
46. 'Notes; Hints; Observations taken from daily life etc. etc. by Joseph Cowen Edinburgh July 1846', MS notebook, item F12, Cowen Collection. See also F19, a paper on the nobility, presented by Cowen in Edinburgh in 1846.
47. 'Report read at Soirée 18 June 1849', MS, D31, Cowen Collection.
48. Item D42, Cowen Collection.
49. Ibid.
50. Ibid.
51. Ibid.
52. Joseph Cowen, Jr., 'Address delivered on May 10th, 1852', item D57, Cowen Collection.
53. 'The Members of the Winlaton Literary Scientific and Mechanics' Institution to the Public generally of Winlaton and Neighbourhoods', August 1847, Item D16, Cowen Collection.
54. W.E. Adams, *Memoirs of a Social Atom*, with an introduction by John Saville, New York 1968, pp. 118, 261–3, 280. See also A.R. Schoyen, *The Chartist Challenge*, pp. 226, 231, 234–6, 242.

5 MID-VICTORIAN URBAN CULTURE

As the ideological conflict between the middle and working classes abated somewhat in the course of the 1840s, a consensus on fundamental values emerged in the cities and provided the foundation of a cohesive and well-integrated culture. By the middle of the century a vast network of institutions had already come into being, devoted to the great goal accepted by all – the moral and intellectual improvement of the individual. Men of all classes agreed on the traits that ought to be cultivated in the individual: rationality, knowledge, moral rectitude, self-reliance, independence, and a devotion to education and self-culture. The ideal of improvement pervaded the common life of the community, not only on formal public occasions but also in the activities of everyday life. Even apart from the contrast to the ideological dissonance of the 1830s and 1840s, mid-Victorian urban culture was noteworthy in its cohesiveness, in the extent to which its official values commanded assent, and in the degree to which these values were embodied in interconnected institutions, roles, and ritual. Underlying this complex social whole was a sensibility of high moral aspiration; the mid-Victorians put the highest value on the pursuit of moral ideals in the life of the community. To a remarkable degree, they had sanctified their social values, and the object of worship was the community itself. It was a culture given to self-congratulation, to the official celebration of every action taken in fulfilment of the sacred purposes of the community. Just as the middle and working classes had participated in the shaping of this culture, so they joined in its litany and ritual.[1]

The mid-Victorian city was not only a community united by common purposes, however, but also an arena in which contending social classes confronted each other in conflict. Most visible were the continual clashes between employers and trade unions. Even more pervasive was the collision between divergent class versions of the values to which all men gave their allegiance. Inevitably, the content of 'improvement', for example, varied widely with its location on the social scale. The formal universality of official values was eroded by the steady pressure of class, status and power. Woven into mid-Victorian cultural patterns were roles derived from a social structure in which the middle-class was dominant. Implicit in the system was the assumption that in the short run – this side of utopia – working men would continue to play a subordinate role in relation to the middle classes, that they would receive an education appropriate to their inferior status, and that they would willingly accept the leadership of their betters. But working men who had been reared in the traditions of early-Victorian radicalism refused to accept the middle-class version of consensus values. They rejected middle-class propaganda, fought efforts to destroy trade unions, and insisted that all men should be treated equally regardless of class.

While abandoning the early-Victorian demand for political and social transformation, class-conscious working men gave their allegiance to a distinct subculture, which embodied the basic values of early-Victorian radicalism. Central to those ideals was the pursuit of moral and intellectual improvement in behalf of working-class independence and self-respect. Implicit in the subculture was a continuing protest against a society that systematically excluded the mass of the people from full participation in the heritage of the community. Various working-class institutions — trade unions, friendly societies, co-operatives — served the purposes of the radical tradition. As a result, despite the fundamental weakness of their position, working men enjoyed a remarkable degree of success in resisting middle-class hegemony and in sustaining their commitment to democratic and egalitarian values. They certainly had not surrendered to 'middle-class values'.

But the democratic and egalitarian values of the working-class sub-culture survived only within the limits imposed by the culture as a whole and by the underlying structure of power and status. While working men were quite capable of recognising and rejecting overt middle-class propaganda, they were vulnerable to legitimising tendencies inherent in the mid-Victorian ethos. Thus the widespread inclination to celebrate the most minor activity concerned with individual improvement tended to cast a warm glow over the society as a whole, with all its imperfections, inequalities, and injustices. Blanketed in this soothing atmosphere, the spirit of protest and criticism lost its edge. Moreover, the sensibility of aspiration encouraged the substitution of earnestness of sentiment and language as an end in itself, detached from specific objectives. High-minded talk about progress and improvement blunted the force of working-class radicalism and softened the subculture that it had helped to create. In addition to such difficulties inherent in the culture as a whole, and apart from the operation of mechanisms of social and ideological domination, radical working men also had to contend with the fact that middle-class progressives and improvers were expressing their own ideals in rather similar language. In this situation the differences between radicalism and liberalism tended to be fudged. Thus, a number of interlocking social and cultural processes weakened the radical impulse to independence and equality and assimilated working-class efforts to patterns that presupposed subordination and inequality.

This chapter will sketch two salient characteristics of mid-Victorian urban culture — its remarkable cohesion and distinctive sensibility of aspiration — with particular attention to the intellectual forces that shaped it. We shall be concerned with the end product of a single process, which resolved the early-Victorian ideological crisis, created a broad consensus, and built a cohesive culture on that consensual base. An important factor in these developments was the presence of the same intellectual forces both in working-class radicalism and middle-class liberalism and in the emerging cultural patterns. As was noted in chapters 2–4, the two contending ideologies shared a great deal of common ground to begin with. With the mellowing of middle-class liberalism in the 1840s and the decline in working-class agitation, the area of agreement was enlarged. Moreover, the chief intellectual components of working-class radicalism were also at the core of the culture that was taking shape in the middle decades of the nineteenth century. Thus, working-class radicalism was organically connected with mid-Victorian urban culture, just as since the 1790s it had developed and acquired its character within the broader cultural framework of England as a whole.

Precisely because the causal impact of social structure is so evident in the process that shaped mid-Victorian urban culture, this chapter will emphasise the fact that intellectual forces independent of the immediate socio-economic situation – in the sense that they were the product of developments reaching into the remote past – also exercised a profound influence. This is by way of reaffirming the familiar historical axiom that cultural patterns cannot be 'derived' from a given social structure, however much they may reflect it; nor can they be reduced to the status of manifestations of something else presumed to be more fundamental. A given class structure is compatible with a vast number of cultural patterns, which it conditions but does not determine. While the middle-class was a necessary cause of many important aspects of the mid-Victorian cities, it was not a sufficient cause. Some characteristics of mid-Victorianism that at first glance appear to be intrinsically 'middle-class' in fact had more complex origins. Finally, intellectual forces are not merely 'causes' producing separate and discrete 'effects', but themselves become constituents of the phenomenon they are affecting. The complex amalgam of mid-Victorianism was compounded of elements derived from the Enlightenment, evangelicalism, and romanticism.

On the other hand, of course, these intellectual forces did not operate in isolation, but in a particular social and institutional structure that decisively affected the end result. Chapter 6 sketches the matrix of power and status in which the contours of mid-Victorian urban culture took shape. Chapter 7 describes the moral and intellectual hegemony exercised by the middle-class in the social and cultural setting of the industrial towns. Chapters 8 and 9 deal with the working-class subculture and two institutions that enabled working men to maintain a degree of independence and to offer some resistance to ideological and social domination by the middle-class. The last chapter examines the activity of the working-class radical movement in this milieu.

Finally, in considering the cultural configuration of mid-Victorian cities, it may be well to have in mind the rather different ideological pattern that developed in Europe after 1848.[2] Similar social and intellectual forces, operating under other historical circumstances, produced a different result on the Continent. In France and in Germany the middle and working classes achieved a momentary unity on the eve of 1848. The June days in Paris symbolise the shattering of that factitious alliance. Both in Germany and in France there ensued what has been called a new 'toughness of mind', a conscious rejection of pre-1848 idealism. New currents of positivism and materialism displaced the remnants of romanticism. Individuals and social groups set out to base their behaviour on a realistic assessment of the facts of social and economic life. In England, by contrast, much of the pre-1848 mood persisted, but the idiom of utopian idealism now provided a gloss to existing social and institutional arrangements.

(1) *Consensus and Cohesion*

Since class differences and class conflicts were so conspicuous in the public life of the mid-Victorian cities, it is necessary to emphasise the cohesiveness of the culture within which transactions between the classes were carried on. One is struck by the congruence between official consensus values and the institutional structure, by the tendency of all classes to invoke shared ideals on every conceivable occasion, and by the extent to which a common outlook was embedded in recurring patterns of activity. As much as men might differ on important points of principle, they were clearly members of a community sharing common purposes. Such phenomena have to be understood, in part, in terms of the perspective of Durkheim, who emphasised the importance of processes inherent in society as a whole, especially the inclination to invest its purposes with a sacred character. The historian, however, is interested in the particular constellation of circumstances that produced consensus and cohesiveness in cities that had been torn by intense social and ideological conflict.

Three intellectual forces were instrumental in creating the consensual foundations of mid-Victorian urban culture — the Enlightenment, evangelicalism and romanticism. Each the product of a long history, exercising their influence in continual and varied interplay, they contributed to the belief in individual improvement as the highest goal of the community and shaped the values of the improvement ethic. From the Enlightenment came the conception of man as a fundamentally rational creature, capable of infinite progress if he will take knowledge and reason as his guides. It followed that a society ought to cultivate the intellectual development of its members through education and the diffusion of knowledge. Since virtue was a necessary concomitant of reason, the intellectual and moral improvement of the individual constituted a single indissoluble objective. As was noted in chapter 2 above, evangelicalism exercised a parallel influence, albeit with primary emphasis on morality. There was an underlying affinity between the theology of progressive sanctification and the rationalist belief in perfectibility based on reason. Coming later, romantic currents of thought and feeling were of lesser importance, although they provided reinforcement and a distinctive coloration. Romanticism enlarged the ideal of improvement by defining it in terms of the development of the self in its totality.

The emergence of consensus was accompanied by a muting of early-Victorian ideological conflict. Fundamental to these interconnected developments was the presence within working-class radicalism of a number of strands that were easily woven into the mid-Victorian cultural fabric. The same elements were also present in middle-class liberalism. The legacy of the Enlightenment was of pre-eminent importance in these processes of change, because it was involved both in the creation and the resolution of the early-Victorian ideological crisis. Having magnified the social and ideological tensions inherent in industrialisation, the traditions of the Enlightenment also contributed to a narrowing of the gap between radicalism and liberalism. During the period of maximum strain there took place both an intensification of the conflict and the emergence of the common ground on which it was to be resolved. Working-class radicalism had received from the Enlightenment not only the intellectual weapons that were to be directed against the established order but also ideas and beliefs that later were to form the core of the mid-Victorian ethos. The working-class commitment to such consensus values was to be so strong because they had been central to the ideology of the Left at the very outset. Since the 1790s popular radicalism had taken it for granted that the intellectual development of the individual was the hallmark of a good society. That idea, in turn, had been inextricably linked to the rationalist premise that the diffusion of sound political knowledge and the pursuit of the politics of reason would contribute to the creation of a society that fostered the development of free men. Thus there was a predisposition among working-class radicals to accept at face value the rationalist claims of a more benign middle-class liberalism, which also rested on the ideals of the Enlightenment.

In this aspect of the process of ideological adjustment and accommodation, evangelical and romantic elements played a subordinate role, as they had in the evolution of working-class radicalism to begin with. Evangelical attitudes and sentiments probably served as an emollient, softening the astringent side of popular radicalism, thus mediating the transition to mid-Victorianism. The softening process, with undertones of sentimentality, was also affected by romanticism, which had significantly influenced the radical temper of the 1830s and 1840s. Along with the Enlightenment then, these intellectual forces moved working-class radicalism along the road to mid-Victorianism.

Once a consensus was established both the working and middle classes joined in the ceremonial celebration of the values of the community. The resulting proliferation of ritual forms provides the most visible evidence of the cohesiveness of the culture. At their innumerable meetings leaders of the multifarious institutions of the mid-Victorian cities engaged in a ceaseless affirmation of the improvement ethic in all its forms. There took place an unending incantation of consensus values on every conceivable occasion. Whether the meetings were organised by the middle classes, the working classes, or both, similar patterns prevailed. Above all, the participants were celebrating their common faith and renewing shared aspirations. The meetings were interludes of reassurance in a situation where the gap between high goals and immediate reality was all too conspicuous. They exalted social harmony at a time of conflict and set their face against discord of any kind. Every effort was made to get participation by all classes. No week passed in the larger cities without regular meetings, anniversary meetings, soirées, and lectures, complete with chairmen, resolutions, toasts, speeches, and minutes, all duly recorded in the press. At such meetings representatives of the middle classes enjoyed a perfect opportunity to act out on the platform their cultural role — lending a hand to respectable working men in the enterprise of improvement.

Even working-class institutions, which had been established by working men to provide for their own needs and to defend radical values against a middle-class jealous of its pre-eminence, conformed very closely to the dominant ritual pattern in their public meetings. While maintaining their independence and asserting the worth of the working-class, these institutions were as zealous as any in proclaiming their commitment to consensus values. This was quite consistent with the overall posture of the working-class subculture, which was simply seeking a truly egalitarian version of the professed goals of the community. Inevitably, however, the end product put more stress on consensus than on criticism. And that, after all, was the point of public meetings in this setting. One form of trade union militancy was the denunciation of employers who disparaged the working-class character. This was often done at public meetings where the trade unionists dwelt on moral and intellectual achievements of working men. They were not at all averse to the presence of a bourgeois figure on the platform to lend support to their case. The friendly societies, free from direct conflict with the middle classes, were even more eager to proclaim the achievements of the working classes. Their public meetings were frequently attended by local dignitaries, singing the praises of the membership. Working men also followed a similar ritual pattern when in the 1860s they formed manhood suffrage associations to demand the vote.

The co-operative societies took particular pride in their soirées, social meetings, and anniversaries: 'More enjoyable tea parties and festival gatherings can hardly be imagined than those originating in Co-operation.' For the historian their meetings are of considerable interest, because they illustrate a number of facets of the culture into which the co-operative movement was so very well integrated. More than other working-class institutions, the co-operative societies combined a commitment to consensus values with a continual critique of capitalist ideology and practice; and they expressed their criticism of capitalism in forms that were perfectly congruent with the culture as a whole. They certainly left no doubt about their conviction that the competitive system was 'fundamentally wrong' and ought to be transformed. Even in the staid pages of the annual report of the Manchester Co-operative Society the labour theory of value was invoked in support of the contention that the mass of the people ought to receive as their reward the 'whole result' of their exertions: 'The increase of wealth has not brought the mass of the people (who are essential to the creation of wealth) their proportionate share of its reward.' The ultimate objective of the co-operative movement was to transform the competitive system: 'Co-operation rightly understood is the lever with which to peacefully revolutionise society — to put Right where it ought to be, and to displace Might from its usurped throne.' Co-operation was to be a fulcrum from which working men 'will resolve to spin the world into a new orbit'.[3]

Despite such genuinely radical intentions, however, the meetings of the co-operative societies reflected a culture so secure in its fundamental values that even the most severe critics operated very much within the omnipresent atmosphere of consensus. In August 1861, for example, 3,000 persons attended an inaugural celebration of the establishment of the Blackburn Redemption Co-operative Manufacturing Company. The chief resolution was introduced by Ernest Jones, a radical whose Chartism remained undiluted: 'That the Redemption Company is started in a determination to endeavour to settle the long disputed questions of strikes and lockouts, to show the public the best means of progress for the factory operative, and then to cultivate a better feeling amongst all classes of the community, and advance the prospects of its members, by securing a safe investment for their money, and giving them a better opportunity for intellectual, social, and moral advancement.' At such meetings it was standard for speakers to point with pride to 'the good moral effect that was produced on a man by joining a co-operative society'. Both in the middle-class press and the working-class press the proceedings tended to be described according to a fixed form, as in the account of a co-operative tea party in the Oddfellows Hall at Ashton-under-Lyne: 'A very respectable body of working people enjoyed themselves over a cup of tea.' In this instance, the secretary's report, after announcing the accession of over 200 new members in the first six months of the year, proceeded along familiar lines: 'The spirit and energy exhibited in the success of our store is fully developing the principles of co-operation, and is producing those great efforts referred to by Messrs Cobden and Bright — the freedom and good fellowship of the working classes.' The members were never permitted to forget that great principles were involved in the mundane business of co-operative retailing. A visitor from the co-operative store in Oldham remarked that the working man's 'time, money, and talents should be spent in co-operation and for the elevation of the working class'.[4]

The leaders of the co-operative societies described their ultimate objectives in the quasi-religious diction of mid-Victorianism: 'The co-operative movement . . . will produce plenty instead of want, harmony instead of discord, love instead of hatred; substitute progressive knowledge for ignorance, morality and honesty for falsehood, vice, and crime.' Whereas competition 'fosters the worst feelings in the human heart', co-operation is in accord 'with the best feelings of human nature'. The Manchester Co-operative Society's denunciation of economic inequality was accompanied by the affirmation that the members value co-operation because 'it enhances not only our wealth, but our moral responsibility'. In publishing the report the editor set it in a consensus framework: 'Co-operation is daily taking firmer ground amongst the working people of England as their leading social institution, because it ensures not only abundant work and fair wages, but education, recreation, and the rights of Englishmen . . . It supplies [a workman] and his family with pure food and strong clothing; and in its higher developments promises those enjoyments, social and political, that make life desirable, home happy, the people contented, and the nation great and prosperous.'[5]

Like other working-class institutions the co-operatives followed the usual pattern of inviting local dignitaries to attend their annual meetings and sometimes to give speeches. The society at Darwen put out a formal invitation, in italic type, to a co-operative soirée to mark the opening of a new co-operative hall. Among those attending were to be 'several influential Gentlemen', and a J.P. was to take the chair. By the

1860s representatives of the middle-class were in regular attendence at such meetings. They found it an excellent occasion for preaching consensus values in a favourable setting. At the annual co-operative festival in Bradford, a councillor presided and took the opportunity to deliver a standard speech. 'As an employer of labour,' he began grandly, 'there was not the smallest jealousy on his part — and he believed the same feeling existed to a very great extent amongst the other employers in Bradford — of the co-operative movement, or of any movement which tended to elevate the working men of this country.' Thomas Potter, a wholesale draper who did business with the Manchester Co-operative Society, obviously enjoyed every moment of the speech that he delivered at its annual meeting in 1864. He began by praising their business acumen and their insistence on buying only goods of high quality. Using the familiar language of working-class radicalism, he also praised them in terms that confirmed their conviction that they were contributing to substantial social change. 'I would next call your attention to the fact that Co-operative societies, above all other societies, tend to raise working people in the scale of society; and this not by the promise of premiums or prizes — nor by being petted, pampered, and patronised — nor even by charity of one kind or another — but they are raised by self-reliance and Co-operation.'[6]

The basic ceremonial pattern in the cities appears most conspicuously in activities initiated by the middle classes. In such cases, of course, socially determined roles were very much in evidence; the platform rhetoric had a distinctly ideological cast to it, and working-class participation reflected relations of subordination. Nevertheless, such meetings must also be understood as community festivals, religious events celebrating a common secular faith. A case in point is the laying of the foundation stone for a new building for the mechanics' institute in Newcastle-on-Tyne in 1865.[7] It was the sort of event that recurred again and again, in various forms, in the Victorian cities. In this instance, one is struck, first of all, by the scale of the proceedings. The day's activities began with a procession to the building site, where the ceremony was held; in the evening came a dinner and then a public meeting. The three separate gatherings ensured that no one failed to realise the importance of the occasion. When the building was finally finished in 1868, another day of ceremonial activity ensued. The same sort of thing had taken place in 1862, when the opening of the campaign to raise funds was announced. That six-year interval serves as a reminder that the Victorian middle classes were by no means eager to provide money for the projects that aroused such outpourings of platform enthusiasm. In Newcastle, as in other cities, there was a considerable disproportion between such ostentatious community activity and the results actually achieved. The new building was a modest affair, not very well located. A critic contrasted the actual character of the building with the fanfare of the day's ceremonies: 'The prospect from the windows will be charming. In the front the fine workshops, with their unique windows, of Messrs Atkinson and Philipson, will be visible, and behind the eye will behold a dirty back lane and shabby houses.' The institute, founded in 1824, had been moribund for some time, and it was hoped that the new building would revivify it. The fact that it took three years to raise the £3,000 indicated a lack of strong support. Moreover, the day's proceedings were not nearly so well attended as had been hoped. There was a distinct air of ineffectuality about the whole affair. Nevertheless, as the critic pointed out, 'the papers in the morning will be full of glorification'. That glorification, like the ceremonies that it dealt with, was not contrived. It was integral to a culture that prized its high aspirations.

'Yesterday was a red-letter day in the history of the Newcastle Mechanics' Institution', announced the *Northern Daily Express*, and proceeded to devote page after page to a reverent account of the series of events. There had been some concern about the weather, but around noon it had brightened up a little; the weather was dull, but on the whole favourable. The results of the elaborate preparations were very much in evidence. 'The merry tones of the bells were at this time taking their prominent part in the rejoicings on the important occasion, and the principal streets of the town presented a very animated appearance.' Flags and banners were on display, especially along the route of the procession. Local dignitaries, reinforced by Sir George Grey, M.P., assembled in the Council chambers in preparation for the procession, which was scheduled to begin at 2.30 p.m. It took almost a whole column in the *Express* to list the groups and individuals in the line of march. 'Starting from the Town Hall, which was gaily bedecked with colours and flags of England, America, France, and nearly every other European country, together with long strings of pendants and banners, the procession turned into Mosley Street at a pretty brisk pace.' The police were hard pressed to manage the 'dense crowd of the line of the procession' and to keep it in the order in which it had been formed. Traffic had been diverted in order to leave enough room for the procession and the spectators. At three o'clock the procession reached the building site and the ceremony of laying the stone began. Sir George was presented with a specially engraved trowel. 'The trowel was a magnificent specimen of art. The handle was of ivory, and the blade of gold. . . . At the top of the trowel was engraved the borough arms, and at the foot Sir George's crest, surrounded with the garter.' He then laid the stone and delivered a speech, The band played one verse of 'God Save the Queen' and the assemblage dispersed. That evening members of the Newcastle officialdom gathered for dinner, toasts and speeches. This was followed by a public meeting in the town hall. There were a number of speeches and resolutions, along with the presentation of a memorial to Sir George Grey by the members of the mechanics' institution: 'We thank you for the courtesy you have shown us this day, and at the same time respectfully congratulate you, sir, as one in authority, and for ourselves gratefully acknowledge the prosperity and peace and goodwill among men, which, under Divine Providence, at present reign not only in this district but throughout our common country.'[8]

The ideological character of the last sentence is plain enough. As a direct reflection of the social structure, the language of the memorial can serve as a textbook example of the sort of phenomenon dealt with by Pareto as well as Marx. Yet the total ceremonial pattern of which the memorial was a part can by no means be understood solely in terms of class relations. The ritual activity of the mid-Victorian cities also reflects an aspect of social reality that was stressed by Durkheim.

A central insight in Durkheim's thought is his conception of society as a unified whole, greater than the sum of its parts, generating common ideals endowed with a sacred character and expressed in cult and ritual.[9] Inherent in every society is the tendency to sanctify its social values. 'Once a goal is pursued by a whole people,' wrote Durkheim, 'it acquires, as a result of this unanimous adherence, a sort of moral supremacy which raises it far above private goals and thereby gives it a religious character.'[10] He interpreted religion as an expression of society's worship of itself and as an embodiment of values and aspirations created by the society. Analysing the various ritual forms in which collective values are expressed, Durkheim sought to show how every society develops ways of 'upholding and reaffirming at regular intervals the collective sentiments and the collective ideas which make its unity and its personality'. The *conscience collective* is the binding force of a society: 'All that societies require in order to hold together is that their members fix their eyes on the same end and come together in a single faith.'[11] Thus, for Durkheim the cohesion of a society is a function of its collective consciousness, which assumes a 'religious' form.

From this perspective Durkheim approached the historical question of the emergence of new forms of social solidarity in the course of the transition from traditional to modern society. In the *Division of Labour* he described what he called the 'mechanical solidarity' characteristic of traditional societies, in which a single corpus of values and beliefs, common to every member of the society, pervaded every aspect of social life. As a result of the development of division of labour along with the ideological proliferation generated by the French Revolution, however, traditional forms of solidarity were undermined. Durkheim perceived nineteenth-century Europe as in a transitional state, moving towards what he called 'organic solidarity'. A new collective consciousness was growing into being. In contrast to the intellectual and moral homogeneity characteristic of traditional societies, nineteenth-century Europe put a premium on diversity in values and celebrated the emancipation of the individual from custom and tradition. In place of monolithic orthodoxies had come the 'cult of the individual' and the exaltation of free thought. But it was precisely this 'moral individualism' that Durkheim identified as a new form of social cohesion. The cult of the individual had become the focus of common belief in the collective consciousness. Durkheim argued that the new individualism, derived from Christian morality, embodied in new form the sacredness inherent in the highest social values.[12]

In a brilliant essay published in 1898, 'Individualism and the Intellectuals', Durkheim depicted liberalism as the secular religion that provides the social cohesion of modern industrial society. The immediate context of the essay was a refutation of the views of the anti-Dreyfusards, who argued that the individualism of 1789 had undermined Christianity, the only body of beliefs capable of maintaining order. Restating his premise that 'a society cannot hold together unless there exists among its members a certain intellectual and moral community', Durkheim noted that although Christianity had traditionally performed that function, historical changes had made it impossible for it to continue, and a new religion was required. Against the clerical reactionaries, Durkheim argued that 'the only possible candidate is precisely this religion of humanity whose rational expression is individualist morality'. It was not a matter of advocating the establishment of such a religion, for it had already worked its way into the social fabric: 'The liberalism of the eighteenth century which is, after all, what is basically at issue, is not simply an armchair theory, a philosophical construction. It has entered into the facts, it has penetrated our institutions and our customs, it has become part of our whole life . . . ' He proceeded to set forth the religious aspects of nineteenth-century liberalism or 'individualism', as he called it in the essay. Above all, 'it is a religion of which man is, at the same time, both believer and God'. Its doctrines reflect many of the essential characteristics of traditional religion: 'The human person, whose definition serves as the touchstone according to which good must be distinguished from evil, is considered as sacred, in what one might call the ritual sense of the word. It has something of that transcendental majesty which the churches of all times have given to their Gods.' In other words, 'This religion of humanity has all that is required to speak to its believers in a tone that is no less imperative than the religions it replaces.'[13]

The thesis of Durkheim's essay is clearly overdrawn, both in form and content. Intent on turning the tables on right-wing ideologues who had been bemoaning the social consequences of the rationalist erosion of the Christian faith, he could not avoid the hyperbole inherent in that sort of an intellectual enterprise. Nevertheless, his main point — the unifying and stabilising function of liberalism — stands up very well indeed. Moreover, although his lyrical account of the religion of humanity seems remote from the reality of German liberalism, for example, it corresponds closely to the consensus liberalism of the mid-Victorian cities. If we ask why this was so, however, we shall not find the answer in Durkheim's theory, but in specific historical forces and circumstances.

(2) *The Sensibility of Aspiration*

The mid-Victorian propensity for the public proclamation of high ideals reflected a distinctive sensibility: moral earnestness and high seriousness, the exaltation of aspiration and striving, an emphasis on noble feelings and sentiments, and an ostentatious idealism and optimism. Such traits bear the impress of evangelicalism and romanticism. While the dominant ethos was utilitarian and rationalist at the core, its spirit owed a great deal to the afterglow of the evangelical revival and to a vestigial romanticism. Since these aspects of mid-Victorianism are, for good reason, associated with the middle-class, their broader historical origins have to be kept in mind. They were the product of a cultural inheritance common to all classes, although the middle-class embraced them with special zeal and left its stamp on their dominant manifestations. Hence working men who displayed similar traits were not *ipso facto* submitting to the intellectual tutelage of their superiors. In this instance, as in others, working-class radicalism, like middle-class liberalism, embodied elements derived from a common culture inherited from the past.[14]

There is no reason to dispute Canon Smyth's judgement that evangelicalism was the primary cause of the moral earnestness so characteristic of the Victorians.[15] From this source came the over-powering inclination to find moral significance in every corner of human life, individual and social. From the evangelical legacy — and the older Puritan traditions that it carried on — came the characteristic moral tone of the high Victorian age. It contributed directly to the tendency to exalt and worship the values of the society, to celebrate every attempt to achieve them, and to sanctify the activity devoted to those ends. To be sure, the Enlightenment had been endowed with a full measure of idealism and moral intensity. The Puritan temper of the utilitarians has often been noted. Conversely, the ethical intensity of the Enlightenment had non-Christian roots in Greek humanism and rationalism. From the Enlightenment the Victorians inherited a pre-occupation with principle and from the evangelical revival an overriding concern with morality. This double dose of high seriousness, in turn, was magnified by the enthusiasm of romanticism, with its emphasis on sentiment and feeling. While romanticism in England did not approach the sort of domination that it achieved in German intellectual life in the first half of the nineteenth century, the romantic spirit, especially as expressed by the Lake poets, entered English culture and infused it with new attitudes.[16] Even such severe critics of romanticism as Macaulay came under its sway. In interaction with other intellectual forces, it contributed to the mid-Victorian affinity for high aspiration and noble sentiment.

A glance at the literary culture of mid-Victorian England may provide an illustration of these themes, while also reminding us of a broader cultural reality common to England as a whole. Writers such as Tennyson and Ruskin clearly have to be understood in terms of a mid-Victorian culture that was not limited to one class or region. That is, they were manifestations of an historically created culture which, in diverse forms, was common to squire and bourgeois, nobleman and artisan, village and city. Reared in a Lincolnshire rectory, Tennyson wrote verse that expressed to perfection the ideals and values of the Victorian middle classes. But in his complex response to an increasingly bourgeois society an inherited literary tradition was clearly a major factor. Similarly, the culture of the cities and the working-class sub-culture drew on a broader 'mid-Victorian' cultural reality. As T.S. Eliot put it, 'The culture of the individual is dependent upon the culture of a group or class, and . . . the culture of the group or class is dependent upon the culture of the whole society to which that group or class belongs. Therefore, it is the culture of the society that is fundamental.'[17] Before turning to the role of class in shaping the social values of the cities, it is well to have in mind other con-stituents of mid-Victorianism.

Walter Houghton and other literary scholars have traced the develop-ment of the mentality of aspiration. Its romantic origins are symbolised in Shelley's observation that reason by itself is an insufficient basis for morality: 'Until the mind can love and admire and trust, and hope and endure, reasoned principles of moral conduct are seeds cast upon the highway of life, which the unconscious passengers trample into dust.' Accordingly, he hoped that his poetry would acquaint his readers with 'beautiful idealisms of moral excellence'. A decade later Thomas Arnold, echoing the same theme, praised poetry as a stimulus to 'all the highest and purest feelings of our nature', and Bulwer-Lytton exhorted writers 'to inculcate a venerating enthusiasm for the true and ethereal springs of Greatness and of Virtue', thus helping to 'refine the coarse and to ennoble the low'. Twenty years later such sentiments had become cultural commonplaces, the common coin of official rhetoric.

The expression of 'high feelings' and 'noble aims' — as Mill called them in his inaugural lecture at St Andrews — had become routine.[18]

Tennyson's *In Memoriam*, 'one of the cardinal documents of the mid-Victorian mind', is a poetic incarnation of the values of his age.[19] Plunged into despair by Hallam's death and troubled by religious doubts raised by recent developments in science, Tennyson resolved this crisis of belief by reaffirming his faith, not in orthodox Christianity, but in an amalgam of Christian pantheism and progressive optimism.

> Ring out the old, ring in the new,
>   Ring, happy bells, across the snow;
>   The year is going, let him go;
> Ring out the false, ring in the true.
>
> Ring out the grief that saps the mind,
>   For those that here we see no more;
>   Ring out the feud of rich and poor,
> Ring in redress to all mankind.
>
> Ring out a slowly dying cause,
>   And ancient forms of party strife;
>   Ring in the nobler modes of life,
> With sweeter manners, purer laws.
>
> Ring out the want, the care, the sin,
>   The faithless coldness of the times;
>   Ring out, ring out my mournful rimes,
> But ring the fuller minstrel in.
>
> Ring out false pride in place and blood,
>   The civic slander and the spite;
>   Ring in the love of truth and right,
> Ring in the common love of good.
>
> Ring out old shapes of foul disease;
>   Ring out the narrowing lust of gold;
>   Ring out the thousand wars of old,
> Ring in the thousand years of peace.
>
> Ring in the valiant man and free,
>   The larger heart, the kindlier hand;
>   Ring out the darkness of the land,
> Ring in the Christ that is to be.

That passage is a crystallisation of the sensibility of aspiration. Tennyson's diction, which sounds so consciously 'poetic' today, was a direct reflection of the culture as a whole. Removed from the context of the poem, his words echo the standard pieties of tract, sermon, and anniversary speech: nobler modes of life, sweeter manners, purer laws, the love of truth and right, the larger heart, the kindlier hand, the valiant man and free, redress to all mankind. The passage also expressed a sense of unease at a reality that belied such high hopes: the feud of rich and poor; the want, the care, the sin, the faithless coldness of the times; false pride, civic slander, spite; the darkness of the land. To decry thus the ills and vices of the day was also very much a part of the mid-Victorian outlook. Hence Tennyson's middle-class readers were not put off by the reference to 'the narrowing lust for gold'. They too in principle disapproved of mere acquisitiveness, untouched by higher goals. Such negative observations, however, merely served as a foil for the note of affirmation that Tennyson sounded so well.

Well before the Victorian age, painting also had been enlisted in the cause of moral instruction and the elevation of the feelings. The chief vehicle was the genre picture, which told a story and pointed a moral. David Wilkie, the leading figure in the field in the early nineteenth century, was praised for his ability to 'raise our passions without touching the brink of all we hate'. A popular painter of the next generation was acclaimed for 'the union of the most exalted sentiment with the utmost perfection of colour'. Increasingly, however, emphasis came to be put on subject matter rather than on colour or form. Characteristically, these tendencies were elevated to the level of principle. In 1856 Burne-Jones described the viewer's duty to seek out the story in a picture: 'When shall we learn to read a picture as we do a poem, to find some story from it, some little atom of human interest that may feed our heart within, lest the outer influences of the day crush them from good thoughts?' For the viewer who wished to take this advice, there was no lack of paintings that were instructive, elevating, and imbued with 'tender refinement'. Even landscapes were expected to combine moral and aesthetic values.[20]

Nowhere did the preoccupation with the morality of art receive more emphatic expression than in Ruskin's *Modern Painters*. In this and other respects Ruskin is of great interest to the student of mid-Victorian thought.[21] Coming from a devoutly evangelical background, his subsequent intellectual development was steeped in romanticism. Hence his mind reflects, with noteworthy richness, the major motifs in the intellectual life of his day. Moreover, unlike other middle-class intellectuals, he refused to be content with mere affirmation and brought his critical intelligence to bear on the failure of English society to actualise its ideals.

The title of a famous chapter in *Modern Painters*, 'The Moral Landscape', by itself sums up a host of assumptions that Ruskin shared with his contemporaries. In a letter written in 1844 he announced his conclusion that landscape art 'might become an instrument of gigantic moral power', and that he would devote his utmost labour to 'the demonstration of this high function'. He would spend his time 'directing the public to expect and the artist to intend — an earnest and elevating *moral* influence in all that they admire and achieve'. In this as in innumerable other passages Ruskin embodies both the values and the diction of his age. 'Let then every picture be painted with earnest intention of impressing on the spectator some elevated emotion, and exhibiting to him some one particular, but exalted, beauty.' He reminded his readers that 'the sensation of beauty' is neither sensual nor intellectual, 'but is dependent on a pure, right, and open state of the heart, both for its truth and for its intensity'. The perception of beauty must be received 'with a pure heart'; otherwise the 'sense of beauty sinks into the servant of lust'. A love of nature, he had no doubt, would contribute to 'nobleness and beauty of character'.[22] Whatever the subject, the same solid Victorian words recur: noble, earnest, elevating, pure, exalted.

Ruskin's definition of poetry encapsulates a great deal of the high Victorian view of life. Both the idiom and the substance are resonant of the culture of which he was so impressive a product. He argued that it was the function of poetry to suggest noble grounds for the noble emotions, which he defined as follows: 'I mean, by the noble emotions, those four principal sacred passions — Love, Veneration, Admiration, and Joy (this latter especially, if unselfish); and their opposites — Hatred, Indignation (or Scorn), Horror, and Grief — this last, when unselfish becoming Compassion. These passions in their various combinations constitute what is called "poetical feelings", when they are felt on noble grounds, that is, on great and true grounds.'[23]

Ruskin's definition of the 'sublime', departing from the views expressed by Edmund Burke in the middle of the eighteenth century, makes explicit a cluster of characteristically Victorian attitudes: 'Anything which elevates the mind is sublime, and elevation of mind is produced by the contemplation of greatness of any kind; but chiefly, of course, by the greatness of the noblest things.' Ruskin was not likely to encounter dissent on that point. He could proceed with his usual authority: 'Sublimity is, therefore, only another word for the effect of greatness upon the feelings.' Contemplation of the sublime not only elevates the mind but 'renders meanness of thought impossible'.[24]

Like so many of the great Victorians, Ruskin was an acute critic of the characteristic vices and weaknesses associated with his culture. Above all, he described the evasions, subterfuges, and deceptions to which men were forced to resort in order to preserve their overheated 'idealism' in the real world. Ruskin deplored the widespread tendency to take refuge in idealised fantasies: 'The pursuit, by the imagination, of beautiful and strange thoughts or subjects, to the exclusion of painful or common ones, is called among us, in these modern days, the pursuit of "*the ideal*"; . . . ' He showed how men used the device of 'visionary satisfaction' to remain at ease in their world. He described 'a general readiness to take delight in anything past, future, or far off, or somewhere else, rather than in things now, near, and here,' thus being able 'to build all our satisfaction on things as they are *not*'. Beyond that, 'a fear of disagreeable facts' could easily develop into 'a species of instinctive terror at all truth, and love of glosses, veils, and decorative lies of every sort'. He inveighed against 'this base habit − the abuse of the imagination, in allowing it to find its whole delight in the impossible and untrue; . . . '[25]

Determined to keep their eyes fixed on 'the valiant man and free, the larger heart, the kindlier hand', the Victorians did not wish their vision of man's higher nature to be dimmed by scepticism or cynicism. They took refuge in what Houghton has dissected under the heading of 'moral optimism'. As an example of the Victorian preference for what a later age was to call 'positive thinking', he cites a contemporary description of Charles Kingsley lecturing at Cambridge in 1860: 'He loved men and women, you felt that. He never sneered at their faults. He had a deep, sad pity for them; . . . he had such a warm, passionate admiration for fine deeds.' The Victorians wished to cultivate what a writer in 1863 characterised as 'the faculty of admiration, the source of some of our truest enjoyments and most elevated emotions', and to preserve a capacity for being 'overwhelmed by the presence of the sublime'. For George Eliot the moral currency comprised 'all the grander deeds and aims of men . . . every sacred, heroic, and pathetic theme which serves to make up the treasures of human admiration, hope and love'. It must not be debased by the 'burlesquing spirit'.[26] Failure and defeat also had their contribution to make in the moral economy of striving and aspiration. As Jerome Buckley put it, in commenting on Browning, 'The major voice of aspiration was inevitably one that had mastered the logic of ebullient acceptance.' 'Rabbi Ben Ezra' summed up the Victorian determination to remain serenely affirmative in mood.[27]

> Then welcome each rebuff
> That turns earth's smoothness rough,
> Each sting that bids nor sit nor stand but go!
> Be our joys three-parts pain!
> Strive, and hold cheap the strain;

> Learn, nor account the pang; dare, never
>   grudge the throe.
>
> For thence — a paradox
> Which comforts while it mocks —
> Shall life succeed in that it seems to fail:
> What I aspired to be,
> And was not, comforts me;
> A brute I might have been, but would not
>   sink i' the scale.

Having embraced such exalted ideals, the mid-Victorians were vulnerable to processes of routinisation and decay. Incessant repetition tended to empty high principles of their content. The most familiar of the Victorian responses to a cultural situation that placed intolerable demands on human nature was a rampant sentimentality, so vividly manifest in art, literature, drama, religion, and ideology. The Victorians displayed all the classic symptoms on a vast scale: an excess of emotion and feeling disproportionate to the object; an eagerness to indulge in such responses; an inclination to stereotyped words and gestures empty of genuine emotional content. They eagerly gave way to the emotions that they thought they ought to feel or wanted to feel. Novels, poems, and plays fed their appetite for vicarious emotional **experience**. What they believed in most deeply they could not refrain from sentimentalising.[28]

Dickens' account of the death of little Nell in *The Old Curiosity Shop* has come to exemplify the sentimental mode in the early-Victorian novel. His art accurately reflected his own attitudes and those of his readers. In a letter to a friend whose daughter had died young, Dickens expressed the hope that the time would come when the father would be able 'to reflect with a grateful heart that those who yield most promise and are most richly endowed, commonly die young, as though from the first they were the objects of the Almighty's peculiar love and care'. As Steven Marcus has pointed out, this passage 'reveals Dickens' sentimentality as a condition of spirit in which doubt and pain and affirmation co-exist, and in which affirmation is commanded forcefully, willfully, to prevail'.[29] Even Thackeray, who satirised the foibles of early-Victorianism, admired Dickens' depiction of the death of Little Nell. Despite his sceptical temper, he, too, could not avoid the sort of sentimental indulgence inherent in the culture. In *The Newcomes* he used any number of images that have been aptly characterised as 'the stock-in-trade of the sentimentalist', as, for example, in a passage depicting 'strong men, alone on their knees, with streaming eyes and broken accents, [who] implore Heaven for those little ones, who were prattling at their sides but a few hours since'.[30]

The mid-Victorian age suffered from multiple symptoms of romanticism in decline. From a debased romanticism came banality as well as sentimentality; once vital modes of thought and feeling were congealed into standardised phrases and gestures. Spontaneity and vividness of expression gave way to heavy-handed repetition. What had been ineffable became explicit, flat, and routine. Keats' nightingale became Landseer's deer. As Peter Conrad put it, 'The waking dreams of the romantics became the higher feelings of the Victorians.'[31] Whereas in 1808 Turner had been praised for his grasp of 'the mysteries of the arcana of affinities between art and moral sentiment', by the 1840s those connections were neither mysterious nor arcane.[32] Turner's ability to rouse 'the sublimest feelings of our mind' gave way to a spate of paintings that pursued that end in a stolid and heavy-handed fashion, quite lacking in his nuances and subtleties. In every aspect of the culture the expression of noble aspirations came to be expected and required, a conventional component in the apparatus of propriety. High-flown language, removed from a context of genuine passion, became the ornamental rhetoric of public occasions, and sentiment degenerated into sentimentality.

While sentimentality was characteristic of the culture as a whole, like so many other aspects of mid-Victorian England it took on a distinctly bourgeois coloration. For the middle classes the tension between extravagant idealism and the squalor and poverty of the real world was especially acute. One response was ideological, that is, the effort to convince the working classes that they were in fact rather well off and that if they were not, they had only themselves to blame (see chapter 7(2)). Another response involved an attempt to convince themselves that all was right with the world. In this social context, the middle classes indulged in the cultural bent for rationalisation, evasion and self-deception. Ruskin's comments about 'glosses, veils, and decorative lies' apply with special force to the propertied classes, who enjoyed immense privileges denied to the vast majority, whose condition made a mockery of the accepted professions of high aspiration. Sentimentality enabled the middle classes to remain spiritually comfortable in a world that was very much at odds with their wishful thinking and insistent optimism. All too often they used their high aims as a means of idealising the real world, thus hoping — and sometimes pretending — that all was moving in the right direction. Wherever they looked they found what they wanted and hoped for: the nobler emotions, lofty sentiments, and a striving after the good. Their Calvinism long since diluted, they comforted themselves with a cheerful Pelagianism, somewhat nervously maintained in the face of an underlying anxiety and even guilt. In their homes they surrounded themselves with soothing and reassuring objects. They welcomed evidence of goodness, kindness, and sweetness. Although they did not ignore poverty, pain, and death, they insisted that such matters be handled sentimentally, so that the proper feelings could be evoked and then put aside. Sentimentalisation of the dismal side of life served to distance them from reality. and to insulate them from genuine contact with aspects of the world that were at odds with their ideals.

Sentimentality as a mechanism of evasion is most conspicuous in the paintings that were turned out for the middle-class market. Scenes of tranquil domesticity abounded. While the plight of the poor was by no means ignored, it took the form of a sentimentalised social realism, designed to trigger a respectably 'compassionate' response in the viewer. In art as in other areas, however, the middle-class preferred solid affirmation. A case in point is the Royal Academy exhibition of 1863. The reviewer in the *Art Journal* classified one group of paintings under the heading, 'Scenes Domestic — Grave and Gay', and gave them high praise: 'England, happy in her homes, and joyous in her snug firesides, is equally fortunate in a school of Art sacred to the hallowed relations of domestic life'. Another group, 'Subjects Poetic and Imaginative', included Millais' *My First Sermon*, a rather sentimental treatment of childhood that was praised by the Archbishop of Canterbury, who said that he had been touched by 'the playfulness, the innocence, the purity, and may I not add, the piety of childhood'. The innocence of children was a theme that enabled the viewer to make a ready escape from the poverty and squalor of so much of the adult world.[33]

Working-class radicals also had to come to terms with a culture that put such a premium on the expression of noble sentiments and high ideals. Many aspects of radicalism were vulnerable to assimilation to cultural patterns that celebrated aspiration for its own sake. Thus, the romantic utopianism of the age of protest was liable to transformation into the routine celebration of improvement activities ostensibly devoted to the eventual creation of a new society. The old radical language persisted, but it came to be applied to the business of co-operatives, friendly societies, and trade unions in an inegalitarian society. Thus, the career of working-class radicalism has to be understood, in part, as a manifestation of a broader Victorian tendency to make hopefulness and aspiration a means of being comfortable in a world that fell far short of extravagantly high expectations. To a degree, acculturation meant deradicalisation.

But working-class radicalism had a great deal more to contend with than the pitfalls of mid-Victorianism. The consciousness of working men was also conditioned by their situation in a structure of power and status. Their weakness, economic vulnerability, and low status were fundamental conditions of their thought and action. These structural factors were operative quite apart from the ideological activity of the middle classes.

Notes

1. On the mid-Victorian period as a whole, see Asa Briggs, *The Age of Improvement*, London 1959, pp. 394–523, and *Victorian People*, London 1954; W.L. Burn, *The Age of Equipoise*, London 1964; Geoffrey Best, *Mid-Victorian Britain, 1851–1875*, London 1971; G.K. Clark, *The Making of Victorian England* London 1962. See also Asa Briggs, *Victorian Cities*, London 1963; H.J. Dyos and M. Wolff, eds., *The Victorian City*, London 1973; J.F.C. Harrison, *Learning and Living, 1790–1960*, Toronto 1961.
2. Gordon Wright, *France in Modern Times*, pp. 235–40; Hajo Holborn, *A History of Modern Germany 1840–1945*, New York 1969, pp. 116–18.
3. *Working Man*, 7 December 1861, 1 January 1862; *Co-operator*, 15 August 1865.
4. *Working Man*, 9 and 23 August, 19 October 1861.
5. Ibid., 1 January 1862; *Co-operator*, April 1864.
6. The invitation from the society at Darwen is in the Holyoake collection, Bishopsgate Institute; *Leeds Mercury*, 11 April 1864; *Co-operator*, April and June 1864.
7. *Northern Daily Express*, 20 April 1865.
8. Ibid.
9. See Anthony Giddens, *Capitalism and Modern Social Theory: An Analysis of the Writings of Marx, Durkheim, and Max Weber*, Cambridge 1971, pp. 65–118, 185–242; Giddens, ed., *Emile Durkheim: Selected Writings*, Cambridge 1972; Steven Lukes, *Emile Durkheim*, New York 1972; Raymond Aron, *Main Currents in Sociological Thought*, II, Anchor edition, New York 1970, pp. 11–113.
10. Steven Lukes, 'Durkheim's "Individualism and the Intellectuals" ', *Political Studies*, XVII, 1969, 25. Lukes' article includes a translation of Durkheim's essay.
11. Ibid., p. 23; Durkheim, *The Elementary Forms of Religious Life*, New York 1915, p. 427.
12. Durkheim, *The Division of Labor in Society*, New York 1933, p. 172.
13. Durkheim, 'Individualism', loc. cit.
14. See Raymond Williams, *Culture and Society 1780–1950*, New York 1960, pp. 338–47. 'The body of intellectual and imaginative work which each generation receives as its traditional culture is always, and necessarily, something more than the product of a single class', p. 339.
15. Canon Charles Smyth, 'The Evangelical Discipline', in British Broadcasting Corporation, *Ideas and Beliefs of the Victorians*, London 1949, p. 98. Smyth, however, is discussing only the Evangelical Movement in the Church of England.
16. See G.K. Clark, 'The Romantic Element', loc. cit.; Walter E. Houghton, *The Victorian Frame of Mind, 1830–1870*, New Haven 1957, pp. 36, 130–1, 266–70, 287; William A. Madden, 'The Victorian Sensibility', *Victorian Studies*, VII, 1963. For examples of the complex and various influence of romanticism on early Victorian intellectuals, see John Clive, *Macaulay: The Shaping of the Historian*, New York 1973, pp. 135–6; David Newsome, *Godliness and Good Learning*, London 1961, pp. 1–20; A.P. Stanley, *The Life and Correspondence of Thomas Arnold*, London 1844; John Stuart Mill, *Autobiography*, New York 1924, pp. 93–128, and F.R. Leavis ed., *Mill on Bentham and Coleridge*, London 1950.
17. T.S. Eliot, *Christianity and Culture: The Idea of a Christian Society and Notes towards the Definition of Culture*, Harvest Book edition, New York, n.d., p. 93.

18. Graham Hough, *The Romantic Poets*, London 1958, p. 150; Houghton, pp. 263–4.

19. William Clyde DeVane, ed., *Selections from Tennyson*, New York 1940, pp. 167–8. See also G.M. Young, *Victorian England: Portrait of an Age,* London 1953, p. 75; T.S. Eliot, *Selected Essays*, New York 1950, pp. 286–95; Jerome Buckley, *The Victorian Temper*, New York 1964, pp. 66–86.

20. Helene E. Roberts, 'Art Reviewing in the Early Nineteenth-Century Art Periodicals', *Victorian Periodicals Newsletter*, no. 19, 1973; Jeremy Maas, *Victorian Painters*, New York 1969, pp. 104–21, 226–57; Christopher Forbes, *The Royal Academy (1837–1902) Revisited: Victorian Paintings from the Forbes Magazine Collection*, New York 1974; Peter Conrad, *The Victorian Treasure House*, London 1973, p. 56.

21. See John D. Rosenberg, *The Darkening Glass*, New York 1961; Buckley, pp. 143–60; Henry Ladd, *The Victorian Morality of Art: An Analysis of Ruskin's Esthetic*, New York 1932.

22. Ruskin to the Rev. Osborne Gordon, 10 March 1844, in E.T. Cook and Alexander Wedderburn, eds., *The Works of John Ruskin,* London 1903–12, III, 665–7; Ruskin, *Modern Painters*, 3 vols., Boston, n.d., part II, section VI, chapter III; part III, section I, chapter II; part IV, chapter XVII.

23. Ibid., part IV, chapter I.

24. Ibid., part I, section II, chapter III.

25. Ibid., part IV, chapter IV.

26. Houghton, pp. 297–301.

27. Buckley, p. 89.

28. See Humphry House, *All in Due Time*, London 1955, pp. 140–50; Conrad, pp. 35–77; Kathleen Tillotson, *Novels of the Eighteen-Forties*, Oxford 1956, pp. 46–64; Clark, 225–9; Houghton, pp. 273–81; Roberts, p. 18.

29. Steven Marcus, *Dickens: From Pickwick to Dombey,* New York 1965, p. 161.

30. Russell A. Fraser, 'Sentimentality in Thackeray's "The Newcomes"', *Nineteenth Century Fiction*, IV, 1949–50, 187–95.

31. Conrad, p. 76.

32. Roberts, p. 14.

33. Maas, pp. 104–8. See also Forbes, pp. 42–6, 52–4, 70–1, and *passim*.

6 POWER AND STATUS RELATIONS

The cultural patterns that pervaded the mid-Victorian cities presupposed and reflected an underlying structure of power and status that remained substantially unchanged throughout the nineteenth century. Class relations permeated the culture and its values. In this area there is much to be said for the Marxist emphasis on the 'primacy' of the socio-economic base. By the same token, a tendency to minimise the importance of power relations is a weakness in the Parsonian tradition of functionalist sociology. In this instance, as in others, the Victorians themselves are a sound guide. In a characteristically moral idiom John Stuart Mill described realistically how 'the higher classes of this or any other country' are conditioned to behave: 'All privileged and powerful classes, as such, have used their power in the interest of their own selfishness, and have indulged their self-importance in despising, and not in lovingly caring for, those who were, in their estimation, degraded, by being under the necessity of working for their benefit.' Noting the 'intensely selfish feelings engendered by power', he concluded that the evil 'cannot be eradicated, until the power itself is withdrawn'.[1]

Working-class weakness and middle-class power were central facts in every aspect of life in the Victorian cities. That weakness was the product of a number of interacting factors — first and foremost economic dependence on potential employers. That dependence, particularly at a time of endemic cyclical unemployment, was virtually absolute. A weak bargaining position meant that wages usually hovered at the subsistence level. Even the skilled craftsman who commanded a higher wage was vulnerable to dips in the trade cycle. That vulnerability was magnified by the 1834 Poor Law. Moreover, as a result of centuries of economic and social weakness, the working man had acquired a status, sanctioned by custom and tradition, which marked him off as inferior. Inherent in the established structure of power and status relations was the assumption that the working classes were inferior to their superiors, intellectually, morally, and otherwise. That assumption was difficult to dislodge, even for a radical working man proud of himself and his class. He was caught in a social framework that assigned him a social role that presupposed subordination and deference.

(1) *Labour and the Law*
The law provides a good vantage point from which to describe the position of the working classes in the social structure. With unexampled clarity and starkness, the law lays bare the anatomy of power in the mid-

Victorian cities. In the statutes dealing with masters, servants and trade unions, and in cases based on such statutes and on the common law as well, the subordinate position of the working man is precisely defined and elucidated. In such cases the judges tended to make explicit social presuppositions and values usually expressed more euphemistically. They took as their premise the notion that in relations with servants the authority of the master must be supreme. Like the rest of their class, the judges took for granted the impropriety of attempts by working men, whether individually or in combination, to question the decisions of their employers. The result was class law, to which the principle of equal protection was foreign. For the historian it presents an invaluable summary, concrete and coherent, of the framework of status and power within which the working classes were contained; it brings into sharp focus the values and attitudes inherent in the system of social relations.

The master and servant laws, which defined the legal relationship between employers and workmen until 1875, translated into statutory provisions the implications of the traditional status of the working-class.[2] A long series of statutes, beginning with the Statute of Labourers in 1349 and culminating in the Master and Servant Act of 1823, enacted a double standard, designed to favour the master at the expense of the servant. If a workman broke his contract, he had committed a crime and was liable to three months' imprisonment. If the master broke the contract, he might be sued in a civil proceeding. That basic inequity was overlaid with others, implicit in the conception of the servant as a person whose first duty is obedience to the will of his master. The master's role was to command, the servant's to obey. The master and servant laws were intended to preserve this natural and proper relationship by extending to the master every assistance in disciplining and controlling servants who perversely refused to behave in a properly obedient fashion. What mattered was the maintenance of traditional patterns of deference and subordination; the liberal principle of equal protection of the laws was ignored. The evident contradiction between social reality and professed principle, which Tory governments mitigated in 1867 and removed in 1875, underlines the pervasive influence of the underlying structure of power and status.

The statutory lineage of the master and servant laws can be traced to the second section of the Statute of Labourers of 1349, which provided for the imprisonment of a workman or servant who departed from service before the time agreed upon. The principle was reaffirmed in the important statutes of 1746 and 1766, as well as in several minor statutes, prior to its final embodiment in 4 George IV c. 34. The antiquity of the legal principles underlying the Victorian master and servant laws does not mean that we are dealing with a statutory anachronism accidentally perpetuating the harshness of the law of feudal society, for the principles were re-enacted in a series of statutes in the eighteenth century before being fully confirmed once again in 1823. Moreover, the law of 1823 was in several respects more stringent than its Elizabethan and eighteenth-century predecessors. In the Elizabethan Statute of Artificers, for example, the punitive provisions are accompanied by paternalist expressions of concern for the well-being of the labourer. The paternalist tone was still conspicuous in the middle of the eighteenth century when Parliament decided that the Statute of Artificers was in certain respects 'insufficient and defective', and passed an Act facilitating the recovery of wages by making it possible to admit the servant's oath in evidence in such suits. By contrast, in the Acts of 1766 and 1823, all the emphasis was on a tighter regulation of servants. The Statute of 1766, entitled 'An Act for better regulating Apprentices and Persons working under Contract', included a preamble that cited the grievances of the masters, indicating a new attention to the disciplinary function of the law. The maximum sentence for a servant who broke his contract was increased from one month to three. Moreover, the statute introduced the provision that the Victorian artisan was to find so galling: the Justice of the Peace was empowered, on complaint by the employer, to issue a warrant for the summary arrest of the servant complained of.[3]

The Master and Servant Law of 1823 modified the eighteenth-century statutes by strengthening even further the disciplinary powers of the magistrates. While repeating the clause of the 1766 Act referring to any person who 'having entered into such Service shall absent himself or herself from his or her Service before the Term of his or her Contract', the 1823 Act added the words 'whether such Contract shall be in Writing or not in Writing'. It added a new provision, to deal with persons who, having signed a contract, failed to 'enter into or commence his or her Service', and made it a crime for a servant to 'neglect to fulfil' a contract. The law did make one concession to the servant. The servant suing for recovery of wages no longer had to serve a summons on the master himself, but now could serve the master's agent. On the other hand, the master's agent was now entitled to make a complaint of breach of contract to the Justice of the Peace. Thus, legal principles derived from medieval social and economic relations had been sharpened and intensified to serve the needs of employers in a capitalist society.[4]

In a dictum in the case of Spain v. Arnott in 1817, Lord Ellenborough stated bluntly just what the master and servant laws were all about: 'The question really comes to this, whether the master or the servant is to have the superior authority.' In treating this rhetorical question, Lord Ellenborough left no doubt that the purpose of such laws was to maintain the 'superior authority' of the master. The same point was made with equal clarity some years later by a company lawyer testifying before a select committee in 1866. He argued that since the purpose of the master and servant laws was 'the preservation of the necessary subordination and discipline, generally speaking in large works or establishments', it was necessary to retain in the statutes 'a certain punitive element [imprisonment], and of the influence *a priori*, so to speak, of the law, upon the relation of master and servant'.[5]

Leading cases in 1826, 1830, and 1833 reaffirmed the principle that 'the year must be completed before the servant is entitled to be paid'.[6] In the first of these cases Justice Abbott removed any doubt about the generality of the ruling. This meant that if a servant were hired without any agreement as to term, it was assumed that the term was a year. Thus the master found it easy, if he wished, to dismiss a man without any wages. As late as 1858, Lord Ellenborough's dictum was invoked in a case that sustained an employer's action in breaking a one-year contract after only one month on the grounds that the servant was incompetent. ' "The master is not bound to keep him on as a burthensome and useless servant to the end of the year." And it appears to us that there is no material difference between a servant who will not and a servant who cannot, perform the duty for which he was hired.' Behind all these rulings lay the conviction that under no circumstances must the servant be permitted to get the upper hand in his dealings with his master. Justice would be done only after the prior claims of the master were met.

A good example of the disciplinary function of the master and servant acts is the ruling of the Court of Queen's Bench in 1857 in the case of Hawley v. Baker.[7] The defendant, Baker, was a potter who quit his job after giving his employer one month's notice. His employer objected that the notice was insufficient, and on his complaint Baker was committed for a month 'to the treadmill'. On leaving prison, Baker refused to return to work. His employer again brought him before the magistrates, who sent him back to jail for another month. The case was appealed and reached the Court of Queen's Bench, which ruled unanimously against Baker. On appeal to the Court of Exchequer, the decision was reversed, and Baker was freed. The reversal by no means settled the legal issue, however, for in a subsequent case, in which a defendant invoked the ruling of Exchequer in Baker's case, the Court of Queen's Bench stood by its earlier ruling, and held that the defendant was liable to a second imprisonment and to re-imprisonment as often as he refused to return to his work. Clearly, on this view, the law of master and servant was not designed simply to punish offences, but to compel servants to submit to the will of their masters.

In a multitude of cases that never reached the high courts, magistrates interpreted and applied the master and servant laws in much the same way, as instruments for maintaining 'the relation between master and servant'. An appropriate newspaper headline for news of such cases was 'Caution to Workmen'.[8] It was reported that a not infrequent observation for a magistrate to make was: 'I do not sentence you exactly for what you have done, but to make an example for others.' Some masters took an exceedingly broad view of their rights under the law. In 1864 the Justices at Driffield convicted a man for disobeying his employer's orders to attend a place of worship once every Sunday. Although this case was untypical – and the *Solicitors Journal* denounced the decision – it was by no means out of keeping with the exalted view of the authority of the master underlying the law of master and servant. Even when the servant had a good case, he had to preserve a properly deferential attitude. Counsel for a Hunslet nail maker convinced the court that there were insufficient grounds for proceeding against his client, who had been arrested on a warrant issued on the complaint of the employers. In exercising their disciplinary function, however, the magistrates proposed simply to suspend the warrant conditionally, instead of revoking it. When the lawyer made the mistake of intimating that he would appeal against the suspension, his client was sentenced to fourteen days' imprisonment. Such conceptions of the master-servant relationship encouraged a tendency to use the law in what W.P. Roberts, the trade union solicitor, called 'its torturing process'. 'The law is not always applied as a means of punishing. Frequently, the course is pursued which was pursued in this case [the Barnard Castle case], which was this: the master said, "I can send you to prison for three months with hard labour, will you go back to your work?" So it is, as it were, that exemption from punishment is sold to the man. Those men agreed to go back to their work.'[9]

The procedures followed in master and servant cases were also tainted by the tendency to favour one party at the expense of the other. Here too, equal protection of the laws was sacrificed in a situation where the basic purpose of the statutes in question was the maintenance of a relationship of superiority and subordination. A case that occurred in Middlesbrough, Yorkshire, in September 1864, illustrates the unseemly speed that had become standard procedure. On a Thursday, a group of ironworkers went on strike to demand the dismissal of an objectionable foreman. On Saturday they were hailed before the magistrates and charged with leaving their work without notice. When their lawyer arrived on Monday to defend them, he found that judgement had already been given against them on Saturday, and that only the sentencing remained. This was the usual practice. Being under sentence was an inducement to the men to abandon their strike and return to work. When the strikers' lawyer, W.P. Roberts, complained that the men had had no time to make a defence, the mayor, from the bench, said that his remarks on that subject 'were in bad taste and out of place'.[10] The reference to 'bad taste' was the usual indication that the bourgeois sense of social propriety had been offended.

The Middlesbrough case is revealing, because it involved employers and employees who were on the best of terms. The dispute was settled when the offending foreman resigned. Apparently, the employers had been unaware of his behaviour, which they would never have condoned. The strikers, even after their shabby treatment by the magistrates, spoke highly of their employers. Thus, the procedure followed in this case cannot be attributed to the bitterness of a long strike, but to the routine application of the master and servant law. The strikers were not being victimised because of the anger of their masters; they were being treated in the customary way.

Because breach of contract by a servant was a crime, the accused working man felt the full rigour of criminal procedure designed to protect society against felons. When an employer complained that his servant had broken his contract, the statute of 1823 empowered the Justice of the Peace to 'issue his Warrant for the apprehending every such Servant'. Under a procedure that was mandatory until 1848, and permissive until 1867, the accused working man was often treated like a common criminal: arrested, handcuffed, and jailed pending a hearing. Often he was not even told what he was accused of. 'The warrant is not left with him, he is merely told, "Come along and you'll know when you get into court"; that is the common phrase.' In the Barnard Castle case, half a dozen men were taken out of their beds and put into a cell three miles away. The next day they were given the usual choice between returning to work or being sentenced. Thus, a man might be 'fetched out of bed between four and five o'clock in the morning, and tried and convicted by twelve o'clock the same day, before his friends knew where he had gone to'.[11] Although cases of this sort were infrequent, they illustrate the position of a working man in a system designed to maintain the superior authority of the master.

Being a working man meant being subject to laws that were not only drafted in the interest of the master class, but also interpreted and applied by members of that class. Sheffield working men found little to choose between the borough magistrates 'more or less connected with trade' and county magistrates 'more or less intimate with the borough magistrates'. W.P. Roberts complained that 'in nine cases out of ten, the employer and the justices live within two or three miles of each other, and in a vast number of cases in the north, the magistrates are every one of them directly interested in the matter'. From the Petty Sessions to the High Court, judges interpreted the law in terms of the social values and presuppositions of the propertied classes. With the best will in the world, it was difficult for magistrates to overcome a normal class sympathy with the prosecuting employer. Roberts described this as 'a natural rather than an unfair sympathy. They see the masters in an elevated position; they see the workmen in a degraded position; and human nature is human nature'.[12] The accused working man was not likely to be a victim of sheer callousness or insensitiveness to the claims of justice. He was up against a socially determined sense of propriety that necessarily led justices to see the case from the point of view of the employer.

The master and servant laws were a temptation to unscrupulous employers, and abuses inevitably occurred. A few examples need to be mentioned, not in order to imply that such practices were widespread, but in order to illustrate the sort of thing that was permitted by a legal system that reflected so directly the interests of the employing classes. During a strike in Liverpool a group of employers brought in sixteen men from North Staffordshire, without telling them that they were to be used as strike breakers. When the men arrived in Liverpool and heard about the strike, they refused to work. They were arrested under the Master and Servant Act and imprisoned for eighteen hours before the case was dismissed, on the grounds that the employers had neglected to sign the contract. A trade union leader cited a Staffordshire case in which a potter was imprisoned for two weeks for neglect of work, despite the fact that he had a doctor's certificate stating that he was too ill to work. Even when the master knew he had no case he could victimise a workman by abusing the law. According to testimony presented in 1866, a Wolverhampton employer induced a Sheffield workman to go to Wolverhampton by promising steady employment at higher wages. When the promised employment did not materialise, the workman left and returned to Sheffield. On complaint by the employer, the police brought the man back to Wolverhampton for trial. The magistrates dismissed the case, but the man was left stranded without funds. He had no redress.[13]

In testimony before a select committee in 1866, George Odger emphasised the threat posed by the master and servant laws to skilled craftsmen proud of 'their position in life'. Such a man was likely to be 'terrified with the thought that his employer would feel disposed to have him before a magistrate for this breach of contract, and this would be prejudicial to the man's position in society, as well as calculated to embarrass his home and family'. According to W.P. Roberts, the law was constantly used by masters 'as a taunt, and a very horrible one; "I will send you to prison for three months", and it is most painful to hear it, especially when one knows that the man who uses the threat is an acquaintance of the magistrate before whom the case will be brought'.[14]

Even when the judiciary interpreted a contract even-handedly, the controlling factor remained the vast disparity in power between the two contracting parties to begin with. The 'servant' in search of work was in no position to haggle over terms. When asked to sign an agreement that required him to give six months' notice, while the employer was required to give only one month's notice, he had little choice but to sign. A trade unionist's description of the manner in which a contract was entered into depicts the social and economic reality: 'A man goes into a shop, he is very much reduced in circumstances, he knows not what to do, he immediately enters into a written agreement, or partly printed and partly written, and filled up at the moment, or a general agreement is hung upon the wall of the workshop, which he does not stop to enquire into. He knows nothing of its purport till he is told that he has broken it, and finds a police officer at his heels.'[15] From the moment that he enquired about terms of service to the time that the terms of the contract come to be enforced, the workman found that law and custom tended to maintain the authority of the master.

In addition to the master and servant laws, which applied to all working men, the law severely restricted the activities of those men who joined trade unions. In this case also the same principle applied: the function of the law was to maintain the superior authority of the master. Trade unions had to be curbed, because they threatened to upset the traditional relationship, in which the master, bargaining individually with workmen, held all the high cards. Underlying the statutes, the common law, and judicial dicta was a strong sense of the impropriety of any trade union action that promised to be effective. To be sure, after 1824 trade unions ceased to be illegal by statute, but the range of permissible activity was narrowly circumscribed, and at common law they remained under a cloud. Both trade union law and its interpretation reflected the status of working men in Victorian society.[16]

The basic statute governing trade unions in mid-Victorian England was the Combination Act of 1825.[17] Its primary purpose was restrictive, in that it was passed to correct the permissiveness of the Act of 1824, which had repealed previous statutes prohibiting combinations. Parliament's decision to stiffen the restrictions on the newly legalised trade unions was indicated in the preamble to the Act of 1825 which complained of the ineffectiveness of certain provisions in the Act of 1824 'for protecting the free Employment of Capital and Labour, and for punishing Combinations interfering with such Freedom, by means of Violence, Threats, or Intimidation'. It noted that 'such Combinations are injurious to Trade and Commerce, dangerous to the Tranquility of the Country, and especially prejudicial to the Interest of all who are concerned in them'. In this spirit was enacted Section 3, which made it a criminal offence to use molestation, obstruction, intimidation, threats or violence to force workers to strike or force employers to make any change in the mode of conducting their business. Section 4 exempted from punishment under the Act persons who met together to agree on the wages they would demand for their work or the hours for which they would work. On the basis of Section 4, the courts ruled that it was not illegal for workmen to strike for better wages and hours. Thus workmen might combine together to agree on the wages and hours that they would demand, and they might stop work if the employer refused their demands. Interpretations of Section 3, however, made it virtually impossible to conduct such a strike effectively without coming into conflict with the statute.

Section 3 of the Combination Act of 1825 set forth a long list of vaguely defined offences that a trade unionist might commit against other workmen or against employers. Up to three months' imprisonment was provided for any person who 'shall by violence . . . or by threats or intimidation, or by molesting or in any way obstructing another, force or endeavour to force' any workman to depart from his work before it is finished. In the corresponding section of the Act of 1824, the specified actions were indictable only if they were done 'wilfully or maliciously'. The omission of these words made convictions much easier and Section 3 narrowed the range of the permissible trade union activity in the course of a strike. In addition, the use of Section 3 in connection with the common law of conspiracy further reinforced the inhibiting effect of the statute. A trade unionist might be indicted not only for committing one of the offences specified in the Act, but also for conspiring to commit one of those offences. Conspiracy to commit an illegal act was a common law misdemeanour, punishable at the discretion of the court. Hence, a conviction for conspiracy might result in a sentence that exceeded the three months' maximum provided for a violation of the Act itself. Trade unions were particularly vulnerable to prosecution for conspiracy to commit the various illegal acts specified in Section 3. Moreover, whereas an action done by one individual might not be deemed to be 'molestation', for example, the same action done in combination would appear in a different light, and be indictable. In the leading case of R.v. Duffield, Mr Justice Erle ruled that persuading workmen to go on strike would constitute a conspiracy to commit the 'molestation' forbidden by Section 3: 'I take it for granted that if a manufacturer has a manufactory . . . [and] if persons conspire together to take away all his workmen, that would necessarily be an obstruction to him that would necessarily be a molesting of him in his manufactory.' Like Erle, the law took a great deal for granted in its perception of proper relations between employers and workmen.[18]

The common law also displayed considerable hostility to trade union activity. At common law trade unions were conspiracies in restraint of trade, and therefore unlawful, although not criminal, and their agreements could not be enforced in the courts. When the Court of Queen's Bench so ruled in 1867 in Hornby v. Close, the ruling came as a surprise, since it had been widely assumed that the Combination Act of 1825 had legalised trade unions, and since trade unions had not been prosecuted as conspiracies in restraint of trade. In fact, however, one of the purposes of the Act of 1825 had been to repeal the sweeping exemption from common law prosecution that had been enacted the previous year. In the event, trade unions were not so prosecuted, because it was more convenient to proceed under Section 3 of the Act. Yet the taint of common law illegality remained and — together with long-standing social prejudices — coloured judicial interpretations of the statute. To be sure, judges differed in their conclusions, but lack of legal precision did not impair the inhibiting effect of the common law. The point was that the law, reflecting the interests and values of the employers, was unfriendly. Hence trade unions operated at their peril. In addition, they were also liable to prosecution under the common law for conspiracy to 'injure'. And their vulnerability was compounded by the readiness of judges to take social norms as the premises of legal interpretations. In 1861 Mr Justice Hill explained why the announcement by a group of workmen that they were planning to quit work unless their demands were met, constituted a conspiracy to injure their employer. While conceding their right to make such an announcement as individuals, he added; 'If, however, they act in combination, not honestly or independently, but by way of conspiracy in order to coerce their employer . . . that combination is illegal.'[19] The judge's casual assumption that working men in combination were *ipso facto* not acting 'honestly or independently' illustrates the tendency to regard as grossly improper any working-class effort to depart from traditional standards of subservience.

The law of employer liability also reflected the inferior status of the working classes. The working man who was injured in the course of his employment had virtually no remedy under the law, for the cards were stacked in favour of the employer. If a working man was injured in an industrial accident, he could claim compensation from his employer only if he could prove negligence, and only if he himself had not been negligent. The application of these common law rules had worked no great hardship in a pre-industrial society, but they left working men vulnerable to the effects of dangerous machinery created by the Industrial Revolution. If, for example, a workman were injured as a result of a fall caused by defective tackle, he had no remedy. He could not sue the contractor who had sold the tackle to the employer, because the contractor was a stranger to the contract; and he could not sue his employer, because the latter had not been negligent. In any case, the burden of strict proof of negligence had to be borne by the working man. This not only resulted in verdicts in favour of masters, but also tended to discourage injured workmen from bringing suits in the first place.[20]

Even if the plaintiff was able to prove negligence on the part of the employer, he could not collect damages if his own negligence had contributed in any way to the accident. Even if the employer's negligence had been much greater than his own, the injured workman could not collect damages. The interpretation of this rule in 1837 in Priestley v. Fowler worked an even greater hardship on the injured man. The court ruled that if a workman was aware of the danger caused by the negligence of his master, and nevertheless continued the work, his knowledge constituted contributory negligence and thus prevented the collection of damages. The ruling was subsequently applied in a Liverpool case, where a labourer had been hired to fill sugar moulds and hoist them up to higher floors in a warehouse by means of machinery. At first a safe method was used; then the employer economised, and adopted an inferior method. When the labourer used the new system, the mould fell on his head and killed him. Because the labourer had realised the danger involved, his wife was unable to collect any damages. In another case, a widow lost three sons when the rope carrying their cart down the mine shaft broke. She was unable to collect damages, because the men had been warned by a fellow employee that they ought to test the rope before descending. They had shown negligence in not testing the rope. The employer who had permitted the defective rope to be used did not have to pay a farthing in damages.[21]

Insensitivity to the rights of the workman appeared in another rule of employer liability law, namely that which prevented the employee from claiming damages from his employer for an injury caused by negligence of a fellow-workman. The inequity of this rule lay in the fact that it denied the workman a remedy that was available to someone not employed by the firm. If a stranger suffered an injury as the result of the negligence of an employee, he might sue the employer for damages. Under the ruling in Hutchinson v. York in 1850, however, an employee was denied this right. The judges held that a servant takes a job with a knowledge of the risks involved, including risks arising from negligence of fellow-servants.[22]

(2) *Poor Relief*

The working man who had the misfortune to lose his job experienced working-class weakness and vulnerability at its most extreme. With good reason it has been suggested that 'fear of the sack' was a major component in the working-class consciousness. At any moment, the working man might be 'launched into the abyss of pauperism, from whence . . . but few return'.[23] Here also the law defines the situation with precision. Under the 1834 Poor Law the unemployed working man, while not denied relief, was to be given it in such a way as to remind him of the stigma that he had incurred and to dissuade him from further transgressions in the future. As in the case of the master and servant laws, this legislation incorporated the social attitudes and prejudices of the propertied classes. The basic idea was that the working man who found himself out of work had thereby demonstrated his moral inadequacy. That attitude, sanctioned by the majesty of the law, and embodied in the administration of the Act enveloped not only 'the poor' but the working-class as a whole. The 1834 Poor Law constituted an official definition of the unique working-class potential for social immorality. It was difficult for working men to escape the the reach, either in theory or in practice, of that officially proclaimed conception of 'the poor'.

Middle-class power confronted working-class weakness most directly in the area of poor relief. Every working man, even the most skilled, was in a financially precarious situation; in the face of prolonged unemployment, he could expect only limited assistance from his friendly society. Hence the possibility of having to apply for poor relief was a very real one. In dealing with unemployed working men the middle classes exercised the vast authority conferred by the 1834 Poor Law. Local administration of the poor law exemplified that characteristic mid-Victorian tendency to blend a more benevolent rhetoric with unchanging social relations and attitudes. On the one hand, the spirit of 1834 had receded: the law was not conceived primarily as an instrument for coercing indolent and depraved working men into properly industrious behaviour. Almost from the very beginning the good sense of local men had prevailed against the doctrinaire rigidity of Somerset House, and neither the mandatory workhouse test nor the prohibition of outdoor relief was enforced. Many guardians even provided outdoor relief to supplement inadequate wages, despite the law. Yet they retained the authority to 'offer the house'. They would decide how much relief to offer, to whom, and under what conditions.[24]

After the official abandonment of the prohibition on outdoor relief, many local boards of guardians continued to urge a more lenient and humane policy. In 1853, for example, local boards requested a modification of the order governing the administration of outdoor relief in the manufacturing districts. A series of memorials from local guardians called for a recognition of special conditions created by cyclical fluctuations. Two articles were singled out for criticism:

Article 5, prohibiting payments to supplement wages, and Article 6, which provided that able-bodied males receiving outdoor relief 'shall be set to work by the guardians'. The Leeds guardians argued that the restriction in Article 5 'is unnecessarily stringent and severe upon the industrious poor, . . . that its operation will be felt to be extremely harsh in those manufacturing communities where, from the sudden vicissitudes of trade, men with families are suddenly reduced from full work to very, very short time'. The Oldham guardians complained that Article 5 was 'both unjustly and unnecessarily stringent and severe upon the industrious poor'. Bolton requested an exemption from its provisions. The Bradford guardians wanted the discretionary authority to exempt industrious working men from both Articles 5 and 6. They objected to forcing a person to 'leave his work and submit to a kind of labour as a test of destitution, for which he is unfitted by his previous habits'. They were afraid that such a working man might be 'brought into association with persons whose moral conduct is contaminating'.[25]

As the comment from the Bradford guardians suggests, however, there was no intention of surrendering the broad powers conferred by the law. Those powers would be used discriminatingly so as to reward the deserving poor while punishing those 'whose moral conduct is contaminating'. In distinguishing between the deserving and undeserving the poor law was a perfect instrument for sustaining the cult of respectability. Working men who had demonstrated their 'respectability' to the satisfaction of their superiors would be honoured and praised in good times and provided with the help that they deserved when they fell on bad times. For working men who carried their independence too far and appeared recalcitrant, the guardians were still empowered to 'offer the house' as a precondition of relief.

Leeds illustrates the inherent severity of the poor law, even when administered humanely by the standards of the day. According to the testimony of Alfred Moore, the relieving officer, Leeds was proud of the generosity with which the law was administered there: 'If there is any outcry about a poor person being stringently dealt with, the rate payers are rather in favour of an increase in the relief than of diminishing.' Confident that no parish was more 'liberal' than Leeds, he proceeded to describe what constituted a generous policy. When asked what he would do with an able-bodied man and his wife, with four children, he replied, 'He will appear before the Board, and they will make an order to put him to test-work, and he has to be paid half in money and half in kind.' At the end of the week, the pauper would receive seven shillings, half of it in money. 'To maintain six of them?' he was asked. Moore replied in the affirmative, and pointed out that the hours were limited: the pauper worked only from eight until four.

He also expressed the opinion that 'great good' had come of the use of the labour test since the order of 1852. According to Moore, the great virtue of the labour test — along with the possibility of invoking the workhouse test — was that it served 'to prevent imposture', provided that the relieving officers were vigilant in the performance of their duty. Another device for guarding against 'imposture' was the requirement that the applicant provide detailed information, whereupon a representative of the guardians would 'go and visit the case, to see if every part of the statement is strictly correct'.[26]

In Leicester, the poor law was administered in a manner that remained quite close to the spirit of 1834. The clerk of the board of guardians engaged in an illuminating colloquy with a member of a select committee who shared his views: 'Is there not a feeling of self-respect growing up amongst the working people that it is disgraceful to apply to the parish for relief, and that they ought to maintain themselves? — Yes, except in the case of those who are hereditary paupers. — Those represent the depraved set of people who have grown up under the demoralising system which existed in former times? — Yes.' The clerk replied in an unqualified affirmative to a question that embodied the original Chadwickian view of the law: 'Therefore the stringency of the administration of the poor law does tend to promote the moral elevation of the working people by causing them to try to improve their condition?'[27] The law was responsible for persuading working men to subscribe to friendly societies in order to avoid being subjected to the workhouse test, which continued in Leicester after it had been abandoned elsewhere.

Both in Leicester and in Leeds the guardians tried to deal more favourably with working men who had proved that they were deserving by their membership of a friendly society. In Leeds the relieving officer described the policy in characteristically positive terms: 'If there is not sufficient coming in from the sick fund, then of course, relief is given; and these men are perhaps more liberally dealt with than the others would be in consequence of their provident habits.' The clerk of the Leicester board of guardians justified such supplementary payments to friendly society members on the more pragmatic grounds that if the man did not belong to a club then he would have to be supported exclusively by the parish. But the same policy was in effect: 'We enquire of the parties what they are receiving from the club; where a man is applying through illness, having a very large family, and it is manifest that whatever he is getting from the club is insufficient for their support, we then give them additional relief.'[28] The guardian would decide how much a 'pauper' needed and deserved.

Perhaps the most ironic feature fo the Poor Law Amendment Act of 1834 was the perpetuation of the main features of the old law of

settlement and removal, in violation of one of the central principles of
1834 – the encouragement of mobility in the labour market. Until
1846 a parish was obligated to relieve only those paupers who were
'settled' in the parish. For all practical purposes a settlement could be
acquired only by birth or apprenticeship. Persons who applied for relief
in a parish where they did not have a 'settlement' could be 'removed' to
their original parish. After 1846 the 'settlement' could be acquired by
five years' residence. Despite this relaxation of the law, the threat of
'removal' remained for a considerable proportion of English working
men. The early-Victorian period had been characterised by a great deal
of internal migration. In sixty-two towns in England and Wales in 1851,
immigrants made up two million out of three and a half million
inhabitants. This meant that a large number of working men were
vulnerable to removal. Even after the relaxation of the law in 1846, a
large number of removals took place. In 1849 over 40,000 persons were
affected by the 13,387 removal orders issued in that year. Thus the
threat of removal was yet another weapon in the middle-class
arsenal.[29]

Local authorities enforced the law of removal with some rigour.
The relieving officer in Leeds, while rejecting the whole principle of
settlement, did not permit his objections to the law to interfere with
its execution. He mentioned a case in which a man lived in Leeds for
a long period of time, thus acquiring a settlement under the Act of
1846 and subsequent Acts, but who left Leeds to find employment in
another town when work was slack. This broke his Leeds residence. In
the event that he returned to Leeds and became a pauper in three years,
he would be subject to removal. In reply to questions from the select
committee, the relieving officer made it plain that he would make an
exception only in the case of the aged: 'If he was in the vigour of life,
or the head of a family, would you remove him? – Yes, certainly . . .
Suppose he happened to have been living in Leeds for four years and a
half, and had gone away as I have supposed, and then returned to Leeds,
and then became a pauper, would you remove him and his family? –
Yes, if the magistrate granted the order. – You would get rid of him
in any way you could? – I do not say that – But by process of law? –
Yes, it is the law which gives us the power.'[30] This was only one of a
number of powers that the poor law gave to the middle classes.

Even skilled artisans, in the years of mid-Victorian prosperity, were
vulnerable to economic fluctuations. Statistics available for one group
of labour aristocrats, the iron moulders, show that joblessness was an
omnipresent threat. From 1853 to 1875 there were only five years
of 'full employment', when fewer than 5 per cent of the Iron Moulders
Society were idle. There were eleven years when unemployment rose
over 10 per cent, and in three of these years it approached 20 per cent.

When unemployment struck, even these labour aristocrats, backed by a strong trade society, felt the lash of the poor law. It made no difference that the iron moulder in receipt of 'tramping benefit' was practising the sort of labour mobility that Chadwick had originally hoped to encourage. For the local middle classes, he was just another pauper. In 1848 a meeting of the Warwickshire branches of the society complained that travellers 'are confined to the Tramps' room like beasts to their dens . . . and by the inhabitants of the towns through which they pass, they are stigmatised with the utmost ridicule and contempt . . . many when they return home . . . are arrested by the parish authorities, and by them destined to the treadmill for two or three months, for what is termed "neglect of family", who have been compelled to ask for relief'.[31] Even if this was an exceptional case, it was well within the framework of poor law policy.

The skilled craftsmen of the Sheffield metal trades were all too well aware of the limits of mid-Victorian prosperity. Three mild trade depressions strained existing relief resources, and soup kitchens, supported by public subscription, were set up in the poorer sections of the city. The Duke of Norfolk provided some relief employment on his own initiative. At the same time, trade unions and friendly societies made 'prodigious efforts' to keep their members out of the workhouse and to save them from having to apply for poor relief. Hence, as Pollard has pointed out, even by the end of the century 'unemployment had lost little of its terror'.[32]

Even a working man in possession of a job was liable to incur the stigma of pauperism if he could not afford to pay for the medical care required by a member of his family and was forced to apply for medical relief under the poor law. According to the poor law board, 'the receipt of medical relief constitutes a pauper, be it in what form it may, whether it be medical relief, or relief in food or money, or in any other form'. In principle, the medical relief system was humane: in time of sickness, no one should lack the necessary medical care, medicine, and food. In the context of the Victorian poor law, however, a man who applied for medical relief for his sick child had to accept the degrading status of pauper in order to receive it. As a result, many working men preferred to rely on the medical care provided by their benefit society, despite the fact that they would be treated by a doctor whose pay was likely to be 'very inferior in amount' to that received by the medical officers of the poor law unions. If the working man sought out the poor law doctor for his child, he might be classified as 'dissolute' or worse. At least, that was the attitude expressed by the Treasurer of Salford in testimony before a select committee on the franchise in 1862. The committee was trying to find out the rental level to which the borough franchise might 'safely' be reduced without enfranchising undesirables. In search of an objective criterion, a member of the committee asked the Treasurer what proportion of persons renting houses between 2s 9d and 3s per week would be in receipt of medical relief when they were ill. His reply took note of the assumptions underlying the question: 'I believe there are a considerable number of dissolute persons who pay this rent; and of course out of the ten thousand persons who would be brought into the franchise as a new element, there must be many disorderly persons, and those would be the parties of course to avail themselves of relief from charitable persons.'[33] In sum, the working man who had to apply for medical relief would 'of course' be dissolute or disorderly.

The structural relations reflected in the law affected both attitudes and behaviour in the mid-Victorian cities. On this foundation rested the hegemony that the middle-class exercised over the working classes.

Notes

1.   John Stuart Mill, *Principles of Political Economy*, London 1892, p. 456. See also Anthony Giddens, ' "Power" in the Recent Writings of Talcott Parsons', *Sociology*, II, 1968; Ralf Dahrendorf, *Class and Class Conflict in Industrial Society*, Stanford 1959, pp. 157–65; David Lockwood, 'Some Remarks on "The Social System"', *British Journal of Sociology*, VII, 1956; Tom Bottomore, 'Out of This World', *New York Review*, 6 November 1969.
2.   See Daphne Simon, 'Master and Servant', in John Saville, ed., *Democracy and the Labour Movement*, London 1954, pp. 160–200; A.S. Diamond, *The Law of Master and Servant*, 2nd edition, London 1946; Charles M. Smith, *A Treatise on the Law of Master and Servant*, London 1852; O. Kahn-Freund, 'Legal Framework', in Allan Flanders and H.A. Clegg, eds., *The System of Industrial Relations in Great Britain*, Oxford 1954, pp. 42–7.
3.   5 Eliz. c. 4; 20 Geo. II c. 19; 6 Geo. III c. 25.
4.   4 Geo. IV c. 34.
5.   2 Stark. 256–258; *Report from the Select Committee on Master and Servant*, 1866, Q. 2311.
6.   Harmer v. Cornelius, English Reports, vol. CXLI, Common Pleas XIX, 94; see also Huttman v. Boulnois, 2 Car. & P. 511.
7.   *Report on Master and Servant*, Q. 1374–97, 1667–9.
8.   *Leeds Mercury*, 23 August 1864.
9.   *Report on Master and Servant*, Q. 2220; and 1665 Leeds Mercury, 15 September and 21 April 1864.
10. Ibid., 27 and 28 September 1864.
11. *Report on Master and Servant*, Q. 1665, 797–830.
12. Ibid., Q. 1866, 1683.
13. Ibid., Q. 1069, 1383.
14. Ibid., Q. 1813, 2220.
15. Ibid., Q. 1178–9.
16. R.Y. Hedges and Allan Winterbottom, *The Legal History of Trade Unionism*, London 1930.
17. 6.Geo. IV, c. 129. See Hedges and Winterbottom, pp. 19–51.
18. 5 Cox 431.

19. Walsby v. Anley, 3 El. and El. 516. See also Hedges and Winterbottom, pp. 13–17, 42–5; David Harrison, *Conspiracy as a Crime and as a Tort in English Law*, London 1924, pp. 114–48.

20. Vernon Lushington, 'On the Liability of Master to Servant in Cases of Accident', National Association for the Promotion of Social Science, *Transactions*, London 1862, p. 190.

21. Ibid., p. 193.

22. Ibid., pp. 194–5.

23. *Parliamentary Papers*, 1852, LXXXIV, 104.

24. M.E. Rose, 'Poor Law Administration in the West Riding of Yorkshire, 1820–1855', Oxford D. Phil., 1965, shows the continuity of local policy before and after 1834. See also Rose's article, 'The Allowance System under the New Poor Law', *Economic History Review*, 2nd ser., XIX, 1966, and 'The New Poor Law in an Industrial Area', in R. Hartwell, ed., *The Industrial Revolution*, New York 1970.

25. *Parliamentary Papers*, 1852, LXXXXIV, 84, 123, 162. See also Public Record Office, MH 12/9098, for Newcastle-on-Tyne, and 12/6178 on Rochdale.

26. *Report on the Select Committee on Irremovable Poor*, 1860, Q. 2402–96.

27. Ibid., Q. 1915–2134; *Victoria County History of Leicestershire*, IV, 257–307; P.R.O, MH 12/6476, Leicester Guardians to Poor Law Board, 3 March 1852, defends the discipline of the workhouse as 'more irksome to the able-bodied and consequently a greater check upon pauperism'.

28. *Report on Irremovable Poor*, Q. 2133. In Basford Union a stonecutter in receipt of 16s for a family of seven, applied for an additional sum for his wife and was given 2s 6d, with the comment: 'This man is considered a very steady person.' Application and Report Book, Basford Union, 1850, Nottingham County Record Office.

29. George Nicholls, *History of the English Poor Law*, London 1898, p. 435; Arthur Redford, *Labour Migration in England, 1800–1850*, London 1926, pp. 54–8.

30. *Report on Irremovable Poor*, Q. 2585–90.

31. H.J. Fyrth and H. Collins, *The Foundry Workers*, Manchester 1959, p. 54.

32. Sidney Pollard, *A History of Labour in Sheffield*, Liverpool 1959, pp. 39–40, 72, 110–12.

33. Select Committee on the Poor Law, *Second Report*, 1862, Q. 3863. Select Committee on the Franchise, *Report*, 1860, Q. 3047.

7 MIDDLE-CLASS HEGEMONY

The middle classes dominated the Victorian city and left their mark on every aspect of its common life.[1] They confront us with two faces, each reflecting their unrivalled ascendancy. On the one hand, they were earnest and articulate spokesmen for the highest values of the community, especially the ideal of improvement for all. As such they were exemplars of a culture that esteemed the public pursuit of moral ideals. They preached the gospel of improvement and prized good works done in that cause. On the other hand, merchants, manufacturers, and professional men also constituted a ruling class, exercising dominion over the wage earners below them. Their social values and their behaviour reflected the imperatives inherent in their position in the class structure. Implicit in their articulation of formally universal consensus values were social presuppositions that bent them into the shape required by an inegalitarian society; differential social roles assumed middle-class pre-eminence. They also engaged in overtly ideological activity — explicitly directed to the defence of their privileged position against the working-class challenge.

In this social and cultural setting the middle classes established a moral and intellectual hegemony. They secured a substantial degree of popular acquiescence in their conception of consensus values and class relations, not by imposing an ideology through propaganda, but by putting to good use the various advantages accruing to the dominant class in this culture. A number of interlocking elements legitimised middle-class pre-eminence and eroded working-class radical ideology. First of all, merely by playing the idealised social role of leaders in the common enterprise of improvement, merchants and manufacturers were justifying their implicit claim to continued superiority. Secondly, as community spokesmen acclaiming the progress that was being made towards shared goals, they were confirming the legitimacy of underlying social and economic arrangements. They most effectively consolidated their hegemony when they were not engaged in defensive propaganda directed against working-class radicalism. Third, the structure of power and status ensured that the middle-class version of consensus values would be embedded in the cultural pattern of the mid-Victorian cities. The end product of the moral and intellectual improvement of the working classes would be the 'respectable working man': educated well enough to understand the reasoned arguments of his social superiors, to respect their accomplishments, and to strive to get on in the world within the limits set from above. While the habitual deference that the villager accorded to the squire was officially banished from the manufacturing towns, new forms of subordination emerged, ostensibly based on the reasoned acceptance of demonstrably valid ideas and policies. Finally, middle-class hegemony was sustained by intertwined social and institutional forms that moulded working-class behaviour to the contours of the class structure.

In France and Germany also the middle-class exercised hegemony over the working-class, but in a different form. The pre-1848 liberals consciously turned away from their earlier idealism and took up a more 'realistic' and conservative position. In France the transition from 'romantic utopianism to a tougher minded mood' is exemplified by the career of Emile Ollivier, who jettisoned the advanced republicanism that he had espoused in the 1840s. His biographer has described Ollivier's determination to reject 'sentimentality and the whole romantic approach' so as to base his conduct on a rational and scientific assessment of social reality. Thus, Ollivier came to prefer what he called 'a feeling for realities' rather than the approach of the 'theorising egoist'. In Germany a major segment of the liberal movement formally abandoned *vormärzlich* idealism in favour of a position that exalted the middle-class and demanded its dominance in the state. Men like August von Rochau, for example, defined liberalism simply in terms of the triumph of the middle-class. An activist radical in his youth who spent ten years in exile before 1848, von Rochau took a very different line in 1853 in a book that popularised the term *Realpolitik*. His liberalism rested on a realistic acceptance of the primacy of social forces. On that basis he argued that the state must represent the class of 'wealth, opinion, and intelligence'. When working men applied for membership in the *National Verein* in 1863, they were turned away.[2] In England the National Reform Union was welcoming them. While the English middle classes were in fact no less tough-minded than their European counterparts, their realism was sheathed in velvet.

The pursuit of profit was the primary concern of mid-Victorian businessmen and they did not permit ancillary interests to interfere. It could be said of most of them, as it was of Richard Smith, a Nottingham manufacturer, that 'his ruling passion through life was a desire to gain wealth'.[3] The pious Methodist who was confiding to his journal a description of his recently deceased friend and employer hastened to qualify this judgement somewhat: 'Or more properly it was the passion which would have ruled on every occasion and with absolute power had not religion kept a check upon it and moderated its operation.' But religion had no easy task of it: 'He was really fond of making money, and this led him sometimes to deviate slightly from what I considered the path of perfect honour.' Smith made plain to his employee just where he stood on the matter of money. ' "Money is not my object", I said to him one day when he increased my salary, and I shall never forget how emphatically he replied, "Then it ought to be, George — it *ought* to be." ' When he parted with his money Smith expected something in exchange: 'As a Methodist, he was useful in various offices, and always liberal in his givings. His liberality was surprising to anyone who knew his fondness for money. But he invariably tried to keep a leading position in the Church, and as he could not accomplish it otherwise, he did it by giving his cash.' Smith's life was centred on his business: 'He was exceedingly industrious, and never seemed contented unless hard at work.' Six working men served as pallbearers at his funeral.

Like Smith the Victorian middle classes conducted their affairs with mixed motives and values, combined in varying proportions. Without neglecting their profits or reducing their privileges, they also responded, however sporadically and fitfully, to the imperatives of their culture. The disparate claims of class and culture introduced a deep ambivalence into their relations with the working classes. While paying their employees the lowest wages and exercising the maximum authority, they hoped for harmony, cordiality and even affection. They made the most of the hegemonic possibilities inherent in the social and cultural patterns of the mid-Victorian cities.

(1) *The Gospel of Improvement*

As the high priests of mid-Victorian culture middle-class leaders preached the gospel of improvement. In countless secular sermons they affirmed the overriding ideal of the community — the pursuit of progress and advancement for all. They presided over the ritual and litany of the established forms of public worship. In this milieu the middle-class defined its social role in terms of the shared ideals of a culture that prized high aspiration. Members of the middle-class proudly assumed leadership in the enterprise of improvement, extending a helping hand to those less fortunate, who had further to go in the quest for the highest qualities of mind and spirit. In this spirit they took on the mission of elevating the working classes, not to keep them in their place, but to fulfil the highest aims of mid-Victorian society. Their hegemony rested on the pride they could take in thus acting in behalf of high principle.

Edward Baines, Jr. was second to none as a preacher of the gospel of improvement. As editor of the *Leeds Mercury* and as the head of the Yorkshire Union of Mechanics' Institutes, he was an eloquent spokesman for nonconformist liberalism in the West Riding. One of the talks that Baines was in the habit of giving on his visit to mechanics' institutes was entitled 'On the Advantages and Pleasure of Institutions for the Promotion of Mental Improvement, and on the Spirit of the Student'.[4] In the text of this secular sermon, written out and revised in his own hand, Baines touched on the main themes of the culture. He opened his remarks with a standard reference to the presence of men from all classes in the institutes: 'There are few spectacles more interesting and delightful than an assembly, composed of persons of various ranks, occupations, and ages, drawn together by the desire of mutually promoting their intellectual and moral improvement.' From this commonplace beginning, he moved on to a lyrical passage celebrating 'the man upon whose soul Knowledge has beamed with its sweet and salutary influences. He walks erect with his face towards heaven, pursuing truth, seeing clearly the path of duty, enjoying the beauties and wonders of nature, distinguishing the evil from the good, and the false from true, appreciating justly the faculties bestowed upon him, and employing them for wise and noble purposes'. By contrast, Baines shuddered with revulsion at the 'criminality of the man whom his maker has endowed with the lofty powers of reason, and who ungratefully and shamefully neglects to cultivate them. . . . To neglect those talents is to despise them, and to despise them is to mock their Author'. The mechanics' institute was a great deal more than an agency of adult education: it was the incarnation of the sacred values of a Christian and liberal community.

Like Baines, official spokesmen for the ideals of the community on public occasions came from the upper middle class of the great towns, the new urban patriciate that had established itself by the 1850s. But the same sensibility of exalted aspiration also found insistent expression at a lower social level, among the middling and lower middle classes. For the social historian the *Surrey Street Circuit Reporter*, with its platitudes and heavy-handed prose, provides even more vivid evidence of the texture of the dominant ethos. Especially noteworthy is the extent to which these Sheffield Methodists were preoccupied with secular values and interests. The mid-Victorian tendency to moralise and spiritualise material reality is conspicuously present. The *Reporter* for November 1868 opens with a paean to the 'hives of industry in Sheffield', which are acclaimed as illustrations of 'colossal power, the superiority of mind over material things'. The city is itself evidence of the fact that 'happily we have passed away from the old barbaric notion that power lived in bone and brawn, thews, and sinews'. In the present day the 'true type of personal power' does not reside in high birth or even in wealth. 'The hard-hearted and close-handed money lender cannot reach the vital interests of being: he only touches the outer rim. Hence men turn to a culturedintellect, and say that "intellectual stature is the true stature of a man".' To be sure, the reader is warned that 'the tree of knowledge is not the tree of life. He who lives for intellect alone, lives beneath a cold sky'. But the theme so central to classic Methodism has been translated into a sentimental mid-Victorian idiom: 'There is something higher than mere mental culture, and this is moral power: its seat is in the heart, its companion is an enlightened and peaceful conscience, its central law is love; and its pulses act in a thousand ways — it denounces wrong, asserts right, places the standard of moral principle high and yields to it allegiance; it is the law of heaven for earth and all time and all being.' The main message, however, is the triumph, power and omnipresence of mind in the economic and political life of the day: 'The impulses of thought are far-felt and permanent. What stately and strong monuments of mind power are around us. A word — a thought passes from you: it lives in ages, becomes a seedling and germ to give birth to the unknown and untold. Thoughts live as watchwords in temptation and stimulants in struggle; they are not the mausoleums of the thinker, but his immortal incarnation, . . . ; this it is that sways its wand over popular assemblies, decrees judicial judgements, directs statesmen, rules cabinets, charms our evenings, guides our history, and beguiles the student till his lamp pales before the light of day.'[5]

The middle-class defined its social role in terms of the ideal of moral and intellectual improvement for all. The obligation of men who had already reached a high level of personal development was 'to ameliorate the condition of the people, and to promote the physical, intellectual, or moral well-being of the masses'. By the 1850s talk about elevating the working classes was so common that it could be suggested that 'reading and writing articles on the "elevation of the working classes" are good, but *work* is infinitely better'. It was usual to take note of the good works already being achieved in this area, while recognising that more needed to be done: 'One of the most hopeful signs in English society is the active interest which is now shown in the welfare of the humbler classes. It is, we think, widely felt that some more serious effort must be employed in their behalf. Their condition presses on the nation's conscience.' Other spokesmen were even more optimistic about the extent of benevolent activity under way in behalf of the well-being of the working classes. 'The well-informed and the benevolent of all classes seem moved by a noble desire to instruct the ignorant, and to reclaim the vicious.' The Manchester area was praised for the institutions that had been established by the inhabitants and dedicated to 'religion, to science, to education, to the improvement of the tastes and habits of the people'.[6]

Inevitably, middle-class improvers took an ostentatiously high-minded and even 'spiritual' approach to the task of elevating and instructing the working classes. An article on 'Our Working Classes', for example, reflects the outlook of Baines and of Surrey Street Methodism. If the author was overdoing it a bit even for the 1850s, his excesses do no more than overstate recurring cultural themes. The article was addressed to a large question, grandly stated: 'How then are the masses to be educated to a living consciousness of the dignity and purposes of human nature?' The answer was to be found in 'education of the spiritual nature, the invigorating of the moral forces of the soul . . . and the enlightenment of the understanding . . . In a word, we want the workman . . . to stand out in visible *bas relief* from the mass, and to realise the perfection of his being in the culture of his every mental and moral faculty in the service of his fellow-men'. The common mind 'must be made to feel the vitalising influence of living earnestness in the persons of those who have grasped the true idea of progress for themselves, and are striving to reduce it to conscious reality'. Similar tone prevails in leading articles in the newspapers of the manufacturing districts: 'We have faith in truth — in its vitality, and in the power of honest manly action; and we have confidence in nothing else as means of improving and elevating our fellow-men.' A few weeks later another leader explained the value of poetry for 'educating our masses'. Poetry would 'do much to elevate their thoughts, refine their tastes, and improve their habits'.[7]

The propertied classes and their spokesmen tended to describe in glowing terms the most limited activity concerned with the intellectual and moral improvement of the working classes. Churchmen and dissenters, ministers and laymen joined the chorus of praise. The Rector of St Matthias's, Salford, president of the working men's club, described the purpose of the second annual industrial and art exhibit sponsored by the club: 'These exhibitions ought not to be lightly skimmed over, for, if the people were to advance in the appreciation of what was great and good and noble, they must study such collections . . . The object of that exhibition was to afford to working men who employed their leisure hours in making works of utility or beauty an opportunity of showing the products of their labour and skill; and, on the other hand, it was intended to set before them higher types of thought and expression, so as to lead them by degrees to a keener appreciation of the beautiful, and to induce them to imitate the specimens of more perfect art.' A clergyman extolled the beneficent influence of penny banks: 'God alone knows the incidental good done by these Penny Savings Banks — *of men led to save* — of men led to think — of men led to be respectable — of men learning self respect — and so made more ready to hear the Good Tidings of the Gospel of Christ.'[8]

The innumerable ceremonial events provided middle-class spokesmen with an opportunity to extol working men for their efforts at improvement. With the usual hyperbole the opening of a reading room was greeted as an event that would bring about the most profound changes: 'Whatever may rescue men of toiling hands and brains, from the stupifying atmosphere of tap-rooms, and gin-palaces, and allure them to agencies which may educate the heart, enlarge their sympathies, and elevate their tastes, so that HOME shall become to them a more holy and beautiful house — this we hail with deepest joy.' The guest speaker expatiated on the slogan, 'Success to the working men of Keswick'. Working-class efforts at managing their own affairs drew high praise. In this pattern, an M.P. at the first annual soirée of the Middleton mechanics' institute singled out the Huddersfield institute which was managed primarily by working men. The expression of quasi-populist sentiments had become convention on such occasions. An account of the opening of a new lecture room asked readers to remember 'that amidst all our British grandeur, "the richest crown-pearls in a nation hang from labour's reeking brows".' The president of the British Association for the Advancement of Science, in an address to 'the working classes of Nottingham', announced that he wanted to be described as a 'working man'. The middle-class image of itself and its relation to the working classes had changed a great deal since the 1830s.[9]

The Surrey Street Methodists were not to be outdone in their glorification of working men who had embraced the sacred cause of improvement, as, for example, at the annual opening of their Christian and educational institute: 'The man of the future will have to be a widely different being, educationally, from the man of the present. The market of this world will have less and less demand for the mere animal in our nature, and more and more for the intellectual; the brutal and the coarse will be left in the rear of the van of human progress, and young men of mental culture will stand abreast of the times to aid this.' Readers were urged to be active in recruitment. 'The class lists will be out in a few days, get them, circulate them, post them in your factories, do this with a conviction that in advancing the mental culture of those around you, you are destroying ignorance and intemperance — . . . you are cheering homes by intelligence and refinement — you are raising youth to the dignity of man, which is the highest end in the social state.' Newly enfranchised working men, having been admitted to 'that noble peerage', were exhorted to 'inaugurate into the history of your country a kingdom of principles — pure, protestant and holy'. Inevitably, they were also asked to set an example for others: 'Let your conduct go to prove the value of the right use of moral power. Let each live in such a style as this; then your presence will reprove vice and your breath quicken virtue; you will become a depository of helps to some and a pillar of hope to others.'[10]

Proud of their leadership in the enterprise of improvement, the middle classes projected a self-image of earnest benevolence They took particular pride in the achievements of that small band of men who lived up to the aspirations of the idealised social role defined by their culture. The resulting self-confidence was no small factor in the hegemony exercised by the middle-class.

Edward Akroyd of Halifax had good reason to take satisfaction in the activities that he described to the Newcastle Commission in 1859: 'I have taken an active part in the establishment of mechanics' institutes, day and Sunday schools, also of working-men's colleges. I maintain and have the management of six day schools, five Sunday schools, two evening schools, and one working-man's college; also two public libraries, containing about 7,000 volumes, for the use of the working classes. The day and evening schools, and the working-man's college contain at present 188 scholars and students. The Sunday schools contain 667 scholars.' There were many others who were entitled to take comparable pride in their efforts 'to promote the improvement of the working classes', as did Edward Baines in his testimony before a select committee on the franchise in 1860. A working-class tribute to Joseph Platt of Oldham sums up the ideal of the middle-class improver: 'He was a benefactor of his native town, a dutiful son, an indulgent husband, a tender father . . . As one of the proprietors of the Hartford Iron Works, his ingenuity, urbanity, and generosity endeared him to the workmen by whom this tablet is erected as an expression of their admiration of his character as a master, as a philanthropist, and a Christian.'[11]

The middle-class role in improving the working classes was acted out ceremonially on those frequent occasions that marked the founding of a new institution or the completion of a year's work. In January 1864, for example, a group of progressive businessmen of Leeds assembled to lend their support to a newly-established working men's hall. A building had been purchased and this meeting was intended to raise money to furnish and operate it. From the platform the sponsors of the meeting described to the assembled working men what they proposed to do. 'Their object was to provide a place in which the working men could assemble and feel themselves at home', read newspapers, books and periodicals, listen to songs and concerts, and 'have friendly intercourse without being surrounded by any of the attractions of vice'.   It was also intended to give working men 'an opportunity, if they were so disposed, of elevating themselves by educating their minds in such education classes as they proposed to have, and by listening to lectures and readings'. The sponsors flattered working-class independence in the new mode that had replaced the hostility of 1834: 'They desired that the working men should feel that that was their institution, and not an institution of any class above them. (Hear, hear.) If employers of labour and others united with them in that movement, it was not to take the management out of their hands, but to give them that friendly help which they might perhaps need, and which would enable them to carry out the better their own wishes and purposes.' Just three months later the mayor presided over a soirée celebrating the successful operation of the working men's hall. In his speech he reminded the members that 'their thanks were due to the gentlemen who had used their influence in establishing this institution in Leeds, that "union is strength", and that the success or failure solely depended upon themselves'. At the soirée, a representative of the Leeds Working Men's Institute reported on the activity of that organisation in the first three months of the year. He announced that 'with certain of the members there had been altered homes, refurnished dwellings, children better clad, and families frequenting places of worship, where before there had been nothing but raggedness, wretchedness, and misery'. He expressed the belief that working men's institutions 'would effect, if generally adopted, a complete renovation in our social system; and he was happy to think that where they had one common object in view — raising the working classes to a higher level — there would be no rivalry in establishing them'.[12] It was a familiar pattern; modest activity and utopian rhetoric; middle-class pre-eminence and working-class gratitude.

These ceremonial transactions between the classes also reflected the middle-class desire for a community characterised by genuinely harmonious and friendly relations. In itself this was not surprising, since the harmony of interests among those classes had been a basic tenet of political economy and liberal ideology from the beginning. What is noteworthy, however, was the mid-Victorian obsession with the achievement of 'cordial' relations between the classes. Looking back anxiously on the disorders of the early-Victorian decades, the middle classes were not content merely with tranquillity, but hoped for something grander. They wanted something more than mere submission or rational acquiescence from the working classes: they wished for a pure and noble relationship between those of different station. A Norwich minister expressed this social ideal in the form of a familiar comparison between the mid-1860s and the generation that preceded it. He took satisfaction in the fact that there had come into being 'a far better spirit between classes, and a sounder feeling of trust in the men, both as between themselves and as regards employers and the richer orders. As elsewhere there has been far greater personal intercourse between the labouring and higher classes of late years than formerly, which has tended to a more human feeling on both sides'. It was commonplace to call for more intimate and friendly communication between masters and men'. 'It is high time', wrote a factory owner, 'that these struggles of physical strength and brute force should give way to reason and more kindly feeling.'[13]

Samuel Smiles shared this mid-Victorian aspiration to the achievement of class harmony through a universal commitment to the enterprise of improvement. His *Self-Help*, published in 1859, was the best known of all the books of advice and counsel for the working classes. Even in his own day Smiles was the most celebrated expositor of the mid-Victorian social gospel. In the conventional wisdom of later generations, Smiles was to become the archetype of bourgeois ideology, self-serving, smug and hypocritical. While Smiles certainly deserves his reputation as an exemplar of mid-Victorianism, he was by no means the cardboard figure of popular mythology. Historical scholarship, beginning with Asa Briggs' perceptive essay, has underlined the complexity of Smiles' thought. His early radicalism has been demonstrated, and we have been reminded that he was capable not only of rejecting laissez-faire dogmatism but deriding it. In sum, Smiles exemplifies a complex culture that resists generalisation.[14]

The first point to be made about *Self-Help* is that it did not preach a narrowly economic creed, urging workmen to work hard in order to get on in the world, and providing helpful advice to that end. In fact, as a representative expression of mid-Victorian culture, its primary emphasis was on the moral and intellectual development of the individual; and the end product of self-help was depicted as an individual of unsurpassed nobility of mind and character. Smiles celebrated self-culture for its own sake and rebuked those who saw it 'too exclusively as a means of "getting on" '. He had little sympathy for those who 'have perhaps looked upon knowledge in the light of a marketable commodity, and are consequently mortified because it does not sell as they expected it would do'. He warned them against becoming disappointed in the work of self-culture when 'they do not "get on" in the world so fast as they think they deserve to do'. To be sure, Smiles noted that from the point of view of advancing in the world 'education is one of the best investments of time and labour'. Nevertheless, he pointed out that 'the great majority of men, in all times, however, enlightened', must necessarily remain working men. Smiles, of course, took a very high line on the matter of the intrinsic value of self-culture for such men: 'We can elevate the condition of labour by allying it to noble thoughts, which confer a grace upon the lowliest as well as highest rank. . . . Even though self-culture may not bring wealth, it will at all events give one the companionship of elevated thoughts.'[15]

There was a great deal in Smiles to which even radical working men might subscribe. For that matter, there was a great deal that would be acceptable to many moralists. His observations on respectability, for example, were unexceptionable. On the one hand, he denounced 'average worldly respectability' and tried to develop an acceptable version. 'The respectable man is one worthy of regard, literally worth turning to look at. But the respectability that consists in merely keeping up appearances is not worth looking at in any sense. Far better and more respectable is the good poor man than the bad rich one —

better the humble silent man than the agreeable well-appointed rogue who keeps his gig.' In this connection he reiterated a theme that recurs in his writings and in mid-Victorian social idealism as a whole: what really matters is not material success but the development of mind and character. 'The highest object of life we take to be to form a manly character, and to work out the best development possible, of body and spirit — of mind, conscience, heart, and soul. This is the end: all else ought to be regarded but as the means.' He did his best to redefine 'success' in these terms: 'That is not the most successful life in which a man gets the most pleasure, the most money, the most power or place, honour or fame; but that in which a man gets the most manhood, and performs the greatest amount of useful work and of human duty.' He also tried to keep money in its proper place, subordinate to nobler things: 'Money is power after its sort, it is true; but intelligence, public spirit, and moral virtue, are powers too, and far nobler ones.' Smiles' vestigial radicalism emerged in his indignation at those whose only concern was the acquisition of wealth. 'The manner in which many allow themselves to be sacrificed to their love of wealth reminds one of the cupidity of the monkey — that caricature of our species.' Smiles conceded that 'worldly success, measured by the accumulation of money is no doubt a very dazzling thing; and all men are naturally more or less the admirers of worldly success'. But he emphasised that wealth must not be mistaken for virtue. 'Though men of persevering, sharp, dexterous and unscrupulous habits, ever on the watch to push opportunities, may and do "get on" in the world, yet it is quite possible that they may not possess the slightest elevation of character, nor a particle of real goodness. He who recognises no higher logic than that of the shilling may become a very rich man, and yet remain all the while an exceedingly poor creature. For riches are no proof whatever of moral worth; and their glitter often serves only to draw attention to the worthlessness of their possessor, as the light of the glow-worm reveals the grub.'[16]

In contrast to the spirit of 1834 — which he, unlike so many other middle-class spokesmen, had rejected at the very outset — Smiles did not single out the vices of the working classes, but subjected all ranks to his stern moralism. Thus on the subject of those who failed to recognise the value of self-culture for its own sake, he did not limit himself to strictures about working men who were too eager to 'get on', but took the propertied classes to task as well: 'The same low idea of self-culture is but too prevalent in other classes, and is encouraged by the false views of life which are always more or less current in society. But to regard self-culture either as a means of getting past others in the world or of intellectual dissipation and amusement, rather than as a power to elevate the character and expand the spiritual nature, is to place it on a very low level.'[17] If anything, Smiles' Puritanism found an even handier target among the classes that had enough time and money for the pursuit of pleasure.

Smiles tried to treat class differences as irrelevant to the common humanity of men. His advice applied equally to all men, regardless of class. He drew examples from all society levels. He singled out instances of noble behaviour among the common people, but only to underline the universality of his message. Hence it is fitting that *Self-Help* should end with a chapter inviting all men to aspire to be true gentlemen: 'Riches and rank have no necessary connexion with genuine gentlemanly qualities. The poor man may be a true gentleman — in spirit and in daily life. He may be honest, truthful, upright, polite, temperate, courageous, self-respecting, and self-helping — that is, be a true gentleman. The poor man with a rich spirit is in all ways superior to the rich man with a poor spirit.' Smiles probably differed from most of his middle-class contemporaries in believing all that he said; there were no unspoken qualifications. He spoke from a background of radicalism and populism. Smiles meant every word of it when he wrote that the qualities of the true gentleman depend 'not upon fashion or manners, but upon moral worth — not on personal possessions, but on personal qualities'.[18] In fact, of course, gentility was primarily a social category, with a gloss of moral qualities. Smiles, however, was not writing as an observer but as a moralist, and was treating the 'gentleman' as a moral ideal.

Smiles and Edward Baines, Jr., both eloquent exponents of the middle-class version of consensus values, arrived at a similar ideological destination by rather different routes. In the 1830s and 1840s Baines and his father, writing from the platform of the *Leeds Mercury*, took a hard line towards the working classes. They acclaimed the new poor law and resisted factory legislation in the name of political economy, while Smiles in the *Leeds Times* denounced the new poor law and rebuked Baines for his hostility to the working classes. By 1859, however, both men were expressing substantially the same type of benevolent middle-class liberalism. Although neither had modified the substance of his ideas, there had been a significant shift in tone and temper. Of the two, Baines was more representative of the middle-class as a whole. He had gradually shucked off the spirit of 1834 and adopted an increasingly positive and optimistic view of the working classes; in a sense, he was moving towards Smiles on the ideological continuum. For his part, Smiles maintained the fundamentals of his early-Victorian outlook, but the note of protest and indignation had faded away. His genuine sympathy with the working classes remained, but his sense of injustice slackened. He had moved to the right, not so much in policy as in spirit. Thus, he ended up in the same camp as Baines. Like the best of the mid-Victorian middle classes they shared an intense idealism, tinged by complacency and a certain smugness. Like their middle-class contemporaries, Smiles and Baines could not escape the limits imposed by their social situation.

(2) 'Nobler Forms of Authority'

In preaching the gospel of improvement and pursuing good works the middle classes were strengthening their hegemony without necessarily seeking to defend their privileges against the threat from below. In fact, the moral strength of their position rested to a large extent on the fact that they embodied so well the shared ideals of the community. At the same time, of course, the middle classes pursued the grand aims of the culture within a social framework that conditioned every aspect of their outlook and behaviour. Their social values presupposed middle-class pre-eminence and working-class subordination. Implicit in the middle-class version of consensus values was a justification of its privileged position and a rejection of egalitarian alternatives. Their formulation of mid-Victorian ideals reflected a perspective that presupposed the continuing dominance of the middle classes.

In addition to these indirect effects of the class structure, the middle-class also actively sought to impose its own stamp on mid-Victorian cultural patterns. They used the resources of their society and culture to construct new forms of working-class subordination. They imparted a middle-class slant to the ruling ideals of the community as a whole; improvement, self-respect, rationality, and independence were defined in a way that undermined the working-class radical attempt to define them in universal terms. Much of their preaching was animated by the consciously ideological determination to convince working men of Chartist errors and sins. This meant persuading working men to accept the cult of respectability and the myth of success.

In the very act of preaching improvement and elevating the masses, the middle classes were also constructing new forms of working-class subordination. Characteristically, they did so while explicitly rejecting the sort of habitual deference that had characterised the social order of rural England: 'The notion that men would more readily obey legitimate authority because they were utterly ignorant of its claims and their obligations, or that they would better discharge the duties and fulfil the responsibilities Providence had assigned them because they were kept in total darkness as to the reciprocities of social life, will now be universally rejected as the most preposterous of fallacies . . . '[19] Such spokesmen for the new order made it clear, however, that they expected working men to accept leadership from above voluntarily and on the basis of rational choice. In fact, one of the chief signs of 'improvement', not to say 'respectability', was the ability to understand the world as perceived by the educated and progressive middle classes.

Fortified by a self-image of rectitude, rationality, and liberality, they took it for granted that they deserved enthusiastic support from below. There was a corollary to every stock liberal denunciation of Tory-style deference: once working men were enlightened about the duties and responsibilities of each social class, they would understand that legitimate authority was entitled to obedience and would act accordingly. Working men who had been given the opportunity to develop their rational powers would recognise the merits of their superiors and gladly follow their lead.

In keeping with the mid-Victorian ethos, the middle classes sought 'nobler forms of authority'. This phrase occurs in a pamphlet published in 1856 that brings together a number of liberal ideas and attitudes usually found only in fragmentary form.[20] The author expresses a central doctrine of middle-class liberalism in the framework of a progressive view of history: 'The power of sheer naked *will* over dependent classes always gives place to nobler forms of authority as those classes become less rude and ignorant, and more intelligent and moral.' As in the speeches of John Bright, the 'iron despotism of the feudal system' is depicted as giving way to the liberal and rational regime of the present. The 'slow growth of civilisation' involves the replacement of the raw power of the aristocracy by a regime characterised by rationality, morality, and responsiveness to public opinion. The liberal view of history traces the sentimentalised origins of an idealised present: 'As the intellectual, and still more the moral, faculties of the people (and of their rulers) were developed, the government found itself obliged, and at length even disposed, to appeal to reason and the sense of right in its subjects, until, at last, authority came to rest entirely upon an enlightened public opinion.'

Moving easily from the realm of government to 'factory rule', the author of the pamphlet suggests that these new forms of authority have a much broader application. He sounds a theme that recurs in mid-Victorian ideology — upright and independent working men freely assenting to the views of benevolent employers. Characteristically, he notes that the more rational and benign forms of authority will also be a good deal more effective: 'Precisely in proportion as working men and women shall stand erect before their employers, in the unassuming dignity of conscious intelligence and uprightness, so will the bearing of the latter become respectful, losing the tone and manner of command, yet consciously acquiring more and more of the reality of power.' In the spirit of even-handedness required by the mid-Victorian consensus, he points out that employers were to blame for much of the 'perverseness' of working-class behaviour, which originated in 'a natural resentment against a still lingering though greatly mitigated peremptoriness, hauteur, harshness and selfishness among employers'.

He attributes the considerable improvement that has since taken place, such as the end of machine breaking, to 'increased intelligence, with a kindlier demeanour on the part of capitalists'. While denouncing working-class combinations, he recommends that employers deal with them by a 'conciliatory and healing line of conduct'. Employers ought to 'attract to themselves the better and higher feelings of the Employed, by an unvarying manifestation of respect, of courtesy, and of a benevolent interest in their well-being'. The author's premise was a commonplace of enlightened and progressive middle-class thought: 'We are persuaded that the existing antagonism between these mutually dependent classes, arises chiefly from their isolation, and would soon give place to better sentiments, if a closer union could be effected between them'; and the 'closer union' was to take place on middle-class terms. Cordiality and friendliness would pay off in more effective social control.

In developing new forms of hegemony the middle-class bent consensus values into a shape that conformed to the imperatives of the social structure. Seemingly universal principles were emptied of their universality and re-defined in class terms. This ideological pattern can be seen, for example, in a series of letters written in 1854 by Samuel Robinson, a progressive Manchester manufacturer.[21] In one of the letters, addressed to the workers in his factory, Robinson took as his text a statement made by a judge at the Stafford assizes 'lamenting the separation between class and class as being one great cause of many of our social evils, and insisting on the necessity of closer intercourse as one of the remedies'. In putting out his version of one of the standard social pieties of the day the judge had said, 'If I were asked what is the great want of English society, I would say, in one word, the want is THE WANT OF SYMPATHY.' When trade union leaders seized on this dictum and posted it on the walls of the town, Robinson was moved to comment. While earnestly expressing his most 'cordial' agreement with the judge's remarks, he gave it a distinctly middle-class slant. Reversing the trade union's interpretation, Robinson warned working men not to make the mistake of assuming that what was needed was more sympathy by masters towards men. On the contrary, he explained why the men must develop a more sympathetic understanding of their employers. In the course of his homily Robinson took another con-sensus principle — the independence of the individual — and gave it a middle-class coloration: 'It is not true benevolence to the working classes to do for them anything which tends to foster in them a spirit of dependence upon the acts of others instead of a manly reliance upon their own; to be constantly doing in their behalf what they have the means and the power to do for themselves.' In fact, 'real benevolence will shew itself rather in ready sympathy with every plan formed by yourselves for your own advancement and improvement and by active endeavours to promote it'. Thus, independence was re-defined to mean avoiding reliance on trade unions and concentrating instead on self-improvement.

Behind the middle-class version of consensus ideals lay the assumption that working men occupied a particular position in society, at the base of the social order, and ought to conduct themselves accordingly. From this perspective, the surest sign of moral and intellectual improvement in a working man was his readiness to recognise the merits of middle-class arguments and to accept enlightened leadership from above. If he proved resistant to such arguments or refractory in his relations with his superiors, this was an indication that something had gone awry. A working man who sent off a rather moderate and well-written letter to the *Bradford Observer* found himself none the less the object of editorial rebuke. While the editor conceded that the letter writer was 'a man above the average of his class in point of intelligence', he pointed out that he 'has not yet learnt to govern himself'. The working man had 'evinced a proud and turbulent spirit'. Such an offence could not be tolerated. It seems that the man who wrote the letter had not behaved in the proper manner when applying for poor relief: 'His conduct both towards the Relieving Officer and the Relief Committee was frequently unbecoming a man in his position.' What the middle-classes expected of the improving working man was not pride or turbulence, but humility and moderation. They had in mind the traits described in a *Manchester Guardian* editorial in 1858, congratulating the working-class on having stopped demanding the vote as a cure for all its ills: 'Is it not because education has made the lower classes more intelligent, more self-reliant, more energetic, has taught them to think more justly of their fellow countrymen, to feel ashamed of their former prejudices, and to acknowledge that it rests with them and not with any Government to ameliorate their social condition?' Even in strikes 'moderation and order are generally manifested in their proceedings, and there is a better appreciation of the laws that govern the rise and fall of wages'. This was what the majority of the middle classes meant by working-class rationality and moderation.[22]

One of the more pervasive social assumptions underlying middle-class improving activity was the notion that working men would derive great benefits merely from associating with their social superiors. There was a great deal of talk about the importance of bringing the classes together and overcoming social isolation, all of which tended to confirm and reinforce middle-class claims to superiority. The annual report of the mechanics' institute in Ripon for 1856, describing the establishment of a girls' school to teach domestic economy, is an interesting example of the fusion of the newer attitudes of liberalism with older traditions of Christian charity in a context that underlines the persistence of the social attitudes of a stratified society. Three evening classes per week were provided for the benefit of the 'Daughters of the poor'. The teaching was done by middle-class women, who took 'a real and truly Christian interest' in the welfare of their pupils. The report that described their activity in glowing terms also included a blunt statement of class relations and the social function of charitable activity: 'An intercourse has been established between two Classes; the educated and the uneducated. It must not cease here. Kindness, and Christian charity, or love, are levers of unexpressed power. With these much may be done.' The writer is referring, of course, to the power to do good, but it is also clear from the context that the maintenance of social discipline and the exercise of social power are perceived as essential aspects of the charitable activity. The levers of power 'give admission where doors would otherwise be closed against us; and once in, God working with us, great help may be given to the advancement of that true social reformation, which, in our day, so many efforts are being made to accomplish'. That 'true social reformation' envisaged an extension of the cult of respectability. Such social presuppositions underlay the high-minded intentions of the teachers, who were doing their best to 'inculcate right principles', to open the minds of their pupils 'for the reception of better nourishment than they have been wont to feed upon', and to create a taste for 'what is good, and pure and holy'. It was also taken for granted that their pupils would benefit from 'the refinement introduced by the intercourse with persons of a superior social rank'.[23]

Implicit in middle-class efforts to elevate the working classes and in their ideological accompaniment was a determination to emancipate working men from any vestiges of Chartism or other forms of radicalism. The propertied classes looked back on the Chartist era with dismay and a lingering anxiety. Mid-Victorian panegyrics to class harmony reflected a feeling of relief that the radical threat had been turned aside. The middle classes hoped that they had won the sort of lasting victory over Chartism that an editorial writer had called for in 1848: 'Our governing classes must address themselves to the task of *conquering the will of the Chartists*. This is the only way of putting them down and *keeping them down*. They may be put down by physical force, but they can be kept down only by moral force.'[24]

Although such plain talk soon gave way to a softer mid-Victorian idiom, the basic attitudes persisted. The frequent contrasts that were drawn between the tranquil 1850s and 1860s and the disorders of the previous generation reflect a continuing concern with the working-class Left. Typically, however, spokesmen for the middle-class put the most most positive construction on the changes that had taken place. In mid-Victorian liberal ideology the abandonment of Chartist militancy was extolled as evidence of the progress that had been made since those dark days. The following account of the transformation of Longton, in the Potteries, is typical: 'On political questions the people were excitable and violent. The creed of the lower classes was rabid Chartism; and during elections a most malignant spirit manifested itself. I am proud, however, to say, that Chartism is only known as a thing that was. Improved circumstances and better information have wiped out that stain from the character of the town for ever.' There had been a great change for the better, as public improvement had a beneficial influence on the people: 'Their tastes have been elevated, their ambitions excited, and a desire for progress has been turned into a proper channel. An onward march has been started in good earnest.'[25]

Implicit in the ideology of improvement was a rebuke to working men who, not so long before, had been receptive to Chartist demagoguery. The ideological implications of the improvement ethic could also be made quite explicit: 'The most effectual remedy for all grievances which afflict the working classes is to be found in the increase of their intelligence', and 'the most powerful assertions of the fraternity and equality of men lies in the universal demonstration of moral and intellectual culture'. Similarly, an M.P. addressing a mechanics' institute produced a new and democratic version of the old be-content-with-your-lot theme. While regaling his audience with the prospect of great moral and intellectual benefits, he added that in most cases they would not be accompanied by worldly advancement: 'High positions were not open to all, but those who educated themselves would find the benefit in a moral and religious point of view, in love of their fellows, in the peace in their bosoms, and in their increased usefulness in discharging the duties of this life and in carrying to their homes an amount of honest affection, and intellectual light which did not exist there before.' Usually, however, the gospel of improvement was preached in more positive terms, promising social and economic benefits.[26]

The virtues of self-improvement were usually extolled in a context suggesting that worldly rewards could also be counted on, such as a better paid or more 'respectable' job. Thus Edward Baines, in the lecture quoted above, moved easily from the lofty realm of the mind and spirit to the more practical benefits that would accrue to working men who attended the institutes. 'I have seen young men and boys entering these Institutions in very humble circumstances, with no connexions that could put them forward in life, and having received only the plainest education. They had nothing in their favour but uncorrupted morals and a disposition to improve themselves.' Such men attended regularly, and made rapid progress: 'I have seen their expanding capacity, their refining tastes, their gradual accumulation of knowledge which qualified them to attain proficiency in the arts that depend on mechanical and chemical science.' Whatever the field of endeavour young men of this sort were rewarded with advancement and success: 'I have seen these young persons rise from the workshop to the counting-house, and not a few of them (whom I could name) taken into partnership by their masters or by others who had observed their qualifications. . . . At one of our meetings seven or eight persons in succession, in the situation of masters, rose and declared that they owed their success in life entirely to the knowledge they had acquired and the habits they had formed in our Institution.'[27] Self-improvement would bring success and respectability.

There was also a distinct ideological cast to the advice of Samuel Smiles, despite his genuine idealism and his belief in improvement for all men, regardless of class, for its own sake. Although he was not consciously engaged in propaganda intended to reconcile the working classes to the class structure of mid-Victorian capitalism, his writings tended none the less to justify middle-class predominance and to deflect attention from the problem of inequality and injustice. When Smiles wrote that 'we can elevate the condition of labour by allying it to noble thoughts', he was echoing the Transcendentalist idealism of his youth, and did not have a propagandist purpose in mind. Nevertheless, the effect of such sentiments, which were so common among the more benevolent and progressive members of the middle classes, was to validate the ideological claims of the propertied classes. While cultivation of nobility of mind and character was an admirable goal in itself, it was hardly a remedy for working-class deprivations and disabilities. Even Smiles' even-handedness in imposing the same standards of moral judgement on all men, including the propertied classes, had ideological implications in the context of mid-Victorian society. It encouraged the notion that social morality was primarily a matter of individual behaviour and that social ethics did not encompass the possibility of changes in class structure and class relations. Here also Smiles' line was typical of the high-minded bourgeoisie: whatever problems existed could be resolved by good will on the part of the individuals involved.

Smiles' observations on the working man as gentleman illustrate the contradictions inherent in the formal universality and even egalitarianism of his social ethic. On the face of it — and this is what Smiles himself consciously intended — he was putting aside factitious class differences and inviting working men to aspire not merely to respectability but even to gentility. The moral attributes of the gentleman, he argued, are universal and not confined to any social class. Yet Smiles' good intentions could not burke the fact that 'gentility' or the 'gentleman' is in essence a social category, which originally came into existence as a dividing line to exclude not only the working classes but also most of middling classes. Hence, when Smiles argued — in his most sincerely classless manner — that the traits of the 'gentlemen' are not limited to any one social class, he was thereby validating the basic ideological claim implicit in that social category to begin with, namely that it is moral characteristics which set the 'gentlemen' apart from the non-gentlemen in the population. In fact, Smiles assumed that the propertied classes had already achieved very high levels of 'gentility' and simply took pains to provide examples of outstanding members of the working class who had done the same. 'Even the common soldiers proved themselves gentlemen under their trials', he observed. He also cited a 'memorable illustration of the chivalrous spirit of common men acting in this nineteenth century, of which any age might be proud'.[28] All this, of course, is very much in the mid-Victorian middle-class mode of helping working men to reach the level already attained by their social superiors and praising them when they were successful.

Although Smiles consciously and explicitly rejected the 'materialistic' values of 'getting on', he nevertheless equated the highest success among working men with the achievement of middle-class status. In fact, he ended up moralising the myth of success by suggesting that it was the moral and intellectual traits of the individual that 'really' constituted success. This had the effect on the one hand, of putting a moral gloss on 'success' that was in fact, and inescapably, esteemed for social and economic reasons; and on the other hand, for those who had achieved that kind of success, but who remained working men, this line had a strong be-content-with-your-lot side to it. In an important sense, then, Smiles was one of those 'propagandists who try to persuade their fellow citizens to develop a special kind of social character which will best serve the needs of the day'.[29] He perceived those needs in terms of the social attitudes and interests of the middle classes. Despite his critique of conventional respectability, Smiles' writings were easily assimilated to the omnipresent pattern.

Baines was not at all ambivalent on the subject. He made it plain that the young men who pursued mental cultivation in the mechanics' institutes would be rewarded with respectability and 'success in life'.[30] In linking personal improvement and social advancement he was much closer than Smiles to the cult of respectability.

(3) *The Cult of Respectability*

The mid-Victorian cult of respectability was an extreme expression of the ideological tendencies inherent in the social situation of the dominant middle-class. It had not been contrived by ideologues but had grown organically out of the interplay between the structure of power and status and the distinctive traits of mid-Victorian culture. Although the gospel of respectability was not preached at full strength by every member of the middle-class, it was invariably present in some form. While Smiles and Baines could hardly be described as high priests of the cult, their ideas fitted in rather well at a number of points. As the polar opposite of the values of radicalism, the cult of respectability is essential to an understanding of the setting in which the working-class subculture existed. When a surrender to 'middle-class values' occurred, it assumed this form.

In a society dominated by the middle classes it was natural for working men to look up to them, since they enjoyed higher status, more money, better education and manifold forms of authority. Working men were conditioned to defer to their superiors, emulate their behaviour and manners, and look to them for approval. There was no mistaking the role assigned to them: to work hard, please their boss, accept gratefully the wages offered, and perhaps to strive for slightly better jobs for themselves and their children. There was no place here for genuine working-class independence. On the contrary, totally different attitudes and behaviour patterns — subordination, deference, materialism — were pervasive and inescapable, for they were inherent in the underlying social and economic structure. Even without middle-class propaganda such structural forces would have operated effectively to inhibit working-class efforts to achieve genuine independence. It was very much in the spirit of mid-Victorian urban culture, however, that the middle classes often elevated these norms into a creed that they preached to working men.[31]

The cult of respectability represented a class version of consensus values, cut to the prevailing pattern of power and status. The 'respectable working man' had been created in the middle-class image of what a decent and respectful working man ought to be. The cult of respectability, therefore, offered a sort of mirror image of the values of the working-class subculture. Each of the character traits which the independent working man esteemed was here refracted through a middle-class prism and emerged in a very different form. His proud demand for respect for the worth and dignity of his class was transmuted into a respectability conferred by the middle classes on working men who behaved themselves 'properly'. What the working-class subculture perceived as intrinsic virtues, valuable for their own sake — rationality, morality, civility — became merely the signs of a social status bestowed by the middle classes. In the version handed down from above, 'rationality' came to be identified with an ability to 'understand' the middle-class view of the world. Civility meant toadying to superiors. The aspiration to genuine independence — conceived as an all-embracing moral, intellectual and social ideal — became, in the self-help creed of middle-class propagandists, merely a striving to stay out of the workhouse and to be 'deserving' of aid in the event of misfortune. Thus the impulse to independence was reversed, for the essence of the cult of respectability was an acceptance of the superiority of the middle classes. Finally, the aspiration to improvement was reduced to a desire to get on in the world on terms acceptable to the middle classes.

On the surface, the middle-class invitation to working men to come within the pale of respectability seemed innocent enough. In fact, the offer was made as if it represented the ultimate in generosity: working men were now to be encouraged to aspire to what had long been considered the quintessence of middle-classness. Yet the offer was ambiguous at best and hypocritical at worst. The whole point of the notion of respectability to begin with was to separate the middle classes from the masses by asserting a claim to moral superiority. In theory, to be sure, respectability was a moral ideal unconnected with class: the respectable man was one worthy of respect, because he possessed traits of character which entitled him to admiration and esteem. In reality, respectability was a social category posing as a moral category. Its function was purely ideological: to enable the middle-class to justify its status by asserting a moral superiority and laying claim to virtues which were denied to inferiors. The point of respectability was the automatic attribution of certain moral traits to a particular socio-economic group. To be sure, a member of the middle-class might lose the badge of respectability as a result of improper behaviour; in the absence of evidence to the contrary, however, a member of the middle-class was presumed to possess a character worthy of respect. Implicit in the notion of respectability at the outset was the presumption that the lower orders lacked the virtues inherent in their social superiors. That fundamental assumption remained in full force when the Victorian middle classes extended the cult of respectability to the upper strata of the working classes. The middle classes, in effect, were born respectable, whereas working men had to achieve it through their own efforts. Working men had to prove their respectability. And the middle classes would decide on the success of their efforts. Working men were to receive the Order of Respectability, Second Class. In theory, however, respectability united men of all classes in a common moral status.

The cult of respectability then, undercut the values of the working-class subculture while professing to advance them. In converting character traits into mere badges of status, it confirmed the basic claims of the class system. In making the middle classes the arbiter of moral character, it confirmed the inherent inferiority of the working classes. By converting social traits such as deference and docility into moral virtues it demeaned morality itself.

The best expression of the cult of respectability in its working-class form is to be found, not in secular sermons of middle-class propagandists, but in the writings of working men who had succumbed and who preached the gospel with the zeal of true believers. A case in point is a volume of prize essays by working men, published in 1861. The author of an essay on 'Courtesy', for example, not only takes it for granted that working men wish to 'obtain the respect of those above them', but suggests that this will enable them to 'lessen the distance which is supposed to separate the two classes'. He follows this with the ingenious notion that the rich have already contributed all that can be expected of them to the lessening of this 'distance', and that it is time for working men to do their part: 'It would be well if there were more sympathy shown by the rich towards the poor, and it would be better still if the class distinctions were so far abolished as to enable both parties to associate together in society, and mutually to co-operate with each other, but are we to expect that all the sacrifice is to be made by the higher to the lower?' This appeal to working men to be fair and recognise the extent of the sacrifice made by their betters sets the tone for what follows, as the author urges working men to take the initiative in eliminating class distinctions by earning the respect of their superiors. 'Are they [the rich] to accommodate themselves to rudeness of speech, to uncivil behaviour, or disgusting habits, when these things can be easily avoided by the exercise of thoughtfulness and the practice of courtesy? Rather should we strive to raise ourselves in the social scale, to dignify our nature, to educate and cultivate our mental and moral being. We may be real, though not refined; wise, though not wealthy.'[32] This was a precise statement of just what the middle classes wanted of 'respectable working men'.

Another expression of this point of view is found in the essay by a silk weaver from Kettering. Like other members of the aristocracy of labour, the author takes for granted the importance of elevating the mass of working men. What is noteworthy about his formulation, however, is the extent to which he assumes that elevating the working classes means bringing them a little closer to the moral and intellectual heights that have already been reached by the middle and upper classes; he displays a strong distaste for the manners of the multitude and puts a great deal of emphasis on shared politeness as a bond of equality linking men of different classes. These attitudes colour an otherwise standard mid-Victorian passage of rejoicing at progress made by the working classes during the previous generation: 'Courtesy and politeness have made great advances . . . A marked decorum has superseded the boorish habits of the past generation, and an air of gracefulness has reached even the cottage of the working man, and often invests it with beauty.' He interprets this improvement as 'a greater general approximation to the manners of the upper classes'. And he concludes with the hope that 'the time may come when the rich may have no exclusive title to the designation of "gentleman", but politeness will prevail generally among all ranks and conditions of men, and goodwill, courtesy, and urbanity be among the common virtues of mankind'.[33] In this context, it is plain that the middle classes will be the chief beneficiaries of working-class 'urbanity'.

Another essayist makes quite transparent the class character of his exhortation to working men to be courteous. Lack of cordiality in class relations, as he sees it, is primarily the result of working-class prejudice and rudeness. He complains that working men are all too often unresponsive to the good advice that is coming to them from above: 'When some noble or gentle lecturer comes forward and proposes to cultivate more cordial intercourse between the different ranks of society, the ice may seem to be melted for a time by the heat of temporary enthusiasm; but soon old Prejudice returns with his churlish host, and builds up again the chilly barriers.' Speaking 'for my class', he explains why working men are so reluctant to 'second the endeavours of philanthropic individuals of rank or wealth to establish more amicable relations between their respective classes'. He attributes this stubbornness to 'old grudges and old prejudices'. To be sure, he raps knuckles on both sides: employers are faulted for 'ruthlessly' reducing wages, thus contributing to 'the want of interchange of courtesy and belief in common interests'. But in the same breath he rebukes working men for 'obstinately' attempting to keep up wages.[34] Such seeming even-handedness, of course, like the application of seemingly universal standards of courtesy, had the effect of playing into the hands of employers who would benefit most from working men who 'courteously' refrained from demanding higher wages.

The essay on Self-Education by William Glazier, a carpenter, is noteworthy for the expression of impossibly exalted aspirations in the context of a classically 'ideological' justification of the class structure and its norms. He preaches a sentimentalised and romanticised version of the creed of respectability, in which the contented working man cultivates his mind and spirit, untouched by the squalid world around him. Even the gospel of success is dismissed as too worldly. Education is not to be prized as a means of social advancement, but for its ennobling influence on the soul. The important question, he writes, is 'how shall education be made subservient towards enabling man, whilst abiding in that station of life to which it has pleased God to call him, to become more respected, more influential, more useful and more happy — a fountain of greater blessings to himself, his family, his country, and the world . . . ' At first glance, it seems that we are back with Sarah Trimmer and Hannah More, especially when Glazier refers, in his climax, to 'the great end of being, which, in every station of life, is to glorify God and enjoy Him, and with Him all other things here and hereafter'. But Glazier is interesting precisely because these highly traditional conservative doctrines are clothed in the new ideological forms of the mid-nineteenth century. Whereas the eighteenth-century ideologist was urging the poor to eschew sin and escape poverty, Glazier asks working men to aspire to the ennobling works of the mind and spirit. Now the conquest of sin is merely a first step towards positive achievements: 'He who has accomplished this — who has rendered passions, appetite, and habits subordinate to the will — stands at a vantage ground for all future battlings. Henceforth, all things are easy to him, and he can go on from conquering to conquer. Such a man, however lowly his station, acquires a nobility of character that entitles him to the admiration of the world.'[35] He does not really have to wait for the next world. He has achieved the highest religious-cultural goal in this world, and respectability to boot.

Glazier exemplifies — not as a paradigm, but as a caricature — the ideological implications of sentimental utopianism in mid-Victorian urban culture. He takes the platitudes of aspiration and treats them as self-evident truths. Thus he blandly denies that materialistic motives will have any effect on 'the vast bulk of workers', whom he describes in Pelagian terms remote from the Calvinism of Hannah More: 'We believe that all men are susceptible to some particular influence, or influences, of a pure and elevating character; . . . To seek out, multiply, extend, and bring into operation amongst the mass of the people, these elevating and ennobling influences, unmixed with sordid considerations, is, in our opinion, worthy the profound study of the most exalted intelligence.' He takes the working-class ideal of independence and self-help and dissolves it in a syrupy sentimentality: 'No man, or class of men, will ever rise to the true dignity of our common humanity who hangs on the skirts of others. There will be no real nobility of character, no real and lasting progress — mentally, morally, and socially — without the vigorous exercise of our own capacities and powers.' Carried away by his utopian vision, Glazier even expresses doubts about mechanics' institutes, because they may lead to the 'neglect of home and family duties'. 'Highly as we esteem intellectual improvement, we should deem it dearly bought if its accomplishment weakened the influence of home.' And in the best tradition of preachers advocating what no one would dare to oppose, but which no reasonable man expects to be actualised this side of the after-life, Glazier presents his own programme: 'We would rather see home institutes multiplied a thousandfold than the extension of elaborate organisations for educating the people. The latter have done and are still doing good; but let us rather see fathers, the high priests of knowledge within the temple of Home, and wives and children, the eager and expectant auditors.'[36]

(4) *Popular Education*

In approaching a society that proclaimed its dedication to the ideal of moral and intellectual improvement for all, an obvious touchstone is the sort of education provided for the working classes. When we turn to the system of popular education in the mid-Victorian cities, we are struck, first of all by the wide gap between aspiration and result. In this area the contradiction between formally universal ideals and the imperatives of class structure is particularly conspicuous. Working-class children were given a separate and inferior education, intended to combat tendencies towards subversion and crime. 'Improvement' in this context meant indoctrination in ideas and values congenial to their social superiors. When in the 1850s the elementary schools showed some signs of efficiency, the middle classes complained that the children of the poor were being educated above their station. A second and more surprising aspect of popular education in the cities is the fact that the schools remained outside the prevailing ceremonial and ideological patterns. Instead of being acclaimed as evidence of intellectual progress, they were ignored. The spirit of the poor law, both old and new, continued to pervade the elementary schools, which were untouched by the warmer currents of the improvement ethic. When anxiety about working-class subversion subsided, the schools ceased to arouse much interest. The early-Victorian faith in elementary education – both idealistic and ideological – was drying up. The elementary schools became the grubby stepchildren of the culture, despite the vast increase in public expenditure in the 1850s and 1860s as a result of Kay-Shuttleworth's zeal in the 1840s.[37]

The steady expansion of this system of popular education entailed an inexorable erosion of the values of working-class radicalism. It was difficult to maintain utopian ideals in the face of processes of deradicalisation and socialisation that did not present a target for criticism. Precisely because Chartism and Owenism had embodied so fervent a faith in education – both for its own sake and as an instrument of transformation – the growth of elementary education had to be regarded as a step forward. Although the schools represented at best a drab fusion of the outlook of the S.D.U.K. and the charity schools – both of which had drawn the fire of early-Victorian radicals – they could not, in the mid-Victorian situation, be denounced out of hand. As the working-class radicals continued the old demand for universal education, but without the accompanying insistence on social and political transformation, they fell victim to a reformism that preserved the old rhetoric but set it in a new context emptied of radical content. While they criticised the system of elementary education, their alternative was nothing more than a national system, removed from the denominations. While this was a perfectly rational and practical proposal, it lacked the egalitarian spirit underlying the educational ideas of Bray, Harney, or Lovett.[38]

Working-class radicalism had to contend with the fact that schools are inherently conservative institutions, designed to transmit established values and knowledge and to serve the needs of the society and its ruling groups. By their very nature, they are adjusted to the social and ideological status quo. In mid-Victorian England, as in liberal capitalist societies in general, the schools functioned to train pupils for jobs in an expanding economy, usually somewhat better than those held by their parents. Given this close link to social advancement or mobility, the schools naturally made a virtue of it. But this was not the sort of personal improvement envisaged by the early-Victorian radicals. Far from fostering equality, it tended to encourage an acceptance of the stratification system and even to legitimise it. Thus in their conscious devotion to progress and social advancement, the mid-Victorian schools were performing the classic conservative function of justifying existing social and economic arrangements. They performed this function quite independently of any conscious ideological intention. Merely attending the school meant absorbing the notion that social advancement was something to be striven for. Moreover, parents searching for a 'good' school for their children in a highly stratified society more often than not would find themselves making the decision on social grounds, either avoiding the children of the residuum or seeking out the children of the petty bourgeoisie. These schools were largely staffed by teachers who had climbed out of the working-class, were preoccupied with their status, and who communicated to their pupils an overriding concern with status, advancement, and respectability. All these aspects of the functioning of the elementary schools tended to erode the old radical aspiration while universal education continued to occupy a place of honour in the radical creed.

Located in an urban industrial environment in an expanding economy, the better elementary schools were concerned with providing skills that would enable their pupils to get good jobs and advance themselves. One such institution, operated by the Unitarians of High Pavement Chapel in Nottingham, took pride in the fact that it had 'always been a source of supply for the Warehouses of the Town'. The register notes that one pupil 'went to a situation'; another is described as 'a promising boy, left to go to work'; a common entry is 'to a situation'. The managers of the school perceived the function of the school in practical terms: 'Apart from the general question of what should constitute a good education as a mental discipline, what will fit these young people to run that race of life which in all probability they will be called upon to pursue? To this question the Managers wish to give a practical answer in the course of instruction imparted under their care.' At the prize-giving ceremony, the chairman of the board of governors noted with satisfaction that gentlemen who wanted clerks or servants in their warehouses came to the school to recruit them. Some boys even returned to the school after being out to work for a time, because 'their parents want them well grounded in "practice bills of parcels" '.[39] The school won the highest praise from H.M. Inspector of Schools.

The elementary schools were tied into the stratification system in such a way as to put a premium on status motives. That is, in addition to the straightforward economic motive of getting a job that would pay more money, there was the social motive of preserving a given status or moving to a higher one. This often took the form of separating oneself and one's children from inferior status groups. Specifically, this meant staying clear of the labourers and making contact with the lower middle class. The working man who set out to choose a 'better' school for his child found himself in a position where the conventional judgement on such matters was based on social as well as educational considerations. In some cases, as for example in Bradford and Rochdale, private schools catered to social motives: 'Some [superior day schools], which seem to depend a good deal on the reputation of their gentility, charge from 6d to 1s 3d a week, and draw their chief support from the higher class of artisans and the smaller shopkeepers, who do not wish their children to mix, as they must do in a public school, with companions from a lower stratum of society.' For the most part, however, labour aristocrats were content with the state-supported denominational schools, since the unskilled were usually not able to afford the fees. According to a report on Manchester and Liverpool in 1870, the state-supported denominational schools were composed almost exclusively of children of 'skilled workmen and superior workmen' and 'their social equals, the smallest shopkeepers'. If children of 'the lowest labouring class' appeared at these schools, the other children would depart. The inspector found this pattern readily understandable: 'The skilled and "respectable" working man is, naturally, very unwilling to allow his children to associate with the lowest children of the town, whose habits and language are sometimes filthy, and whose bodies are almost always dirty and often diseased.'[40]

The state-supported schools required the payment of small fees. This standard mid-Victorian practice — intended to stimulate working men to prize what they were receiving — had the effect of emphasising the line that divided 'paupers' from the rest of the working-class. Official policy statements were unequivocal: if a working man falls into 'the pauper or criminal class . . . the State will come to the assistance of his children, will rescue them, and contribute largely both to their maintenance and education'. Thus in education too the stigma of pauperism — that omnipresent incentive to respectability — was very much in evidence. Under the circumstances the artisan was not likely to permit his children 'to mix with the thieves and vagrants of the ragged school'. In this situation egalitarian principles were not in evidence, however much they might still be applied in criticism of the middle classes. The unskilled worker, 'neither wholly independent nor yet quite pauper', found it difficult to pay the fees 'without a painful sacrifice'. Those who made the sacrifice naturally wanted some sort of social and economic return.[41]

The elementary school teachers of the mid-Victorian period had been recruited primarily from the working classes, particularly the more ambitious and active elements. Strenuous efforts had been made to select candidates of impeccable earnestness and respectability. Many of these teachers had been trained under the pupil teacher system established by the minutes of 1846. By 1859, the teachers were working with over 15,000 pupil teachers. Teachers and pupil teachers constituted an important point of contact between the working classes and the official culture.[42]

The elementary school teachers were extremely status conscious and they communicated the ethos of social advancement to their charges. Their professional associations and journals dwelt on the inadequacy of their status in society and on the need to improve it. One of these journals put their case rather crudely in 1853, arguing that the elementary school teachers simply could not do their important work at all effectively unless they were given higher professional status and more money: 'A man's influence must ever be dependent, to a very great extent, upon the respectability of his social position. If you lower this, you materially diminish his power of usefulness. This is especially true in respect of all the learned professions. Besides, unless the position of schoolmaster is made one of respectability, they will never be induced to remain long in the profession.' Even the demand for higher pay was expressed, not in straightforward economic terms but in terms of petty bourgeois status consciousness: 'Now, according to the present constitution of society in this country, there is only one way of raising a man from a position of comparative obscurity to one of respectability; and that is, by giving him the means of maintaining that respectability. There is no use in mincing the matter; we all know this to be the case.' Acceptance of socially determined values — together with rejection of any attempt to insist on other values — was total and other-directed. 'A man cannot hold a respectable position in English society, unless he has the outward requisites and guarantees of that position. The mass of the world look to appearance far more than to anything else. Indeed, the world in general has not time to examine into any intrinsic and personal claims which a man may have to be regarded with consideration.' It would be hard to find a balder acceptance of the cult of respectability.

There was no hint of an egalitarian insistence of the maintenance of self-respect for every person. All that mattered was more money and higher status for schoolmasters, who were now paid no more than 'the commonest mechanic'. 'So long, therefore, as things remain as they are, the schoolmaster will never meet with the respect due to himself and his office, unless he receive a far better remuneration for his services than he does at present.'[43]

While demanding more pay for elementary school teachers, the *Educational Expositor* took a very hard line on their pupils and how they ought to behave. The editor announced grandly that he had to concede that some of the critics of popular education had a point. After the children of the poor have been at elementary school for some time they throw off their 'native civility and do not assume in its place anything of a more polished kind, but, on the contrary, become positively and often intentionally rude'. He much preferred their previous condition of servility: 'In their native untutored state, the lower class of people in his country generally treat their superiors in social ranks with a degree of respect and deference bordering on servility.'[44]

The mid-Victorian elementary schools still bore the stamp of their origins: eighteenth-century charity schools modified by an admixture of utilitarianism. They were intended to handle the children of the poor, a sad lot who had to be raised from the lower depths. Under these circumstances it was very difficult indeed for pupils to avoid what twentieth-century educational jargon calls a 'negative self-image'. An entry in a log book in the 1860s, summarising the characteristics of the students, reflects a recurring preoccupation with class and cleanliness: 'Cleanliness. Commendable considering the class of children and the poverty of many of their parents.' A similar point of view, carried to an extreme, appears in the entries opposite each student's name in the register of the High Pavement Boys' Day School: 'a very dirty boy', 'a very dirty idle boy', 'a quick but dirty boy'. The first three entries in the register set the tone: 'a very good boy', 'a very bad boy', and 'excessive idleness'. Most of the comments, it should be noted, fall into the 'very good' category. Occasionally, the parents come under judgement: 'a nice boy but ungrateful parents'. The schools were acutely conscious of the distinction between the 'respectable' who came to the school and the 'low' who lurked outside. The latter sometimes constituted a physical threat as this log-book entry indicates: 'The gymnasia are a source of great annoyance, as they attract all the dirty big lads of the neighbourhood who climb the palings and lie in wait to enter the playground with the school children, dispossess the children of the swings and are the same time very rude and impertinent. To-day stones were thrown into the school, and the front-door forced open with a great noise.' The teacher certainly had every reason to be furious with the disruption. Inevitably, however, this objectively based indignation expressed itself in social categories — dirty, rude, and impertinent.[45]

The school inspectors were convinced that the system was working well. The following account, provided to a select committee in 1869, is a good statement of what the educational establishment wanted of the teachers and the schools: 'I believe that the mere daily contact with persons so well educated and well mannered as our present school teachers — the product of our excellent training colleges — has had a most beneficial effect upon the present generation of the working classes in England and Wales. I believe that this contact, above all else, is the reason why our labouring classes are now so much more civil, refined, and gentle than they used to be thirty years ago, before the training colleges were in operation.' In Lancashire, he went on, a 'silent revolution' had taken place: 'The change from roughness and semi-barbarism to civilisation which may be seen in such towns as Oldham, Padiham . . . is little short of marvellous.' The spirit of the charity schools, in sentimental mid-Victorian form, lived on: 'I trust that our training colleges may long flourish and supply us with these earnest and duly educated teachers, who, by their religious zeal, their well-informed and active minds, and their gentle manners, may be really fitted for their holy work of forming and instructing the hearts and intellects of our youthful poor.'[46]

The system of popular education was intended, in the most literal sense, as a means of social control. In evidence presented to the Newcastle Commission, which was intent on getting value for money, the inspectors stressed the success of the schools in transforming the children of the working classes into model citizens in a bourgeois liberal society. In his report on Bradford and Rochdale, Inspector Winder described three effects of elementary education on 'the intellectual habits and condition' of the people: 'It has refined their tastes — The desire for coarse and animal pleasures, though still far more rife than it ought to be, is to some extent giving way to more rational recreations. An intelligent love of good music is widely diffused . . . A piano is by no means an uncommon piece of furniture in a working man's house; and I have myself, on several occasions, heard a very tolerable performance in a cottage.' A second effect of popular education noted by Winder was a rubbing-off of working-class roughness: 'It has humanised manners — To judge from the stories current in the neighbourhood, the outlying districts of Rochdale must have been in a condition approaching barbarism within living memory . . . Brutal sports, bull baiting, cock fighting, and the like, once the delight of the people, have almost wholly disappeared; and I was given to understand that a general softening of the harshness of character, which is a serious hindrance to the spread of education, is gradually but certainly in progress.' The third effect described by Winder was the acceptance of middle-class economics. He put it this way: *'It has developed their practical common sense* — Education has set the people thinking on the economic laws under which they live, and on the practical efforts which they can independently put forth for the bettering of their condition. Though there is still a lamentable deficiency in this respect, I was assured that saving habits and prudent foresight are much more common than formerly was the case.' The fundamentals of laissez faire and self-help had been absorbed. Ignoring the co-operative critique of competition, Winder gave the movement the highest praise: 'I consider this to be by far the most striking example of working-class intelligence which came under my notice.'[47]

In his report on Bradford and Rochdale, Winder noted, almost casually, that employers had found that educated working men displayed a 'readiness to learn, and desire to excel'. The inspector for the Dudley area reported that employers had remarked on 'the greater manageability and docility of those who have submitted in any degree to the discipline involved in any kind of schooling'. They showed a 'greater readiness to submit to their employers' judgement'. For their part, inspectors tended to lavish high praise on those schools which secured a full measure of obedience and submission from their pupils. After a visit to the High Pavement school for boys in Nottingham, the inspector wrote a glowing report: 'Each time I visit this School I am struck with the excellence of the Discipline. The bodily training of the Boys, their sustained power of keeping quiet and silent, and the way in which each is doing his work . . . on his own individual resources are admirable features of the School.'[48]

The schools were supplied with textbooks designed to indoctrinate pupils with acceptable ideas and attitudes. Manuals for teachers left no doubt as to exactly what sort of results they were expected to achieve. 'The cultivation of the mind by the instruction afforded in these schools opens and expands the faculties, impresses on the heart a deep sense of moral and religious duty, and produces habits of industry, order, and subordination.' At the bottom of a page in *Daily Lesson Book Number Two* of the British and Foreign School Society appeared this 'hint' for the teacher: 'Lesson. Nations and individuals increase in useful knowledge, only by the judicious employment of time.' The teacher was directed as follows: 'The MORAL LESSON should now be faithfully given. The *hint* at the foot of the page should for this purpose be taken. The attention of the children will then be called first to the early times when men wrote on bark or leaves — their condition will be noticed — their disadvantages — the absence of the light of truth among them, etc., then the state of England many hundred years ago should be explained

— thankfulness for present mercies should be excited — the responsibility connected with superior advantages urged, all which will naturally lead to the specific lesson given in the note.' Progressive history, detached from its original radical context, had been enlisted in the idealisation of contemporary England and its infinite capacity for further improvement.[49]

(5) *The Temperance Movement*

Middle-class hegemony in the mid-Victorian cities found a most direct expression in the temperance movement. Earnest working men joined with the middling classes in extolling the virtue of total abstinence and in inviting the less fortunate to come within the pale of respectability by renouncing drink. In the temperance movement consensus values assumed a narrowly middle-class form, as the improvement enterprise was defined primarily in terms of assisting working men to overcome the personal deficiencies that supposedly prevented them from reaching the moral and intellectual level of their social superiors. But the postulate of inherent working-class inferiority — so characteristic of the provident societies and the new poor law of the 1830s — now appeared in a much more positive mid-Victorian setting, with a new emphasis on the possibility of moving upward on 'the scale of being'. And working men who had crossed the great divide were invited to join in the work of reclaiming the residuum. Thus, in the temperance movement working men themselves had become the chief votaries of the cult of respectability, in which virtue was treated chiefly as a sign of status.

As was noted in chapter 2, however, the original involvement of working men in the teetotal agitation was remote indeed from mid-Victorian respectability. Teetotalism originated in an effort to transform the existing temperance movement, which combined an anti-spirits programme with the established procedures of traditional philanthropy. In short order, the teetotallers took over the movement and set it on a new course. They insisted on nothing less than total abstinence; the pledge was to be the sign of a total reformation of the individual; and members of the teetotal society would aggressively seek out converts by the most direct means. The dynamism behind the new movement came from class-conscious working men, hostile to every form of deference. Teetotal Chartists took up the cause because it demonstrated the moral capacity of working men, who had been maligned for so long by their social superiors. From these origins the teetotal cause acquired a prestige among working men that it was to retain even after the movement had entered a new phase.

Even in the early years of the movement teetotal working men directed their zeal to respectable ends and conformed to emerging

patterns of improvement activity. Working men who joined the
temperance societies were caught up in the cycle of business, including
a ceaseless round of meetings. In Leeds over a dozen branches met
regularly and also sent delegates to weekly meetings of the parent
group. Like Leeds, Newcastle had its own temperance periodical, which
exhorted its readers to redoubled efforts: 'Up and be doing, dear
friends, get *soundly* connected to Teetotalism, by *attending* meetings;
buying tracts and periodicals; *subscribing* towards rent, printing, etc.;
and above all, regularly . . . labouring in this part of the Lord's
vineyard.' They formed ancillary groups: a mutual improvement
society in Rochdale, a benefit society, and a musical and popular lecture
society in Newcastle, and a circulating library and reading room in the
Leylands branch of the Leeds society. They organised special events: a
cheap trip to Liverpool, a temperance gala at the Leeds Fair, a
temperance love feast, or a festival to celebrate the opening of the
circulating library at Leylands. They watched over their members to see
that there was no backsliding; among the officers at Newcastle was a
discipline secretary; Rochdale had a system for visiting errant members.
And they carried the message to outsiders. The town would be divided
into districts for visiting and the distribution of tracts. The Newcastle
society reached out to the surrounding towns: 'By way of breaking up
the fallow ground in this contemplated field of moral culture,
simultaneous meetings were held on Christmas Day in nearly all
villages within twelve miles of the town.' In 1847 the Newcastle society
held a special demonstration at which speeches were delivered exclusively by working men.[50]

Although the temperance movement catered for working men, it
did so with a strong bias in favour of conventional respectability.
Working-class pride often got twisted into a distinctly middle-class
shape, as for example, at the demonstration of working men in
Newcastle in 1847. One of the speakers flattered his fellow participants:
'When he looked round the platform, he thought they were all middle-
class men. (Cheers.)' The speaker was a hatter who was doing rather well
in his own business. He told the audience that a friend of his, when told
that he was one of the 'working men' who had agreed to speak at the
demonstration, expressed surprise: 'But you're one of the middle
classes.' The latter's comment on this at the meeting was, in effect, that
he was still a working man, despite the achievement of middle-classness.
'What made him a middle-class man? Teetotalism.' Another speaker, a
glassmaker, sounded a more plaintive note: 'Although he was not
ashamed of being called a working man, he hoped his friends around
him would look to higher and greater things. Why should they not
aspire to be prime ministers, M.P.'s and privy councillors, as well as
anybody else?' In fact, working men who participated in the

temperance movement tended to be socially mobile, albeit on a rather small scale. Some had entered the labour aristocracy from a lower stratum of the working-class; others had moved into the lower middle and middling classes. Some moved on in the world during their period of membership, like George Dodds, a flax dresser, who participated in the formation of the Newcastle Teetotal Society and later became a city councillor.[51]

But the initial appeal of the temperance movement was to working-class idealism. It reflected and in turn reinforced, the strength of the ethic of improvement among the working classes. Abstinence was only a means to greater ends. 'Woeful experience has abundantly shown that it is of little use to reclaim men from habits of idleness and vice, unless means are taken to furnish them with employment of a purer and nobler kind.' It was necessary first of all, to take the reformed drunkard by the hand and 'endeavour to implant and cultivate those moral motives which afford the best security for adherence to the pledge. This can best be effected by the establishment of societies for mutual instruction and improvement, libraries, lectures, and other similar objects'. Thus the new movement eagerly associated itself with the apparatus of improvement. 'We are glad to see that such societies are springing up, in connection with the Temperance cause, in many places around us. At Leeds, a Mental Improvement Society has recently been formed.' A temperance missionary, looking back on a month of intensive activity, explained what more could be done by others in the movement: 'Attend the meetings when the local advocates speak, and especially the humblest of his class; you will thus encourage them to improve their minds and fit themselves for greater usefulness, and also putting a check to that vicious pursuit of coffee-house gambling.' Theirs was an educational enterprise. 'The teetotal reformation is a great educational effort — . . . to change the pernicious usages of society — to improve the moral habits of the people — to teach them right and economical application of their resources.' Hence, 'No true friend to the education of the people can, with consistency refrain from helping forward the temperance reformation.' And the temperance reformers, in turn, supported Sunday schools and other aspects of education. In Newcastle, a temperance friendly society published an almanack, *The Northern Temperance and Rechabite Almanack, for the Year of Our Lord 1842, Being . . . the 8th year of Teetotalism and 7th of Rechabitism,* which included a poem: 'The Teetotal Boy: Recitation for a Sunday School Anniversary or Teetotal Meeting.' An engraving depicted a Sunday school examination, with this caption: 'The Teetotal Boy; or, the Reformed Drunkard's Child at the Sunday School Examination.'[52]

By the 1840s the temperance movement had settled into a routine that reflected middle-class social patterns. Members of the local societies concentrated on meetings of the faithful, rather than on active proseletysing. Working-class participation became more passive. Full-time agents were hired, and the old pattern of exhortation, visiting, and tract distribution reappeared, but with a much broader social base drawn from the ranks of the middling classes and respectable working men. The local temperance societies assumed a sectarian character, with affinities to the nonconformist groups with which they often became closely affiliated. Sometimes they built a temperance hall, which usually looked very much like a nonconformist chapel. To pay for this sort of thing money had to be raised. By the 1850s the temperance societies were soliciting funds from the upper-middle-class people who had left the movement a few years before. Their success in raising money was a sign that teetotalism was now respectable. They took pride in this, as in Leicester, for example: 'These facts demonstrate that when the Temperance societies work worthily and energetically, and aim at great objects, they may rely upon the assistance and support of the philanthropic public; for it is worthy of note that the greater portion of the money raised for the purpose of achieving the above results was advanced by gentlemen who were never influenced by the expectation of "dividends"; they also show the great importance of perseverance under difficulties, and in opposition to the fears of some of our best friends.'[53]

The evolution of the temperance movement exemplifies, in rather extreme form, the routinisation and institutionalisation of early-Victorian idealism that was so prominent in the process that moulded mid-Victorian culture. In the course of the 1840s the movement adapted itself to the stolid and drab cultural patterns that were taking shape in the cities. In his *Reminiscences* Livesey mourned the changes that had occurred during his lifetime: 'There is a great contrast betwixt the present and the past — betwixt the spirit, the activity, the devotedness, the liberality, the self-sacrifice, and the success connected with the first five years compared to what we witness at the present day.' He noted that the decline in numbers and enthusiasm had been accompanied by a rise in complacency and self-congratulation: 'In the early days we felt that we were really engaged in a "Temperance *reformation*". We gave heart and soul to it. The conflict was fierce; and the resistance, manifested in hostile opposition, served only to fire our zeal. We seemed as if we would turn the world upside down. We scarcely feel in this mood now.' Livesey deplored the disappearance of working men as teetotal missionaries and their replacement by men professionally involved in the movement. 'Our working men — sawyers, mechanics, and men of all trades — were constant speakers at the meetings; they went everywhere, and no others were listened to with equal attention. Instead of these fearless heroes, reverend gentlemen and professional lecturers, to a great extent, have taken their place (more so in Scotland than here), although for penetrating the masses and benefiting the millions, there is no agency equal to the plain, pointed, short, unvarnished speech of the teetotal artisan.' In Leeds, some twenty years after the dramatic triumph of the new teetotal forces, the movement carried on a mood of determined dutifulness. 'At the present time there is not much excitement on the Temperance question in this town; but still the work is going on. About ten meetings are held every week, besides the Bands of Hope. The Ladies Association employs a Temperance missionary, who devotes his time to visiting, collecting subscriptions and holding meetings.' The 'missionary' had just held the first of a series of Saturday evening meetings where 'amusement is blended with instruction'. 'It is an attempt to supply working men with a cheap means of rational enjoyment apart from the public house; the evening's entertainment consisted of music, singing, recitation, and Temperance addresses.' This was part of the standard round of activities in the local temperance societies.[54]

With the hiring of agents to carry on the work full-time, the temperance societies adopted the outlook and practices of the religious bodies concerned with the welfare of the working classes. The agents devoted themselves to visiting, exhortation, and the distribution of tracts. In regular reports the societies announced in detail exactly what had been accomplished. The agent of the Hull Temperance League had been on the job less than a year when a summary of his activities was issued. He had delivered twenty-one prepared lectures and eighty-three addresses in the open air or in the lecture rooms of the league. He also was on duty daily in the office. His employers were particularly pleased with the fact that he had spent a great deal of time in 'domiciliary or house-to-house visitation', which enabled him to 'present the claims of the temperance reformation to the hearts and homes of our artisan population'. On these visits he secured thirty-nine pledges out of a total of eighty-one. In his journal he made the point that the value of the visits ought not to be measured solely in terms of pledges: 'The full advantage resulting from the system of visitation cannot be fully estimated or anticipated, there being generally a tendency towards improvement according to its opportunities for conversation which does not immediately become evidenced in our pledge-books. A timely visit and persuasive remonstrance have often secured the wavering on the side of virtue, and sustained the weak in their endeavours to break from the destroyer.' In Leicester the agent organised his work more efficiently by getting a roster from the constabulary: 'Having by permission gained access to the police books and the borough prison, he was enabled to pay visits to the most dissolute and abandoned characters that infested the locality, and in a great number of cases succeeded in inducing them to sign the pledge and cast off their old habits.'[55]

In some societies the members themselves took an active part in the work of visiting. This was cited as a sign of a flourishing society, as in Burslem, in contrast to nearby societies that were in a state of decline: 'Occupation is found for every member of the committee of some kind or other. Visiting takes place from house to house and the committee are divided into couples for that purpose.' Many societies mentioned the sort of discipline characteristic of the nonconformist sects, and members who failed to attend regularly were themselves 'visited' and dismissed if lack of attendance persisted. The society in Ashton-under-Lyne proudly reported the sort of individual participation that was probably become increasingly rare as the professional agents took over: 'For several months Mr Brown has energetically laboured in our town, upon his own responsibility, to extend our principles. He has made a great impression upon the working classes, and caused hundreds to visit our Hall who had never done so before . . . Very kindly Mr Broom holds a weekly Reading Class for the working classes, without the slightest expense to them.' The working men expressed their gratitude with a tea party.[56]

The temperance societies participated in the various forms of improvement activity aimed at the working classes. In 1854 in Leicester the members of the 'Temperance, Elocution, and Mutual Improvement Class' presented a series of entertainments. Three years later the society was busy with mutual instruction classes 'to train the young in various branches of elementary education'. It was pointed out that 'one young man, who owes his mental elevation mainly to his union with this institution, is now studying for the ministry'. The establishment of a penny bank by the Leeds Band of Hope and Youths Society was accompanied by the standard expression of confidence in the great things being accomplished: 'It is not sufficient merely to exhort the working classes to exercise economy and forethought, there must be inducements held out, and feasible plans adopted to encourage the formation of habits of providing for the season of adversity and affliction.'[57]

The temperance societies contributed more than their share of the organised ceremonial that was so conspicuous a part of the public life of the mid-Victorian cities. In addition to the usual anniversary meetings and processions, temperance festivals were a special feature of the movement. These sometimes assumed vast proportions, as at the Liverpool and Birkenhead temperance festival in the spring of 1856. In contrast to the spontaneity and informality of the movement in the 1830s, the dominant note now was co-ordination and inter-group co-operation. The festival was organised by a co-ordinating committee: 'Upwards of thirty societies, including the Ladies Total Abstinence Association, the Sons of Temperance, the Central Band of Hope, the Birkenhead Auxiliary of the United Kingdom Alliance, the Birkenhead and Liverpool Tents, and the St George and Iona Temples, were each represented by a member of the General Committee, upon whom devolved the entire management of the whole of the festivities.' The proceedings began on a Monday with a grand temperance procession of the participating societies. Tuesday brought a flower show and a performance by a Welsh choir, followed by a poultry exhibition on Wednesday. On Thursday handbell ringers competed for prizes. On Friday the English and Welsh choral societies gave a concert. Throughout the week a bazaar was in operation, including gymnastic exhibitions, a tent devoted to mesmeric performances, and various amusements, 'too innumerable to mention'.

The official account of the festival in a temperance journal was an integral part of the proceedings, whereby the faithful rejoiced in their faith and in the fellowship of the saints. Intent on proving their 'respectability' − in the most general sense − both to themselves and to outsiders, temperance spokesmen consciously projected an image that reflected what they took to be the basic values of the community. The *Weekly Record*'s description of the festival at Liverpool and Birkenhead combined the familiar sentimental tone with a note of defensiveness.

> Among the numerous arrivals, through the medium of bands, and bows, and ribbons, and medals, we soon discover the lovers of Temperance. Here they are young and old, male and female, the very picture of happiness. Who says a teetotaller cannot be happy? Who dares to call them poor, and thin, and lean, and miserable? Look at these, sir! They do not look as if they were strangers to happiness and comfort, at any rate. The majority are composed of young men and women, whose healthy and neat appearance betoken demonstratively the agreement of abstinence with their various constitutions, mental and physical. Their *bon mots* and ringing peals of laughter as they land on the platform evince a state of feeling quite the opposite of melancholy. It is manifest that they do not want wine, or gin, or beer, to heighten their elevation.[58]

A poem entitled 'Acrostic: the Birkenhead Temperance Festival' struck the note of cheerful optimism that the movement was striving for:

> Be this a time of cheerfulness, of harmony and joy;

> In works of true philanthropy we now our hands employ.
> Right glad are we to see the crowds beneath our banners come,
> Keeping this happy Festival, and 'feeling quite at home'.
> Endeavour we, by every means, the noble cause to spread,
> Nor shall we then have spent in vain the week at Birkenhead.
> Hail to the Star of Temperance, which on our land has risen,
> Ere long it will have useless made the Workhouse and the Prison.[59]

Despite Livesey's complaint about trends in the temperance movements throughout the country, his own group in Preston was moving in the same direction. Livesey himself spoke in the new accents of earnestness and even deference to elites whose support was needed. In a letter to the Mayor of Preston, Livesey and a colleague summarised 'the progress of temperance in Preston'. They quoted with gratitude a statement by the mayor in which he congratulated the temperance movement on having contributed to a decrease in crime and drunkenness in the borough. They continued in a tone that was rather different from Livesey in the 1830s: 'We trust you will not think us exceeding the bounds of propriety if, with your excellent testimony as to the increase of sobriety before us, we lay before you and the public generally the recent extraordinary efforts of the Preston Temperance Society, which we know to have contributed considerably to this most gratifying result.' They concluded with a rather unctuous statement linking temperance with the official mid-Victorian values.

> No less acceptable, we trust, will this statement be to your worship, who, by patronising every movement and association connected with the religious, moral, and social improvement of the town, has demonstrated that the personal labour, pecuniary resources, and official influence of the chief magistrate of a borough can be concentrated upon objects infinitely more valuable to the well-being of society than the mere 'hospitalities' with which the office of mayor is by some too often associated. No greater honour could be desired, we conceive, than to have the rule of a sober town; and encouraged by your approval and that of the respectable inhabitants of the borough, we assure you it is the ambition and anxious desire of all the working teetotallers and of our committee to make Preston a model in this respect.[60]

The round of activities that occupied the temperance movement in the mid-Victorian cities is clearly set forth in Livesey's summary of what was going on in Preston, where the movement was flourishing. A new hall had been opened. When the Tuesday-night meetings overflowed,

Sunday-night meetings were begun, which were also crowded. 'Our members have rapidly increased weekly; and to prevent their return to the public house, and to attract others to come among us, we commenced a Saturday night Temperance concert, which soon became so much crowded that it is now extended to Monday night also. Here our reformed characters enjoy themselves in innocent relaxation, and, by listening to and joining in our Temperance melodies, get more and more established in their teetotal principles.' According to Livesey, the movement in Preston was really booming: 'The revival has extended to every part of the town; and such is the anxiety to attend Temperance meetings, that, in addition to the above four in the week, the hall is now open every evening, the other nights being occupied by lectures, Band of Hope gatherings, female meetings or meetings of the "Sons of Temperance". Though the hall will accommodate from 800 to 900 it is found much too small.' Livesey's summary depicts the familiar pattern of highly organised activity that characterised the mid-Victorian temperance movement: 'We have received within the last three months more than a thousand pledges, and during our New Year's Revival Meetings alone 402 names were enrolled in our book. The New Hall, to which a reading room and a bath room are attached, is open from morning to night every day in the week, free to members. In addition to the three divisions of the "Sons of Temperance" and two of the "Rechabites", both secret orders, which provide for sickness and death, already existing, a fourth is to be formed this week. The females are as zealous as the males; they hold their own meetings, and have recently established a division of "the Daughters of Temperance".'[61]

Livesey deplored the fact that the hiring of professional agents had led to a decline in the sort of militant proselytising by teetotal working men that characterised the early days of the movement. He pointed with pride to the persistence of extensive working-class participation in the movement in Preston in the 1850s. But his description indicates that there, as in other cities, working men were involved in a movement that had gradually changed its character.

The work is chiefly carried on by the unpaid efforts of our working men, many of them being reformed characters, whose plain speeches produce a deep impression on those of their own class. They are at work agitating the cause after the hours of labour every night; and inclement as has been the weather, they still continue their Sunday afternoon meetings in various parts of the town, especially in those places most noted for drinking. Tracts and publications have been distributed by tens of thousands; and on Saturday nights from ten to twelve, and on Sunday nights from eight to ten o'clock (notorious hours for drinking), our friends and young converts turn out to distribute tracts to all they meet affected with liquor.[62]

These working men were volunteers in the service of middle-class respectability.

The mid-Victorian temperance movement was a central component of the cult of respectability. Working men who involved themselves in it found it virtually impossible to escape the implications of the narrowly middle-class version of consensus values that permeated the movement. Here was the classic case of wretched working men being assisted to achieve that degree of self-help that would raise them towards their betters. The agent of the Leeds Temperance Society was voicing what he knew to be the views of his employers when he took a line reminiscent of the provident societies and the principles of 1834: 'The idea seems to be now generally impressed upon the minds of the working classes especially, that our system is a good one, and worthy of their adoption. Tracts are received with thankfulness, and I have good reason to believe, perused with attention.'[63]

But the temperance movement posed a subtler threat to the values and ideology of the working-class subculture. This was the tendency to associate the movement with the highest ideals of the culture while at the same time linking it to social motives and mechanisms of less exalted sort. In a tract on temperance published by the Chambers brothers, Dr Lees set out from the high ground of improvement.

It is clear, that to operate advantageously on the masses, their moral, intellectual, and physical condition must be raised. Let the friends of Temperance direct their energies to these objects. Wherever an effort is making to establish schools, to substitute harmless public entertainments for what are vicious, to remedy social grievances and disorders, to encourage a love of the fine arts, to rouse the fancy and stimulate the moral and religious sentiments — there let the friends of Temperance be foremost. Putting away all petty and sectarian differences, let them be seen uniting with philanthropic men generally in everything which can tend to elevate the people in the scale of being. Keeping before them what has already been attained by one section of the community, let them endeavour to bring up the other to the same standard.

Lees moved easily from a reference to the 'scale of being' to the suggestion that working men should emulate their social superiors who had already reached that high level, and strive to win their approval: 'What that standard is, cannot be too emphatically told: it is that degree of *self-respect and regard for public approbation*, which, independently of higher motives, lift men above a habitual indulgence in mean and sensual enjoyments, and stimulate them, by self-denial and perseverance, to attain a position equally consolatory to their own feelings, and respectable in the eyes of their fellow-creatures.' Thus, in the name of realism, Lees assimilated the desire for self-respect to the cult of respectability, with its emphasis on winning the good opinion of the middle classes. 'Let these things be pressed unremittingly on the consideration of the managers of all kinds of Temperance associations, and generally on all who wish well to social improvement.'[64] The means to social improvement was to be an appeal to the social motives of working men, not to the idealism so esteemed by the teetotal movement of the 1830s.

The preceding passage from Dr Lees' tract was quoted approvingly in a pamphlet by G. J. Holyoake. As a radical critic of society and as a militant exponent of working-class secularism, Holyoake was not at all in tune with a movement that combined Christianity and respectability. Yet he was committed to the temperance cause as one of the many avenues of improvement that would necessarily have the support of any true friend of the working classes. For Holyoake and other working-class radicals individual improvement, through temperance and other means, was a fundamental value whose validity was self-evident. He disagreed with Lees only in rejecting a legislative solution to the problem. As a rationalist who regarded virtue as 'the child of reason, not of force', Holyoake was confident that the temperance cause needed 'neither coercion nor scolding'.[65] In practice it was difficult for Holyoake and other working-class radicals to keep their temperance activity free from entanglement with the middle-class version, which had such a different social connotation.

This chapter, concerned with aspects of middle-class hegemony in the mid-Victorian cities, has singled out the temperance movement for attention, because it illustrates the way in which the radical belief in individual improvement was vulnerable to assimilation to cultural patterns determined by the middle-class. A more pervasive manifestation of the moral and intellectual ascendancy of the middle-class was the chapel, with which the temperance movement had such close ties and affinities. Although generalisation in this area is difficult, it seems probable that the 1850s and 1860s saw an increasing involvement of the upper and middle strata of the working-class with Nonconformist congregations that were dominated by the middling and lower middle classes. Here working men were particularly susceptible to the cult of respectability. Moreover, the Sunday schools, both Nonconformist and Anglican, brought all segments of the working-class into contact with the hegemonic activity of the middle-class. Finally, the various religious institutions concerned with rescuing and elevating the poor — home missions, domestic missions, clothing clubs, Dorcas societies, etc. — also contributed significantly to the maintenance of middle-class pre-eminence.

Under these circumstances even working men who remained aloof from church and chapel found it difficult to preserve their moral and intellectual independence.

Notes

1.   Aspects of middle-class values and ideology are treated in the following: E.P. Hennock, *Fit and Proper Persons*, London 1973; John Vincent, *The Formation of the Liberal Party 1857–1868*, London 1966; John Foster, *Class Struggle and the Industrial Revolution*, London 1974; Asa Briggs, *Victorian Cities*, London 1963; Donald Read, *Cobden and Bright*, New York 1968. For Gramsci's formulation of the concept of hegemony, see Gwyn Williams, 'The Concept of "egemonia" in the Thought of Antonio Gramsci', *Journal of the History of Ideas*, XXI, 1960; Thomas R. Bates, 'Gramsci and the Theory of Hegemony', ibid., XXXVI, 1975, John Cammett, *Antonio Gramsci and the Origins of Italian Communism*, Stanford 1967, pp. 204–6; Gramsci, *Selections from the Prison Notebooks*, New York 1971, pp. 12–13, 55–60, 160–1.

2.   Theodore Zeldin, *Emile Ollivier and the Liberal Empire of Napoleon III*, Oxford 1963, pp. 1–40; Gordon Wright, *France in Modern Times*, New York 1960, pp. 238–9; Leonard Krieger, *The German Idea of Freedom*, Boston 1957, pp. 341–58. Hajo Holborn, *History of Modern Germany 1840–1945*, New York 1969, pp. 116–19.

3.   Journal of George Harwood, February 1865, MS, Nottingham Public Library.

4.   MS, Archives Department, Leeds Public Libraries. See also Derek Fraser, 'Edward Baines', in Patricia Hollis, ed., *Pressure from Without in Early Victorian England*, London 1974.

5.   *Surrey Street Circuit Reporter*, November 1868.

6.   *Manchester Papers*, September 1856; *Papers for the School Master*, March 1851; Joseph Hibbert, *A Lecture upon Hyde*, Hyde 1856.

7.   *Manchester Papers*, September 1856; *Bradford Review*, 18 January and 13 February 1858.

8.   *Manchester Guardian*, 3 September 1856; *Home Mission Field of the Church of England*, no. 10, June 1860.

9.   *British Workman*, 1 November 1855; *Oldham Chronicle*, 8 January 1859, cutting in Samuel Bamford, Diary, MS, Manchester Reference Library; *Nottingham Daily Guardian*, 30 August 1866.

10.   *Surrey Street Circuit Reporter*, August 1868.

11.   *Report of the Commissioners Appointed to Inquire into the State of Popular Education in England*, London 1861, V, 15; *Parliamentary Papers*, 1860, XII, Q. 3456; Tait, *Oldham Lyceum*, p. 47.

12.   *Leeds Mercury*, 6 January and 6 April 1864.

13.   J.M. Ludlow and Lloyd Jones, *Progress of the Working Class 1832–1867*, London 1867, p. 293; Samuel Robinson, *Letters to the Persons Working in the Dukinfield Old Mill*, 1854.

14.   Asa Briggs, *Victorian People*, London 1954, pp. 124–49, and his introduction to Samuel Smiles, *Self-Help*, London 1958; Alexander Tyrrell, 'Class Consciousness

in Early Victorian Britain: Samuel Smiles, Leeds Politics, and the Self-Help Creed', *Journal of British Studies*, 1970; A.W. Coats, ed., *The Classical Economists and Economic Policy*, London 1971, pp. 180–9.

15. Smiles, *Self-Help*, pp. 315–16.
16. Ibid., pp. 298–300.
17. Ibid., p. 316.
18. Ibid., pp. 372–4.
19. Tait, *Oldham Lyceum*, p. 25, quoting annual report of 1850.
20. Arbitrator, *Employers and Employed*, Manchester 1856, John Rylands Library.
21. Samuel Robinson, *Letters to the Persons Working in the Dukinfield Old Mill*, 1854.
22. *Bradford Observer*, 20 April 1848; *Manchester Guardian*, 15 October 1858.
23. Yorkshire Union of Mechanics' Institutes, *Annual Report*, 1856; James Hole, *Light, More Light!*, London 1860, p. 50.
24. *Bradford Observer*, 8 June 1848.
25. Factory Inspectors, *Report for the Period Ending 31 October 1864*, p. 58.
26. John Kitching, *A Lecture Addressed to Working Men, on the Opportunities which they Have for Improving their Minds*, York 1860; *Oldham Chronicle*, 8 January 1859.
27. 'On the Advantages and Pleasures of Institutions for the Promotion of Mental Improvement . . . '
28. Smiles, *Self-Help*, pp. 378–80.
29. Briggs, *Victorian People*, p. 125.
30. Baines, 'Mental Improvement'.
31. Geoffrey Best, *Mid-Victorian Britain 1851–1875*, London 1971, pp. 256–63; G.M. Young, *Victorian England: Portrait of an Age*, Oxford 1953, pp. 12–25.
32. *Social Science: Being Selections from John Cassell's Prize Essays by Working Men and Women*, London 1861, pp. 216–17.
33. Ibid., pp. 186–7.
34. Ibid., pp. 200–3.
35. Ibid., pp. 1–10.
36. Ibid.
37. See Mary Sturt, *The Education of the People*, London 1967; John Hurt, *Education in Evolution*, London 1971; J.M. Goldstrom, *Education: Elementary Education 1780–1900*, Newton Abbot 1972; Frank Smith, *A History of Elementary Education, 1760–1902*, London 1931; Brian Simon, *Studies in the History of Education 1780–1870*, London 1960, pp. 337–50.
38. See W.P. McCann, 'Trade Unionists, Artisans and the 1870 Education Act', *British Journal of Educational Studies*, XVIII, 1970; Simon, pp. 350–67.
39. High Pavement Boys' Day School, Minutes of the Committee, 1873; Register of Students; Log Book, 31 October 1864; MSS, Nottingham University Library.
40. *Report of the Commissioners Appointed to Inquire into the State of Popular Education in England*, London 1861, vol. II, 183; *Parliamentary Papers*, 1870, LIV, 128, 174.
41. Ibid., 128; *Report on Popular Education*, 1861, II, 218.
42. Asher Tropp, *The School Teachers*, London 1957, pp. 5–77.
43. *Educational Expositor*, vol. VI, 1853.
44. Ibid.
45. Hulme Operatives Day School, Minute Book, MS, Manchester Reference Library; High Pavement Boys' Day School, Register of Students, MS, University of Nottingham Library.
46. *Parliamentary Papers*, 1870, XX, 155.
47. *Report on Popular Education*, 1861, II, 240–2.

48. Ibid., 257; High Pavement Boys' Day School, Log Book, includes the Inspector's report of 6 January 1866, MS, University of Nottingham Library.

49. British and Foreign School Society, *A Handbook to the Borough Road Schools*, London 1857. British and Foreign School Society, *Daily Lesson Book Number Two*, London 1842.

50. Newcastle Temperance Society, *Third Annual Report*. See Brian Harrison, *Drink and the Victorians*, London 1971.

51. *Testimony for the Millions, Being Speeches of Working Men, Delivered at the Temperance Demonstration*, Newcastle-on-Tyne 1847.

52. *Leeds Temperance Herald,* 1 April 1837; *National Temperance Magazine,* September 1845; *Northern Temperance Almanack*, 1844; *The Northern Temperance and Rechabite Almanack, for the Year of Our Lord 1842, Being . . . the 8th Year of Teetotalism and 7th of Rechabitism.*

53. *Weekly Record*, 21 March 1857.

54. Joseph Livesey, *Reminiscences*, pp. 37–8; *Weekly Record*, 13 September 1856.

55. *Weekly Record*, 19 April 1856.

56. Ibid., 11 July 1857, 3 May 1856.

57. *British Temperance Advocate*, June 1854; *Weekly Record*, 28 March 1857.

58. Ibid., 24 May 1856.

59. Ibid.

60. Ibid., 7 March 1857.

61. Ibid.

62. Ibid.

63. Leeds Temperance Society, *Nineteenth Report*, Leeds 1850.

64. G.J. Holyoake, *The Social Means of Promoting Temperance*, n.d. [1859].

65. Ibid.

8 THE WORKING-CLASS SUBCULTURE

Mid-Victorian working men did not passively acquiesce in middle-class hegemony. A robust working-class subculture, cradled in the traditions of early–Victorian radicalism, encouraged resistance and independence. Although the aspiration to structural change had disappeared, there persisted a cluster of values and attitudes that constituted an alternative to middle-class ideology: class consciousness and pride, rejection of subordination and deference, and a realistic scepticism in the face of middle-class propaganda and pretensions. The keystone of the working-class value system was independence, in various forms. Without attempting to change the class structure, the 'independent working man' sought to mitigate its effects and to maintain a degree of freedom from the controls imposed from above. His values had developed to a large extent in opposition to a continuum of middle-class attitudes towards the working classes, ranging from outright contempt and hostility to smug condescension. Central to the subculture was an assertion of the worth and dignity of working men, and their right to develop their faculties to the fullest. Implicit in it was a denial of the middle-class claim to social, intellectual, and moral superiority. In this context the commitment to individual improvement, so prominent in the traditions of radicalism, persisted as an egalitarian alternative to the middle-class version of consensus values. Institutions such as trade unions, friendly societies and co-operative societies helped sustain the values of the subculture while at the same time enabling working men to be somewhat less dependent on the economic system. Thus there was a widespread effort to maintain working-class independence and self-respect in a society where power and status were concentrated in the hands of the propertied classes.

To be sure, mid-Victorian working men did not spend their waking hours in the earnest pursuit of high ideals. They had more than enough to do to keep their jobs, stay on good terms with employers, and eke out a livelihood. There is no reason to exempt working men from the scepticism that we bestow on the ostentatious idealism of the other Victorians. Yet it would be a mistake to see no more than conventional rhetorical frosting in their incessant expressions of principle. A number of circumstances combined to give genuine substance to the official values of the working-class subculture. First of all, idealism functioned as a weapon in continuing class conflict, latent and overt. In confrontation with a middle-class that was aggressively insisting on the validity and purity of its social philosophy, working men who prized

their independence were forced into the counter-assertion of an alternative. Second, mid-Victorian culture encouraged men of all classes not
only to affirm high ideals but to take them seriously. In this matter the
historical distance separating us from the Victorian age exceeds the
chronological. Third, the momentum of early-Victorian radicalism,
with its impassioned and utopian devotion to principle, also contributed
to the idealism of the working-class subculture.

But the idealism that kept alive the old radical values brought with it
a vulnerability to processes of assimilation and attenuation. To the
extent that working men were imbued with the sentimental idealism of
the culture as a whole, their affirmations of principle were liable to
become just another standardised expression of high-minded aspiration.
The working-class subculture was vulnerable to a cultural style that
put a premium on the mere avowal of moral ideals. The incessant
reiteration of a few principles carried the possibility, to which the
culture as a whole was so susceptible, of routinisation and banality.
At the same time, the idealistic orientation of the working-class subculture also generated a disposition to accept at face value middle-class
formulations of consensus ideals. Finally, quite apart from the social
and ideological activity of the middle-class, working men were very
well integrated into a culture given to the proclamation of its grand
purposes and to the celebration of activity devoted to those ends.
Deeply involved in the network of institutions devoted to the cause
of improvement, they were necessarily predisposed to accept the
implicit claim that substantial improvement for all was in fact being
achieved. Caught up in the mid-Victorian tendency to inflate the
moral significance of routine and limited activity, working men came
to perceive their own institutions as contributing not only to specific
working-class objectives but also to the great ends of the community
as a whole. In accepting these cultural patterns working men also
tended to accept the legitimacy of the social roles and presuppositions
that were interwoven with them.

In this cultural milieu it was difficult for working men to maintain
their ideological independence in the face of an amiable middle-class
version of consensus values. At every turn they encountered middle-
class improvers and liberals who were articulating similar principles but
in subtly different form. Whereas working-class radicalism had demanded
opportunities for working-class improvement in the course of a critique
of a society that systematically denied such opportunities to the mass
of the people, middle-class activity on behalf of 'elevating the masses'
presupposed working-class subordination and social roles that reflected
the social structure. In the name of progress and improvement for all,
the middle-class was constructing new forms of deference. Unlike
traditional ideologies, which explained to the common people why they

ought to be content with their wretched lot, the middle-class liberal formulation of consensus values did not operate as a sedative to dull the pain, either by diverting attention to the hope of bliss in the after life or by inducing resignation to the inevitability imposed by Providence or the laws of political economy. On the contrary, the primary emphasis was on the pursuit of higher and better things. Everyone, working men above all, was in the fortunate position of being able to move ahead without limit, morally, intellectually, and socially. Middle-class spokesmen had co-opted the rhetoric of equality. Articulating the goals of the community in formally universal terms that veiled inegalitarian presuppositions, they invited all men to join in the common enterprise of progress. Improvement was equally accessible to all, although working men were starting at a lower level. Thus mid-Victorian liberalism presented an elusive target to working men who had learned to recognise the self-serving character of political economy and the gospel of success.

When, in the name of high principle, working men were invited to pursue improvement and advancement on middle-class terms, it was difficult to refuse. Progressive merchants and manufacturers depicted the goals of improvement in language that was similar to that of working-class radicalism: the fostering of independence, self-reliance, and self-respect. Many traits of the working-class social character, as defined by a generation of radicals in opposition to a system of class domination, now found a place in the middle-class model of the 'respectable working man'. It was not easy to distinguish the working man who valued knowledge and education as means to genuine independence from someone who simply conformed to the image prescribed by his superiors. Virtues that were prized for their own sake could easily be bent into an unintended form and given a different significance. The pursuit of self-respect could and often did lead to the cult of respectability. Moreover, the upper strata of the working-class, the most articulate exponents of radical values, were also the most susceptible to the social pressure to separate themselves from the mass below and to identify with the petty bourgeoisie above. Thus social as well as ideological forces predisposed them to embrace the cult of respectability. Despite these circumstances, however, democratic and egalitarian values were kept alive in a subculture that successfully withstood the full consolidation of middle-class hegemony.

'Working-class subculture' is a methodological construct that is intended to provide a means of describing the presence among mid-Victorian working men of values and attitudes that were very much of the culture as a whole and yet distinct from the dominant middle-class version of the prevailing ethos. Such a construct is not a vehicle for quasi-scientific generalisation, but is designed to encompass considerable diversity in form and content. The examples discussed in the following sections, therefore, are not offered as instances of a monolithic 'working-class subculture' but as diverse manifestations of values and attitudes shared, to varying degrees, by mid-Victorian working men. The evidence would seem to suggest that some such values were widely accepted in principle by working-class strata above the 'residuum'. My research tends to bear out Geoffrey Best's comment on William Lovett and Thomas Cooper: 'They certainly did not speak for the whole of their class but I share a general impression that more of their class thought like this than during any earlier or later periods in the century.'[1]

(1) *Independence and Self-Respect*

The cluster of traits prized by the working-class subculture — rationality, civility, morality, self-respect, responsibility — has to be understood in the context of an aspiration to genuine independence and freedom. Rationality was admired not only for its own sake, but also because it connoted intellectual freedom and the ability to make independent judgements. Civility meant neighbourliness, good fellowship, and mutuality among equals. Morality meant the observance of proper standards of behaviour in interpersonal relations, especially within the family. Responsibility meant looking after the needs of one's family in a society where economic insecurity was an overriding fact of working-class existence. The working man's contribution to a friendly society represented a conscious and responsible decision, not a surrender to 'middle-class values'.

Although there was, of course, no 'typical' Victorian working man, certain ideas and attitudes tend to recur in various contexts. Occasionally a number of familiar themes are compactly expressed in a few sentences, as in a passage from the autobiography of Robert Lowery, a Chartist who later became active in the temperance movement. Lowery's statement can serve as a point of departure for a consideration of the values of the working-class subculture: 'It is in the very nature of the intelligent and virtuous to feel self-respect, and the claims of manhood as man. They can bear poverty and exclusion from the ranks of the wealthy. They know they are not equals in wealth, but they cannot bear insult, and to be told that because they are not their equals in wealth they are not capable of being equal in intelligence, integrity, and manhood.'[2] This passage makes explicit a number of attitudes which are clearly present, although often only implicitly, in working-class documents of the period. First there is the egalitarian assertion of equal moral and intellectual potential among all men, regardless of class. The tone of the passage is not at all deferential, but populist. The 'claims of manhood' are made in the face of a middle-class denial of such claims, whether explicitly in the form of 'insult', or implicitly in attitude, gesture and tone of voice. Lowery demands respect, on the basis of demonstrated virtue and intelligence. It is a demand for respect for moral and intellectual qualities, regardless of class status. All this is remote from the cult of respectability.

Ordinary working men were quite aware of the operation of the class system and the working-class subculture embodied a continuing effort to resist the imposition of a narrowly middle-class version of shared ideals. Two letters written by an ironworker's wife during a strike in 1866 illustrate the way in which working men combined a commitment to consensus values with an assertion of working-class independence and a critique of the shortcomings of the middle classes. In their exposure of middle-class hypocrisy, the letters provide a vivid picture of a social system which took pride in the profession of the highest moral ideals only to have them abandoned in practice when they conflicted with class interest.[3]

In a scathing indictment of employers' bad faith, the ironworker's wife contrasted their platform rhetoric with their actual behaviour: 'We are told that we ought to live in good houses, clothe and educate our children properly; and yet at every opportunity the masters have, they come down upon us for a reduction. Well, the Lord forgive them for their cruelty this time.' She recalled the patronising attitude of the middle-class improvers towards working men: 'We are told of the extravagance, wickedness, and immorality of the working classes, and how we have kept ourselves "quiet and peaceable during these trying times", just as if we were some species of wild beast, whom it was the special province of these platform reformers to keep right.' She pointed out that their tune would change as soon as they decided that they needed working-class support in a political movement: 'But wait, Sir, until this reform agitation takes place; then we shall hear of all the good qualities possessed by the workmen. All our virtues will be discovered then.' She found the same sort of hypocrisy among the ministers and elders of the chapels and churches, and concluded that the poor could expect sympathy only from each other: 'We know by this time how many of our pastors, deacons, and elders have visited us in our troubles; we know how many of them have studied "Mrs Grundy" more than the teachings of Christ; . . . I know many of you have worked hard at your sewing meetings, bazaars, and in many other ways, to free your little Bethels from debt. Which of them, and how many of your ministers and leaders have come to you in your affliction and asked if you had bread in your cupboards? Have they not rather given you the cold shoulder, and all their sympathies have gone to the oppressor?'

She was appalled by the fact that when the strike was broken the steadiest and most respected working men were fired. 'And who are the men who are singled out? Not the men who can leave their work to drink during hours and waste the property of their employers, but steady, intelligent, and upright men who try to do justly towards master and man.' Because they had served as delegates to other towns in an attempt to win support for the strike, their high moral character was not enough to get them their jobs back. 'Does it not appear a mockery and a sham to talk to the working man of "mechanics' institutes", "reading rooms", and "clubs", when we know from bitter experience that whenever a working man takes advantage of the same he becomes the target for all to shoot at.' She had just about lost all faith in the employing class: 'There was far more meant in the words of that Staffordshire employer "than met the ear" when he asked the question, "What do the working classes want with reading rooms and mechanics' institutes; all they require is the gin palace and the beer house." Does it not seem that there was a premium held out to the man to keep himself as low as possible in morality; no inducement to advance himself. It appears so paltry and mean to take revenge in such a way upon their best workmen.'

The ironworker's wife, like many mid-Victorian working men, had no illusions about masters who 'so often break the faith'. She was especially contemptuous of their pious talk of improvement for the working classes. Her commitment to the familiar cultural values, so similar to the official line, was not the result of middle-class propaganda, but in spite of it. She was expressing an aspiration to independence and emancipation, in the best tradition of working-class radicalism.

Beneath the often abstract and formal language of the 'intelligent working man' lay a clearsighted awareness of social realities, especially the actual attitudes of the middle classes. Working men were quite capable of recognising the cult of respectability for what it was, despite its superficial resemblance to many of their own values. Although for the most part one finds only scattered and indirect indications of this sort of thing, occasionally one runs across a document which discloses more fully this realistic and hard-headed component of the working-class subculture. A case in point is a letter written by an apprentice to his master after seven years of service in a Sheffield warehouse.[4] The apprentice made it plain, on the one hand, that his master's conduct had always been 'gentlemanly', and that he had provided the best food and excellent lodgings. What bothered him, however, was that the master had the cheek to reproach his apprentice for 'loving money'. This was too much, and he proceeded to explain to his former master exactly what social values were actually dominant in the warehouse: 'The one lesson taught everyone, by every arrangement in your establishment, was to preach up the importance of money . . . morning, noon, and night, the staple topic of admiration was wealth. He that had obtained it no matter how, was "the fortunate", the "respectable man", the "honourable and high minded person"; while he that was poor, was the constant object of sneer, or pity, or lampoon.' As for the complaint that he loved money, the apprentice asked: 'How was it possible for a young man that ate with you, and worked at your elbow, to escape being mammonised?' In fact, all masters taught the same lesson: 'That one lesson every day and everywhere, on every occasion, and to every man, woman, and child, is the paramount value of money, respectability, station and pleasure.'

This sort of realism, reinforced by resentment at middle-class pretensions to superiority, led to widespread working-class resistance to the preaching of middle-class improvers. Here also much of the evidence is necessarily indirect, since prudence required the appearance of acquiescence in the line handed down from above. But there would seem to be good reason to take at face value the complaint of a prize essayist, who had himself succumbed to the blandishments of the middle classes, that many working men were hostile to high-minded pleas for more cordial relations between classes. There were thousands of 'malcontents', he said, who were given to comments of this sort to philanthropists who wanted to improve the working classes: 'You make laws in your own favour; you lay burdens on our shoulders that you will not touch with your fingers; you overtask us; you underpay us; and when we receive our miserable pittance of wages, you would have us make our obeisance and say, "Thank you, sir." Go to; enjoy your rank and wealth, and if you do us no good in the way of bettering our circumstances, never mind mending our manners ; let us alone.'[5] Although the essayist attributed these views primarily to the worst paid operatives, they were undoubtedly widespread also among the more affluent, who were tired of sweet talk from above about elevating the masses.

Far from being confined to occasional carping by failures and malcontents, criticism of middle-class propaganda and pretensions was an established pattern of the working-class subculture. It represented a continuing effort to assert an egalitarian version of the consensus values in the face of constant middle-class pressure to give them a narrow class form. William Aitken illustrates the readiness of working men to reject the myths and propaganda with which they were being deluged by the middle classes. A provincial grand master of the Oddfellows, Aitken exemplifies the responsible and 'respectable' leader of a working-class institution that was deeply committed to the official values of the culture. Throughout his life, however, he remained faithful to his class and to the values underlying his youthful radicalism. In 1825, at the age of eleven, Aitken worked as a piecer in a cotton mill. When he became active in the short time movement, he was fired. He then turned

to school teaching, and continued his participation in the factory movement and in Chartism. The *Northern Star* described him as a man who
'has suffered considerably from the rampant enemies of man's rights'.[6]
Although in occupational and economic terms, he may be said to have
moved out of the working-class, he displayed few signs of '*embourgeoisement*'. When he rose to a position of leadership in the Oddfellows, he
remained an eloquent spokesman for radical values. In that spirit he
denounced Benjamin Franklin's platitudes.

Aitken attacked both political economy and the gospel of success in
his article on Franklin. Dismissing as 'absurdity' the maxim, 'Early to
bed and early to rise, makes a man healthy, wealthy, and wise', Aitken
pointed out that 'the great bulk of mankind are hard workers, go to
bed "early", and rise "early", but the work that millions endure
destroys their "health", the small earnings they receive do not find them
the necessaries of life, to say nothing of "wealth", and they have not
time, by study and an exhausted daily frame to make themselves
"wise".' Thousands of men and women, 'labouring hard from year end
to year end, are under-fed, under-clothed, and badly housed', and 'the
small amount of money earned by the multitude of workers prevents
them paying any great sum of money for the teaching of their children'.
As for the maxim, 'There are no gains without pains', Aitken reversed it:
'There are many pains with few gains, and plenty gains with few pains.'
That is, 'The multitude of hard workers have the "pains", minus the
"gains", while the usurer ... the speculators in consols, money dealers
generally, and a shoal of others of the same kith and kin, have the
"gains", minus the "pains".'[7]

A similar example of the ability of working men to see through the
ideological mystification practised by middle-class propagandists turns
up in the minute book of a mutual improvement society in Manchester
in the 1860s, composed of Sunday school teachers and students over
the age of sixteen. Their acceptance of the dominant value system was
accompanied by a criticism of the social order and a rejection of
attempts to explain away its deficiencies. In August 1863, following
the usual practice of the group, a member read an essay that served as
the basis for discussion.[8] He took the negative on the question, 'Are
the working men of England treated as men and do they get a fair
day's wage for a fair day's work?' In the essay he denounced 'the evil
effects arising from the working man not being paid sufficient for his
labour to enable him to keep his wife at home to nurse and train up his
children in the way they ought to go'. Not only spinners, but also 'too
many mechanics, both fitters and turners are working for little over
20/- per week'. 'The self-acting minders ... are a class much to be
pitied for the long tedious hours which they work and the miserable
wages they receive.' The minutes summarise his remarks: 'He requests

us, if we would believe, to go and see for ourselves the men and women who work in our cotton mills, for then we would see them pale, worn and withered. Men who if they had not been worked harder than the slave would have been robust, healthy looking men.' The essayist was equally blunt in dealing with the second part of the topic: 'Let those . . . who think that the men are treated as they ought, ask themselves whether it is right after a man has served his master faithfully and given him the best of his days to turn him off when he sees the frost of years begin to whiten his hair or when his sight begins to fail him? And yet, there are plenty of firms who claim respectability who do such things. As a result, because their wages have been so low, and through no fault of their own, men have to end their days in our workhouses.' He cited another example, based on personal knowledge, in which a cotton spinner was sacked immediately when he took the trouble to give his employer advance notice that he was going to take a better job with another firm.

The essayist also explained the disastrous effect of low wages on family life. If young working men decided to wait until they were able to support a wife before getting married, 'they must wait until the end of their days'. When a man did marry, his wife would have to go out to work. According to the minutes, the essayist 'pictured in piteous words — where married women who have for the better support of their families to work in our cotton mills and leave their young children out to nurse and the nurses in many cases drug them to sleep — thus ensuring to us in years to come a sickly and weakly generation'. He concluded by advising working men to 'combine into Unions and promising them if they do not that the days of Feudalism or worse than that will come when we shall lose the proud name of Free-born English Men'.

In the debate that ensued, not much opposition developed. An attempt at rebuttal, citing the laws of supply and demand, evoked a spirited rejoinder from another member of the group, who argued that the essayist had merely stated the facts: 'His arguments were chiefly brought from the cotton operatives. The men of England undoubtedly are slaves and every cotton lord, he can prove, wastes a generation in ten years.' When the adjourned debate resumed two weeks later, the same speaker disposed of the rags to riches myth: 'We point out to him one or two rich men who have risen from humble ranks, but we forget to tell him of the many hundreds who though they have been persevering, hard working men have not risen.' These young men had not been taken in by the myth of success. On the contrary, they took pride in rejecting its grandiose claims.

Even working-class rhetoric which at first glance seems indistinguishable from the preachments of middle-class improvers on closer inspection turns out to be rather different. A case in point is a letter supporting a proposal for the creation of a system of secular education, written by a a working man who was also a Wesleyan local preacher. Although the writer perceived himself in terms of that thoroughly mid-Victorian category, 'the intelligent working man', he did not speak the language of deference. On the contrary, the burden of his letter was that the Wesleyan ministers who opposed secular education were merely expressing the views of the rich and had failed to consult the poorer members of the congregation. 'As a member and local preacher in the body, I move and have continual intercourse with my own order — operatives and artisans of intelligence — who complain to be so misrepresented. The fact is, our opinions are unascertained; we are never consulted.' He contrasted the views of 'the Wesleyan artisan and the Wesleyan poor' with those of 'the Plutocracy' who dominated the congregation. In this populist vein he delivered a paean to education which combined official pieties with an anti-Establishment bias: 'The tendency is to imbue the mind with a power which enables the possessor to estimate true excellence, and begets the aspiration which is necessary to a personal attainment of it. It tends to check that fulsome cant and fanaticism which degrades the Christian Church — to induce that self-respect so salutary in social life, in restraining from excess of all kinds.'[9]

Underlying the demand for respect so pervasive in the working-class subculture was resentment at the casual assumption of superiority on the part of the middle classes. Quite often, therefore, what appear to be the clichés of respectability actually functioned as a defence of working men against the strictures being levelled at them by their 'betters'. An official of the Oddfellows praising members for 'their independence, their moral manhood, and their general probity' was engaged in the unending enterprise of refuting middle-class critics. Increasingly in the course of the 1850s working men had to contend with more subtle forms of condescension, in addition to the 'insults' that concerned Lowery. The patronage that was often extended so aggressively to 'deserving' working men carried with it such a presumption of class superiority that even the studiously respectful author of one of Cassell's prize essays was moved to write rather plaintively that although some members of the middle classes 'may have amassed considerable wealth, and thereby have attained a better position in society, it does not follow that they are necessarily more intelligent, or better workers in the cause [of mechanics' institutes] than many of the working men, who take such a lively and active interest in the progress of such institutions'.[10]

In these circumstances the class consciousness and class pride so prominent in the radical movements of the first half of the nineteenth century persisted into the mid-Victorian decades. Among the more militant such sentiments took the form of scornful criticism of working men who had defected to the cult of respectability. Those who pursued the sort of 'respect' bestowed by the middle classes as a reward for docility and conformity found themselves under attack in Harney's *Friend of the People*: 'We have known such — men of some ability, and more self-conceit, who, having made some little progress from misery and obscurity, have forthwith aped "the respectables", offered themselves for purchase to those who had occasion for needy and unscrupulous instruments, and turned their backs upon the class from whom they sprang. Gerald Massey is not one of this rotten tribe.' This passage occurs in a review of a volume of Massey's poetry. In the sentimental mid-Victorian idiom the reviewer praised Massey for not having deserted his class: 'Entertaining a high opinion of Gerald Massey's poetry, there is that about him which we esteem of much greater value than the noblest gifts ever bestowed by Genius on her favourite sons; we allude to his chivalrous devotion to his order — the long-suffering children of Labour.'[11]

Although the demand for a transformation of the social and political system had been abandoned, the co-operative societies provided an institutional vehicle for continuing the old critique of a competitive and acquisitive society. For many working men the co-operative shops were not only a means of buying necessities at a lower price but also a way of preserving a vision of a social order emancipated from the vices of competition. In the face of the overwhelming power of Victorian capitalism, the co-operative movement sought to maintain the working-class values of mutuality and fellowship and to proclaim the possibility of an alternative social order. The co-operators' criticism of the competitive system had a real bite to it. Taking a properly Victorian moral stance, they announced that competition was 'not only a defective but an evil principle, and not calculated to produce that justice between man and man, and that social happiness in society, that human nature requires'. Their view of Victorian society was free of the soothing platitudes of platform rhetoric: 'We see that the fruits of competition are selfishness, discord, contention, and strife; ignorance, vice, and crime in all the forms that misdirected and prostituted human ingenuity can devise.' Where the official line was class harmony, the co-operatives pointed to distrust and conflict: 'It were hopeless to expect man ever to be extricated from the ice-bound grasp of selfishness, so long as competition regulates either social or commercial affairs. Every glance at the results traceable to competitive strife, confirms our opinion that it is unworthy of an honest people.' In principle, the co-operative movement remained committed to the eventual achievement of a total change of system: nothing less than the replacement of competition by co-operation. It was sometimes suggested that shopkeeping was only the first phase in the co-operative movement. The second phase in the movement would bring much more fundamental changes: then the working-class will 'begin to see that the evils and anomalies by which we are surrounded are in the *system*, and not in the *men* who are engaged in it', and that 'we are individually rather the victims than the agents in this system of cursed competition and strife'.[12]

James Hole, an Owenite who took the lead in establishing a co-operative society in Leeds in the mid-1840s, illustrates the two aspects of the working-class subculture with which this chapter is concerned: a continuing commitment to the traditions of radicalism that combined shrewd realism and utopian optimism. His *Lectures on Social Science and the Organisation of Labour* provides a systematic statement of ideas and values usually expressed only in fragmentary form. To be sure, Hole himself was not a working man, but a *petit bourgeois*. Nevertheless, as an advocate of radical social transformation he was very much a man of the Left. In 1845 he was a founding member of the Leeds Redemption Society, one of a number of Owenite societies formed in the late 1840s to enable 'the Working Classes to work out their own Redemption by Union amongst themselves'. The Leeds society consisted of both Owenites and Radicals. In 1848 Hole became secretary of the Yorkshire Union of Mechanics' Institutes and thereafter devoted himself primarily to the adult education movement. Despite his affiliation with an institution that was the incarnation of middle-class liberalism, however, Hole did not abandon his radicalism. The *Lectures* reaffirmed the principles and aspirations of Owenism along with its critique of the social and economic system. Like other early-Victorian spokesmen of the working-class Left, however, Hole gave up the hope of the transformation of society and concentrated on improvement and reform within the existing order. His *Lectures* illustrate the tension between radicalism and mid-Victorianism that underlay the working-class subculture.[13]

Like many mid-Victorian working men Hole combined a soft and sentimental diction with a shrewd assessment of social reality; and a *de facto* acceptance of the social order with a continuing commitment to egalitarian values. Although his eyes were fixed on distant spiritual horizons, Hole never lost sight of the underlying structure of power and status or failed to perceive it as an obstacle to the achievement of his social ideals. He was under no illusions about the situation in which working men found themselves: 'Their weakness invites oppression; irresponsible power and the abuse of it being inseparably linked.' From this realistic vantage point Hole denounced the 'tremendous degradation of rendering one man dependent for his bread, and that of those near and dear to him, on the whim and caprice of his fellow creature'. His mid-Victorian rhetoric was accompanied by an acute perception of class relationships and a total rejection of the pretensions of the bourgeoisie. 'It cannot be', Hole wrote, 'that a child of God in his true estate of being should enter the presence of his fellows, as tho' he were an interloper, a mere grub or worm on whom it were a condescension for the great man to tread.' The 'serf-like' relation between employer and employed had 'repressed the sentiments of self-respect and moral responsibility'. He also made it plain that social inequality was not conducive to the virtues of which the Victorians were so fond: 'Consider how little of true nobleness and independence can lodge in the breast of the worker, entering his employer's presence as a socially inferior being, not daring to express his thoughts if conscious that they differed from his Master's, and who must take note of his slightest word, lest he smile at an inopportune moment.' Hole never let his reader forget that it was power that counted: 'The relation between master and servant approaches slavery in the degree in which the servant is deficient in counteractive force.'[14]

Hole was just as realistic in his assessment of the middle-class and its ideology. He dismissed the arguments of political economy as impudent rationalisations. 'The right of the capitalist to grasp all he can, and give his workmen as little as he can, is only surpassed in injustice by the impudence with which it is avowed and defended.' Hole was willing to make no concessions to ruling economic doctrine: 'The master who makes the most he can out of his labourers, differs but in degree from the slave driver, and the principle of political economy justifies the slavery of Greece and Rome as much as it does the system of modern labour.' While giving the mill owners credit for good intentions in their contributions to schools, chapels and soup kitchens, Hole considered their philanthropic efforts misplaced. Such 'mistaken philanthropy . . . often saps the spirit of independence in the labourer, and ultimately increases the evil. The labourer *wants* work, the means of earning his own comforts'. Hole also made short shrift of the success myth. He pointed out that the system was still fundamentally defective even though it permitted an occasional workman to escape from the ranks; such an isolated event 'is no compensation of the system − the one prize cannot atone for the nine hundred and ninety-nine blanks'. He called instead for the 'introduction of just and fraternal arrangements' which 'might possibly turn all into prizes'. He denounced a system in which the way a man is treated 'depends not on what he *is*, but on what he *has*'.[15]

Yet Hole hoped that the social system whose evils he described so well would be transformed gradually but inexorably by the improving institutions of the mid-Victorian cities. He illustrates, in somewhat extreme form, the inner logic that led radical working men to transfer their utopian idealism to the celebration of minuscule increments of improvement. Seeking to maintain a socialist position in the *Lectures*, he deplored the inferior education provided to the mass of the people under the existing system and called for the creation of a regime of genuine social and cultural equality: 'Socialism proclaims that the life of the masses ought not to be one dull blank, unhallowed by noble thought or lofty sentiment, its course purely animal, swallowed up in the drudgery of labour, or buried in the mire of sensuality . . . It announces that both man's inner and outer life may be raised and beautified — that the abuses of property may be remedied, and more humane relations established among men.' The young Marx had projected a similar vision of the socialist utopia in his Paris writings a few years before. Hole, however, took a rather different view of how these socialist principles might be realised. Having concentrated on the adverse moral and intellectual consequences of capitalism, and having emphasised the fact that socialism would raise the cultural level of all men, and having rejected any hint of revolutionary action to transform the existing social and economic order, Hole moved easily into a position where he became convinced that any number of working-class activities might contribute substantially to the achievement of the utopia that he envisaged. Thus he found 'true exemplifications of Socialism' in the various movements whose object was 'to elevate the masses of Society'.[16]

Hole had in mind 'Working Associations, Mechanics' Institutes, Co-operative stores, Flour-mills, Freehold-land societies, and the like'. Even if they did not accomplish much, such organisations were nevertheless of great value, because they demonstrated 'the vast latent power of association'. In model lodging houses, baths and wash-houses, and mechanics' institutes, he found 'the germ of those magnificent organisations which the world will one day witness'. In the name of practicality and common sense, he argued that 'it is not the part of wise men to *wait* for the realisation of large schemes, but to seize present opportunities and make the most of them'. What linked such diverse activities to socialism was 'the principle of Association, or co-operation'. They were part of a grand design: 'Each of these various movements is (often unconscious of its promoters) working out the parts of a grand problem the solution of which can only be arrived at experimentally.' One could move slowly, in confidence that intellectual improvement was an all-powerful engine of progress. 'The degree of association of which men are capable, depends on the height of moral and intellectual cultivation to which they may have attained.' Having put his faith in the principle of association, Hole gave free rein to his utopian optimism. Here was an 'instrument in the hands of the working classes' which 'requires only their own active participation'; they have the 'means of emancipation in their hands'.[17] He defined the idea so broadly that just about any aspect of working-class activity could be interpreted as an important aspect of the overall movement towards socialism.

Thus the realism that distinguished Hole's analysis of the existing social system was blunted by a number of optimistic assumptions that encouraged the expectation that 'socialism' might be achieved through the day-to-day co-operation of men of good will associated on behalf of improving activity. His trenchant analysis of the human consequences of excessive social dependence was considerably softened by his assumption that the majority of working men 'are dependent because they are ignorant', and that 'no employer can despise or oppress a man with as much soul as himself'. This sort of wishful thinking was part of the legacy that Hole had inherited from early-Victorian radicalism. His rationalist faith led him to the conclusion that 'even in their present state, the diffusion of intelligence ameliorates the servile conditions of labour'. In the best tradition of Enlightenment rationalism he concluded that 'the only effectual mode of arriving at social organisation is by the dissemination of Ideas'.[18]

Starting from an exceedingly radical perspective, Hole ended up advising the working classes to continue the sort of improving activity which they were also being urged to carry on by spokesmen for the middle classes. To be sure, he hoped for a totally different result in the long run, and he took a highly unfavourable view of the capitalist society in which this activity was taking place. Nevertheless, he ended up praising the basic institutions of mid-Victorian culture in the name of socialism and co-operation.

(2) *The Perils of Idealism*

Although the working-class subculture was strong enough to repulse the overt threat posed by the cult of respectability and middle-class propaganda, it was vulnerable to more subtle patterns of acculturation. Radical values were subject to various mechanisms which tended to attenuate their egalitarian thrust while assimilating them to middle-class models that presupposed inequality and subordination. Even working men who maintained their commitment to the traditions of radicalism were exposed to cultural processes that tended to weaken their efforts by shifting their direction and significance. Under these circumstances, therefore, there was a constant tension between the values of the working-class subculture and the countervailing tendencies of both the social structure and the culture as a whole. Although the cult of respectability did not triumph, the forces that produced it were an ever-present threat to the integrity of radical values, especially because of certain aspects of the working-class subculture: the inclination to sentimental idealism, the tendency to apply such ideals in an exaggerated estimation of the significance of minor activity directed to individual improvement, and the resultant overlapping with the middle-class version of consensus values.

In their efforts to maintain radical values in an inhospitable society, many working men, responding to the patterns of the culture of which they were very much a part, embraced an intense idealism, often in sentimental form. They projected an idealised image of the independent working man, characterised by nobility of character, altruism, spirituality, and total dedication to the highest intellectual and moral ideals for their own sake. The following passage reflects, in somewhat extreme form, the readiness of working-class spokesmen to express their aims in the standard idiom of mid-Victorianism: 'Let us faithfully attend to the culture of our being, that we may in the economy of moral influence under which we live, be the almoners of blessing, truth, and freedom to people yet unborn. That we may realise a position so important, so God-like, we must cultivate the divine element within us — we must aim at intellectual and moral greatness.'[19] Such language did not necessarily reflect psychological or ideological softness. On the contrary, it was often used as a means of criticising the middle classes and the social order which they dominated. It enabled working men to counter middle-class claims to superiority by capturing the market in idealism. Working-class pride and self-confidence were bolstered while the middle classes were tarred with the brush of materialism and acquisitiveness. On the face of it, this appeared to be a good pre-emptive bid in idealism. In fact, however, working men were in danger of overplaying their hand. In making so much of nobility of character and spirituality of soul, working-class spokesmen could easily be overtrumped. To the extent that their words became a mere incantation they could not compete with a middle-class that delighted in glorifying high aims to be achieved in the infinite future. In his idealism, as in his earnest rationalism, the independent working men had little purchase from which to resist tendencies that were in fact undermining his fundamental values. In projecting an idealised social character as a means of outflanking middle-class pretensions to superiority, working men were in danger of losing all contact with the enemy forces.

William Aitken, whose critique of the gospel of success has been noted above, subscribed to a rather sentimental creed as an alternative. In this spirit he deplored the fact that many of Franklin's sayings tended to 'harden the heart of mankind, encase it in adamant, destroy the great Christian maxims, and foster a narrowness of mind between man and man'. He contrasted the 'selfish maxims of the Doctor' with the 'touching, beautiful, and simple doctrines of the New Testament', which tend to 'soften the heart, teach us to be kind to each other, and inculcate in the bosoms of all the God-like feeling of charity'. Thus, Aitken put his faith in individual goodwill and charity, stimulated by high principle. All this was very much in the style of mid-Victorian culture. The very principles to which he was appealing in his criticism of Franklin led him to a position that was indistinguishable in substance from the official ethos. In calling for adherence to the principles of the New Testament, he was buttressing a premise which justified the expectation of significant improvement without radical social and economic change — the capacity of the middle classes to respond to moral appeals.

In the very first issue of the *Oddfellows' Magazine* Aitken had written a story which exemplifies the gentle and sentimental idealism underlying his radicalism. The title of the tale bespeaks a familiar Victorian genre: 'The Factory Beggar Girl: A True Story.'[20] In the winter of 1841 the author met a factory girl, whose hand had been cut off as a result of an accident at the mill, and who had been discharged by the works manager. The author went directly to the mill owner, who reinstated the girl. Aitken drew a standard moral: 'This is another proof of the necessity of gentlemen who employ large numbers of people, being careful to whom they delegate their power. It also proves the necessity of the working classes appealing to the fountain head, in a proper and decorous manner, when they have anything whereof to complain, and experience proves that many of the misunderstandings that exist between employers and employed would be removed.' Thus Aitken shared the mid-Victorian assumption that the social system was fundamentally sound, and required only more virtuous and under-standing behaviour on the part of all classes. In this context, therefore, criticism of the middle classes for not behaving properly — as for example in preaching Franklin's sort of materialism — lends authority to the implicit ideological justification of existing social arrangements and inequalities.

The ironworker's wife, whose denunciation of perfidious employers was quoted above, also based her criticism of the middle classes on a highly idealised working-class version of the creed of improvement and self-help. Quite aware of the suffering inflicted on working men by the employing class, she had no alternative to offer except her faith in the capacity of the individual to overcome all difficulties by maintaining his strength of mind and character. 'I would like to tell you what I think all this teaches us — and it is that all our help, all our salvation lies in ourselves. We have proved it by experience. It lies not with our masters, nor with our churches, but in our cultivation of those higher qualities which are lying dormant in our natures.'[21] Here, as elsewhere, the ideal of individual improvement is not presented as a means of seeking middle-class approval; on the contrary, her point is that working-class self-help is necessary because the middle classes have shown that they cannot be relied upon. The mid-Victorian reference to the 'higher qualities' is made in a context of class consciousness and pride; the high-flown language has not been adopted because it is what the middle classes consider proper.

Similarly, the specific remedy which the ironworker's wife offers to working men — temperance — is put forth in the same breath with a rebuke to employers who encourage their employees to drink. 'Many of you can redeem yourself and bring peace and happiness to your homes and hearts . . . by giving up the beerhouses. That's where your salvation lies. Oh, I blush to own that many of you are ready to lick the hands of those masters who have starved you the last nineteen weeks if they would give you a pot of beer.' Thrift also will dispose of many of the ills of the working classes: 'We have the Post Office Savings Bank, which will take in one shilling per week; or we have Co-operative societies, which will take threepence per week; so there is no excuse for us not saving something. There is not one amongst us but might save something if we give up the beerhouse.' Temperance and thrift are the traits of the independent working man, who refuses to truckle to unscrupulous masters who seek to prey on his weaknesses. Drink, the English worker's curse, has made him the 'Caliban' of society: 'There is no hope for you until you have the moral courage to throw off the yoke of bondage this strong drink imposes on you, and let your intellects which have been given to you for high and noble purposes, have free play. Will the day ever come when English workmen will know their power; will be too noble to degrade themselves as they do; . . . but will be able to stand erect in the image of God, as he was first made.'

The ironworker's wife reflected a working-class subculture in which idealistic aspiration had been transferred to various institutions of improvement, ranging from co-operative societies to temperance groups. As a result, many working men tended to bestow extravagant praise on rather limited activity on the grounds that it contributed to the achievement of the utopian goals that they continued to proclaim. Thus, working-class idealism fitted neatly into a culture that delighted in the proclamation of noble aspirations and the celebration of whatever seemed remotely associated with their achievement. In this mood a friendly society set its purposes in a cosmic and providential framework: 'Seeing, then, that the association of our species was originally designed by the great Creator of all things, it is reasonable to infer that the constant progression of man is the aim of the Deity; and the nearer we approach to social perfection, the nearer shall we be to the ultimate design of Providence.'[22] In sum, working men shared with the culture as a whole the sensibility of sentimental aspiration. Even those working-class radicals whose rhetoric occurred in the context of an attack on middle-class ideology were caught up in a cultural pattern that drew the sting from their protest by associating it with more of the same.

Of the various working-class institutions involved in some aspect of the improvement enterprise, the co-operative societies were the most hostile to the theory and practice of capitalism. Precisely because their aspirations were so pure, however, they were particularly vulnerable to the mid-Victorian tendency to take comfort from the mere affirmation of high principles.[23] Founded in the utopian atmosphere of the 1840s, they were to flourish in the more complacent mood of the 1860s. Their initial utopianism was transmuted into a ritualised optimism about what was being accomplished by a network of retail shops. Faithful to the values of the working-class subculture, the co-operative societies were also very much exposed to the hazards of mid-Victorianism. In this setting, it was tempting to be content with 'disseminating the sublime and heaven-born truths of CO-OPERATION'. It was gratifying simply to reiterate the sort of formula that appeared in the annual report of the Halifax Co-operative Society in 1852: 'In conclusion, we have to exhort you to continue steadfast in the cause to which you are by this experiment committed; knowing that your labour will not be in vain in the holy work of the social and political elevation and ultimate emancipation of your class.' They were confident in the ultimate success of their holy work because they knew that there is 'a strong vitality in the principle of co-operation, which has power to overcome whole ages of inertia, bad habits, and ignorance'.[24]

Reinforcing their faith in the efficacy of principles was the conviction among some-co-operators that they were part of a progressive process which would automatically lead onward and upward. 'Civilisation is all a *process of gradual development*; we cannot *jump to perfection by kangaroo leaps*, but must . . . toil on from a *less* to a *greater* state of perfection.' Such gradualist utopianism was a recurring motif in the movement. Another writer, while commending co-operation to everyone who 'yearns to see inequality and injustice buried for ever', depicted that process in bland and sentimental terms: 'Whilst being a medium for the administration of justice to each other, Co-operation will do much to engraft the maxims of honesty and right in the trunk of the mind, and indelibly impress them upon the heart. And surely there is abundant necessity that the cheerful smiles of justice, with their exhilarating influences, should be allowed full exercise, in order to give strength and resolution to the tremulous, and inspire the distrustful with confidence.' As a matter of course, the co-operative movement increasingly tended to perceive its everyday activity in terms which assimilated it to established cultural patterns. The announcement that co-operation is a lever to revolutionise society was followed by the statement that 'a real earnest co-operator joins a store or a society to raise the moral, social, and political standard of his class'. This did not mean materialism, however, for 'the real co-operator inquires less about the dividend, but is anxious to see a library, a reading-room, a sick-fund organised'. When a speaker at the annual soirée of the Plymouth Co-operative Society called for the removal of the 'degrading dualism now existing between employer and employed', he did so in a 'neat and earnest speech'. Embedded in a soft cultural setting, the co-operative movement's critique of competitive capitalism lost its edge and tended to become just another component of the rhetoric of aspiration.[25]

In the mid-Victorian manner the co-operators combined an overblown rhetoric with a deep-seated moderation both in theory and in practice. It was assumed that rationality required the rejection of extremes that lay outside the boundaries of acceptable aspiration. An account of the sort of men joining the movement in the mid-1850s describes them as 'a class of sober, thinking, and reading men — men who oppose the raving of political quacks as strongly as they do the wretched pleadings of a false political economy'. They would protest against injustice in a rational and moderate manner. 'These men do not believe that they and their children are to be always mere drudges, labouring to accumulate fortunes for others; nor do they believe that they are to escape from their present situation by violent speed or unlawful action.' His readers were assured that they could escape their present situation 'by uniting their means, and, in accordance with sound business rules, working patiently, soberly, and on a ground of true equity . . .' In a pamphlet aptly entitled *The Economic and Moral Advantages of Co-operation in the Provision of Food*, the former Owenite John Holmes described the advantages that accrue to men who abandon buying on credit and instead pay cash at a co-operative store. 'They become independent, and feel morally as well as socially elevated.' Through such moderate and sensible activity great moral ends could be achieved.[26]

An equally modest proposal, couched in terms of an exalted idealism, was all that the Sheffield apprentice could offer as an alternative to his master's 'mammonism'.[27] He invited his master to live up to professed values and contribute vigorously to the cause of improvement: 'Now, sir, do stoop to be advised. Change your policy. Try what Education can do towards recovering morality to the working classes, and integrity to trade. A few pounds and a frequent word on popular Education, would send your young people to places of improvement like the People's College, instead of places of amusement, where principles are first sodden and then defied; while the feelings rush in rapid decline, from the tenderness of youth, to the cold and callous selfism of hacknied vice.' This blend of romanticism, rationalism, and Puritanism overlapped middle-class ideology at a number of points.

Given the mid-Victorian consensus, such a blurring of the distinction between independent working-class values and the doctrines of middle-class ideology was inevitable. Both classes shared a belief in the moral and intellectual improvement of the individual as a social goal of overriding importance. They also agreed on the moral and intellectual traits that should be cultivated. As a result, even working men who were trying to give a populist and egalitarian form to the values of the culture often sounded as if they were merely echoing the standard line taken by middle-class ideologists.

Even the virtues most esteemed by the working-class subculture could easily be bent into a form congenial to the highly stratified society of the mid-Victorian cities. A case in point is the working man who took seriously the cluster of values rooted directly in the Enlightenment: faith in reason, education, knowledge, and intellectual improvement. In principle, his commitment to these rationalist values was a means of affirming the worth and intellectual potential of the working-class, as part of a demand for access to education and knowledge which had been monopolised by the propertied classes. These values had become lodged in the working-class subculture in the context of a radical protest against social and intellectual obscurantism which regarded the spread of knowledge among the common people as pernicious. By the mid-Victorian period, however, this commitment to rationalist values brought some unanticipated consequences of an essentially conservative character. Now that the value of education and knowledge was officially proclaimed at every turn, especially by the more progressive and idealistic spokesmen of the middle classes, working men who asserted the old rationalist values were echoing the middle-class line. Moreover, in the process they were lending credence to the implicit claim that the society was in fact devoted to intellectual improvement for all. Finally, in this instance as in others, traits which the working man prized for their own sake were also being touted by the preachers of respectability as signs that the working classes were now emulating their betters and were beginning to approach that high level of morality and intellect.

The long-standing working-class defence against overt obloquy from above did not work against the more subtle mid-Victorian forms of derogation. In fact, the old radical insistence on the virtues of the working classes now was all too readily assimilated to the newer patterns of middle-class hegemony. Although the middle classes had not really adopted a more favourable view of their inferiors, they had abandoned the sort of condemnation of working-class vices encouraged by the spirit of 1834. Now they took the more genial line of inviting the élite of the working classes to come within the pale of respectability. Working men who pointed with pride to members of their class who had made great moral and intellectual advances were refuting out-of-date insults. In so doing they were in danger of falling in with newer ways in which the middle-class asserted its superiority by condescending praise for those superior working men who had succeeded in rising above the level of their class.

G.J. Holyoake, who had started out on the far Left as an Owenite lecturer in the 1840s, illustrates the difficulty of the attempt to preserve the old radical values and aspirations in the mid-Victorian situation. In 1866, as editor of *The Working Man*, he was still advocating working-class causes with the same militancy and inveighing against the injustices suffered by working men in a society which preferred competition to co-operation. Yet Holyoake's seemingly unexceptionable radicalism was in fact rather well adapted to cultural patterns that tended to assimilate and deradicalise the principles of the early Victorian Left.

The Working Man often displayed a tendency to sentimentalise and trivialise the ideals of working-class radicalism. In an editorial entitled 'Diversity of the Working Class', for example, sentimental praise of working men is laid on with great gusto: 'The working class is becoming the formidable class — not formidable as was formerly feared, in the sense of being dangerous, but formidable in vastness and beneficence. It is the great creating class.' The rest of the editorial makes it plain just how remote in spirit this is from earlier variations on the theme that labour is the source of all wealth, for it proceeds to argue that anyone who works hard enough deserves the honour of inclusion among the working-class. 'Even poets, considering how many of them labour at stubborn metres, may take rank among the working classes.' The writer accepts at face value one of the more canting practices of mid-Victorian platform oratory — upper or middle-class speakers announcing to working-class audiences that they are all working men: 'It is now no uncommon thing to hear noblemen, and persons of high high social station, tell audiences at mechanics' institutions, that they (the speakers) too are working men. Gentlemen now claim to be considered as working as hard as any mechanic, and it must be owned that great numbers of them do so work.' The implication of this line was that the intellectual and moral characteristics of English working men had raised the status of the term: 'The British workingman aspires to be . . . intelligent, saving, thinking, and improving; as well as industrious. Indeed, "working man" is becoming a name of honour.'[28]

Another journal, also called *The Working Man*, affiliated with the co-operative movement, was intended to be a 'popular organ which shall be really representative of the people', and it posed a number of questions that suggested a distinctly radical posture: 'How is it that the working body of the land, the main supporter and creator of its wealth and greatness, although by far including the greatest number of its inhabitants, is in that degraded state of subjection to the minority which we witness? . . . How is it that after all these sacrifices, they are despised and insulted?'[29] Radical criticism of the social order persisted, but in an almost vestigial state, smothered by pap. Thus, we find one writer pointing out how 'the rich classes, our masters, rulers and governors, all co-operate . . . to support and uphold their present unjust system of coercive laws and customs, which make and keep them rich and the poor poor'. The working classes, he adds, should learn a lesson from this. But the lesson turns out to be a mid-Victorian parody of an older tradition: the working classes should also co-operate 'to obtain JUSTICE for themselves — not by violence or any unbecoming means, but solely by the dignity and force of moral truth. Justice should be their motto, their polar star, their guide!' But they must be careful to advocate justice 'in a proper manner', for then 'all honest men and women would join in the request, which, in such a case could not possibly be long withheld'. The writer concludes with a fascinating passage in which the language of working-class radicalism has been sentimentalised and idealised into nullity: 'Working Men, herein is the proper object of your co-operation — herein is your emancipation — your regeneration — your duty and your honour. Herein you may emulate one another in doing good to all, and exercise your patience, your faith, your hope, your charity and love for all mankind, and with the assurance of success and reward, greater than you have ever yet contemplated.'[30] The writer had not 'sold out', nor had he been 'bribed' by the bourgeoisie. He simply was indulging in mid-Victorianism.

It took considerable effort to maintain the old radical values in the face of the cloying embrace of mid-Victorian culture. But it was possible. Another contributor to *The Working Man*, for example, wrote in a critical spirit that was up to the standard of his predecessors and successors on the Left, albeit not without the note of resolute optimism characteristic of the age. 'Gordius' enlisted inflated rhetoric in an attack on rationalisations that purported to justify the existing order. He denounced the 'laboured sophistry and mental prostitution' which had been resorted to by those 'whose unrighteous aim it is to win reconciliation with the victims of an unjust social system, in order the more easily to perpetuate and complete the dependence or slavery of a portion of the human family'. With these ringing words, he began a letter on the subject, 'Employer and Employed — Are Their Interests Identical?' His answer was a flat negative: 'Selfishness, nursed by an inveterate greed of gain, and a desire to govern and domineer on the one hand, and a conscious independence wrought by a false sense of inferiority on the other hand, destroys all sincere reciprocity of feeling, all manly virtue, and all moral beauty.' His comments on political economy were worthy of Bronterre O'Brien: ' "Buy cheap and sell dear" is the theory and practice of that school of political economists whose false teaching and foul dealing have imposed upon the credulity of the employed by making them believe their social, political, moral, and intellectual degradation to be the result of their own vicious natures, and not of a system of competition in which everyday life demonstrates the subjugation of the interests of one section of the human family to that of the other.'[31]

Like other spokesmen for the values of the working-class subculture, however, Gordius too could not completely avoid the conservative implications of ideas that were central to his creed. In the name of independence and class pride he insisted that working men themselves may become 'the authors of a lasting, and almost unlimited improvement of their own condition of life'. He clearly was not urging contentment with low wages, for he complained that far too many working men were 'so accustomed to middle-class preachments and privations as to be content with the barest and coarsest necessaries of life'.[32] His call to self-improvement was an appeal to working men to raise their sights above the limits defined by their social superiors. Nevertheless, his optimistic talk about individual improvement had undercut the radical thrust of his argument by ignoring the severe restrictions imposed by the social and economic system. Moreover, he was a bit out of date in suggesting that middle-class spokesmen were preaching contentment in privation; optimism had become the dominant ideological theme. Finally, like other mid-Victorian radicals, Gordius himself contributed to the official optimism by his confidence that the evils which he had diagnosed so trenchantly would eventually be removed almost automatically by the spread of knowledge among the working classes. By supporting popular education and greater communication of knowledge the middle classes were promoting 'increased power in the people', which was bound to bring in its wake unlimited progress towards a society free from greed, selfishness, and intellectual degradation.

Notes

1.   Geoffrey Best, *Mid-Victorian Britain*, London 1971, p. 259. See also J.M. Ludlow and Lloyd Jones, *The Progress of the Working Class 1832–1867*, London 1867.
2.   *Weekly Record* 26 July 1856.
3.   *The Following Letters and Answers Appeared in the Daily Newspapers Concerning the Ironworkers' Lockout, 1866*, Gateshead 1867. Ludlow Collection, Goldsmiths Library, University of London.
4.   *People's College Journal*, 1846, No. 1.
5.   *Social Science: Being Selections from John Cassell's Prize Essays by Working Men and Women*, London 1861, pp. 200–1.

6.   *Northern Star*, 5 April 1845; for Aitken's biography see *Oddfellows' Magazine*, July 1857; his report to Lovett from Ashton-under-Lyne in 1839 is in Add. MSS 34245A, f.19.

7.   *Oddfellows' Magazine*, April 1859.

8.   St Peter's Mutual Improvement Society, Minute Book, 13 August 1863, MS, Manchester Reference Library.

9.   *Manchester Guardian*, 1 May 1850.

10.   *Social Science: Being Selections from John Cassell's Prize Essays by Working Men and Women*, London 1861.

11.   *Friend of the People*, 26 April 1851.

12.   *Working Man*, 1 January 1862; *Co-operator,* April 1864.

13.   J.F.C. Harrison, *Social Reform in Victorian Leeds: The Work of James Hole*, Leeds 1954.

14.   James Hole, *Lectures on Social Science and the Organisation of Labour*, London 1851, pp. 143–4.

15.   Ibid., pp. 143–5, 158–9.

16.   Ibid., pp. viii, 147, 160.

17.   Ibid., pp. viii, 148.

18.   Ibid., p. 143; Harrison, p. 23. On Hole's significance as a transitional figure in the decade 1846–56, see ibid., p. 26.

19.   *Foresters' Miscellaniy*, March 1850.

20.   *Oddfellows' Magazine*, I, no. 1, 1857.

21.   *Letters Concerning the Ironworkers' Lockout.*

22.   *General Laws for the Government of the Ancient Order of Foresters,* 1865.

23.   See Sidney Pollard, 'Nineteenth-Century Co-operation: From Community Building to Shopkeeping', in Asa Briggs and John Saville, eds., *Essays in Labour History*, London 1960; G.D.H. Cole, *A Century of Co-operation*, London 1944.

24.   *Co-operator*, June 1860; Halifax Workingmen's Co-operative Society, *Report for the Half Year Ending 1 May 1852*, Halifax 1852.

25.   *Christian Socialist*, 27 December 1851; *Co-operator*, June 1860; *Working Man*, 7 December 1861, 1 February 1862.

26.   *Co-operative Commercial Circular*, 1 February 1854; John Holmes, *The Economic and Moral Advantages of Co-operation in the Provision of Food*, Leeds 1857.

27.   *People's College Journal*, no. 1, 1846.

28.   *Working Man*, 13 January 1866.

29.   *Workman*, 5 July 1861. The title was changed to *Working Man* in the next issue.

30.   Ibid., 1 November 1862.

31.   Ibid., 1 January 1862.

32.   Ibid., 1 July 1862.

9 TRADE UNIONS AND FRIENDLY SOCIETIES

Trade unions and friendly societies were first and foremost a response to practical necessity. In order to stay afloat and maintain a degree of independence in a hostile social and economic environment, working men had to resort to some sort of collective action. Through trade unions labour aristocrats could defend their interests against the superior power of employers. Through friendly societies the mass of working men could pool meagre resources and make provision against misfortune. In performing these practical functions both institutions were also able to give substance to the values of the working-class subculture. Both trade unions and friendly societies operated within a framework of consensus and carried on their activities in ways congruent with pervasive cultural patterns.

In different ways each of these institutions also reflected the social and ideological conflicts that pervaded the well-integrated culture of the mid-Victorian cities. To varying degrees both trade unions and friendly societies found themselves at odds with the dominant middle-class and its ideology. Even the friendly societies, perfectly attuned to the motifs of the mid-Victorian ethos, experienced the tension between the formal universality of consensus ideals and the reality of class and status. Justly proud of their efforts at self-help, they were dismayed to find that the middle-class often depreciated their activity and continued to treat working men with condescension and derision. The trade unions came into direct conflict with middle-class power in a way that undercut the received doctrine of social harmony. Hence they stood in an even more ambivalent relationship to the culture of which they were a part.

(1) Trade Unions and Class Conflict

Trade unions were focal points of class conflict in a society that exalted social harmony.[1] In their encounter with trade unionism employers displayed none of the high principles that characterised their platform rhetoric. Social realities that were blurred or wished away by consensus idealism here came vividly into the open. When an employer confronted a newly established trade union, he set out to smash it as soon as possible and wasted no 'civility' in the process: lock-outs, victimisation, legal repression, blacklegs, and blacklists were the order of the day. Labour aristocrats who were genuinely interested in behaving rationally, responsibly, and courteously found out that the only trait that really counted with their masters was subservience. Trade unionists came face to face with the reality of class domination. The chasm between masters and men, between middle-class and working-class, was shown to be as deep as ever, despite the preaching of liberalism. While trade unionists accepted consensus values, they saw that shared social ideals did not have the same meaning for employers.

The extent of class conflict on the trade union front is a reminder of the complexity of the processes which transformed early-Victorian agitation into mid-Victorian stability. The same forces of economic improvement and expansion that had contributed to a relaxation of the tensions of the 1830s and 1840s had also created conditions for the growth of trade unions, which threatened to disrupt the new equilibrium. While economic change had taken the edge off early-Victorian discontent, it had also brought into being more direct forms of class confrontation. Moreover, the trade unions were composed of a labour aristocracy, that segment of the working-class most closely attuned to consensus values.

In counterpoint to the cultural affirmation of class harmony, clashes between masters and workmen were an omnipresent feature of the collective life of the mid-Victorian cities. Although workmen spent most of their time on the job and not on strike, the prospect of a strike or lock-out was inherent in the trade union situation at this time. Even in quiet periods, when strikes or lock-outs were rare, the memory of past disputes and the possibility of new outbreaks were always present. And there were many occasions in the 1850s and 1860s when labour conflicts were prevalent indeed. Trade unions seldom enjoyed more than peaceful coexistence with employers; the trade dispute, either latent or active, was the norm. In the area of labour relations the mid-Victorian period was anything but an age of calm and stability.

Since trade unions threatened to shift the pattern of power relations, employers were bound to resist, not merely for economic reasons, but because trade unionism offended their sense of the fitness of things. When working men organised to bargain collectively, they were rejecting the 'place' that had been assigned them since time immemorial. However respectful the demeanour of their members, trade unions were obviously chipping away at the prerogatives of the bourgeoisie; in principle, the predominance of the employer class was at stake. Moreover, trade union activity denied the social harmony that was one of the most cherished of mid-Victorian pieties. Trade union members were openly refusing to play their proper role of co-operating amiably with benevolent and helpful superiors. There could be no mistaking the challenge, and the middle classes reacted accordingly. Employers made no secret of the fact that they considered trade unionism an alien force, quite out of place in a well-ordered universe. They would accept it only under compulsion. As one employer put it in testimony before the Royal Commission on Trade Unions, 'I am for having them all abolished.'

This position was often supported by an idealised picture of relations between masters and men before the appearance of trade unions. According to a survey made in 1860, most masters were agreed that 'Trade Unions have destroyed the proper relation — one of affectionate dependence — of the operative towards his master'.[2] It was a common complaint that trade unions tended to 'separate masters and men, rather than unite them in friendly feeling and for the promotion of the common good in the trade'. Inevitably, they were pronounced 'bad in morality', as well as 'antagonistic to progression in every way'.[3]

Even as late as 1867 employers were still quite hostile to that most respectable of New Model unions, the Amalgamated Society of Engineers. A director of the Atlas Works in Manchester looked back wistfully to the idyllic days before the A.S.E. had disrupted the peaceful scene: 'I thought in 1851—52, which was the time of the great lock-out or strike, as it may be termed, as viewed from either side, that then was the great turning point in the amicable personal relations which one had with one's workpeople, and since then it has been rather dealing with a corporate body than with individuals. Before 1851—52 one knew almost every workman in the place by name, and dealt with him individually.' A leading question from a member of the Royal Commission helped the witness to a neat conclusion to his tale of paradise lost: 'Dealing with individuals you acted under the tie of humanity towards them? — Yes, and I think that it was rarely that any dispute arose . . . it was an affair between man and man.' By 1867 most of the men in the plant had joined the union, but it was still unrecognised by the firm. Asked about his views on conciliation, the witness replied that he would accept it only 'if you would remove the action of the trade unions'. In a similar vein, the head of a great shipbuilding firm in Jarrow depicted the baleful impact of trade unionism on a previously perfect situation. He conceded that a trade union might win an advance in wages sooner than would have been the case without a union, but he argued that the advance that came without trade union efforts would be 'much more permanent' and free from the other pernicious consequences of trade unionism: 'I think that when the demand comes through a trade union it creates a bad feeling, and breaks up all good feeling between employer and employed.'[4] The trade unions were blamed for introducing the cash nexus into warm and friendly relations that had previously obtained between the owner and each of his 5,000 workers.

Economic orthodoxy reinforced the natural reluctance of employers to accept trade unionism. Trade unions, in one common interpretation of the laws of political economy, constituted an improper, if not immoral, interference with the free play of the market in labour. The conviction that they constituted an 'interference with the natural adjustment of the rate of wages' underlay the *Leeds Mercury*'s criticism of trade unions: 'Until the formation of the union, the price of labour had fluctuated naturally according to the relation of supply and demand. An intelligible standard was fixed for both sides — the master gave the smallest price for which he could buy labour, and the men got the largest price for which they could sell their labour.' With the abstractness so characteristic of middle-class liberalism, the writer ignored the effect of disparity in power on the bargaining process and insisted that the standard 'inflicted no injustice', for 'the law of supply and demand, if left to itself, is quite certain . . . to procure the workman a share in the master's gains'. The rigidity of the *Mercury*'s position is of interest to the historian not as an example of class bias (for that is obvious), but as an example of the persisting strength of the formulations of classical economics. The metaphors speak eloquently:

> Without unions on either side the wages of the workmen ebb and flow with the prosperity of the master just as inevitably as the tides of the moon. The harmony is perfect, and strikes, lock-outs, discords, and the whole train of evils they bring after them, are unknown. How different where the union enters. Both sides may be perfectly honest and just, but a false principle of regulation is brought in, a mode of calculation no more comparable in simplicity or exactness with that we have indicated, than the wild guesses and artificial systems of astrology are comparable with the beautiful accuracy and truthfulness of astronomy.[5]

When a trade union first appeared in an industry, the immediate response of employers was to crush it by whatever means promised to be effective, including the full coercive power of the law. The men might be locked out until they agreed to capitulate and renounce the union, and the capitulation might be formalised in 'the Document'. Occasionally company unions were formed. Employer associations developed a united front against the enemy. Strikers were prevented from getting employment elsewhere and often were evicted from company houses. When the strike was over, trade union leaders were blacklisted. In fact, 'victimisation' was a technical term in trade union terminology. The rules of the local unions in the cotton industry are replete with references to it. One union provided for the payment of a sum 'to every man sacrificed through having obeyed the order of the Executive Council or his own local Council, such as going on deputations or left out at the end of a strike or lock-out'. A lace workers' union had a special benefit, larger than the unemployment benefit, which was paid to men who had been discharged because of union affiliation.[6]

The Amalgamated Society of Engineers illustrates the basic pattern of mid-Victorian labour relations: an initial confrontation in which employers sought to destroy the union, followed by varying degrees of grudging acceptance and lingering hostility. In 1851 it was forced into a long and bitter strike that almost ended in disaster. The union was surprised by the strength of the employers' resistance: 'The most respected employers in the trade, as well as the hard masters, had gone against them.' Having taken employer rhetoric at face value, the leaders of the A.S.E. learned a lesson. The best that they could get was a truce, which lasted until 1866, when the employers made another attempt to destroy the union.[7]

On the surface, the pattern in the cotton industry seemed more peaceful. After the bitter strikes of the early 1850s, an effective *modus vivendi* was worked out. In the 1860s employers were making virtually no use of the master and servant laws against trade unions. By the early 1870s an exceedingly stable relationship, involving detailed and highly technical negotiations, had been worked out between employers and unions. G.D.H. Cole has pointed out that the employers in the cotton industry, 'the pioneers of the new Capitalism, were the first to accept Trade Unionism as a useful agency for collective bargaining about wages and conditions'. In 1874 a spokesman for employers in the Blackburn area painted a very favourable picture of trade unionism to the Royal Commission. He estimated that the majority of workers in the area were union members, 'and the fact is that we do not object to their being in union as we now have the system of meeting their representatives. We often settle disputes more readily through the instrumentality of a meeting of the committees than we otherwise should'. He was most pleased with the leaders of the unions: 'The unions generally have, in our district, a secretary who is a respectable and reasonable man, and . . . in many cases, through his instrumentality and that of our secretary alone, the disputes are prevented from going very far.' Although strikes occurred, they were 'somewhat differently conducted from those in other trades', and there had never been much picketing. In contrast to the situation then prevailing in the iron trade, strikes were usually settled by negotiation.[8]

Even in the cotton industry, however, we find the familiar pattern of hostility and distrust throughout most of the mid-Victorian period. Acceptance of trade unions was less than universal. In 1867 the Royal Commission summarised as follows the reply of the secretary of the Cotton Spinners to questions about union relations with employers: 'Ordinarily recognised by employers. Some of the branches . . . are recognised by a considerable number of employers.' Moreover, the secretary's reply to questions about 'wants' showed that 'recognition' was of a rather limited sort: 'If managers gave up interfering to prevent workmen from seeing their employers, and if employers (instead of discharging their men, as they too frequently have done, for merely trying to get an interview) were to show a willingness to meet them and consider any question in dispute', satisfactory working rules could be adopted and disputes would be less frequent. The secretary of the Preston branch of the Power-Loom Weavers' Association reported the same strained relations with employers. Among the 'objects' of the association that he described to the Royal Commission was 'to render assistance to strikes when such become necessary . . . and also to members who may be made victims through furthering the objects of the society'. He pointed out that there had been more than a hundred court cases 'for stoppage of wages, illegal dismissal, and assaults'.[9]

The cotton unions had achieved this limited acceptance only after the bitter conflicts of the 1850s and the cotton famine of the early 1860s. In 1853 the cotton industry was a long way from the truce that prevailed in 1867. The Preston lock-out, which lasted from September 1853 to April 1854, was still fresh in the mind of the secretary of the Preston branch of the Power-Loom Weavers' Association when he reported to the Royal Commission in 1867 on the 'causes' that had led to the formation of the union: 'The tyranny to which the men were forced to submit from the defenceless position of the trade after the "great" lock-out of 1853–54'. Although the occasion of the lock-out was a dispute over wages, the basic issue in Preston was trade unionism. Another attempt by employers to resist trade unions produced an extremely long strike in 1859. The masters took exception to the fact that the paid secretary of the union was to be 'the only medium of communication between employer and employed', and 'indignantly refused to submit to such humiliating conditions'. They received a great deal of support from other manufacturers 'on the express ground that the dispute was not a mere question of wages, but one of dictation'.[10]

To be sure, mid-Victorian employers did not enjoy trade disputes. They would have preferred harmonious relations based on mutual trust and rationality. From time to time, some of them discovered that trade unions could be handled effectively and entered into a bargaining relationship. The term 'New Model employers' has been coined to describe them. Even they, however, accorded trade unions no more than grudging acceptance.[11]

A brief account of a lock-out in the iron industry in the Leeds area in 1864 will illustrate more concretely certain patterns of employer-employee relations in the mid-Victorian cities. In this instance employers who were threatened with unionisation responded in the usual way by mobilising all their powers of resistance. It made no difference that many of the Leeds employers were known for their good works, or that Leeds was proud of the relationship which prevailed between masters and men. A long struggle ensued, marked by the importation of foreign blacklegs. It ended in a defeat for the union.

Until November 1863 the ironworkers of Leeds had been unorganised. Then they joined the National Association of Puddlers, established under the leadership of John Kane at Gateshead a few months before. The rules of the new union announced that 'funds shall be used to resist oppression and for raising prices'. Another rule stated that the union would defend the interests of men who had been discharged for trade union activity. When the dispute broke out in April 1864 the issue was simply 'whether the men shall or shall not connect themselves with a trades' union'. Demands for higher wages were only the occasion for the lock-out. After demands were presented to several firms, the employers decided to break the union. On 9 April they posted notices requiring men to sign a declaration promising not to associate with a trade union as a condition of continuing employment. The men refused to sign; they were locked out on 25 April. With the exception of two firms, where the declaration was not required, all the ironworks in the district shut down. Workers in the Bradford area issued handbills denouncing the declaration. The placards concluded with this colloquy: 'Mate, have you signed?' 'No, nor never will!' 'Nor me either; for being a freeborn Briton, and not a Virginian slave, no man shall say "must" to me.'[12]

The immediate response of the ironworkers was quite conciliatory. While refusing to sign the declaration, they went out of their way to disclaim any intention of interfering in management decisions. John Kane and the membership as a whole were careful to dissociate themselves from a leader of the Leeds branch of the union, who had written a threatening letter to an employer demanding the discharge of one worker who had not yet (prior to the lock-out) joined the union. Even the *Leeds Mercury* expressed its gratification that the men were 'animated one and all with a disposition to conciliation'. But the employers were adamant and refused to see representatives of the union. This was perfectly consistent, since the purpose of the lock-out was to break the union. But it prevented any kind of a negotiated settlement. The responsibility for the long lock-out rested directly with intransigent employers. Confronted by a union that did not approach them with the soothing deference that they expected, they decided to fight. It made no difference that the Leeds ironworkers were respectable skilled artisans of the familiar type. Their union did not know its place. It had to be broken.

The locked out ironworkers found some middle-class support, but efforts at mediation came to nought. In Bradford they met with a group of political and religious figures and denounced the declaration. In an attempt to find a way out of the impasse a middle-class deputation appointed at the meeting – including the National Reform Union leader John Priestman – had an interview with the managers of one of the Bradford iron works. The meeting seemed to be making progress, but nothing came of it. The deputation did succeed in getting one 'concession', which understandably did not serve to mollify the workers. The employers intimated that 'the kind of union they would approve, and of which they were willing to become honorary members, would be a union for subscribing to a sick or superannuation fund, but they should desire such a union to be limited to their own workmen, and would object to any assistance being given to men out on strike elsewhere'. On 10 May the Rev. George Onions reported to the Bradford ironworkers that the employers refused any concessions, and insisted on the declaration.

By June, the employers in Leeds and in Bradford had persuaded many workers to sign the declaration and return to work. Policemen were hired to protect the men on the way home, and in some instances sleeping accommodation was provided at the works. There were a few cases of violence committed on workers who returned. Kane complained that men who did not return were evicted from their homes. About forty or fifty puddlers had been imported from Belgium to help break the union. By September the employers had won. The mills were operating again, with men who had signed the declaration. The union had spent £17,000 to no avail.[13]

Some working men took a sardonic view of the behaviour of employers who were well known for their devotion to progress and philanthropy. Just after the lock-out was initiated, a letter writer noted that the leading inhabitants of the Leeds area had attended the soirée for the working men's hall on 4 April. He summarised the speech of the Rev. G.W. Conder who said that 'owing to the vast amount of knowledge which had been imparted to the working classes during late years, the contentions which existed in bygone times between employers and employed would never, he believed, occur in future, as they now considered matters in a more sensible and intelligent light'. Other speakers apparently took much the same line, which led the letter writer to remark, 'Now, what are we to think when we look at these things, and remember that, a few hours after this, some of the gentlemen who took so active a part in the proceedings of that meeting were running about trying to break up the Ironworkers' Association?'[14] This was fair comment. Although the middle-class improvers were not being hypocritical, their principles were certainly compartmentalised. Where questions of power and status were involved, the liberal writ did not run.

A revealing indication of the employers' unyielding hostility to the principles of trade unionism was the Gladstonian legislation of 1871. Trade union leaders rightly condemned Gladstone's Criminal Law

Amendment Act of 1871 as 'class legislation'. Moreover, harsh amendments introduced in the House of Lords, and opposed by the Liberal government, were supported not only by Edward Baines but also by Alfred Illingworth, a 'New Model employer' of Bradford. The T.U.C. complained that men like Joseph Cowen and George Dixon, whose support they had expected, were conspicuous by their absence. Even George Howell was prompted to remark, 'In fact we must create a Working Class Party, for Whig, Tory and Middle Class Radicals ignore our wants and requirements.'[15]

In order to defend the Criminal Law Amendment Act against agitation mounted by the trade unions, the National Federation of Associated Employers of Labour was founded in 1873. It included the major industrialists, among them Edward Akroyd of Halifax, a man rightly proud of his devotion to the cause of working-class improvement, and Titus Salt, a New Model employer from Bradford. The Federation put out a journal, which for the next eight years 'kept up a relentless and frequently vitriolic assault on trade unionism'. Emphasising its purely defensive intentions, the Federation announced that 'preparation for "industrial war" will be a new guarantee of industrial peace'.[16] The cold war phraseology was quite consistent with the attitudes of employers throughout the mid-Victorian period.

(2) *Trade Unions and Working-Class Values*

Institutionally and ideologically the trade unions resisted middle-class domination and maintained a firm commitment to the values of the working-class subculture. In confrontation with hostile employers, trade unionists took a realistic view of their situation and refused to accept at face value the ideological claims of their antagonists. Yet they conducted their 'struggle for acceptance' without deviating from established cultural forms. Hence the trade unions exemplify the antinomies so characteristic of mid-Victorian urban culture. While denouncing the 'oppression' and 'aggression' of the employers, they nevertheless took for granted the willingness of a society dominated by the middle-class to foster the moral and intellectual improvement of the individual. They continued to place the highest value on morality and rationality, despite the fact that employers showed little respect for such traits when displayed by militant trade unionists. They showed forbearance towards employers who took every opportunity to crush them. While exceptionally well integrated into the culture, they were engaged in endemic conflict that belied the official faith in social harmony.

The trade unions were part of a broader working-class movement concerned with asserting the worth of the common people in a society that worshipped status and money. Hence they acted not only as bargaining agents, engaged in power struggles with employers, but also as spokesmen for the working-class against the middle-class. The trade unions' emphasis on the virtues of their members was not so much a bargaining ploy, intended to convey an impression of conciliation, but rather part of the long-standing defence of working men against obloquy from above. Along with the pursuit of better wages and conditions, trade unions were asserting the radical impulse to self-respect, independence and, to a degree, equality.

Clashes between trade unions and employers were an important factor in maintaining the radicalism and class consciousness of the labour aristocracy and countering divisive forces that tended to separate it from other working men. A noteworthy aspect of the mid-Victorian situation was the fact that trade unions were composed of skilled men who were most vulnerable to *'embourgeoisement'* and the cult of respectability. By virtue of their trade union involvement, however, these men were brought into direct contact with the coercive force that lay behind middle-class liberal ideology. While their socio-economic characteristics dictated a preoccupation with narrow craft interests and a sense of superiority to the less skilled, their continuing battles with the employer class fostered a broader class consciousness and strengthened their political radicalism. Trade disputes were perceived in terms of ideological categories — capital and labour, employers and workmen, masters and servants — that strengthened the class consciousness of the labour aristocracy. Attacks on middle-class behaviour and ideology reinforced the radical values of the working-class subculture. Indirectly, such ideological conflict was also conducive to the notion, usually only tacit, that eventually a society free from class domination might be attained. Although the pragmatic temper of the trade unions precluded the utopian hope for a transformation of the social order, they nevertheless preserved to some small degree the vision of a somewhat different society. Both in theory and in practice the trade unions resisted middle-class hegemony — but within the framework of the culture of which they were very much a part.

Trade unionists were under no illusions about their employers. They knew that weak and unorganised working men would be taken advantage of. The announcement of the formation of a new amalgamated union in 1866 made explicit what the membership knew from immediate experience: 'Seeing our defenceless position whilst isolated, we think it high time to take some steps to improve our social condition.' Organisation was a matter of necessity, since unorganised working men were liable to suffer 'very severely indeed from various causes, causes over which, disunited, they had no control whatever'. The very existence of trade unions was based on a recognition of the clashing interests of masters and men: 'No demand, however reasonable, will be granted by the majority of employers but through the pressure which strikes bring to bear upon them.' Beyond such a pragmatic awareness of the facts of life, the trade unions were often compelled to reject the ideological and social claims advanced by employers.[17]

The omnipresence of labour disputes, some bitter and protracted, encouraged the development of a critical attitude towards the pretensions and power of employers. This ideological militancy encompassed not only a criticism of the teachings of political economy but a class-conscious denunciation of the injustices practised by 'capitalists' or masters. The statement of a new union formed in 1866 that it was intended 'for the protection of Labour's right against Capital's overwhelming might' was typical of the rhetoric generated by the trade conflicts of the 1860s. A house painter described the 'gigantic struggle . . . going on through the country in defence of the rights and privileges of labour . . . The mighty colossus of labour is fighting a battle against the merciless power of capital'. He was confident that the 'struggle now going on will result in the final triumph of the working man'. The Wolverhampton Trades Council called for united action 'to rebut the lock-out system now so prevalent with the capitalists'. Even the moderate leaders of the London bricklayers denounced social and economic inequality in language that echoed Chartism and Owenism. Taking as their premise the principle that 'labour is the primary source of all wealth', they deplored the fact that 'one class is made subservient to the other, and has to do double work, because they provide subsistence to the idlers'. Because the idlers 'have got the law-making power in their hands', they have been able to 'keep down the real producers'. Mid-Victorian trade unionists did not have to be instructed in class antagonism: it was part of their social existence. Hence they responded favourably to the newer anti-capitalist rhetoric, as well as to the persisting legacy of an older social radicalism.[18]

A pragmatic recognition of the facts of life was strong enough to dispose of political economy in practice even when it might be accepted in theory. Trade union leaders who accepted in principle the validity of the laws of political economy did not permit this to interfere with their efforts to get the best bargain out of employers. Charles Blake of the Chain Makers Union, for example, subscribed without reservation to the axioms of 'political science': 'Nothing can alter the action of the law of supply and demand, which governs the rate of wage.' Hence, 'Trade unions cannot . . . raise wages beyond what the market will afford their employers to pay them.' But Blake did not stop there and take middle-class economic theory as an invitation to working-class passivity, for he added in the same sentence, 'but this much they can accomplish viz. − to secure the best price for their labour that the state of the market will afford.' To get the best price for their labour workers could not rely on the automatic operation of the law of supply and demand: 'Men who are not united and active can never secure this. Union will obtain it for them.' That allowed considerable latitude for trade union action, especially in view of employers' readiness to cut wages at the first sign of a drop in the price of their product and to keep them low in a rising market. The function of trade unions was to combat employers. The principles of political economy were bent to support that purpose or they were rejected.[19]

As proper mid-Victorians, however, trade unionists were uncomfortable with ideological and social conflict that was so at odds with the consensus ideal of harmony, rationality, and cordiality. To a remarkable degree they continued to believe in the possibility of cordial and harmonious relations between employers and employees: rationality and civility on both sides might remove the differences that momentarily divided them. They continued to nourish the hope, if not the expectation, that their opponents might eventually come round and live up to the standards that they all agreed on. Partly from principle, and partly as a means of gaining recognition from employers, trade unions supported various conciliation and arbitration schemes in the 1860s.

The chainmakers of the Newcastle-upon-Tyne area were by no means a passive group. In 1859, for example, they dispatched an organising mission to the midlands, and a bitter strike resulted. Their militancy, however, did not preclude the hope that masters and men might somehow agree on a plan that would 'remove contention'. An editorial in their journal in 1858 articulates one of the fundamental articles of mid-Victorian social doctrine: the notion that if only the parties to a dispute would follow the dictates of reason, then senseless trials of strength would be avoided. 'This is called the "age of intelligence", we ought to forget the lower, and evoke the higher attributes of our nature. Let the employed be respectful and temperate in all their transactions with those whom they serve, and let employers cultivate a gentle demeanour, and the sympathies and affections of their workmen.' In industrial relations, as in other fields, Victorians of all classes believed that difficulties and conflicts were attributable to the deficiencies of individuals. In this instance the editorial writer, more in sorrow than in anger, deplored 'the insults that are given by haughty and arrogant masters'. Such behaviour was the cause of industrial conflict: 'We believe that strikes in many cases arise from the bitter feeling, which is too often the normal condition between masters and workmen, and if the former would unbend a little, and in all their transactions treat their men with the same courtesy that they display in their intercourse with the rest of the world, one fruitful source of strikes would be removed.' The writer recommended a system of arbitration for the chainmaking trade, in the hope that employers and employees would then 'learn to know each other better, and more kindly feelings would spring up than exist now'.[20] Trade unionists were reluctant to reject out of hand the middle-class insistence on its desire for friendly relations. Like the chainmakers, other trade unions combined considerable militancy in relations with employers with the acceptance of values which came rather close to the middle-class definition of respectable working-class behaviour.

The Stonemasons' Society, the largest union in the building trades, illustrates the dualism of social militancy and cultural conformity that pervaded the trade union movement as a whole. It had been 'designed as a fighting organisation' and in the 1850s battled for higher wages and shorter hours. Richard Harnott, who has been described as 'perhaps the most typical and influential Trade Union leader of the time', became general secretary in 1847 and steadily built up the strength of the organisation.[21] Harnott's prefaces to successive editions of the union's rules show the persistence of a spirit of militancy, independence and realism along with a steady expansion in the rhetoric of improvement and even respectability.

In 1849, as in the ensuing decades, the stonemasons avowed their determination to 'resist the oppressors' and combat 'tyranny and injustice'. In 1852 Harnott's preface included a realistic appreciation of the union's power position and its implications: 'Generally speaking, we have nothing to expect, in the present state of society, from the justice or humanity of employers and capitalists; our past experience gives ample proof of that.' The only answer was the application of counter-force; the association was intended to 'bring the whole power of the body to bear' in protecting members who individually were utterly powerless. Even in 1855, when Harnott was beginning to speak in softer mid-Victorian accents, he emphasised the need to 'keep firm the barrier of defence, and to protect ourselves against the selfish and unprincipled proceedings of the capitalist'. In the 1860s too, Harnott described the association's continuing effort to secure 'a guarantee against evils arising from . . . oppression of capital', and for 'protection against aggression on the rights and privileges of the trade'.

Harnott's prefaces also reflect a continuing process of Victorianisation. Without lessening the militancy of his defence of the interests of his members, Harnott expressed his aims in terms of consensus values and attitudes. At the very outset in 1849 he referred to 'that friendly feeling which ought ever to exist between the employer and employed', and emphasised that the union was intended to take action, 'without trenching in the least on the privileges of any honourable employer'. Starting from that conventional piety, Harnott proceeded to enlarge upon the virtues of the association as an agency of improvement. In 1855 he noted that 'a great and glorious change has been wrought by our united exertions, and by our associating together frequently much good has been done towards improving the moral character of our order'. By 1862 Harnott's words had a most familiar ring: 'Progression being the order of the day, it is highly necessary that the hardy son of toil should endeavour to raise himself in the moral sphere of society, for the mutual benefit of himself and fellow-workmen.' Shorter hours would allow 'more time for the cultivation of our minds'. By 1868 Harnott's preface included a full statement of the ethic of improvement, in justification of the traditional activities of the union: 'Every individual who has chosen the calling of an operative mason has a direct interest in common with those similarly engaged, and as an intelligent and rational being is in duty bound' to make provision 'for the cultivation and development of those high and noble faculties with which his Creator has endowed him. Without the realisation of these worthy objects set forth, man cannot feel that he has attained the full stature of an independent manhood, a feeling essential to his full development and highest usefulness.'[22]

In many instances the ritual reiteration of cultural pieties functioned as an ideological weapon in the confrontation between employers and employees. In mid-Victorian society conflict had to be conducted in terms of high principle. Hence one function of the incessant professions of working-class idealism and zeal for improvement was to show that employers, on the contrary, were animated primarily by a narrow class interest. In response to the moral aggressiveness of the middle classes the trade unions emphasised their own moral purity. By a continuing reaffirmation to their commitment to consensus values, they were building up their moral position. It was a way of putting down employers and asking them to practise what they preached. Thus it was standard practice to blame employers for violating the official canons of cordiality and reason. A newly established trade union in Birmingham in 1874 stated that they were organising only because 'aggressions have repeatedly been made' on the trade in the previous thirty years. Their motives were pure: 'We are not actuated by any spirit of antagonism towards our employers, for we believe that the steps we are now taking will have an influence in establishing a more friendly feeling between employer and employed.' Adapting the social harmony theme to their own purposes they piously announced that they expected 'the co-operation of our employers, for a trade association rightly established cannot fail to be beneficial' to both employers and employed, since their interests are identical. The Preston Carpenters took a similar line in their Rules in 1864: 'When we consider man as a rational and intelligible [sic] being, his most refined enjoyments and greatest comforts are those which spring from the proper elevation of his mind, and the society of his fellow men. It therefore follows, that well regulated societies of the working classes, founded upon just and honourable principles towards their employers and each other, will be the most likely means to benefit themselves and society in general.'[23]

While the more extravagant statements of trade unionist moderation and respectability may have been dictated by prudential considerations, they nevertheless reflected widespread working-class acceptance of consensus values. The presence of such deeply internalised values is especially evident in the case of trade unionists who were consciously maintaining a militant posture in their relations with employers, and not at all intent on reassuring public opinion. Thus the radical house painter quoted above defined trade disputes not only in terms of the class struggle between capital and labour, but also in terms of cultural categories that tended to blunt his militancy. While noting that employers made concessions only when compelled to, even in response to moderate and reasonable demands, he went on to express the hope that employers would show greater appreciation of the good qualities of their employees. He clothed his point in properly mid-Victorian language:

In this age of marvellous progress and intellectual advancement, when mind predominates and rules the actions of men, does it not frequently happen that labour finds it difficult to enforce a due appreciation of its value, and impress upon the mind of the capitalist the old and salutary truth, 'That the labourer is worthy of his hire', and the working man is a rational being guided by something more than instinct and acting under other powers than physical strength, and having within him something higher than his stomach.

In this vein, he naturally singled out for emphasis the 'moral changes' that have been brought about by the struggle in the building trades.[24]

In April 1864 George Potter, editor of the *Bee-Hive* and spokesman for 'forward policies' in trade unionism, travelled to Leeds to address the carpenters, who were demanding higher wages and shorter hours. While delivering the sort of militant speech that the occasion called for, Potter put the case for trade unions in standard mid-Victorian terms. His argument for shorter hours took as its premise the line put out by the middle-class improvers who were so vocal in Leeds: 'If the hours of work were reduced it would enable men to improve their minds, and working men required time for instruction, and intellectual improvement was obtained by them under great difficulties. But they were making headway . . . They are becoming more intelligent, more thoughtful, and more provident. (Loud cheers.) They . . . were working out with great earnestness and determination their social and political emancipation. (Loud cheers.)' While this was not uttered in a servile or even 'moderate' manner, it reflected the widespread trade union tendency to operate within the framework of mid-Victorian consensus. Along the same lines, Potter also made the point that improved behaviour on both sides would be helpful. He assured the carpenters that if they pressed their demands in a 'straightforward manner', their employers would respond in a 'conciliatory spirit'. He hoped for a 'good feeling' between masters and men: 'Frankness and cordiality will win working men's hearts, and a ready explanation will often remove misgivings and dissatisfaction. Were there more trust, and greater sympathy between classes, there would be less disposition to turn out on the part of the men, and a more accommodating spirit on the part of masters and others'. In view of the behaviour of Leeds employers in the 1860s, Potter had to stretch a point in order to take this line. But take it he did, confident that 'a liberal employer will always find his return in the goodwill of his workmen', while 'a tyrannical master earns only fear and hatred of all those brought under his control'.[25] In this attempt to combine firmness with conciliation Potter was very representative of the mid-Victorian trade union movement.

As one would expect, the Amalgamated Society of Engineers made every effort to persuade the 'liberal employer' that he could count on the goodwill of his workmen. Exemplar of what the Webbs called the 'new spirit' in trade unionism in the 1850s and 1860s, it was imbued with consensus values and took pride in the respectability of its members. Typical of the 'New Model' unions that provided unemployment, sickness, and death benefits in return for fairly high weekly contributions from members, the A.S.E. was wary of strikes. Even this thoroughly mid-Victorian institution, however, did not passively submit to middle-class ideology or embrace the cult of respectability. Faithful to the values of the working-class subculture, it existed in a state of tension with a social and ideological system dominated by the middle-class.

The friendly society function, so prominent in the A.S.E. and other unions of that type, was not a reflection of middle-class 'individualism', but a response to practical necessity. It was one means, however tenuous, of meeting the threat of destitution in the economic system. In addition, in the spirit of the working-class subculture, the friendly benefits represented a conscious effort to sustain the self-respect of working men who had to contend with the demeaning apparatus of poor relief. In an address to prospective members the council of the A.S.E. explained that the society's benefits were intended to protect workmen against poor laws that had been designed 'to prevent men from having recourse to them', payments being made so grudgingly that their purpose seemed to be 'to degrade and disgust the recipients'. The address underlined one of the central facts underlying the working class subculture: to be relieved as a pauper 'humiliates a man in his own eyes, . . . disgraces him in the eyes of others . . . and breaks down every sense of personal dignity and independence'. By contrast, the point of trade union benefits was to enable a man to 'maintain his self-respect'. The trade unionist could 'feel proud of his prudence and foresight' in taking steps in good times that would save him from having to apply for relief to men whose interest it was to treat him 'rudely and harshly'.[26] Like other trade unionists then, the engineers entertained no illusions about the beneficence of the social and economic system. Their union was intended to help them make the best of it.

Although the leaders of the A.S.E. were reluctant, on practical grounds, to engage in strike activity, they did not hesitate out of confidence in the good intentions of employers or out of a belief in the teachings of political economy. In fact, in 1855 the council held that the 'trade advantages' conferred by the society were 'of even greater importance' than the benefits paid out to individuals. It emphasised the necessity for collective action in preference to individual selfishness: 'For the many, the amelioration of the condition of each individual and the elevation of his social position, is not to be obtained singly, but only by the growing prosperity of the mass. Efforts made without concert are powerless but power springs from the combined action of thousands.'[27] As for political economy, the council noted that it was correct to attribute a fall in wages to an oversupply of labour. But it also pointed out that wages do not in fact tend to rise at the same rate when labour is in short supply. At the very least, some sort of combination was necessary to get wages up again after they had fallen.

While the A.S.E. was committed to the mid-Victorian radical ideal of the independent working man, worthy of respect and emulation, it was not always able to prevent the erosion of that ideal by the ever-present middle-class version. On the one hand, for example, the council's appeal to members in the address of 1855 represented a characteristic statement of working-class values in terms that reflected the culture as a whole: 'It is for them to enhance the character of the Society by their demeanour in their workshop as well as in their home lives . . . And it is for them to watch over the minds among them and to give them such direction as will make the men of the future honourable, useful, independent, and united members of a great, powerful, and thriving industrial community.' Whereas the Chartists and Owenites had hoped to achieve working-class independence and self-respect by somehow transforming a repressive social system, the A.S.E. pursued the objective indirectly, by building up the power of the union. Once that ideal had been removed from the context of early-Victorian radicalism and protest, however, it was vulnerable to social and cultural pressures.

The council of the A.S.E. was not always able to avoid the demeanour of Uncle Tom. In the 1855 address, for example, the employers were assured in fulsome terms that they had nothing to fear from the society, which was 'not intended, nor adapted, to damage their interests, but rather to advance them, by elevating the character of their workmen, and proportionately lessening their own responsibilities'. Trade union members would perform their work 'more skilfully' and would be 'more anxious than others to fulfil the duties properly belonging to their position'.[28]

While the A.S.E. was pursuing its policy of pressure and conciliation, the ironworkers in the 1860s were locked in savage conflict with unyielding employers who refused to accept unionisation. Their leader in the struggle was John Kane, a man second to none in militancy. Born in Northumberland in 1819, he went to work at the age of seven. At the age of fifteen he took a job in an ironworks at Gateshead, near Newcastle-on-Tyne. He participated in the Chartist movement and made an unsuccessful attempt to form a trade union in 1842. In the 1850s he continued to be active in the cause of political radicalism and was a leading figure in the Northern Political Union, which under the leadership of Joseph Cowen, Jr. advocated manhood suffrage. But Kane was very much his own man. On one occasion he rejected an invitation from Cowen to speak at a meeting to pass resolutions that were to be presented to Parliament in a petition. He objected to the fact that Cecil Headlam, the M.P. who had been selected to present the petition, had refused to associate himself even with the moderate reformers. Kane described Headlam as 'a miserable Government Hack, such a one I hold in the most unmitigated contempt'. So long as they insisted on entrusting the petition to Headlam, he wrote, 'It would be a Burlesque for me to speak to such a subject.' In the 1860s Kane stood firm throughout the struggle and later regaled the Royal Commission on trade unions with an account of blacklegs, blacklisting, and evictions.[29]

Like other mid-Victorian trade union leaders, however, Kane was compelled to struggle very hard indeed merely for acceptance of the existence of his organisation. Recognition was the basic issue in the multiple disputes in which the ironworkers were engaged in the 1860s. Kane finally secured *de facto* recognition when the employers were persuaded by one of their number, David Dale, to agree to a system of conciliation. In form, however, trade union officials still did not participate in the new conciliation process; this begrudging attitude was, as we have seen, typical of the employer class as a whole. For all the limitations of the system, however, Kane accepted it and bent every effort to make it work. As a supporter of conciliation he denounced wildcat strikes and defended the rationality of the arbitration procedure. Moreover, he and his union became fervent supporters of the whole apparatus of improvement in which mid-Victorian working men had become involved. A case in point is the meeting held in Darlington in 1870 to establish a working men's club. The description of the event in the *Ironworkers' Journal* depicts a standardised cultural ritual, which recurred on countless similar occasions: conflicts of class and status were forgotten in a communal celebration of shared values. Usually, such lyrical accounts occurred in the middle-class press. In this instance, however, we find the same tone in a trade union journal.

The initiative for the establishment of a working men's club, to be affiliated with Henry Solly's movement, came from the ironworkers' 1870 conference, which passed a resolution inviting him to visit the iron works of the north of England. An employer, David Dale, arranged for Solly's first visit to Darlington, when a small club was organised. The next step is described by the official journal of the ironworkers.

> In the centre and north end of the town a number of employers and workmen held several meetings to consider how they could best stem the tide of intemperance and immorality, and promote the social and moral improvement of the working men at the north end of the town, where the iron works are situated. A committee, composed of delegates from each of the works and one employer, was appointed to make arrangements for the holding of a large tea meeting and demonstration, which took place during the Christmas holidays.

The meeting turned out well: 'This was a most successful gathering, there being not less than a thousand working men with their wives and sweethearts present. The night was bitter cold, the place of meeting a large workshop which was kindly lent by Mr Wilson.' A number of gentlemen addressed the meeting 'at considerable length', and a joint committee of workmen and employers was set up to find suitable premises for a club, which was opened several months later.

The account concluded with a comment, in the usual style, on the progress that had been made: 'It may be said with perfect safety that there is not a town better supplied with the means for social and intellectual improvement and enjoyment than the rising town of Darlington, with a population of 28,000. There will shortly be three working men's clubs, a Church of England institute, a good mechanics' institute in the centre of the town, and another large institute for the benefit of the men employed by the North Eastern Railway Company . . . ' The journal also printed a more detailed account of a meeting held at Consett, attended by both Dale and John Kane. Its explanation of the reason for publishing the account illustrates something of the way in which the leaders of the working classes had come to treat their followers primarily as persons in need of individual improvement: 'Many of the ironworkers are strangers to the higher enjoyments which only cultivated minds can appreciate. We long to see the time when our ironworkers will find a cheaper, a purer, and a higher kind of enjoyment than is to be found where the pot and pipe are the books that are provided by Mr Boniface for the *special benefit* of the working men.'[30]

In inviting the working men at Consett to set up a club of their own, Kane delivered a homily on the standard values of the official culture. He began by urging the working men themselves to take the first steps, instead of simply complaining about the lack of a club. 'Let them do this, and then they might look to the Consett Iron Company doing something for them. (Hear, hear.) The co-operation of the company was very desirable, but the workmen would have to take the initiative.' In justifying the club, he put a great deal of emphasis on the importance of preventing drunkenness: 'The temptation to lead men to drink was not a party question, and everything here seemed to be in favour of the public-house . . . Those who wanted beer in the club and those who do not should co-operate in the work, and could do so without giving up any of their ideas on the question of temperance; but the less of drink there was provided in connection with the club the better. (Applause.)' Like countless middle-class speakers, this militant trade union leader stressed the value of intellectual improvement: 'Working men should have a place of resort for receiving instruction, etc., as they should learn to be thinkers as well as workers. What had been accomplished at Darlington could be done here.' He did not think that the puddlers, who got enough exercise at work, needed a gymnasium: 'The development of the muscular part of man is desirable, but not at the neglect of his intellect. (Hear, hear.) They wanted one thing more than muscular games, they needed mental improvement. They required quiet games, the use of a good library, and a newsroom.' The workmen of Consett should not be content merely to go to and from work: 'They should have higher aspirations and aims, and these could be gratified by establishing a working man's club.'

Even more striking, from a trade union leader — however committed to the arbitration system — is Kane's stress on the connection between knowledge gained through the club and an understanding attitude towards management.

The establishment of a club would spread intelligence amongst the workmen, and make them lose the charm which some unfortunate people still retained for ruinous and unfortunate strikes. (Hear, hear.) He never yet found strikes pay any party connected with them; . . . The action of the board of Arbitration was always a question of reason and comparison; it was not what they thought the workmen should have, but what the selling prices of finished iron could afford, so that the invested capital and management, on the one hand, and the value of labour on the other hand, could be fairly adjusted without strikes or lock-outs.

He then took his seat 'amid much applause'.

(3) *Friendly Societies*

Of all working-class institutions the friendly societies were most in harmony with the culture as a whole. They were actively engaged on behalf of values that were central to consensus liberalism: self-help, thrift, prudence, decorum, independence. They were deeply imbued with the soft and sentimental spirit of mid-Victorianism. Precisely because they were so well integrated into the culture, however, the friendly societies exemplify all the more vividly the tensions within mid-Victorian society. Because they were so eager to accept middle-class preaching at face value, they were all the more disappointed at the reality of middle-class behaviour. Their leaders could be trenchant in their denunciation of the cant and snobbery of the propertied classes. Although the friendly societies were totally committed to consensus values, they pursued them within the framework of a working-class subculture that prized genuine independence and self-respect. Their activity was not an expression of acquiescence in class rule, but an attempt to achieve a degree of emancipation from its constraints.

In a numerical sense friendly societies were the most representative of working-class institutions. According to an estimate made in 1872, there were 32,000 societies with some four million members. Preeminent among them were the 'affiliated orders', in which a central headquarters presided over the activities of numerous branches. The largest was the Manchester Unity of Oddfellows, which included over 400,000 members in 1872. Close behind was the Ancient Order of Foresters. All told, the affiliated orders accounted for almost a third of friendly society membership. They catered to the upper strata of the working-class. A study of the Manchester Unity of Oddfellows in the late 1840s shows a high proportion of members from the building trades and the traditional handicrafts. The leadership of the affiliated orders came from self-made men of working-class background who had moved into the ranks of the middling classes.[31]

The primary purpose of the friendly societies was to provide working men with a modest amount of sickness and life insurance. The member made a small contribution and was eligible for benefits. When sick, he received a benefit that usually amounted to about a third of his ordinary wage. In many cases he could call on the services of a doctor hired by the society on a contract basis. On the death of a member, his family received a sum that made possible a decent burial. The Oddfellows had a more extended series of benefits: for the death of the member or his wife; for the relief of members in sickness and in old age; for temporary assistance to the widows and children of deceased members; for assistance to members when travelling in search of employment; and 'for assisting members in distressed circumstances'. At the other extreme there were 'burial clubs' with a much more limited function.[32]

An important secondary purpose of the friendly societies was to provide regular occasions for conviviality and fellowship. The monthly meeting, at which the premium was paid, was a festive occasion. It was often held in a public house, so that alcohol enhanced the merriment. In the affiliated societies there was an additional element of mysterious ceremonies and regalia. They saw themselves as a means of 'making the leisure hours of an agreeable and pleasant character'. The laws of the Oddfellows stated proudly that 'there cannot be any meetings imagined of a more delightful and gratifying kind'. The Foresters too announced that they 'assemble to promote the social happiness of our brethren and to relieve our minds occasionally from the pressure of care with temperate conviviality'.[33]

Even more than most Victorian institutions the friendly societies infused their activity with the highest social and moral significance, and took satisfaction in the pursuit of the most sacred goals of mankind: 'What are its objects?' asked a manual of Oddfellowship in 1858. 'The relief of sickness and distress; the support of the widow and orphan; our own social and moral elevation — the holiest and best objects which mere human agency can hope to achieve!' Their rules evoke the mood of a Victorian print: 'Joy and friendship rise through the flowery fields of pleasure, under the mild restraint of Morality, whilst her sister Reason leads her by the hand.' Even conviviality contributed to the higher purposes esteemed by the culture:

> The lodge is always considered as sacred ground; and no sooner do those, who in any other place might meet together as enemies, enter into its precincts, than their bad feelings seem to vanish as if by magic, and in their stead, the desire to promote the well-being and happiness of all, reigns predominant. We see mingling together men of all nations and creeds, and every grade of politics; and all behaving in a respectful and friendly manner

towards each other. The prejudices which are engendered by being born in a different land, the sectarian feeling which is apt to prevail amongst religious enthusiasts, and heart burnings of violent political partisans, are all for a time obliterated and forgotten by those who meet together in the temples of Oddfellowship.

Yet the next sentence, characteristically, is defensive: 'There must, then, be some great and good moral principle amongst us by the aid of which we can accomplish all this; there must be some powerful and virtuous influence connected with the Order, which neither the slanders of the malicious, the arguments of the prejudiced, nor the sneers of the ignorant, can prevent from having a vast and beneficial effect upon the destinies of mankind.'[34]

The origins of the friendly societies were depicted in the same extravagant terms: 'Is it not, then, our duty while in this world to make each other as comfortable and happy as we can? It is this noble feeling which first prompted the formation of friendly and sick societies. To administer to the wants of a sick-bed — to ease the feelings of a dying pillow, were objects which first prompted a few illiterate and poor men to form themselves into small bodies for the uniting of their pence in aid of each other. These were the Godlike germs from which our society and others of a like nature were formed.'[35] The Oddfellows' song,[36] intended to be sung to the air of the French national anthem, 'Partant pour la Syrie', represents an only slightly more lyrical version of the commonplaces of official discourse:

LOVE, FRIENDSHIP, AND TRUTH
by Edward L. Hart

When sickness lays the strong man low,
   And on his fever'd bed,
He hears his children weeping by,
   And vainly asking bread,
In simple guise comes charity,
   That troubled head to soothe;
A motto on her garment spreads,
   'Tis Friendship, Love, and Truth!

When by a lov'd child's cold dead clay
   The mourners sadly stand,
And see a mother's poor relief
   In grasping its small hand,
Comes charity, with saddened smile,
   As innocent as youth;

And still the words that round her shine
  Are Friendship, Love, and Truth!

That close black veil, that choking sigh,
  Those tears of scalding rain;
That child who weeps, scarce knowing why;
  That sad funereal train;
What mean they, that they dim the air
  With gloom and dark despair?
Is there no hope for answer to
  A widow's heart-breathed prayer?

Yea; God hath bidden man arise,
  And see the labour done,
That wipes the orphan's streaming eyes,
  That checks the grief begun.
Then shining like an angel bright,
  Comes charity to soothe;
A motto still her garments bear,
  'Tis Friendship, Love, and Truth!

God bless the honest hearts and brave,
  That never heed man's sneer,
But do the work their Master bids,
  To lessen sorrow here;
And may our Order ever stand,
  In prime and strength of youth;
And may we never false become
  To Friendship, Love, and Truth!

In addition to their own benefit activity the friendly societies founded mutual improvement societies, institutes, and literary institutions in connection with the lodges. The provincial district grand master of the Birmingham district described improvement activity in 1845: 'We are going on most gloriously in this district with our library and schools, and we have every reason to believe that, in a short time, we shall have the most valuable and useful literary institution in the town.' Lodges that did not go so far as to form an institute arranged lecture series. A lodge in Lewes in 1860 set up a committee to plan a programme of essays and readings: 'It is highly desirable to blend instruction with amusement, so as to enhance the moral and intellectual character of the brethren.' The title of a paper read to the City of London lodge during the winter of 1862–3 illustrates the friendly societies' attitude towards improvement in the 1840s and 1850s: 'On the importance of the culture and development of the mental faculties, and the expediency of the Manchester Unity encouraging the intellectual improvement of its members.' It was a matter of pride that among the best Sunday school teachers were 'some whose minds were first cultivated by a benefit society'. The Oddfellows were active in philanthropy. A lodge in Oldham sponsored a series of concerts for the people in the working man's hall. The proceeds went to the widows and orphans fund. In Bradford a lodge raised money to furnish a ward in the infirmary. The formal presentation was made with the usual ceremony, including appropriate comments by a clergyman: 'And who could look around on the manner in which this was fitted up without perceiving the march of improvement?'[37]

Unlike the co-operatives, the friendly societies were totally committed to the mid-Victorian social order and its values. Their own involvement with fellowship and conviviality made them especially responsive to the cultural yearning for class harmony. They hoped to be able to do something to 'soften down the asperity and rancour too frequently engendered by excited enthusiasm, or ill-regulated party zeal'. In an extended metaphor, one friendly society leader compared the class structure to an ancient temple: 'The pedestals of the columns are the great mass of the nation – the sturdy artisans and manly toilers, who are in themselves a sustaining power; the shafts typify the solidity of the middle classes; the capitals may represent the nobility, whose grandeur exalts.' Underlying the various components was a higher unity: 'The pediment exhibits alike the traditions of plebeian and patrician; and above them all, in fair proportions, is the national idea – the choral unity – it holds forth to the eyes of mankind.' In this case, the working classes received no more than a tepidly populist tribute: 'Our business is low down in this grand pile; we are with the pedestals, who, often unseen, still give strength and permanence to the superstructure. We write of the working men who crowd our busy thoroughfares, and hum in our national hive; and it is of their working lives and working homes we would wish for a brief space to be heard.'[38]

One expression of this positive and acquiescient attitude was a tendency to sentimentalise social reality and to romanticise relations between employers and employees. A case in point is a description of a walk through a Manchester warehouse, which is treated as a magnificent totality in which 'each animated atom has its particular place and use, tending to the unity of the whole', so that it is of the utmost importance that every workman in the place 'should execute his business with precision, with punctuality and with vigour'. 'His heart and hand should go in unison; he must feel an interest in what he does, even though he be (as it were) the lowest step in the commercial ladder.' This sort of ideologising is very much in the mid-Victorian mood: the workman is to be instructed in the exalted character of his work, despite his humble position on the ladder. In this scenario, both employers and employees come on like the heroes in a contemporary melodrama: 'Good masters make good men; and the best proof that the principals in our Manchester warehouses are what they should be is the perfect concord which exists between them and their subordinates.' The author describes working men of truly remarkable generosity: 'I have known a case where a firm was temporarily restricted for cash, and the fact being bruited somehow, the warehousemen, high and low, down to the very porters, packers, and errand-lads, contributed (in the most unpretending and deferential manner) their savings; and a round sum was collected and timidly presented to those in power!' They turned over several hundred pounds, and the employers 'never forgot'. The author also describes workmen who arrive well before opening time, and who 'remain *until they were ordered off*'.[39]

Friendly society publications included a generous serving of hortatory articles and stories. *The Loyal Ancient Shepherds' Quarterly Magazine* announced its didactic purpose: 'The comparatively un-educated mind must receive something to incite it onward and upward.' To that end, it published such tales as 'Will Woodward, the Hatter; and the Benefit Society'. Woodward was able to join the society only after overcoming a number of difficulties. But there was a happy ending: 'He is now one of the most intelligent and efficient officers of his Order, and all his efforts are in the direction of educational and moral reforms among the brotherhood.' In the *Oddfellows' Magazine* there were poems, such as 'Good Deeds Never Die', and there was a special page for younger readers which was to include 'moral and scientific truths to be impressed on your minds to make you better boys and girls'. 'The Up Hill Way: A Story in Four Chapters' was the story of a man falsely suspected of robbery. 'Mary Hartley or the Odd-Fellow's Wife: A Tale of a Working Man's Friendly Society', by Charles Hardwick, ran the gamut of official social values. Hartley joins the society against Mary's wishes. He is disabled in a fire, in which he rescues the mill owner, and later is killed by a flood. Mary then realises the benefits of Oddfellowship. The mill owner becomes an honorary member after he is assured that the society has no trade union ambitions. He is told, by the doctor who serves the society, that he need have no fear of a turn-out: 'The operatives of Lingfield already love you for your previous kindness; but when I announce the course you have taken on this subject, not a single man will leave his work. Sympathy and kindness form an infinitely stronger link than force and terror in the chain which unites the employer and employed.'[40]

Despite their total commitment to consensus values, the friendly societies had by no means abdicated their critical faculties or abandoned their quest for genuine independence. They had no trouble distinguishing between the professions of the middle classes and their actual behaviour and attitudes. They did not forget the social and economic disabilities that working men were burdened with. Working men supported friendly societies primarily in order to do something about such disabilities; the high moral ends came as a bonus. Thus the friendly societies were an authentic expression of a working-class subculture which sought to bring within the reach of working men the values professed by the society, by removing some of the obstacles interposed by that society. Along with the cloying rhetoric went a stubborn determination to stick to their principles in the face of middle-class resistance and hypocrisy.

The function of the friendly societies brought them into the most direct contact with the harshest side of middle-class social attitudes: treatment of the poor. The whole point of such societies was to prevent a man from falling into the hands of either the poor law guardians or the charity people. On this subject the leaders of the friendly societies did not mince words. They denounced an 'age of cant' and 'pseudo-philanthropy'. The head of the Foresters derided those who showed a great philanthropic interest in the criminal law while remaining indifferent to the plight of the poor: 'In Christian Britain, were it not that there is a fearful hereafter, it were far better to be a highwayman and a murderer than to be driven to the parish to ask for relief. In the one case the thief has some care taken of him – he has a comfortable room provided for him in prison – his food is of a good description.' The historian of the Oddfellows spelled out the consequences of the 'cold and heartless nostrums' of the political economists: 'The face of the country has been covered with barracks for lodging paupers, by which means the working man has been taught to look upon himself as a *thing* depending upon others, rather than as a being whose labour and industrious habits added dignity to his position in society.'[41]

In this context have to be understood the seemingly abstract statements of high purpose, to the effect, for example, that their members were to be made 'FREE, INDEPENDENT and CIVILISED'. The statement that 'the very object of a benevolent society is to make a man free' has to be understood not only as consensus liberalism but also as an indication of a determination to do something about the most immediate limitation on freedom in the concrete. Similarly, the assertion that benevolent institutions 'speak most in favour of liberty, and independence, and civilisation' encompassed specific working-class disabilities: a man is not free when he lacks the money to get his children an education or when he has to rely on the 'cold and merciless hand of the parish surgeon to examine his pulse and prescribe for his ailments'. Sentimental language was also useful in illuminating the dark side of Victorian life: 'Thus have thousands been left to pine and die for the cupidity of parish officials or hardhearted guardians.' In rescuing a man from the callousness and cruelty of the poor law, the club 'tends to make a man free'. If this was a rather limited freedom, that limitation reflected the objective characteristics of the social order rather than subjective illusions of friendly society members. The same applies to the modest degree of 'independence' aspired to in the following: 'A man can afford to be independent when he knows his wife and children have the means, should anything happen to him, of following his remains to their last home in respectability. His mind is relieved from a great weight as he puts on one side the few halfpence weekly to pay into his "club".' [42]

The friendly societies were intended to overcome not only the cruelty of the poor law but also 'the degradation of charity', which threatened 'to destroy the principle of self-respect'. Another historian of the movement displayed a similar hostility to the whole tradition of charity: 'Charity, forebearance, and humiliation have been the daily theme of many among the smooth faced and well fed ministers of the gospel, men who are in the habit of preaching in the fashionable language of soft flattery to the rich, and are ever threatening the poor with eternal punishment.' Charles Hardwick, a Past Grand Master of the Oddfellows, spoke scornfully about the psychologically self-serving character of middle-class philanthropy: 'It is quite possible to nurse and fondle a virtuous impulse until it degenerates into a mere selfish enjoyment of the "pleasure of doing good".' He denounced as 'social turpitude' the practice of 'trumpeting forth a man's own virtue, or the virtue of his class, by a course of bullying of the poor, and angrily lecturing them *en masse* on *their* ignorance and *their* vices, real and imaginary, exaggerated or otherwise'. The middle classes were constantly proclaiming their own philanthropic virtues, while in fact they did not do very much for the poor, who were really forced to rely on their own efforts. 'They generally prefer to *talk* very eloquently about the duty of loving one's neighbours as oneself, and leave the *bona fide* practical *loving* to said neighbour, and to very poor people, the latter of whom, somehow, or other, often contrive to carry out this doctrine with more truthfulness of heart than "their betters".' [43]

Hardwick also pointed out that anyone who broke the consensus and discussed the actual behaviour of the middle classes was soon made to realise that such comments were inappropriate. Whoever wishes 'to castigate arrogant spiritual pride with a meek and lowly mask upon its face' is 'liable to the unpleasant charge of wilfully wounding the sincere convictions of well-meaning men', for 'it is considered very shocking indeed to use free speech upon the peccadilloes of "respectable" proprietors of well-filled purses'. To criticise them in plain language 'is to proclaim yourself at once a low fellow, utterly unacquainted with the ways of the world or the usages of polite society'. There was far too much 'toadying of wealthy scoundrelism'.[44]

An official description of the aims of benevolent societies includes a vivid picture of the class system as experienced by a proud and independent working man. In this case it was suggested that a member might find in his club a momentary sanctuary from the abrasiveness of the class system that dominated his working hours:

> His wife sees her husband rise by five in the morning and work perhaps until seven or eight at night — she sees the man of her choice despised by the great and trampled upon by the proud — she sees wealth wallowing in luxury, and the cat, or dog, or horse of the employer more cared for than her spouse; but though amid the every-day transactions of life *he* may have to submit to many indignities which under other circumstances his proud soul would revolt against: yet there is *one* consolation, there is one place in this world where even he — firm and lowly though he is — where he is somebody, and where he is on an equality with the highest, and that is at his club.[45]

In absolute terms, this must be pronounced a rather small consolation. But more substantial rewards were simply not available. The best that a man could hope for was to preserve some small measure of dignity and independence. The friendly society contributed to the achievement of that objective, however limited. It was not a manifestation of surrender to the middle classes.

The friendly societies took a populist pride in the fact that they were composed of working men. An official summary of the annual meeting of the Oddfellows in 1858 is typical: 'Here we see how working men — we claim no higher title, though we have noblemen, members of parliament, ministers of religion, authors, artists and professors of science, working with and among us — can, without assistance from the state, and by means of their own money, carry the principles of our association into actual every-day practice.' Theirs was 'essentially a working-man's society'. The Foresters saw themselves in similar terms: 'Most of our members are working men. A class not less important than any in the community, but certainly possessing fewer advantages than do many others.' Such references to the working-class character of the order were often defensive, however, and accompanied by expressions of regret that the virtues of friendly societies had not always been properly recognised by the middle and upper classes.[46]

As a matter of class pride the friendly societies exhorted their members to achieve the virtues esteemed by the working-class subculture. 'A good Forester is a man who, jealous of his rights as a citizen, maintains them in a temperate, manly, and decorous manner;

and at the same time, he knows his duties too, performs them well, and pays a ready and willing obedience to his country's laws — neither cringing nor servile on the one hand, nor wild and factious on the other.' In this vein, the Forester was reminded not to be forgetful of 'the dignity of his manhood and character as a rational being'. Hence he must avoid brawling, drinking, and 'absurd and disgusting speech'. Every member of the Order ought to be 'honest, sober, and industrious'.[47] Such traits as these had no necessary connection with the quest for middle-class respectability.

A more detailed picture of the ideal type of 'independent working-man' is found in 'a few words of serious advice' offered by an editor to the younger members of the Order of Foresters. He spelled out the duties enjoined upon them by the initiation ceremony. 'Has your education been neglected? strive to improve it . . . in our opinion the first and grand thing to be done is to get information. This is the touchstone of all greatness.' The editor also put a great deal of emphasis on the obligation to bring the blessings of knowledge to the less fortunate: 'In addition to storing your own mind with knowledge, endeavour to disperse it to others. Assist in Sunday schools and evening schools.' Thus the model working man was expected to play an improving role in relation to the lower strata of the working class. 'If you alleviate one sorrow: if you comfort one sick bed: if you relieve one famishing family, you then meet with gratitude . . . Go with me to your deserving recipients of parish relief, and I will find you plenty to do.'[48]

The friendly societies tended to define the independent working man by separating him from the lower strata of the working-class, but without seeking to deny his working-class character. On the contrary, his class consciousness was fostered by contrasting him with his social superiors, who were often depicted as stubbornly refusing to recognise his true worth. In urging the young Forester to do good works among the poor, the editor reminded him that he must not expect much in the way of praise from above: 'The great men of the land may look down upon you with pity — may be with contempt — but your reward, even in this world will be far superior to that which princes can bestow . . . You will have the thanks and prayers of the widow.'[49] The friendly societies nourished a deep resentment at the refusal of the middle classes to acknowledge their virtues.

Provoked by niggling criticism of the actuarial shortcomings of the friendly societies, even so compulsively moderate and positive a man as Charles Hardwick was moved to cut through the customary rhetoric and speak some plain truths about the realities of Victorian life. Outraged by the way that *The Times* had been harping on the deficiencies of the societies, he pointed out all that the working classes had accomplished by their own efforts, without any assistance from the philanthropic and charitable groups that were so free with carping advice and complaint: 'The vast amount of provident effort made by the best section of the operative population of Great Britain . . . has preserved an honourable independence in the hearts and homes of thousands of noble but unfortunate working men stricken by the breath of sickness; an effort which has practically done more to elevate them in the scale of manhood, than hundreds of praise-bespattered but impotent efforts to drill free men into a kind of docile, social militia.' Working men had every reason to resent their 'continually being spoken of *en masse* as if all were the mere outscourings of the jail or the parish workhouse'. He thought it odd that after years of boasting about advances in popular education there should suddenly occur a load outcry about the 'depravity of the *working* classes'.[50]

Even in asserting the traditional radical values of the working-class subculture, however, the friendly societies could not avoid paralleling and often reinforcing the middle-class propaganda line and the values determined by the structure of power and status. Like other working-class institutions, they could provide their members with no more than a limited independence and self-respect. For these modest gains they had to pay a fairly high price in accommodation to the social and psychological claims made by their superiors. For example, it was in the best traditions of working-class radicalism for the friendly societies to take pride in the fact that they included men from varying social and economic levels who met together 'upon an equality' with each other. In that egalitarian tradition, they emphasised that the various offices in the society were equally open to all men, solely on the basis of their ability: 'It is the brightest ornament in our excellent institution that its offices are open to all . . . The only qualifications required are honesty of character and regularity of attendance.' Great pride was expressed in the fact that at one lodge the Chief Ranger was a chimney sweep. Yet statements which in this context had a democratic resonance inevitably contained overtones that suggested the rather different implications of the success myth: 'You ask if you shall ever attain those offices. That depends upon yourself. The way is open to you,and to all others; but to reach the highest honour (Grand Master) you will have to prove yourself worthy of it by a long course of labour.' Moreover, the celebration of social diversity in the name of equality could all too easily involve the acceptance of some extremely inegalitarian presuppositions: 'The very fact of the benefit society taking a man from the lowest rank and placing him upon an equality with others, his superiors in mental accomplishments and in more comfortable and easy circumstances in society, this very fact tends to elevate the human mind and increase the civilisation of the country.' Although in theory every man has been placed 'upon an equality' with every other, the whole point of the comment is that this is a marvellous thing because men of higher rank are also superior in mental and moral traits.[51] It is assumed that merely associating with one's superiors at such meetings will lead to immediate improvement. Beneath the grand talk lies the familiar mid-Victorian assumption that hobnobbing with people of higher social status would produce elevation of mind and character.

The friendly societies were also vulnerable to the unintended consequences of their attempt to defend themselves against middle-class criticism. Hardwick and other friendly-society leaders very much wanted the approval of the middle classes whose deficiencies they saw so clearly. And in the act of refuting criticism from above, they inevitably came to accept much of the substance of the middle-class view of the proper position of the working classes in the social order. They came to portray their virtues not so much in terms of the genuine independence demanded by the working-class subculture, but rather in terms more congenial to the propertied classes. Hardwick, for example, at the annual dinner of the Jolly Sailor lodge in Leeds, argued that the friendly societies were 'a benefit in many ways to the middle and upper classes, and by improving the moral tone and character of the working classes they were a great helpmate to the clergy'. The Foresters too rejoiced at the fact that the 'upper and middle classes' had begun to be impressed by the 'sobriety, good conduct and intelligence' of the members of the Order. This was invariably accompanied by complaints that the newspapers were ignoring the activities of the societies. Hence official spokesmen took every opportunity to bring the virtues of their Order to the attention of the propertied classes. Most stress was put on the fact that members were kept off the relief rolls. But on one occasion Hardwick also pointed to their role in preserving public order, citing the fact that on the occasion of the Queen's visit to Manchester the police did not swear in special constables but simply relied on the assembled members of the friendly societies. Inevitably, then, the friendly societies found themselves actively associating themselves with the middle-class image of proper working-class behaviour.[52]

As the friendly societies stressed the virtuous behaviour of their members, they naturally tended to point up the contrast to working men who remained outside the fold. This very natural tendency, in turn, tended to undermine their moral position as spokesmen for the working classes as a whole and put them close to the middle-class line. Hardwick's defence of the respectability of the upper strata of the working classes involved him in a rather direct acceptance of socially determined values: 'The whole mass of the people *poorer* than themselves are treated as the "working classes", or rather as the "lower orders", forgetful that amongst the millions of British subjects so classed there exists so great a diversity both as regards habits and education as there are languages amongst the nations of the earth.'[53]

Soon the friendly societies began to receive the praise that they craved from the 'middle and upper classes'. An M.P., being initiated into the Oddfellows, expressed his pleasure at joining a society of 'three hundred thousand members, whose duty and business it was to aid each other in manfully fighting the battle of life'. It was gratifying to hear this sort of thing at a time when *The Times* was still so carping in its criticism. The audience was delighted with the warm praise from the platform for the great work being done by the societies: 'It was by prudence and forethought alone that the working man was enabled to raise himself in the scale of society, and become an actual power in the land.' This was standard middle-class liberal propaganda. In other contexts, members of the friendly societies were quite capable of identifying its limitations. In this situation, however, where their merits were being publicly acknowledged, they were not in a mood to be critical. And the leaders of the societies went out of their way to get local dignitaries to participate in their major functions. When the Foresters sponsored a ball in Ashton-under-Lyne in aid of the Widows and Orphans Fund they secured the patronage of the Mayor and the local M.P. The official report noted with pride that 'some of the most respectable and influential gentlemen of the neighbourhood patronised it with their presence, and appeared highly delighted with the proceedings'. The friendly societies were already strongly predisposed in favour of the gospel of success which such respectable and influential gentlemen were wont to preach to working men on public occasions.[54]

The publications of the friendly societies were full of accounts of men who had got on in the world, along with exhortations to others to do the same thing. Since their leaders had been recruited from men who had been so successful, official biographies provided a ready vehicle for this sort of homily: 'Like most men who have to climb from the lowermost rounds of the social ladder, Mr Webb and his partner [his wife] have tasted of the bitters as well as of the sweets of life.' The ladder metaphor and the social values inherent in it were implicit in the life histories of men who were a good deal closer to the social world of the members of the societies than were the grander figures in the writings of Smiles. The biographical sketch of the Rev. Thomas Price, a Provincial Grand Master, is a case in point. He was born in Wales in 1822, the son of a farm bailiff. At an early age he went into domestic service for three years, when he managed to save enough money to apprentice himself to a plumber, painter, and glazier. During the period of his apprenticeship he taught in Sunday school. At the age of twenty-one, having completed his apprenticeship, he received a gift of five pounds from his employer, and set out to walk to London.

He arrived there 'footsore and weary, with only a few shillings remaining of his master's gift'. But he was undaunted. 'The man who before he was fourteen had exhibited such rare self-denial as to save instead of to spend, and to begin his own way in the world unaided, was not the man to quail before difficulties — for had he not determined to conquer fortune and attain a name that should be known among men?' After finding a job as a house painter he spent his leisure time learning the additional skills of gilding and lettering. But he was not content with such narrowly practical studies: 'Now began his first real yearnings after knowledge. He joined a mechanics' institution, and studied hard . . . and thus laid the foundation of that useful sphere in which he has since been so eminent in the Principality.' At the request of the congregation of the chapel in which he was a Sunday school teacher he gave up his trade and entered the Baptist College at Pontypool. In 1845 he became pastor at Aberdare.[55]

The biography of Benjamin Street, a Past Grand Master of the Order, announced the purpose of such biographies: 'A brief detail of the struggles of Mr Street to gain his present respectable position in society, may not be without its value to some of our younger members.' After ten years in service, Street ran two small public houses and then became proprietor of a hotel. His public career in the town of Wirksworth included the familiar features of the role of the middle-class: 'Mr Street has ever been amongst the foremost in supporting, by his subscriptions and exertions, every thing calculated to benefit and improve the town in which he resides. Whether in catering for the amusement of its inhabitants, extending charitable institutions amongst them, or seeking to elevate the moral and mental condition of the youth of his town, Mr Street's exertions have been most conspicuous.'[56] Among other things, he supported the local mechanics' institute from the beginning, and became its treasurer.

Some of the hortatory writings in friendly society publications reflected both the gospel of success and the cult of respectability. An essay, 'Sobriety and Self-Advancement', is as crude a statement as one could find of socially determined values covered with a veneer of moral idealism. Directed to 'adventurers after secular promotion', the message is unequivocal: if you want to get ahead, you will have to stay sober. The reader is advised about exactly what he ought to do if he wants to win the 'glorious laurel' that 'abstinence and industry' has in store for him. 'Husband your earnings in readiness for any bright opening, or to support you during any of those commercial stagnations which are so constantly recurring.' Linked to this were the practical advantages of improving activity: 'Connect yourselves with mechanics' institutions; frequent lecture rooms; and grudge not a weekly outlay on the better and more instructive literature of the day.' Omitting the usual references to the value of this sort of thing for its own sake, the author proceeded directly to the pay-off: 'By and by you will be able to improve your outward respectability — to invest a little of your surplus money in a Building Society, or to purchase your own electoral rights.' The high ideals were tossed in almost as an afterthought: 'And what are these but some of the great and benevolent ends for which we were created?' The same essay included a pre-Smilesian catalogue of men who had made it from humble origins, Franklin, Arkwright, etc. The mill owners of Lancashire were described as 'mainly the self-elevated children of industry'. The 'brightest ornaments' in English life were 'men of obscure and inauspicious origin, whose advancement was the result of undeviating sobriety and unquenchable application'.[57] This was the 'success myth', as Harold Perkin has called it, down to the last detail.

A distinctive and important feature of the friendly societies was the prominence of ceremony in their institutional life. An elaborate and secret ritual complemented the conviviality of the meetings. Much more than other working-class institutions, the friendly societies reached their members through regular meetings, usually every week. Their social and ideological functions were closely tied in with their ceremonial and official business. They conveyed their message earnestly and insistently, while enabling their members to enjoy themselves in the process.

We get a sense of the importance of the lodge nights in the life of a devoted member from an account — idealised, to be sure — in the Foresters' magazine in 1850. We are told that all members of the family, realising the importance of the father's payment, 'ungrudgingly make a sacrifice of part of one of their homely meals to pay into the "club", and when "club" night comes, *all*, aye, *all* are anxious that he should keep "financial" '. That night the member prepares for the meeting as if he were going off to chapel. 'He washes himself, puts on a clean neckcloth, and with shoes or clogs neatly "blacked", as blithe as a lark he goes to his "club".' At the club he meets with others 'situated as he is', and after an hour he returns home 'cheerful and happy'. Even on his return, the ritual continues. His wife and children studiously refrain from questions about 'the one *secret*'. He locks up his copy of the rules for safe keeping, carefully wraps up his regalia and puts it away. Next time it will be brought out 'neatly folded and smooth'. 'If he has been in office, and a medal has been granted to *him*, that is almost idolised by his family.'[58]

The Bolton Unity of Oddfellows published a detailed manual of the procedure to be followed at meetings. The Grand Deacon was directed to open the proceedings by saying: 'I, _____, Grand Deacon of the Ancient Union, do . . . declare this Lodge duly opened for the despatch of business, hoping every Brother will conduct himself with propriety, lest he fall under the lash of our laws, by which we punish the guilty and protect the innocent.' Another formula read as follows: 'In the name and by the blessing of the Supreme Eternal Architect of Heaven and Earth, to whom be all honour and glory, I open this Lodge.' The Brothers were to reply, 'Amen.' The District Grand Master, conducting a catechitical dialogue with a candidate for office, was instructed to say: 'Finding you have not been inattentive to the official Lectures, be pleased to give me a summary account of what may be learned from the sublime themes intended for mental improvement, as handed down to us by the Fathers of the Primitive ages.'[59]

A prospective member of the Oddfellows was made to realise that he was about to enter into quite a complicated enterprise, which required careful explanation by his sponsor: 'You wish to become an Oddfellow. You ask me to see you "made", and let you know all about it.' The applicant had to provide vital statistics, get a certificate of good health from a doctor, and pay his 'earnest money'. Then his sponsor would take him to the lodge house and present him for initiation: 'When we meet, you must pay the rest of the initiation fee, and I, taking the doctor's certificate, shall leave you for a little time, to prepare the members for your reception. I shall tell them I propose you as a member — have known you for many years — believe you to be respectable, and a fit person to become an Oddfellow. Nothing being said against you, the lodge will no doubt resolve that you shall be admitted.' Then the prospective member was brought in for the ceremony of initiation. Since this was secret, the sponsor could not reveal any details, although he added reassuringly that there would be no skeletons, axes or red-hot pokers. It was to be a properly serious proceeding: 'Being introduced to the members, and having taken upon yourself the usual promises, you will listen to a reasonable — but impressive — homily, upon your duties to your Creator, your neighbour, and yourself, and at its close may shake hands with me as a brother.' The new member would receive five books to take home with him after the initiation, rules and laws, along with a contribution book. He was enjoined to study the material carefully.[60]

The new member was also briefed on the sort of thing that he could expect at regular meetings. They began with routine business, and the chairman opened the meeting with a 'stereotyped but businesslike speech'. The minutes of the last meeting were read and approved. There were reports on visits to sick members, and allowances were voted to them. New visitors were appointed, to serve until the next lodge meeting. Death certificates were read, and funeral money was ordered to be paid to the wife or mother. But the new member was reminded that the routine was enlivened by good cheer: 'You observe how, during intervals of business, the chairman has elicited songs and toasts

— he now looks this way, and calls upon you to sing. When you have done he proposes a toast.' Then back to business, as the secretary reads the names of those who will be 'out of limits if not paid for tonight'. A member might volunteer to pay what was owed by a delinquent.

Among the routine business conducted at lodge meetings was the levying of fines on errant members. These were levied for violations of any of the various rules against swearing, intoxication, or — in one case — reading newspapers or books during lodge hours. Other fines concerned failure to obey the rules governing behaviour for sick members. 'Resolved that Brother Cornelius Coward be fined 5/- for being out of his house after hours during receipt of sick pay.' It was possible for members to appeal against an adverse decision to the meeting as a whole. On one occasion a formal trial was held, with 'defendant' and 'plaintiff', when one member was accused of calling another 'you damned Humbug and Hypocrite'. On a more humdrum level the secretary was often asked to 'warn those Brothers who will go bad if not paid for on that lodge night'.[61]

Even without formal ideological exhortation, the meetings of the affiliated orders were well calculated to reinforce consensus values. For one thing, they brought together members from a fairly extensive social range, from the middle reaches of the working-class to the lower middle and middling classes. As has been noted, most of those in the upper strata had started out in 'humble circumstances'. Hence they offered visible proof of the validity of the advice that members were constantly being offered: that thrift, hard work, and self-help could bring substantial rewards. They were the men who also occupied the main offices in the societies. The presence of such men, who had every reason to look favourably on consensus values, had a great deal more impact than homilies on diligence and respectability. Moreover, the societies made much of the fact that men of different social levels were brought together at lodge meetings and treated as equals. This fitted in neatly with their egalitarian orientation. But the societies, like the social order of which they were so very much a part, asserted the principle of equality without calling into question the fact of social stratification. They prized equality of opportunity and limited social mobility, while asserting equality as a moral or religious principle. Their own elaborate hierarchy of offices and ranks directly reflected the values of a stratified society which encouraged limited advancement within a static structure. There could be no mistaking their fondness for the trappings of rank; each office had its own coloured sash, cap, and apron; and advancement in the order was made much of. Here, as in the consensus values of the culture, it was individual merit that really counted: 'It is the brightest ornament in our excellent institution that its offices are open to all . . . The only qualifications required are honesty of character and regularity of attendance.'[62]

Notes

1. See W. Hamish Fraser, *Trade Unions and Society: The Struggle for Acceptance*, London 1974; G.D.H. Cole, 'Some Notes on British Trade Unionism in the Third Quarter of the Nineteenth Century', *International Review of Social History*, 1937; H.A. Clegg et al., *A History of British Trade Unionism since 1889*, I, Oxford, 1964, pp. 1–54; A.E. Musson, *British Trade Unions 1800–1875*, London 1972; Allan Flanders and H.A. Clegg, eds., *The System of Industrial Relations in Great Britain: Its History, Law, and Institutions*, Oxford 1967; National Association for the Promotion of Social Science, *Trades' Societies and Strikes*, London 1860; Sidney and Beatrice Webb, *The History of Trade Unionism*, London 1920.
2. *Trades' Societies and Strikes*, p. 271.
3. Flanders and Clegg, p. 204; *Trades' Societies and Strikes*, p. 603.
4. Royal Commission on Trade Unions, *Tenth Report*, 1867, Q. 19079, 18981–2, 17818.
5. *Leeds Mercury*, 27 April 1864.
6. Norman Cuthbert, *The Lace Makers' Society*, Nottingham 1960, p. 36.
7. James B. Jefferys, *The Story of the Engineers, 1800–1945*, London 1946, p. 79; *Trades' Societies and Strikes*, pp. 169–205; Fraser, chs. 1 and 2.
8. G.D.H. Cole, *Short History*, p. 144; Daphne Simon, 'Master and Servant', in John Saville, ed., *Democracy and the Labour Movement*, London 1954, p. 190; H.A. Turner, *Trade Union Growth Structure and Policy: A Comparative Study of the Cotton Unions*, London 1962.
9. Royal Commission on Trade Unions, *Eleventh Report*, Appendix D.
10. Ibid.; *Trades' Societies and Strikes*, pp. 439–45.
11. Royden Harrison, *Before the Socialists*, London 1965, pp. 27–9; on the diverse attitudes of mid-Victorian employers, see Fraser, pp. 98–119.
12. *Leeds Mercury*, 15 and 26 April 1864.
13. Ibid., 26 and 27 April, 5 May, 4 and 7 June, 13 and 24 September 1864; Royal Commission on Trade Unions, *Fifth Report*, Q. 8415.
14. *Leeds Mercury*, 20 April 1864.
15. Fraser, pp. 160, 191; F.M. Leventhal, *Respectable Radical*, Cambridge, Mass. 1971, p. 153.
16. Fraser, p. 118.
17. *General Rules of the Amalgamated Beamers, Twisters, and Drawers' Association*, London 1866; *Rules of the Leicester and Leicestershire Amalgamated Trimmers' Association, Established May 1866*, Leicester, n.d. Webb Collection, London School of Economics. *Bee-Hive*, 18 August 1866.
18. *General Rules of the Amalgamated Beamers*; *Bee-Hive*, 18 August 1866; resolution of Wolverhampton Trades Council, minutes of London Trades Council, 29 May 1866, Webb collection; London Operative Bricklayers Society, *Report and Balance Sheet*, 1861.
19. *Chain Makers Journal*, March 1859.
20. *Chain Makers Journal*, November 1858.
21. G.D.H. Cole, *Short History*, pp. 172–9.
22. Webb Collection, London School of Economics.
23. *Rules and Regulations of the Scale Beam, Steelyard Weighing Machine and Millmakers Trade Protection Association*, Birmingham 1880, preface dated 1874; Preston Carpenters, *Rules;* Webb Collection. See also Amalgamated Society of

Carpenters, *Eighth Annual Report*.
24. *Bee-Hive*, 18 August 1866.
25. Ibid., 16 and 23 April 1864.
26. Council of the Amalgamated Society of Engineers, *Address*, London 1855.
27. Ibid.
28. Ibid.
29. Webbs, *History*, p. 240; Kane to R.B. Reed, 8 January 1858, item C11, Cowen papers, Newcastle Reference Library.
30. *Ironworkers' Journal*, 1 June 1871.
31. P.H.J.H. Gosden, *The Friendly Societies in England 1815–1875*, Manchester 1961, pp. 71–93, 224.
32. *Laws for the Government of the Independent Order of Oddfellows*, 1855.
33. Ibid.
34. Samuel T. Davies, *Oddfellowship; Its History, Constitution, Principles, and Finances*, Witham 1858, p. 3; Foresters, *General Laws for the Government of the Ancient Order of Foresters*, 1865, p. 4; Oddfellows, *Rules*, 1855, Preface.
35. *Foresters' Miscellany*, December 1850.
36. *Oddfellows' Magazine*, April 1858.
37. Gosden, pp. 151–3; *Foresters' Miscellany*, March 1850; *Bradford Observer*, 22 January 1852; *Manchester Guardian*, 27 April 1850.
38. *Oddfellows' Magazine*, April 1860, July 1858.
39. Ibid., April 1858.
40. *Loyal Ancient Shepherds' Quarterly Magazine*, April 1848, John Rylands Library, Manchester; *Oddfellows' Magazine*, January and October 1857.
41. J. Burn, *An Historical Sketch of the Independent Order of Oddfellows*, Manchester 1845, p. 33.
42. *Foresters' Miscellany*, March 1850.
43. James Spry, *The History of Oddfellowship*, London 1867, Dedication; Burn, *Historical Sketch*; *Oddfellows' Magazine*, October 1860.
44. Ibid.
45. *Foresters' Miscellany*, March 1850.
46. *Oddfellows' Magazine*, July 1858; *Foresters' Miscellany*, December 1852.
47. Foresters, Laws (1865).
48. *Foresters' Miscellany*, December 1850.
49. Ibid.
50. *Oddfellows' Magazine*, October 1860.
51. Ibid., October 1859; *Foresters' Miscellany*, March 1850.
52. *Oddfellows' Magazine*, January 1858; *Foresters' Miscellany*, March 1852.
53. *Oddfellows' Magazine*, April 1857.
54. Ibid., October 1859; *Foresters' Miscellany*, December 1852.
55. *Oddfellows' Magazine*, July 1860, April 1859.
56. Ibid., July 1858.
57. *Foresters' Miscellany*, March 1850.
58. Ibid.
59. *Making Piece and Lectures for District Grand Lodges of the A.N.O. Oddfellows, Bolton Unity*, Huddersfield 1852.
60. *Oddfellows' Magazine*, April 1859.
61. Pleasant Retreat Lodge, Preston District, Minute Book, 8 May 1857, Lancashire Record Office, Preston.
62. *Foresters' Miscellany*, March 1850.

10 WORKING-CLASS RADICALISM AND PARLIAMENTARY REFORM

In the mid-1860s working-class radicals once again organised great demonstrations to demand manhood suffrage.[1] The new agitation, led by the Reform League, reflected the persistence of a militant and class-conscious radicalism. By insisting on manhood suffrage and by maintaining a separate organisation, the movement preserved its independence of the middle-class campaign for an extension of the franchise. Rejecting servility and deference in politics as in social life, the radicals claimed the vote for the working-class as a whole without reservations; they were impatient with liberal attempts to draw a line at some point below £10. The radical resurgence also found expression in a campaign against the master and servant laws. With new vigour the radical movement was asserting the claims of working men in a society dominated by the propertied classes.

Despite substantial continuity with Chartism, however, working-class radicalism had gradually changed its character in the intervening years. While much of the old militancy remained, it had been transposed into a different key. With the abandonment of the Chartist hope — however vague — for some sort of fundamental change as a result of the enactment of the Charter, the significance of the demand for the vote changed drastically. The working-class radicals of the 1860s were offering only a more extensive version of liberal reform. In other ways also, when removed from the Chartist context, radical values and principles tended to take on a consensus coloration, emphasising individual improvement in the present and immediate future. Thus an argument that had been peripheral to Chartism, that working men were worthy of the vote, now moved into the foreground, in the somewhat equivocal form of the assertion that working men had proved themselves deserving of the vote by the improvement that they had achieved during the previous fifteen years. Here the radicals were very close to the middle-class liberal line. Such affinities with liberalism were reinforced by extensive collaboration with middle-class reformers that was rooted in practical necessity and ideological agreement.

The radicals were also vulnerable to deradicalising tendencies inherent in the culture as a whole. Precisely because of its idealism, radicalism was susceptible to the mid-Victorian propensity to sentimentalise principles and to reduce them to litanies of aspiration. In this situation radical values were often indistinguishable from other social pieties, especially since they were so congruent with the prevailing consensus. The old spirit of protest and criticism easily faded. Thus radical agitation was in danger of becoming just one of many socio-religious activities abounding in the mid-Victorian cities. The established forms of militancy — agitation, demonstration, petition — were readily integrated into a culture that was officially committed to remedial reform in response to an enlightened public opinion. The demand for specific reforms tended to reinforce the belief that no abuse could withstand the assault of dedicated reformers, and that grievances were constantly being removed by rational action based on a common devotion to progress for all. Moreover, since radicalism shared the values of the culture as a whole, its agitation for reform strengthened the consensual foundations of the society. Faith in reason, so central to the traditions of the Left, echoed the rationalism of a culture that also rested on an intellectual base derived from the Enlightenment. The old radical belief in knowledge, education, and individual improvement was now being proclaimed, albeit in different form, from every platform and pulpit. In this situation the working-class radical emphasis on failure to actualise these values was overshadowed by continual references to the moral and intellectual improvement that had been achieved by English working men.

(1) *The Acculturation of Working-Class Radicalism*

While working-class radicals in the 1850s continued to assert democratic and egalitarian values in a class-conscious framework, those aspects of early-Victorian radicalism that were most congenial to mid-Victorianism were accentuated. The improvement ethic became increasingly prominent. The temper of radicalism softened as it settled comfortably into a soothing cultural ambience.

The secularist movement in the West Riding in the 1850s certainly preserved intact the social and political radicalism of the early-Victorian decades, combining the demands and aspirations of Chartism and Owenism in the context of a fierce attack on orthodox Christianity. As part of their continuing protest against injustice, the West Riding secularists also urged the cause of individual improvement. Their organ, the *Yorkshire Tribune*, put universal suffrage at the head of its statement of principles, with the rights of labour following immediately, thus emphasising that a man was entitled not only to the vote but also to suitable work which paid an adequate wage. Other principles included the nationalisation of land and 'the accumulation and distribution of wealth on the co-operative or communistic principles of Robert Owen'. 'Sham Manchester Liberals' were dismissed with the comment that they were interested only in the defence of their cotton bales. For their part, the secularists wished to 'rescue the wages-slave from the grasp of the capitalist-employer'. The point of the Charter was to win social rights for working men and to free labour 'from its thraldom to capital'. The secularists were equally uncompromising on the matter of the rights of women, and demanded 'the absolute legal equality of the sexes'. Their radical credentials were impeccable.[2]

Inseparable from the radicalism of the West Riding secularists was a profound commitment to the moral and intellectual improvement of the individual. Concerned about the wretched condition of a high proportion of the working classes, especially as a result of the prevalence of drunkenness, they were convinced that the remedy was to be found in personal effort. They emphasised that if 'the Working Classes . . . are to be saved from the weakness of ignorance, and the thraldom of degradation, it must be through their own energies and by their own efforts'. The *Yorkshire Tribune* preached a populist version of the self-help creed, in which the emphasis was not so much on exhortation to emulation, although this was implicit, but on the latent talents of the common people. Under the heading 'Self-made Men' came a long list including, among others, the following biographical notes: 'Columbus was a weaver, Franklin was a journeyman printer . . . Halley was the son of a soap boiler. Arkwright was a barber. Belzoni, the son of a barber'. Jesus, the Wesleys, and Luther 'all sprung from the ranks of the poor'. The moral drawn had an egalitarian rather than a liberal cast: 'Genius, talent, skill, greatness of character, and expansiveness of mind are not confined to any rank; tho' the world's most eminent men — its brightest genius and its purest benevolence, its truest heroes and its best benefactors — have always come from the cottage — have ever been of the "humbler" classes.' On the one hand then, the humbler classes were in rather poor shape, to say the least. On the other hand, they were quite capable of regenerating themselves, without any help from the government or the middle classes. In this setting, self-help had a radical ring to it, symbolising the independence and inherent worth of the working classes. But it also had obvious affinities to the preaching of middle-class improvers.

The elements that entered into the acculturation of working-class radicalism can be seen most vividly in George Julian Harney, who at the beginning of the 1850s was as firmly planted as ever on the far Left. Throughout the Chartist years he had resisted reformism, insisted on political and social transformation, and hoped for a revolutionary seizure of power by the working classes. Like other working-class radicals, he accepted consensus values while trying to give them an egalitarian form. Moreover, the fusion of rationalism and romanticism was so prominent in Harney's outlook that he was a good deal more in tune with the mid-Victorian sensibility of high aspiration than were the more staid and pragmatic working-class radicals. Harney therefore illustrates in its most extreme form the tension within working-class radicalism in the 1850s and 1860s, for he maintained the traditions of the Left in a form that was at once undiluted and also vulnerable to the acculturating forces at work. He is also noteworthy in that he recognised the processes of deradicalisation that he was unable to arrest.

Looking back on the 1840s from the vantage point of 1851, Harney commented with his usual acuity and vivacity on the profusion of reformist, improving, and even utopian attitudes that had been spawned by the propertied classes. He derided the earnest improvers and their palliatives: ' "Utopia!" exclaims the king, the courtier, the aristocrat, the priest, the usurer; and singing chorus to the same song, "Utopia!" exclaim the "liberal" bourgeois, the "moderate reformer", and the "wait-a-little-longer" progressionist, and all the tribe of cheats, counterfeits, and charlatans who live and flourish by dealing in "philanthropy" and political humbug of every description; affecting to war against the existing system, but always ranging themselves on its side, and against the men who earnestly desire the salvation of humanity.' In an editorial entitled 'Inadequate Remedies for Social Evils', he denounced the sham reformers whose rhetoric concealed a lack of substance, and complained that the working classes were being used 'for the glory of the Lameths, Lafayettes, and Lamartines, and the profit of the bourgeoisie'. Harney had little taste for bourgeois liberals, however earnest, whether French or English. He sought to draw a clear line between them and 'the men who earnestly desire the salvation of humanity'.[3]

In fact, however, Harney shared the sensibility of the reformers that he denounced so vehemently. In the spirit of romantic utopianism he hoped for 'the regeneration of the vast mass of mankind', who were denied 'those rights which should distinguish them from the brute creation'. In properly mid-Victorian fashion, Harney recommended that working men read Tennyson. 'His poetry is a very world of wondrous beauty — purifying and ennobling beauty; and working men should be made acquainted with it that they may get beauty into their souls, and thence into their daily lives.'[4] Although Harney's belief in revolution set him apart from W.J. Linton, the two men shared the romantic utopian outlook of high aspiration. Linton described his socialism as 'touching the deeper spring of human endeavour — *the inherent tendency to aspire towards good*, and so leading on through nobleness to nobleness, from progression to progression, to a higher, and yet a higher and more excellent future. This is the Socialism of the Republican'.[5] This rhetoric was also very much in tune with the mid-Victorian ethos.

Harney shared the consensus faith in education, while trying to counter the use to which it was put in the writings of middle-class propagandists. In a favourable comment on W.J. Fox's annual motion calling for free secular education, Harney dissociated himself from what he called certain ' "Manchester School" fallacies' in the speech, such as the notion 'that "strikes" are the consequence of ignorance; and that education is the remedy for both evils — fallacies eagerly seized upon by *The Times*'. But it was Fox's opponents who continued to draw Harney's heaviest fire. In equating opposition to education with despotism and reaction, Harney echoed the rationalist radicalism of Paine and Carlile: 'Tyrants are the sworn foes of Knowledge. Wherever there is Oppression of any kind, it will be found that the oppressors have recourse to every means to shut out the light of knowledge, and perpetuate the existence of Ignorance.' The difficulty, however, was that the capitalist class which Harney now considered the main enemy was ostentatiously committed to the 'light of knowledge'. Hence, in reaffirming the rationalist values of the Left, he was also reinforcing similar principles in the ideology of Manchester liberalism.[6]

From his position on the far Left, Harney insisted that the radical movement must not be content with anything short of a total trans-formation of the social and political order. He pointed out that the trade unions and co-operatives were powerless 'to accomplish those changes in society and government which are absolutely necessary to redeem the working classes from wages-slavery and political serfdom'. The co-operators have in mind no more than a 'rose-water revolution', and the bourgeoisie would crush even that at the first sign that it was making any progress. Similarly, while the trade unions had 'retarded the ascendency of all-devouring capital', they were nevertheless by their very nature 'impotent to effect any general social change for the advantage of the wealth producers.' To this extent he agreed with Ernest Jones. Unlike Jones, however, Harney felt that these institutions, despite their limitations, were nevertheless contributing to the radical cause in the long run, because they were spreading principles that would eventually triumph and bring about a revolution. His rationalist faith remained unshaken: 'The co-operative and industrial movement will advance the discussion of social principles, and thereby prepare the way for those Social Revolutionists who seek, through Universal Suffrage, the ABOLITION OF CLASSES AND THE SOVEREIGNTY OF LABOUR.' The co-operative movement would give an impetus to 'the general question of Social Regeneration'. While the co-operative societies certainly affirmed the principles that Harney had in mind, neither they nor the trade unions were contributing to anything resembling 'social regeneration'. Harney had optimistically incorporated these reformist institutions into a nominally revolutionary movement whose chief concern in the short run was a diffusion of sound principles. And the assertion of high principle was readily assimilated to similar patterns in the culture as a whole.[7]

Charles Murray, a London shoemaker whose attack on the middle-class was total, uncompromising, and compulsive, also remained very much within the boundaries of mid-Victorianism. A Chartist in his youth, he was one of the founders of the Social Democratic Federation a generation later. In the 1850s, from the vantage point provided by the doctrines of Bronterre O'Brien, he took up a belligerently anti-middle-class position.[8] In 1854 Murray wrote a long letter denouncing G.J. Holyoake for having sacrificed 'right to expediency, truth to respectability' in selling out to Manchester liberalism: 'You found favour in the Middle Classes, whose patronage you doubtless prefer, or you would not have remained . . . so servile a defender of their fraudulent and destructive system of society.' The occasion for this diatribe was an article by Holyoake praising Richard Cobden and defending his claim to be considered a Radical. Murray denied Cobden's right to the title in a sentence that summed up his social and political views: 'If, Sir, you mean by "a Radical" one who advocates the sovereignty of the people, politically and socially, then do I deny that he is a Radical, but only a mere Middle Class agitator, one who seeks to make the Middle Classes the actual rulers of this and every other country, at the expense of all other classes, territorial and industrial.' In the course of the essay he gave the middle classes no quarter. They were not interested in a free press, but only in a cheap press, so that they could 'inundate the country with cheap but false literature', and 'hire all the venal and corrupt writers and political apostates to debase the public mind, by teaching false doctrines on land, money, commerce, religion, politics, etc.' It was 'the respectable Middle Classes' who 'provided for every fellow who forsook his Chartism by giving them employment in Insurance Offices, etc.' These are the men, Murray said scornfully to Holyoake, 'whom you are continually holding up for the admiration of the Working Classes'.[9]

To illustrate the depravity of the middle-class, Murray cited a family history: 'If we trace the history of any family in humble circumstances, of say, six sons, we find that five of them are more or less generous, kind, open hearted, and independent; whereas the sixth one is of a close disposition — mean, grasping, crafty, and slavish. It requires little discernment to prognosticate that the one will become a Middle Class man, if in the course of his life, the slightest chance offers, no matter what the conditions.' In other words, he added, to make sure that no one missed his point, 'the Middle Classes . . . are Middle Class men, generally, because they are naturally bad'. He added a qualification about individuals, but it did not seriously modify his basic line: 'I would have it clearly understood, that I do not blame the individual members (of the Middle Classes) for being such: because it is an unjust and tyrannical form of society, and every man born in it must either be a victimiser or a victim.'

There is a certain charm in Murray's argument, couched in the sentimental idealism so characteristic of the working-class subculture, that the social and economic characteristics of the middle classes prevented them from attaining the ideals which they proclaimed so proudly: 'In order that a man may be suited for a position in the middle ranks of society — in order that a man may be capable of running a race with the world in competing for that position, he must be void of all the finer susceptibilities of our nature; he dare not cultivate the nobler feelings — the more generous passions — the diviner attributes of his nature.'[10] Murray seemed to be on to a good ploy in denying to the middle classes the very virtues which they were preaching so earnestly. But it was no more than a debating point. Murray's argument merely illustrates the extent to which he — like so many working-class radicals — took for granted the validity of the fundamental values and forms of the culture whose rulers he found so uncongenial. In effect, he was assigning to the working-class the role of cultivating 'the nobler feelings'. That was not at all incompatible with the role assigned to working men in the more saccharine forms of middle-class propaganda.

The assimilation of popular radicalism to the forms of mid-Victorian culture, especially the tendency to sentimentality, is particularly evident in poetry, which provides the historian with expressions of cultural platitudes in starker form than usual. A Poem, 'Look Up, Ye Toiling Millions', published in a trade union journal in 1852, states a number of themes that were to be prominent in the 1850s and 1860s. The first stanza opens with the familiar rhetoric of protest:

> Look up, ye toiling millions!
> There are better days in store,
> When the shackles that enslave you
> Shall be loosed for ever more.
> Your long-enduring patience
> Shall receive its just reward,
> In universal freedom,
> Which no armed hosts shall guard.

The next stanza, however, introduced the mid-Victorian note that 'man's moral reformation, and th' enthroning equal laws' would usher in freedom and 'sweep oppression from your tyrant-ridden land'. Knowledge also would contribute to the cause:

> Let ignorance be vanquished,
> With the evil it hath done:
> Give diligence to knowledge,

'Tis a firm and faithful friend,
It makes oppression tremble,
And will crush it in the end.[11]

Although the author was echoing earlier radicals in his confidence that knowledge would destroy oppression, he was nevertheless reducing the old faith to a set of culturally acceptable truisms.

A letter written by a Sunderland working man to the *Bee-Hive* in 1866 illustrates the characteristic mid-Victorian juxtaposition of militant protest and consensus values. In one sentence the writer demands the repeal of 'those laws which favour the employer and trample down the employed'. Such language, with undertones of class struggle, was commonplace among radical working men in the 1860s. The next sentence, describing the sort of 'just and equitable laws' that ought to be enacted, is anti-climactic: 'Laws and systems would be established for the purpose of elevating the great mass of the working and lower class — they would be improved in intelligence, in frugality, in sobriety, and every virtue which dignifies humanity.'[12] Such aspirations, firmly rooted in working-class radical traditions, were not necessarily inconsistent with the acceptance of class conflict. Yet middle-class spokesmen were also calling for the elevation of the working classes in much the same terms. That sort of ideological overlap circumscribed the impact of working-class radicalism.

Lodged in a culture that prized rational reform and renovation to remedy demonstrated grievances, working-class radicalism was vulnerable to assimilation; the whole apparatus of protest and agitation could easily be co-opted and assigned an appropriate role along with other movements devoted to the cause of progress. In this situation demonstrations and demands were liable to lose their edge, and lapse into the blandness, if not the banality, of mid-Victorianism. Robert Lowery, for example, remained loyal to the fundamental principles of Chartism, but in the 1850s his radicalism had been transmuted into a respectable facsimile of Left politics. While continuing to urge demands for the correction of abuses, he depicted such agitation as part of a providential plan for unending progress; a certain amount of discontent was 'a necessity in the normal condition of society', because it led to remedial action. Even the pain caused by social ills was valuable as a stimulus to agitation: 'There is always some wrong, some sin — thence some suffering; this suffering is a blessing . . . Suffering is the divine voice that bids us to be up and find a remedy.' The one unmitigated evil is 'contentment with wrong'. Hence the good man is constantly searching out wrongs that need to be corrected, for this is inherent in the nature of things. 'If we look carefully remedies are to be found for mental, moral, and social evils.' This is in keeping with God's law. 'No evil can beset us but He hath provided a way whereby we may escape. Agitation in a right spirit appears to be our normal state.' Inevitably, as a proper mid-Victorian, Lowery finds the process of complaint and reform to be morally elevating: 'The process of our refining is disturbance — struggles — writhings — heavings, by which the alloy or dross of ignorance and vice is separated from the pure metal.' After a period of commotion and disturbance, the separation is completed, and 'all is placid, the refiner's face is reflected back from the metal — the image of God-like men from the regenerated soul, of God-like men from purified society'.[13] Lowery's radicalism had been assimilated to the ethos of high aspiration and noble striving. Mid-Victorian culture had a niche for a radicalism that adapted itself so well to established patterns.

While most working-class radicals did not embrace mid-Victorianism so totally or so fervently as Lowery, the parliamentary reform agitation of the 1860s fitted perfectly into the culture of which they were very much a part.

(2) *Manhood Suffrage*

Although the agitation for an extension of the franchise was relatively dormant during the 1850s, the issue was still of fundamental importance. In the new culture that had emerged out of the social and ideological conflicts of the Chartist era, this remained a great unresolved question. For working-class radicalism the franchise issue could not be postponed indefinitely, since it continued to be a primary symbol of the demand for equality, justice, and respect. It was the parliamentary reform agitation of the 1860s that settled the question in the towns before the legislation of 1867. It was settled in a way that reflected the culture as a whole — on the basis of a broad consensus, but in the context of class conflict that had been muted somewhat. For working-class radicalism it represented both a triumph and a defeat. On the one hand the parliamentary reform movement embodied a forceful reaffirmation of radical principles and values, which were now supported by middle-class liberalism. On the other hand, however, those values had been established only in the somewhat attenuated form so characteristic of the culture, that is within the limits imposed by the structure of power and status. In parliamentary reform, as in so many other areas, old principles and ideas underwent subtle changes in a new context.

When the franchise once again became a live issue for working-class radicalism in the 1860s, it was in a political and social context that had changed considerably since the 1830s. For one thing, the middle-class radicals had taken up the issue with some enthusiasm. Although in a minority, the main body of progressive middle-class opinion had shifted somewhat to the Left, especially as working men came to be perceived not as enemies but as potential allies against the aristocracy. The only question was how much of an extension, and Liberal opinion ran the gamut from household suffrage to the £6 or £7 rental. As a result, from the standpoint of maintaining their principles undiluted, working-class radicals were now in a much more difficult position than they had been in a generation before. On the one hand, the middle-class radicals were making them an offer that they could hardly refuse: a joint effort to secure a substantial extension of the franchise. On the other hand, if they accepted they would have to pay a price. They could expect something much less than manhood suffrage; this meant giving up a great deal both symbolically and in substance. For another, the middle-class movement, coming from above, was cast in terms that made all too visible the new forms of subordination and deference that had been developing in the cities. There was more than a hint of paternalism, and even condescension.

Working-class radicalism refused to enter the parliamentary reform movement on middle-class terms. Radical working men preserved their independence by insisting on manhood suffrage and by forming their own local associations to conduct an agitation. In this matter, as in others, they did not passively succumb to the middle-class, either ideologically or institutionally. On the national level, the Reform League, run by working men, asserted the cause of manhood suffrage; the National Reform Union had not pre-empted parliamentary reform for household suffrage. The league was an expression of an indigenous working-class radical movement in the cities.[14] Having preserved its ideological and institutional independence, however, working-class radicalism could not shake loose from cultural patterns that gave an unintended shape to its campaign for parliamentary reform; nor could it avoid the implications of a necessary collaboration with middle-class reformers. The conscious efforts of working-class radicals, while note-worthy in themselves, were powerless to prevent the muffling of Chartist militancy. They maintained the old ideals and principles against frontal attacks, but could not preserve the old content in the face of less visible processes of ideological and cultural change and the need for middle-class support.

The approach to parliamentary reform that working-class radicals instinctively rejected — only to be caught up in its implications in the course of the agitation — was a standard middle-class version of consensus values. On this view, the working classes had advanced in knowledge and education during the previous generation; hence a substantial number of working men were clearly qualified to exercise the franchise responsibly and intelligently. Middle-class reformers, long devoted to the cause of the moral and intellectual elevation of the working classes, were bound to do their utmost to support parliamentary reform in an effort to bring qualified working men within the pale of the constitution. Thus, the role of the political reformer corresponded perfectly to the official role of the middle classes in the culture as a whole: assisting working men in the great community enterprise of improvement for all. Filtered through the prism of middle-class attitudes, this approach usually emerged in terms that underlined the social distance between rulers and ruled. It was clear that the middle-class reformer who advocated an extension of the franchise was doing working men a great favour, which he expected them to appreciate. In the literal sense of the word, he was condescending.

Edward Baines, Jr. was the exemplar of the moderate liberal position, which stopped short of household suffrage. In 1865 this was still a relatively advanced line, and he could speak from rather high ground when he appeared in January at the inaugural meeting of a Reform Association just formed by the working men of Bramley. Since he was addressing working men whom he regarded as fit to exercise the franchise, he could flatter them in much the same manner as Cowen, but more stiffly. 'He rejoiced most heartily that the working men of Bramley were doing that which was so very honourable to themselves . . . in demanding what was their reasonable right.'[15] Baines took the line that in 1831 there had been good reason to exclude working men from the franchise on the ground that 'generally the working men were ignorant and destitute of education and intelligence'. But times had changed. Since then there had been a great advance in the intelligence and education of the people. 'The older men amongst the audience knew in what a great variety of ways the amount of cultivated intelligence amongst working men now was immensely greater than it was when they were lads.' He cited the number of savings banks, friendly societies, attendance at churches and chapels, mechanics' institutes, working men's clubs, and literary societies. 'Did any one doubt the good conduct of working men?' M.P.s speaking in the country had been impressed by 'the excellent conduct of working men, their good order, their intelligence'. Finally, he argued that the conferring of the franchise on working men would contribute still further to the ongoing tide of improvement: 'The tendency of the franchise was to elevate the man, and to impress on him a sense of the responsibility which he owed to his country for the conscientious and right and wise exercise of the vote conferred upon him. He believed, therefore, that it would tend to the improvement of those who received the franchise, as well as to the increased stability of our institutions.' As a reformer in the vanguard of opinion at this time, Baines could ignore the problem of his intention to exclude a substantial number of working men as unqualified. His speech was resonant with the highest values of the culture.

A few years before, Baines had taken the chair at a conference of working men from the West Riding to consider parliamentary reform. The main speech was delivered by a Leeds manufacturer, James Marshall, and printed as an appendix to the proceedings of the meeting. The speech is of interest because it embodies so vividely the Bainesian moderate Liberal line, which, as it turned out, failed to satisfy the working-class radicals of Leeds. Marshall advised the assembled working men about the best way to conduct the agitation that they had in mind. In the familiar mid-Victorian Liberal manner, he praised them for their virtues and suggested that they continue along the same lines: 'You are about to make an appeal to the moral sense and public opinion of the whole of your countrymen: not to men of your class only.' Marshall then laid down the 'real grounds on which you may justly claim an extension of the franchise which shall include large numbers of your class now without a vote'. There was no extremist talk of manhood suffrage in his Liberal formula: 'Simply, that the general advance of society in education and intelligence, and especially in moral aims and political knowledge, has qualified large numbers of your class for the exercise of the elective franchise. On this ground it is just to you, and would greatly add to the strength and safety of our institutions, that you should have it.' They must proceed 'temperately and firmly' and reject those who thought it necessary to 'thunder into your ears tremendous denunciations of the tyranny and oppression of the institutions and the government under which you have hitherto lived'.[16] If they conducted this sort of campaign, they would win the support of the middle-class reformers and would gain a substantial extension of franchise.

But this line did not go down at all well with working-class radicals in Leeds. In fact, the starchy attitude of Marshall and Baines was a stimulus to the formation of an independent working-class movement. At the 1861 conference the main resolution was denounced as a 'milk and water' affair by Alderman Carter, a sometime Chartist who had emerged as the leader of the manhood suffrage group in Leeds. In March 1866 he severely criticised Gladstone for the feebleness of his reform proposals. Working men gave their support to the Leeds Manhood Suffrage League, which Carter formed in 1866.[17]

As in Leeds, the founding of manhood suffrage associations in industrial towns in the 1860s attested to the strength of working-class radicalism and its determination to reassert the old principles in pure form, undiluted by concession. While the radicals might accept something less in the short run, there could be no retreat on the question of principle. The working man was entitled to his political rights without any nit-picking about rentals or ratals. On the issue of the franchise there could be no compromising of the principle of equality. In the course of the ensuing parliamentary reform agitation working-class radicals were quick to attack anyone who refused to recognise the inherent worth of their class. In insisting on manhood suffrage, they stood apart from the middle-class moderates and resisted attempts to co-opt them into the Liberal movement. On this great symbolic issue the working-class radicals were determined to stand their ground. As William Smith, secretary of the Nottingham Manhood Suffrage Association put it in a letter, so long as any proposal for parliamentary reform 'falls short of Manhood Suffrage, it should only be accepted as part of the rights of the Masses, and . . . Agitation never ought to cease until the whole is obtained'. Reform League speakers frequently complained that the moderate reformers were proceeding much too slowly. At a reform demonstration in Bradford in January 1867, E.O. Greening demanded 'a complete enfranchisement of the manhood of England', deplored the fact that 'there were a good many Liberals who preferred reform bit by bit', and took issue with the limitations called for by W.E. Forster, M.P. for Bradford. He disposed of such views with a populist anecdote: 'A working man in Lancashire gave it as his opinion that such a mode was like eating peas with a pin (laughter), which, he said, was likely to tire the arm before the stomach was filled. (Hear, hear, and laughter.)' An ageing Nottingham Chartist saw the issue as a matter of principle: 'I shall always stand forward to support the rights of man as vested in himself and not in his house. (Cheers.) I want to do away with that abominable system by which if I am to vote, I am obliged to have a vote through my house and not through my own individual self. (Cheers.)'[18]

In some of the demands for manhood suffrage there even remained echoes of the old Chartist tendency to see the issue in class terms, as part of a broader struggle for the overall emancipation of the working classes. To William Smith it seemed that 'wage slavery is not much more than half way from negro slavery to national and social liberty as it ought to be'. To get there it was necessary not only to win the vote but also to do something about a 'class government' that encourages 'a scheme of education for *middle classes* alone — I should like to know why one class should be educated for Masters and Employers while the more numerous Class are left to be educated by some one almost as uneducated as themselves'.[19] On the whole, however, the working-class radicals in the 1860s did not perceive the franchise issue in terms of such a conflict with the middle-class. Smith had made his comments in a letter. On the platform, co-operation with middle-class reformers was the order of the day. The ideological distance between them had been significantly narrowed since the Chartist years.

A profound change had taken place in the meaning of the radical demand for the vote. Even when Chartist language was still used, it took on a different tone and resonance in the mid-Victorian cultural context.

Where Chartists had perceived the vote as the first step on the road to a radically different political and social order, the mid-Victorian radicals tended to see it as part of a gradual process of steady reform and improvement in the quest for common goals. Whereas the Chartists saw the vote in terms of a shift in power, the mid-Victorian radicals talked in terms of the right to participate responsibly and rationally in the processes of government. Now working men put a very heavy emphasis on their 'worthiness' for the vote. They had improved themselves, according to the most severe standards of the culture, and they insisted on the vote because they were entitled to it. While the Chartists had also defended the virtue of working men against charges levelled at them by their betters, they had conducted their defence more aggressively. The mid-Victorian radicals did so in a softer tone. In the process they tended to forget that the vote was a means to an end. It became an end in itself — a badge that would formally and officially recognise their worthiness.

Working-class radical idealism remained, but it focused on consensus values, and merely attempted to give an egalitarian or populist cast to them. Thus the agitation for parliamentary reform was assimilated to other familiar cultural patterns devoted to common effort on behalf of good causes. In contrast to the Chartist era, middle-class participation was prominent, although working men maintained a separate organisation in the Reform League. At every point the working-class radical agitation for the vote was congruent with prevailing cultural patterns. While conflict with the middle-class was still in the picture, it had been acculturated and deradicalised.

Even when insisting on manhood suffrage, spokesmen for working-class radicalism made their case in an idiom that reflected the ideological and cultural changes since Chartism. E.O. Greening, for example, while demanding the vote for 'the manhood of England' at a Reform League demonstration in January 1867, put his argument in mid-Victorian liberal social categories that brought him to the point of platitude, not to say cant. Thus he refused to put the case in straightforward class terms. 'This was a question, as it appeared to him, which did not concern the working-class of this country exclusively. All classes formed society, and when one large section of our countrymen suffered, the whole of society suffered with it. Society was like the delicate machinery of which it was said that the weakness of the weakest part was equal to the weakness of the whole.' In his next sentence Greening turned from 'the whole of society' to the working classes, but in overblown rhetoric that treated the denial of the franchise as if it were the ultimate in deprivation: 'At the present time the working men of this country were suffering from the social principle of human slavery. By the social principle of human slavery he meant one class of men undertaking to remove from the shoulders of their neighbours and brethren those responsibilities and those duties which God had imposed upon them — in short, one class of men taking upon themselves to do for other men what God intended them to do for themselves. (Hear, hear.)' Greening was simply educing, in a rather heavy-handed way, attitudes implicit in mid-Victorian working-class radicalism, acculturated and domesticated. In this context, Greening's militant language has lost its force and often seems to be no more than the worn-out rhetoric of an out-of-date litany. 'The natural consequence of such a state of things was that, although this was the richest country of which we had any knowledge, either in the past or the present, the amount of pauperism, dependence, and degradation was perfectly appalling.' In illustration, he did not cite the poor law or exploitation but the extent of illiteracy, a deprivation that could be mentioned without raising the hackles of middle-class reformers. Having taken this line, it was fitting that Greening should conclude with words of reassurance to potential allies among the middle classes: 'If the wealthy Liberals assisted the working men to get the power in their hands to exercise the franchise, the working men would not abuse the trust reposed in them, but would more than repay the services rendered by cherishing a feeling of gratitude, which would make them all feel that they were brethren in the land, and that it was no longer a nation divided against itself. (Cheers.)'[20]

Even traditionally subversive labels acquired moderate connotations. At a reform meeting in Huddersfield in 1866, Moore Sykes, a working man active in the Reform League announced, 'I tell you cordially, friends, that I am a leveller.' On the face of it, this seemed radical enough, since he was setting himself apart from a Liberal M.P. who qualified his support for Gladstone's cautious reform proposals by adding that he was no 'Chartist, Communist, or Leveller'. As it turned out, however, Sykes' mid-Victorian gloss on 'leveller' was not so far removed from the Liberal position after all: 'But you will permit me to put my own interpretation upon my own words, if you please. (Hear, hear, and laughter.) I make no war upon the rich man's person but upon his prejudices; I make no war upon the rich man's purse, but his pride.' Echoing a familiar refrain, he asked only that working men be given their due: 'The talent, the intelligence, and the capacity of working men have been vindicated by thousands who have risen from obscurity, and become the admiration of their fellow men. I do not place working men higher than any other class; but I place them . . . as high in intellectual capacity.'[21] This was still egalitarianism, but in culturally acceptable form.

Above all, the reform meetings insisted that working men were worthy of the vote. At the West Riding demonstration of the Reform League in October 1866, the first resolution had Robert Lowe very much in mind: 'That this meeting enters its solemn protest against, and its denial of, the charges of venality, ignorance, drunkenness and indifference to Reform, brought against the working classes during the last session of Parliament.' The conduct of the meeting itself was intended to refute such charges: 'The country must be shown that working men can manage these Demonstrations in an orderly and peaceable manner; and that they are worthy of the position in the State which they are now claiming.' Worthiness meant moderation. Hence the radicals found themselves arguing that reform would contribute to stability and public order. They were going to press for an 'immediate settlement, to maintain the peace and secure the contentment of the country'.[22] Intent on refuting the arguments of their opponents, the radicals ended up making their case in the most respectable mid-Victorian terms. By 1867 even Ernest Jones was depicting parliamentary reform as a 'conservative' measure conducive to stability.

Thus, while working-class radicals were able to dissociate themselves institutionally and programmatically from Liberal reformers, they ended up conducting their agitation in ideological and ritual forms that reflected a culture dominated by the middle classes. The theme of their campaign — that working men were worthy of the vote — corresponded directly to what Marshall and Baines recommended. Without sacrificing principle, they welcomed the active collaboration of middle-class radicals who were willing to support manhood suffrage. Given the exigencies of parliamentary politics, however, they necessarily ended up supporting measures that fell far short of the ultimate goal. Reform League platforms invariably included a number of middle-class liberals and radicals. Hence the League's meetings and demonstrations looked very much like countless other mid-Victorian meetings, at which progressive members of the middle-class — on the platform — collaborated with working men in a cause that represented progress and improvement. In this instance, the middle-class participants could be even more proud of their devotion to principle, since there was still so much opposition to franchise extension among the propertied classes as a whole.

The reform demonstrations arranged by working-class radicals were great ceremonial occasions, festivals celebrating liberalism and the gospel of improvement. They were not merely political events but climactic ritual episodes in the secular religion of the Victorian towns. Lavish attention to detail was required for such vast undertakings to run smoothly, as can be seen in the *Official Programme of Procession, Resolutions, & General Arrangements for the West Riding Demonstration on Woodhouse Moor and in the Town Hall, Leeds, October 8th, 1866*, issued by the Leeds Manhood Suffrage Association.[23] After laying out the order of procession, and describing the duties of general marshals and the marshals to be appointed by each of the groups participating, the circular turned to the order of proceedings on arrival at the moor. 'All the Banner Bearers must immediately arrange themselves six yards in the rear of the Platforms, and continue playing until Half-past Two.' Both the timing and the ritual were precisely specified: 'The first Resolution will be moved and seconded at each Platform, commencing at Half-past two. Two Minutes before Three the Trumpet on the Central Platform will sound a flourish, preparatory to putting the Resolution. The first Resolution will be put at exactly Three o'clock; a second flourish of Trumpets will announce the putting of the Resolution when all in favour of it will hold up both hands.' At the very end of the long meeting the Band was to strike up 'Rule Britannia', and the procession was to re-form and make its way back to the town hall.

The ideological and ritual patterns of the West Riding demonstration were repeated in countless other meetings in cities throughout the country in 1866 and 1867, but with local variations. At Newcastle-on-Tyne, for example, middle-class radicalism was dominated by Joseph Cowen, Jr., who had been an unwavering supporter of manhood suffrage throughout his life. Under these circumstances working-class radicalism remained in his shadow. The reform demonstration of January 1867 was very much Cowen's creature. It was he who decided that there would be maximum participation by working-class speakers, so as to refute once and for all the argument that working men were apathetic about the vote. The striking thing about Newcastle, therefore, was that a vigorous segment of middle-class radicalism had taken liberal principles seriously not merely to the point of accepting manhood suffrage but of demanding it and exulting in its imminence. Absolutely confident of the reliability of the working classes, Cowen and his colleagues preached a bourgeois populism that carried official cultural values to their furthest limits. There was no difficulty in winning working-class support. In fact, working-class radicalism in Newcastle lacked the independence that it had developed in a city like Leeds, where Baines made so visible the class character of the moderate liberal position. Cowen's radicalism, of course, also shared basic middle-class social assumptions, but these were less visible and were softened by a genuinely populist spirit.

The official account in the *Newcastle Chronicle* of the reform demonstration of January 1867 reflects familiar middle-class attitudes, democratic, sentimental, and rather patronising. Noting that some working men in the procession had displayed models of their productions as evidence that they deserved the vote, the writer quickly added a comment that set the tone for the rest of the article: 'If, indeed, their manhood — and a more manly and intelligent-looking body of men could not be found on the face of the earth — were not a sufficient plea for their enfranchisement.' The workmen of Jarrow 'came in hundreds to demand a recognition of their manhood'. A long list of the trades represented concluded with a paean to the 'Northumbrian miners who spend the best part of their lives in the bowels of the earth, among the petrified forests of pre-Adamite ages, but who are still alive to the interests of a country which has reached the present proud pre-eminence among the nations of the earth from the wealth which they laboriously and courageously bring from their noisome caverns where danger and death continually linger'. 'A large number brought their wives and sweethearts with them, and several of the softer sex took their places among the ranks of the Reformers . . . in one of the ranks a stalwart pitman of middle age marched with his hand locked in that of the partner of his joys and sorrows.' The description had the texture of a painting by Frith: 'Nothing could exceed the excellent taste of all the appointments of the Northumbrian miners, or the quiet, unassuming respectability of their demeanour, and there is no doubt that the impression they have made by their appearance and behaviour on this occasion will raise them as a class high in the esteem of their fellow-men.' Other groups of workmen also were praised for being 'well dressed and most respectable in appearance'. One group was described as 'the pick of the skilled mechanics' in Sir William Armstrong's works, 'a body of men . . . more respectable and intelligent in appearance it is scarcely possible to conceive'. This was the middle-class progressive at his most amiable.

The working men who spoke up for manhood suffrage at the meeting did so in a way that conformed rather closely to the image set forth in the *Chronicle*'s description of the participants in the procession. Baines could not have found cause to complain. At the number one platform, the chairman, a millwright, began the proceedings at the sound of a bugle and touched on all the familiar themes. The demonstration proved that working men were not indifferent to the matter of franchise extension; Lowe was denounced as a 'man of disappointed ambition, that libeller of the sons of labour'; if Lowe were to 'put his head out of his cave and see such an array of the stalwart and hardy sons of the North met together, for the purpose of asserting their claims to a just and constitutional right, he might wish that the words had been left in the limbo of things past or to come'.[24] He refuted every possible argument that it would be dangerous to enfranchise working men.

In other towns, as we have noted, working-class radicalism achieved a greater degree of independence and militancy. Nowhere, however, could working men escape the limitations imposed by the social and political pre-eminence of the middle classes. The social and ideological patterns manifested in the parliamentary reform agitation necessarily reflected a culture characterised by middle-class hegemony. The Reform Act of 1867 fell far short not only of the aspirations of Chartism but also its programme.

But the working-class agitation of the 1860s cannot be fully understood if we limit ourselves to the programmatic and electoral categories appropriate to the party politics of a later era. It was very much the product of the historical circumstances characteristic of the middle decades of the nineteenth century. More than most political movements it was an affirmation of faith as well as an attempt to secure specific reforms. The radical faith, expressed so forcefully in Chartism, had assumed a softer form in the setting of mid-Victorian urban culture. Although criticism of middle-class ideology and behaviour continued, existing social arrangements were not called into question. As if in compensation for the decline in militancy, mid-Victorian radicalism proclaimed an even broader vision of progress and liberation for all men. Lincoln and Garibaldi were venerated as leaders in the cause of freedom. The afterglow of romantic idealism suffused the democratic and liberal creed. As in religious movements, the proclamation of the faith became an end in itself. A characteristic expression of mid-Victorian radicalism, reflecting the values of the working-class sub-culture, occurs in an address from the working men of Nottingham to Garibaldi in 1864:

> It is pleasing to us when we can feel we are addressing a man whose life has had one great and beneficent object, and who, in all his struggles, and labours, and aims, has sought to advance that liberty and freedom which have their basis on rational and intelligent principles. Your life has been marked by events of no common kind, some of which excite the sympathy and stir the finer feelings of our common humanity, whilst others command the admiration and approval of our sterner and intellectual natures.[25]

This earnest idealism, so characteristic of both the strength and weakness of mid-Victorian radicalism, was soon to undergo an inevitable historical transformation. But it did not simply fade away. In a different form it was to find expression in the Independent Labour Party, which took root in the working-class subculture of the north of England. The significance of working-class radicalism in the middle third of the nineteenth century is not to be found in subsequent developments, however, but in the quality and intensity of its commitment to democratic and egalitarian principles that still embody the best aspirations of western culture.

Notes

1. See Frances E. Gillespie, *Labor and Politics in England 1850–1867*, Durham, North Carolina 1927; F.M. Leventhal, *Respectable Radical: George Howell and Victorian Working Class Politics*, Cambridge, Mass. 1971; F.B. Smith, *The Making of the Second Reform Bill*, Cambridge 1966; Royden Harrison, *Before the Socialists: Studies in Labour and Politics 1861–1881*, London 1965, and 'The British Labour Movement and the International in 1864', *Socialist Register*, 1964.
2. *Yorkshire Tribune; A Monthly Magazine of Progress*, Holyoake Collection, Bishopsgate Institute. See also Edward Royle, *Victorian Infidels*, Manchester 1974, pp. 179–90.
3. *Red Republican*, 12 October 1850.
4. Martha Vicinus, *Industrial Muse*, New York 1974, p. 104.
5. F.B. Smith, *Radical Artisan*, Manchester 1973, p. 226.
6. *Friend of the People*, 31 May and 22 March 1851.
7. Ibid., 25 January 1851; A.R. Schoyen, *The Chartist Challenge*, London 1958, pp. 218–23; John Saville, *Ernest Jones: Chartist*, London 1952, pp. 47–9.
8. Stan Shipley, *Club Life and Socialism in Mid-Victorian London*, History Workshop pamphlet, Oxford 1971, pp. 1–20.
9. Charles Murray, *A Letter to Mr George Jacob Holyoake*, London 1854, Holyoake Collection, Bishopsgate Institute.
10. Ibid.
11. *Operative*, 24 April 1852.
12. *Bee-Hive*, 22 September 1866.
13. *Weekly Record*, 26 July 1856.
14. See the excellent M.A. thesis by M. Dunsmore, 'The Northern Department of the Reform League', Sheffield, 1962.
15. *Leeds Mercury*, 5 January 1865.
16. *Report of the Yorkshire Reform Conference, 18 and 19 November 1861*, Leeds 1861, pp. 52–5.
17. Ibid., p. 32; Dunsmore, pp. 152–74; for speeches by Carter outside Leeds, see *Oldham Chronicle*, 26 January 1867, *Huddersfield Examiner*, 28 July 1866, and *Bradford Review*, 19 January 1867. At Bradford Carter criticised both self-styled reformers who refused to accept manhood suffrage and also middle-class men of working-class origin who were now flirting with the aristocracy.
18. William Smith to the secretary of the Bradford Reform Union, 26 December 1864, MS, Bradford Reference Library, DB4, Case 1. Both Smith and his correspondent, W.S. Nichols, were active in the temperance movement. *Bradford Review*, 19 January 1867; *Nottingham Review*, 10 February 1865.
19. William Smith to W.S. Nichols, 1 April 1866, MS, Bradford Reference Library.
20. *Bradford Review*, 19 January 1867. In 1868 Greening became an independent candidate for Parliament in Halifax, with the support of the local branch of the Reform League, although George Howell refused to endorse him. See Leventhal, p. 109. A leader of the co-operative movement, Greening was not himself a working man. In 1865 he acted as delegate from the working-class manhood suffrage group in Manchester to the national reform conference; see Gillespie, p. 254.
21. *Huddersfield Examiner*, 24 February 1866; for a speech by Sykes critical of Gladstone, see ibid., 14 April 1866. For the local background, see Dunsmore, p. 230, where the February speech is quoted in part.
22. *Official Programme, of Procession, Resolutions, and General Arrangements*

for the West Riding Reform Demonstration on Woodhouse Moor and in the Town October 8th, 1866, Leeds 1866. Bradford Reference Library, DB 19, Case 17.

23. Ibid.

24. *Newcastle Chronicle*, 29 January 1867. In Bradford the Reform League was dominated by the middle-class radicals. See Dunsmore, pp. 206–11. For the overlapping in membership between the National Reform Union and the Reform League in Bradford, see DB 4, Case 1, and DB 17 Case 19, including the minute book of the Bradford branch of the National Reform Union. On Birmingham, see my article, 'The Origins of the Birmingham Caucus', *Historical Journal*, II, 1959.

25. *Leeds Mercury*, 16 April 1864, See also Gillespie, pp. 217, 250–1; Leventhal, pp. 48–50.

INDEX